IN-SERVICE EDUCATION FOR STAFF DEVELOPMENT

In-Service Education for Staff Development

BEN M. HARRIS
The University of Texas at Austin

ALLYN AND BACON, INC.
BOSTON LONDON SYDNEY TORONTO

Library of Congress Cataloging-in-Publication Data

Harris, Ben M.
    In-service education for staff development / Ben M. Harris.
        p.   cm.
    Bibliography: p.
    Includes index.
    ISBN 0-205-11675-2
    1. Teachers—In-service training—United States.   I. Title.
LB1731.H29 1989   88-14613
371.1′46—dc19   CIP

Printed in the United States of America
10 9 8 7 6 5 4 3 2 1   92 91 90 89 88

To Mom, who knew little of formal schooling, who learned how to rear four children, and who taught me about lifelong learning.

CONTENTS

EXHIBITS

PREFACE

This book is intended as a basic reference, source book, and text for those giving professional leadership to in-service training and staff development programs. The volume emphasizes practical approaches to planning, organizing, and directing training programs for professional staff personnel. Additionally, the book devotes much of its attention to the problems of designing training experiences for improving both acceptance levels and growth rates among participants. Both individualized and group training programs are included.

The focus of the book is upon the training of personnel in school settings with special emphasis on needs of the instructional staff. However, the basic principles and specific techniques presented may well apply to training needs of personnel in hospitals, business and governmental operations, and volunteer civic organizations.

The underlying assumptions utilized by the author are derived both from practical experience and study and from the theory and research relating to teaching, learning, change process, communications, and human relations. Planned programs of in-service education are emphasized in contrast with informal arrangements. Training for implementation of change processes is emphasized throughout the book.

Distinctions among education, training, and staffing as components of staff development programs are developed to clarify operational requirements for each and interfacing possibilities.

This book is directed primarily at administrators, supervisors, training directors, and other personnel with responsibilities for planning and program implementation. As a sourcebook, it is essentially a practical guide to those practices most likely to be successful in school settings. Case illustrations, forms, evaluation instruments, and sample training plans are provided to serve the practitioner. However, a strong base of research and theory in the behavioral sciences and in education is utilized to give readers the professional-level understanding necessary for developing and maintaining in-service training programs of more effective and imaginative kinds.

The eleven chapters in this volume are designed for use in at least three different ways. Chapters 1 and 2 are rather lengthy introductions intended to provide the reader with considerable substantive information and to clearly delineate a point of view. Chapters 9 and 10 are also largely informational and intended to assist the reader in thinking about in-service education as professional leadership in the broader context of law, policy, and educational change process.

In contrast to these informational chapters, all others attempt to assist the reader in practical ways. Specific procedures are illustrated and discussed; poor practices are noted; and alternatives are analyzed. A few briefly annotated references for further study are suggested at the end of each chapter, while an extensive bibliography is also provided to document specific citations and sources.

The appendixes include an array of aids for the reader. Some provide greater detail on the ideas or procedures presented in Chapters 1–11. Throughout this volume the reader is urged to consider using the aids illustrated in the various appendixes, to see if they can contribute to better practice.

ACKNOWLEDGMENTS

To all of my colleagues and students who have encouraged and assisted me in so many ways, I owe continuing thanks. Their specific contributions are too numerous to recognize in detail. Professors Kenneth E. McIntyre and E. Wailand Bessent pioneered an earlier work with this author which still influences me. Many students have reviewed and criticized various chapters. A special set of contributions were made to the development of various chapters by Drs. Jim Kidd, Jimmy Creekmur, Don Killough, Dan McLendon, Jane Hill, Helen Almanza, Judy Lozano-Loredo, Nancy Hagen, Steve Cavender, and Gloria Berry, based on our work together on various studies of current practices.

For unusually faithful and patient clerical and proofreading assistance, I owe special thanks to my wife, Mary Lee Harris, and to Dolores Peyton and Anne Psencik.

1.
The Nature of
In-Service Education

INTRODUCTION

In-service education (ISE), like any other kind of education, has to do with helping people grow, learn, improve, enjoy, think, and do. The title of this book gives a suggestion about the special place of in-service education in the larger arena of education. The phrase "staff development" emphasizes the concern of this book for *staff* as people being served by in-service education. The development of a staff in a school setting suggests important features of in-service education that set it apart from preservice education, but also from general education, vocational training, career education, adult education, and even personal development, as important as all of these may be.

In-service education is any organized effort to improve the performance of personnel in already assigned positions. The unique character of in-service education derives from its concern for *all* personnel, not just those with problems or deficits or unusual promise. In-service efforts are rooted in the belief that all personnel can improve their performance, that people make organizations effective, and that planned programs are most efficient. With no more careful definition than this, let's think about the tasks of helping people grow on the job! There are various approaches, of course, to improving performances of staff members. A tightly worded definition will be suggested later to help us keep on target. But first, why so much concern with people? The vignettes that follow depict diverse situations in schools, where modified performances may be in order. Each vignette depicts a unique individual or group facing ordinary but important problems of professional performance.

1

Vignette 1.   End of the First Year

Bill Thompson has just completed his first year as middle school teacher of the "core" for sixth graders—English, reading, writing, spelling, social studies and advising, including career education. His principal has been talking with him about his new contract for next year with these words: "You've made good progress, Bill. I know you'll work harder next year to improve your teaching still more. I hope you'll start out with a much tighter rein on those kiddos. You know? Start out firm, make sure they know *your* rules. Clarify expectations. Set a no-nonsense tone to the classroom from the very first moment! You'll find that makes all the difference in the world."

As Bill left the principal's office, he felt relieved, he had a new contract and assurances of confidence in him from the principal, he thought. He walked down the hall to his empty room to straighten up and pack his things for the summer. Jack Martinez, eighth-grade math teacher, was in the room across the hall. He was directing several students who were helping him clean and straighten things up. They were joking and laughing. Jack was sitting on a table, talking with a girl. Bill looked in and heard Jack saying, "I'll be back in town, Ellen, by August 2. So call me if you want a bit of help! Okay?"

Bill did not want to interrupt, so he paused just long enough to say, "See you next August, Jack, Mr. Martinez." He went to his room. As well as feeling relieved that he had a new contract and that the principal's evaluation reported no serious problems, he was also glad the year was at an end. He packed the last of his personal belongings and walked into the hall. Jack could still be heard talking with students in the nearby classroom. Bill listened, curious about why Jack's students were staying around. Jack Martinez had been teaching five or six years. He wondered if he'd be better respected after a few years of experience, too!

The school was largely deserted. Report cards had been issued, and most students had gone for the summer. Bill felt a bit sad. Somehow, it hadn't been much fun! Oh, well, he thought, next year will be fine. The first year's the toughest!

The New Teacher

Vignette 1 looks in on the new teacher at the end of his first year. He has performed reasonably well—his principal assures him that a new contract is forthcoming—but still he has ambivalent feelings about himself. He senses that he is not yet competent, but he rationalizes that more experience is all that he lacks. His principal seems unaware of ways to help him grow. Valuable role models are close at hand, but still inaccessible without planning and facilitating. We will return to ways of helping Bill Thompson achieve excellence in later chapters as we describe individual growth planning, demonstrating, and diagnostic and clinical approaches.

Vignette 2. The New Principal's Crisis

Jane Hunt had dreaded this moment. She had heard about such sticky problems and wondered what she'd do when faced with one. Now here she was in the middle of one. She was taking third grader Suzie by the hand down the hall. Her mother had come to the office to take her out of school. Jane has been principal of Airdale Elementary School for almost six months, and this was the first case of a mother asking to take her child out of the school when the father had expressly forbidden it *in writing*. Suzie was crying and pleading with Ms. Hunt, "I'm not s'posed to go with mommy! Daddy said not to let her take me away." Jane tried to be reassuring, "Well, she is your mother, so we must talk with her. Now no need to cry. We'll talk about it together in the office."

"I don't want to talk," Suzie screamed, pulling to release her hand from the principal's grip. Jane had to grab her to exercise her authority and found herself virtually dragging the child down the hall into the office.

Suzie's mother wanted to leave immediately with her daughter. She said, "We're leaving today. We must hurry or we'll miss the plane." Jane Hunt insisted they sit down and talk about the whole situation. Suzie was crying, her mother was irate. "I'm not going to talk with you about our family affairs," the mother blurted out. "It's none of the school's business. She's my flesh and blood, and we're leaving."

Jane was almost pleading for delay! Everything happened so fast. The secretary was out to lunch, so she couldn't even find the letter from the father. What had he said, she wondered. Were they legally separated or not? Was the father the legal guardian? Who registered the child—mother or father? Does that make any difference? What does the policy handbook say to do? Shall I call the superintendent? What will he think of me? Oh, why did I accept this job, anyway?

Training for Leadership

Vignette 2 illustrates concerns for staff members other than classroom teachers. It is true, of course, that most in-service education focuses upon the growth needs of teachers, since they constitute the largest group of staff personnel in any school or college. However, Jane Hunt faces in the midst of crisis one of the many perplexing problems of effective leadership. That this is a crisis situation does not mask her need for opportunities to continue learning about the job of the principal. The legal, public relations, and child welfare ramifications of the situation she faces are numerous. The many alternatives for action are not easily thought of even by experienced administrators, because of changing conditions, new legal developments, and personal stylistic differences. Hence, only through continuing opportunities for in-service education can we hope to provide administrators and

Vignette 3.   Caution! A Team at Work

The team had been organized very carefully. Both experienced and inexperienced teachers were included among the five of them. They had a man on the team, well known as a good disciplinarian. He used to coach basketball and knew how to handle boys. Each team member had his or her own specialization. Helen was their grammarian; George was gung ho for American literature; and Jessie was interested in creative writing. Coach Mead was willing to work mostly on spelling, vocabulary drill, and punctuation, too. Ann was a bit of an oddball, some of her teammates had suggested privately. Her experience was mostly elementary and her major was library science, but she had a recent master's degree in reading and language development.

The team had operated all last year reasonably well. Swift High School was new; the team organization was new for Swifttown schools; and everyone seemed enthusiastic, did their own thing, and had gotten along fairly well. At least, there were no big crises. Now it was late November of the second year! Parents had been asking questions about the English team. "Are the students getting a good program?" "Is it quiet enough in that large room with nearly a hundred students?" "What about college exams—will they be ready to pass them?"

The principal, too, was beginning to raise questions. Last week he had observed in the English team area twice for about fifty minutes each time. He left with some concerns about what seemed to be happening. He asked to be invited to the next team planning meeting, but coach Mead, the team leader, replied that they would not have a formal meeting until after the Christmas holidays and asked, "Would that be okay?"

But the team was meeting *informally* this afternoon just before the Thanksgiving break. All were there except Ann, who had been released early to drive two other teachers to a workshop sponsored by the regional education service center in cooperation with the state unit of the International Reading Association. As the team members talked, they expressed concerns about many things: "Why has he [the principal] started observing in our area all of a sudden?" "What's he want to meet with us for?" "We know what we're doing!" "You know, this team thing may be for the birds after all." "I'm working harder than ever," Helen responded. "I'm afraid parents are getting up tight. Maybe we should begin to concentrate more on grammar and punctuation and vocabulary so the kids will be ready for the SAT," proposed George. "The discipline problems just take so much time. If we could really concentrate on those who want to learn, we could get someplace!" offered Jessie.

supervisors with the deeper and broader understanding required of leaders. In a later chapter the use of simulations, in-basket exercises, and case materials are discussed as especially promising approaches.

A Team of Individual Needs

Vignette 3 focuses on the problems of a teaching team. Here we see illustrated the needs of quite experienced teachers for in-service education. Notice in this situation the common mistake of assuming that teachers could somehow learn to manage a team if they were turned loose. While the diverse needs of each individual on the team are emphasized, in that very diversity are suggested the potential resources for promoting in-service growth.

Never Too Late to Learn

The Elderly Matriarch represents a point of view about the importance of in-service education for all. Long-timers are all too often neglected both as valuable human resources and as individuals who can grow and need opportunities to do so. This vignette also offers just a hint about the informal structures, traditions, and influence patterns that must not be ignored as in-service education is promoted as an essential aspect of the school operation.

The reader will be asked to refer to these four vignettes in connection with various ideas presented in subsequent chapters.

HELPING PEOPLE GROW ON THE JOB

Some will argue that "experience is the best teacher." If so, being on the job is nearly a guarantee of growth. Obviously, in the real world such formulas do not always hold true. For some, each year is a new and vital experience, and hence learning does occur with no special plan or arrangement. But for others many years are the same, except perhaps a bit duller, more boring, or more frustrating and confusing than those that went by before. For most of us the daily routines of the working assignment are neither panacea nor void but a mixed bag. Some on-the-job experiences do offer opportunities for learning, but the need for help in making the most of such experience is often crucially important. A chance to read, to see, to discuss, to analyze as one experiences can greatly enhance the learning process.

But then there is also the problem of assuring appropriate learnings. Experience teaches many things, and some of it is most *unfortunate*. Under certain conditions experience teaches us that so-called good practices

Vignette 4.   Elderly Matriarch

She sat there in the lounge rocking away and drinking her tea. It seemed curious to Wayne Kennamer that only Loreen Cloran ever sat in that old-fashioned rocking chair in the teacher's lounge. He soon learned that she regarded it as personal property. Although no one knew for sure how that old chair had gotten there, they did know it was "reserved" for Ms. Cloran, and she'd tell you "It's my chair" in no uncertain terms. Even the principal, Gordon Eckert, never challenged her right to the chair.

Ms. Cloran was the oldest teacher in town. No one knew how old she was because she wasn't telling, and no one else had been around long enough to remember. Wayne Kennamer, as the new curriculum director for Alpine Cove Schools, soon learned other interesting things about Loreen Cloran. She was the head of the sixth-grade teacher group. She prided herself in teaching "the good old-fashioned way" and made kids "toe the mark." She not only had a reputation for being tough but was highly regarded by many, if not most, parents as an excellent teacher. Furthermore, her students' test scores showed it. Of course, she insisted the principal give her plenty of the good students every year, and if any "boys acted up" she arranged to have them transferred to some other room.

Speaking of rooms, Ms. Cloran had had the same room for at least thirty years. She always refused to move, no matter what other changes took place. To Wayne's amazement, he also discovered that she had another rocking chair in her room. The kids said she used it a lot, too—taught from her chair.

Wayne Kennamer couldn't resist asking about Loreen Cloran. Principal Eckert advised him to ignore her as much as he could and try to get along with her. Wayne took that advice for about a year as he worked with teachers—observing in classrooms, arranging workshops, conducting demonstrations, leading curriculum development meetings. Ms. Cloran generally did not get involved with Wayne either. In fact, she failed to attend any of the activities he arranged unless it was part of a regular faculty meeting. They would chat in the lounge. He'd ask how she was, and she'd brag about her kids' progress or offer some negative feedback about one of his workshops in the form of hearsay! Still, they remained cordial with each other.

In the fall of his second year at Alpine Cove, Wayne was promoting more and better use of visual aids. Some teachers had expressed an interest in the use of 16 millimeter films now readily available from the regional service center, but Alpine Cove's blinds, screens, and projectors were inadequate. Wayne had secured money to remodel several classrooms over the summer. New projectors were purchased, screens were installed, and rolling carts were designed so that even kindergarten children could roll the equipment in and out of the room.

To facilitate training, Wayne began to schedule "open clinics" in the teachers' lounge. He had a projector. Any interested teacher was welcome to come to the lounge any time to get a demonstration and practice operating the new machines. Wayne spent as many hours as he could in the lounge each week to help out and promote the training.

It was predictable, of course! Ms. Loreen Cloran was not happy with all of this. Her lounge break was being disturbed. Those machines were a "nuisance." Having "boys" in the teachers' lounge was "just not right." "We teachers want a bit of privacy and relaxation when we get a break," she contended, obviously speaking for others as well as for herself!

Wayne Kennamer knew he was in trouble. He had to back down and shift his efforts elsewhere. But he also needed to save face. Ms. Cloran became his new challenge.

Wayne only had a short while to decide what to do. Teachers were talking. He decided to find a way to work with and through the "old matriarch." He asked to visit her classroom. She said, "Sure, if you want to!" He did want to, and the visit gave him important insights. He found Ms. Cloran not nearly so tough as she pretended to be. In fact, she was well organized, systematic, friendly, helpful, and task oriented. She did teach from her rocking chair a good bit of the time, but the pointer she held was for pointing, not striking, as some had imagined. Her instruction was text dominated, chalkboard supplemented, and test oriented; but she differentiated assignments, guided learning on a personal basis, and even utilized supplementary materials some. She read stories, kept library books around, and used lots of pictorial material.

When she did get out of her rocking chair, she generally stayed up front, putting material on the chalkboard or pointing to and discussing writing and sketches prepared earlier.

As Wayne departed with a wave and a smile, Loreen Cloran hardly looked up. But a scheme began to develop in his mind. Ms. Cloran had made a comment that struck a spark. One of her students was holding a paper to show, and the teacher said, "You know I must save my legs for later. Don't make me get up! Come over here and show me!"

Wayne Kennamer began to put together *her* need to sit, *her* use of chalkboard and pictorial material, and *his* desire to get overhead projectors into use. He decided on a straightforward approach. He borrowed some of her pictures, made copies of them on transparencies, and showed her the results on the screen. He demonstrated the use of the film roll as a moving chalkboard, emphasizing that she could use simple grease pencils, sit in her rocking chair, and have full command of all the chalkboard she wished.

Only a few weeks later Wayne Kennamer was visiting in Loreen Cloran's room again. This time he had several other teachers with him. They were observing the use of the overhead projector but a lot more also. The old matriarch had become a better teacher and was helping others grow on the job too. She and Wayne had worked together getting much of her regular material onto transparencies. She had developed a transparency file that reduced her use of the chalkboard, which students were now using more. She had a special stand that kept the overhead at the right level, right beside her rocking chair. She beamed as the other teachers watched her use the projector, first as a chalkboard, then for pictorial displays, and then to critique a sample of writing or reinforce a passage from the text.

won't work, or are too much work, or are impractical or too theoretical, despite their successful use right down the hall or across town.

Still another practical concern about helping people grow on the job, rather than just hoping it will occur, has to do with *timing*. Experience often doesn't offer what we need when we need it. Sometimes an experience is beyond our capabilities to absorb or analyze or adapt to our needs. At other times, we urgently need some enlightening experience, like that beautifully responsive youngster who makes a discussion click; but alas, there is no such person in the classroom today, so a chance for success is lost and we experience failure and disappointment. Or perhaps we try something new and promising and it just doesn't succeed. We need someone to provide coaching, feedback, and support, but neither the principal nor our supervisor is on hand to observe and help (Joyce and Showers 1983).

The new staff member is commonly inundated with experiences that tend to confuse and frustrate. Under such conditions learning rates may be reduced, and the person may adopt simplistic survival tactics. Such "successful" surviving may discourage further, later efforts to develop new skills and competencies; the survivor may not wish to take such risks again, let alone continually. Bill Thompson may well accept his principal's advice, and it may work, but how will he learn to function more like Jack Martinez?

Experienced personnel who have survived the trials and tribulations of being new on the job may receive little feedback on their performance they can use to assess the need for further growth. Under such conditions, the illusion may emerge in the mind of the isolated practitioner that his or her performance is quite satisfactory, highly successful, and adequate in all respects. Ms. Loreen Cloran may lose the opportunity to end a career feeling more competent than ever. To be sure, there are always problems, aggravations, even frustrations in the work life of the individual who is isolated in his or her endeavors. But these may be perceived, in the absence of feedback, as situational phenomena rather than as intrapersonal problems that might respond to changes in performance. Or, if the need for change is recognized, it may be sought in a random, rather unsystematic fashion, using only trial-and-error procedures. Furthermore, those changes in performance that ultimately seem to work may be only temporarily adopted if the perception guiding the search is one that holds the situation at fault.

Experience on the job is a good teacher if:

new experiences are provided
intellectual activity is related to the new experiences
negative outcomes are minimized
timing of experiences promotes learning in useful sequence

confusion and *frustration* are prevented
coaching and *feedback* for correcting faulty performance are available
choices of alternatives in performance are made in systematic ways

Assumptions about People

In-service education has no meaning at all except for the assumption that staff members can and will grow beyond minimum expectations of initial employment. It is often necessary to remind ourselves of this fundamental assumption and be careful not to act as if it were not so, as Ms. Cloran's principal seemed to be doing. However, the utility of *raw* experience as in-service education has been called into question. One does learn as the result of experiences, and learning continues throughout an active lifetime (Tyler 1985, 203). If this were not so, people could not survive long in rapidly changing societies. However, raw experience may be woefully inadequate. The team members at Swift High School may well need in-service training to survive.

Exhibit 1–1 presents a set of assumptions that seem a sound basis for approaching the tasks of in-service education. We start, of course, by assuming that on-the-job learning will occur. However, the other assump-

EXHIBIT 1–1. Assumptions Shaping In-Service Education

1. People can and will learn on the job.
2. People experience satisfaction from learning that is clearly perceived as appropriate.
3. People need feedback on their own behavior to make efficient use of experiences for learning (Tyler 1985, 204).
4. People need direct intervention in accomplishing some learning outcomes but not others (Joyce and Showers 1983).
5. People tend to want to learn some things at some times, under certain conditions, and at certain costs (but not under just any combination of these) (Blessing 1979, 29).
6. People are capable of learning anything if the time, conditions, and motivations (rewards) are adequate (Bloom 1976, 7).
7. People learn best those things they perceive to be meaningful, purposeful, and satisfying (Luke 1980).
8. People have developmental as well as situational and personal needs that can help to provide satisfaction (Maslow 1971, 55).
9. People must learn in order to survive in the long run. But they do not have to learn to survive in the short run; instead, they can cope, resist, or endure.
10. People learn in active states under conditions of mild arousal, attentiveness, and even stress.

tions are also stated explicitly and need to be more carefully analyzed if efforts to facilitate and promote in-service education are to be productive.

Assumptions about people's needs for satisfaction and feedback are closely related. Learning outcomes that are not perceived as appropriate are not viewed as potentially satisfying and hence are reluctantly pursued. However, less appropriate learnings once gained are less than truly satisfying and hence do not promote continuation of related kinds of learning activities. Feedback can help change the way people perceive reality and their perceptions of what is appropriate or inappropriate. Hence, it is not sufficient to say, "Well, if it's not appropriate to you, let's forget it." In Vignette 2, had Jane Hunt, a principal, viewed the erupting events in terms of the immediate emotional welfare of the child, she might have perceived bringing the child to the office as quite inappropriate. Instead, she was using the legalistic frame of reference that demanded a different kind of response and may have prevented her from learning enough to make an informed decision. Similarly, the Swift High School English team (Vignette 3), suffering from lack of feedback, is suddenly reacting to its own uncertainty.

The assumption about direct intervention to produce learning is the focal point of many considerations in designing sessions, selecting strategies, and guiding in-service participation by staff members. The issue that arises in connection with this assumption is whether people can guide and direct their own learning as adults or whether this may not be the case. Furthermore, if not all learning can be self-directed, how is the determination of the need for intervention to be made, by whom, and under what conditions? For example, did the principal at Swift High School intervene properly (Vignette 3)? Were the observations he has completed a form of intervention, or were they simply a response to his need to be informed? Did the principal err in not intervening earlier? Was it faulty to assume that learning to function as a team would be a natural outgrowth of sharing the same space and the same students over time?

The assumptions about people wanting to learn and being capable of learning are two sides of the same coin. Bloom's (1976) concept of "mastery learning" has been widely misinterpreted to mean that anyone can learn anything. In a completely abstract, theoretical sense, this may be true. Operationally, however, the time required, the conditions for learning, the prerequisite skills, and the motivation required to persist in a learning task (Tyler 1985) sometimes are too demanding. Similarly, it is true that all people undoubtedly seek to learn. But when, what, how, and at what cost?

Ann, the reading specialist on the Swift High School team, seems ready, willing, and able to learn a variety of things at the conference she is attending. But a three-day conference may not provide adequate time for her to learn what she seeks; the conditions found in a big conference setting may not be conducive to learning; or she may perceive the reactions of her teammates to be so discouraging that she may decide to enjoy the social festivities instead.

The last assumptions in Exhibit 1–1 fit no particular pattern. Each assumption seems important in its own right. Objectives are better attained when perceived to have not only meaning but purpose too, and there is satisfaction in the learning itself. Meaning and purpose are prerequisites of satisfaction in most instances. Satisfactions, however, are sometimes very personal; a sense of satisfaction is derived from having very personal needs met. Various situations demand certain performances and give satisfaction when they are forthcoming. Hence, the teacher who succeeds in enabling most of the students to pass the SAT in order to satisfy most parental expectations may feel satisfied. However, developmental needs are somewhat different. They change as we grow older; our values grow clearer, and life's circumstances may leave us more or less content with our lot in life. For most, the process of maturation is one of identifying new needs that we seek to satisfy with new learning, while old aspirations are left behind, realized or not. Ms. Cloran has no need to demonstrate her basic competence as a teacher, but Bill Thompson does. Ms. Cloran still has her sense of pride in her work, but the physical limitations of aging offer new problems to be faced.

That people must learn in order to survive seems self-evident, yet is a fact overlooked by educators who are constantly concerned with specific learnings. People may not learn as we wish they would, but there are no non-learners (Tyler 1985, 203). Learning is an active process, however, and in-service training can make a difference.

A Rationale for Staff Growth

In-service education is to the school operation what good eating habits and a balanced diet are to human growth and vitality. Without substantial continuing growth in competence in personnel serving in our elementary and secondary schools, the entire concept of accountability has little meaning. The heavy reliance upon *people* to perform nearly all tasks required for building and maintaining quality educational programs is a reality that cannot be treated lightly. It is this reality that gives in-service education both its importance and its urgency. Were it possible to run schools with less dependence upon personnel, as in some industrial operations, in-service growth would be less essential. Were the competencies of school personnel less complex in nature, limited in-service training might suffice. If a ready pool of highly competent people existed, improvements in education could be wrought by firings and replacements with less reliance upon in-service education. If few changes in the operation of the educational system were required in the near future, in-service education could be less of a concern.

If the present certified personnel who are serving in our schools had all come through rigorous four- or five-year programs of *preservice preparation,* in-service preparation might be less urgent. If futurists could assure us that extensive retirements and withdrawals from teaching would permit top quality restaffing of our schools in the near future, then preservice rather than in-service education might be the more urgent need.

None of these conditions seems to prevail in the present or is likely to prevail in the foreseeable future. Significant improvement of education cannot be accomplished, it would seem, without a major programmatic effort at the in-service education of personnel in all elementary and secondary schools. This view is supported, whichever way we turn, when we ask how we can accomplish the improvement of education. The staff is the heart of the operation of schools. Money, materials, time, space, facilities, and curricula—all these are important, too. But initially, in process, and ultimately, the ability of the staff to perform is crucial (Zumwalt 1982, 215).

In contrast with an automated operation, schools are heavily dependent upon human performance for nearly every aspect of their operation. Some might argue that schools are overly dependent on people and urge more efforts toward mechanical means to accomplish at least some of the high-cost operations of teaching. Hence, computer-assisted instruction, self-paced learning materials, and other approaches have been developed. However, these physical technologies have reduced dependence on people very little to date.

So long as people make the crucial difference in the school operation, their in-service education will be a vital concern. Even if a fully qualified, ideally competent staff were available, *time* would gradually erode that competence as conditions change and old competencies become obsolete. Even if new learnings could be gained from on-the-job experiences, staff turnover and the need to speed learning processes for some would still demand in-service education. The real problems confronting schools are enormous in comparison with any ideal conditions. The gap between what is known and what is in practice is enormous in nearly every school setting. The gap between what people can do and what they are potentially capable of doing is also enormous for most staff members. Even the gap between what people are doing and what they want to do is very great for many staff members.

Little has been said about *preservice* education as related to the need for in-service education. It would not be difficult to show the inadequacies of preservice programs for the preparation of teachers or counselors or supervisors. The literature abounds with such criticism. The contributions of preservice programs could also be lauded with references to significant improvements such as microteaching and competency-based training (Enos 1976). Historically, excessive confidence in formal teacher preparation via college or university courses has had a negative effect on in-service education opportunities for school personnel (Edmonds 1963, 6). Phillip Jackson supports this concern by noting that preservice training is "only the first stage of becoming a teacher" (1974, 38). Beginning teachers, administrators, librarians, and superintendents are provided (one hopes) with survival skills, and the public is (one also hopes) protected from "gross incompetence." The demonstration of competence in any complex job assignment is inevitably a matter of in-service education. Preservice education "is primarily an introduction to professional preparation" (Harris et al. 1969, 3). These are the realities, too long ignored, that make in-service education the most important developmental task to which the schools of the nation must attend in the decades ahead.

VARIOUS APPROACHES TO IMPROVEMENT

The improvement of instruction is the essential focus of in-service education. However, it is important to view this in perspective, to recognize the variety of approaches that can be utilized for improving instruction, for in-service education is not the only way. An initial distinction can be made between maintenance and change. The former consumes most of the time, personnel, and other resources allocated to school operations (Harris 1985, 23). The change function, in contrast to the maintenance function of the school operation, is often neglected. But neglected or not, changes can be wrought in diverse ways, each of which warrants special consideration; improving instruction means changing the ongoing operation in some way.

Changes can be *planned* or *unplanned*. In the former instance, we refer to them as developmental efforts or programs. In the instances of unplanned change, they tend to take the form of reactions, protective arrangements, coping mechanisms, and even organized resistance. The problems with unplanned change include the lack of predictability of outcomes and the high percentage of negative outcomes. Planned change offers no guarantees as a panacea, of course. However, when change goals are rationally selected, actions controlled to assure reasonable change rates, and precautions taken to assure minimum negative effect, the chances of improving learning opportunities for students are greatly enhanced.

Within the context of planned change, at least five rather different approaches to improvement are possible. Thinking more specifically about the improvement of instruction process, these approaches include:

1. improving instructional goals and objectives
2. improving instructional resources provided
3. improving the tools for instruction
4. improving the working conditions within which teaching and learning take place
5. improving staff performance

Obviously, the fifth approach relates directly to in-service education. The other four approaches are distinctly different, however, even though they might be utilized in concert with each other.

Improving Goals and Objectives

This approach to improving instruction tends to be most closely associated with curriculum development. It may well involve working with parents, staff, and students to secure changes in the school's instructional priorities. It might involve introducing new units, new lessons, or even new courses into the curriculum. While staff members will undoubtedly gain new knowledge and understanding as a result of working to change goals and objectives, the key outcomes tend to be substantially different. Changes in public perceptions, changes in students' expectations of themselves, changes in documents guiding teaching practices, and changes in content emphasized in classrooms are the direct, primary outcomes being sought in such operations. Concomitant changes in teacher performance are secondary, incidental, or indirect outcomes.

Because the school operation is so inevitably dominated by the people involved, it is virtually impossible to undertake changes in goals and objectives for instruction without also producing in-service growth, too. However, if goal setting is the purpose, in-service growth becomes a concomitant outcome. Furthermore, the in-service training required to assure that new goals and objectives will be fully utilized in skillful ways is essentially another matter. Hence, differentiation is important so that incidental in-service growth associated with curriculum development is not equated with the in-service education requirements for implementing new curricula.

There is another important distinction: Whereas any curriculum development activity is surely going to be productive of in-service growth, the involvement of personnel will necessarily be selective, for all personnel can rarely be involved in all goal setting. However, when the primary objective is effective goal setting and restructuring of instructional objectives, the criteria for selective involvement will be quite different from those used when the primary objective is in-service education. Two quite different outcomes can derive from a single effort, but both are not likely to be optimally served.

At the risk of oversimplification, these distinctions can be illustrated. For instance, the school that seeks to secure public support for family life education in its middle school curriculum will need in-service education for the teachers involved. However, those faculty members working most closely with the parents' advisory committee to study the family life education proposals may need to be those requiring the *least* in-service education. Conversely, planned efforts to introduce career education as an integrated set of objectives throughout the curriculum may waste much time unless in-service education for the staff has been thorough and has preceded the work of introducing new objectives.

The emphasis on these distinctions and the inevitable relationships between improving goals and objectives and in-service education should not cause the reader to lose sight of the importance of each. Instructional improvements can be gained by improving goals and objectives in the absence of other efforts. Such changes inevitably produce others, but curriculum change can be a main effect.

Improving Resources

The resources provided for use in facilitating instruction can substantially and directly improve learning opportunities for students. Resources of directly instruction-related kinds are diverse. Most obvious are fiscal and human resources. Within limits, fiscal resources can be converted into other kinds of resources that offer flexibility and variety in the ways that instruction can be improved. Human resources, while less flexibly employed, are obviously useful.

The use of funds for instructional improvement hardly needs to be illustrated. If money permits an increase in field trips, visiting lecturers, teacher aides, or other instructionally useful resources, there is at least some chance that student opportunities, too, will be enhanced. It is a common belief in educational circles that more money, less categorically budgeted and earmarked for instructional purposes, will improve instruction. Such direct relationships do seem to exist. While money per se is not as powerful as is often thought, using money for instruction is quite obviously a way to stimulate improvements, quite apart from in-service education.

Human resources are a much-neglected resource. Obviously, more money can secure more human resources. But most often, increases in monies available have been utilized primarily to increase salaries. In so doing, increased or improved human resources are *not* assured, regardless of the worthiness of such expenditures for humanitarian, social, economic, or other reasons. Another aspect of this neglect is the failure to utilize human resources readily available for improving instruction with little or no money required. The wealth of human talent available in parents, students, and citizens has long been recognized but only nominally exploited. Peer tutoring, work-study programs, parental involvement, citizen advisory groups, and cooperative vocational programs are but a few of the numerous examples of efforts to utilize available human resources more fully. When these resources are skillfully used and properly coordinated, considerable increases in numbers and varieties of people functioning within the school operation can be attained. Distinct improvements in instruction can be provided in these ways with limited additional funding. In-service education will generally be required to assure efficient use of such human resources. However, the potential for change—for improvements—is essentially that of more people to serve students better.

Improving Instructional Tools

Anthropologists and archaeologists often consider the tools of a society as a crucial indicator of the society's development. Similarly, the tools employed give distinctiveness to each craft, trade, or profession and may well be an indicator of its developmental sophistication. If this is true, teaching in most schools and colleges is only gradually developing, but changes are clearly evident. The tools of nearly all classrooms a century ago would be extremely few and simple—a book or two, a slate, paper, and little more. Two generations ago the motion picture, the library, and the laboratory were added, but the older tools were still predominant. Only one generation has passed since tape recorders, television sets, kits, and games have become parts of the instructional scene.

The opportunities for improving instruction by improving the available tools for teaching and learning continue to be substantial. This seems not to be a neglected area, however. Expenditures in real dollars for instructional materials and equipment have increased enormously in recent decades. One could demonstrate that much of the tool kit for instruction tends to be underutilized. For instance, if one walked into nearly any school in the land at any instructional hour, one would observe a tiny percentage of students using the library. Notice the often locked doors of the language laboratory in many high schools. Notice the continued reliance on a single text in many classrooms, the limited and crude use of films, and the reluctance to employ simulations and games.

The neglect in this tools approach to improvement of instruction has been more in *utilization* than in provisioning. Hence, in-service education may well be an important missing ingredient. Nonetheless, many teachers can make better use of more and different tools. Television sets are still far too scarce in many elementary and secondary schools to facilitate in-classroom instruction. The single basal textbook still dominates some classrooms because school officials will not authorize the multiple adoptions many teachers need to use. If the tools of the teacher were regarded as more important, in-service program activities could better train teachers in their efficient use.

Improving Working Conditions

The condition under which the teaching/learning process is directed has many facets. The physical conditions usually receive the most attention, but other conditions may be even more important. Industrial operations have long attended to breaks, lighting, music, leaves, and other working conditions to improve morale to assure peak productive efficiency among workers. Morale in the school setting is also important, and it extends well beyond teacher morale to students and parents alike.

Many aspects of working conditions involve provisions for basic human needs: a place to rest and relax during off periods; toilet and first-aid facilities close at hand, clean and adequate for both emergency and normal uses; a place to eat without noise and burdensome responsibilities. Pioneers in industrial human relations have demonstrated the importance of people's feelings about their jobs and their place in the factory.

Yet schools often neglect to provide for the simplest of agreeable working conditions from both a humane and an efficiency point of view, in the name of economy, even while splurging on extraneous matters. A recently completed college facility costing $9 million had massive, expensive sliding glass doors throughout but no place to sit and eat in comfort, no telephone privacy, and not a single lounge for instructors or students. Open-space schools can be massive caverns with all the comforts of a factory building, or they can provide alcoves, corners, and special spaces to offer comfort and privacy as well as functionality.

Relating working conditions—physical or psychological—to the improvement of instruction is not easily accomplished. Physical conditions —open space, new equipment, special facilities—offer opportunities or limitations that may still rely on in-service education for productive utilization. The high school team of Vignette 3 is an illustration of unfulfilled teaming within a very modern arrangement of open spaces.

Improving Staff Performance

Improving instruction through change in staff performance can be thought of as virtually synonymous with in-service education. But no, it is not yet so simple. Given a staff group, without change, a fixed entity—then how else does one improve their performance? In-service education is the answer. But suppose people are retiring, resigning, being dismissed, being hired, being reassigned, or being promoted? Each of these conditions constitutes change in staff and is potentially an opportunity for improving instruction (Harris et al. 1985).

The performance of individual staff members tends to be most responsive to change and improvement via in-service education. But staff groups are a slightly different matter. When a third-grade teacher leaves Jane Hunt's Airdale Elementary School, an opportunity to improve instruction is created. When the Swift High School principal begins to search for ways to improve the English team operations, he may well consider reassignments of personnel as an approach right along with in-service education. When Loreen Cloran retires, her unique competencies will not be replaceable, but Wayne Kennamer and Gordon Eckert will have an opportunity for reassignment as well as a replacement. Bill Thompson and Jack Martinez need not work another year separated by a hall from each other; they could become partners, sharing problems and ideas.

In Exhibit 1–2, given in a later section of this chapter, the distinction between staff development through *training* and staff development through *staffing* is shown. The procedures suggested previously relate to staffing, but they have considerable promise for improving instruction.

DEFINING IN-SERVICE EDUCATION

Scholars and practitioners offer many variations of the definition of in-service education. But there is also a great deal of similarity in both concept and terminology used concerning this important developmental task. Both the similarities and the differences are important to recognize. Unfortunately, an extensive array of closely related terms has come into common use in referring to in-service education, and most of these terms are used without definitions. Accordingly, they tend to create confusion regarding possible similarities or variations in meaning.

Among the widely used terms that are used as if they were almost synonymous with the term *in-service education* are:

on-the-job training   continuing education
renewal   professional growth
staff development   professional development
human resource development

Distinctions in meanings can and should be made among these terms. When they are used almost interchangeably, considerable uncertainty is created in the minds of many who are trying to communicate about in-service practices and concepts. Even some commonly used terms may take on special meaning. For instance, Nadler (1974) attempts to differentiate the meaning of *training* as learning, which is job related, from *education,* which is individual related, and from *development,* which is organization related. Obviously, such special meanings attached to commonly used words are very difficult to convey without reiteration, but these distinctions do represent an effort to be more precise about the meanings of terms.

A Definition

Throughout this book, the term "in-service education" is used to mean: *any planned program of learning opportunities afforded staff members of schools, colleges, or other educational agencies for purposes of improving the performance of the individual in already assigned positions.* This definition is intended to be broadly inclusive in certain ways while restricting the operations it embraces in other ways. For instance, no restrictions are implied on the kinds of activities to be provided. However, the purposes of in-service education are clearly restricted to learning outcomes related to the improvement of performances. The use of the term "staff" is unrestrictive, allowing for either broad or narrow application of in-service plans to various staff groups.

The essential terms utilized in this definition set some limits on the nature of in-service education as a task of the school operation.

A planned program is specified, eliminating a wide variety of events that accidentally or incidentally contribute to the purposes of in-service education. In prescribing in-service education as planned and programmatic, the emphasis is placed on designing learning experiences, assessing needs, projecting expectations, budgeting, assigning responsibilities, and evaluating.

Learning opportunities suggest the uniquely educational character of in-service education, distinguishing this task from curriculum development, staffing, public relations, and other tasks that may well be educative but that have quite different goals and objectives. For instance, engaging a staff group in the revision of a scope and sequence chart, selecting new text material, or working with the community to set instructional priorities are all developmental and valuable, and they may produce learning outcomes. However, insofar as the primary objectives of these activities are other than the learning of the staff, they are not included as in-service education under this definition.

Staff members are specified as the persons for whom in-service educational activities are planned. A reference to "teachers" is purposely omitted in this definition. In school settings, most in-service education should be targeted to teacher improvement because teachers are the bulk of the personnel employed. However, in-service education for administrators, aides, volunteers, supervisors, and board members cannot wisely be neglected. Of course, in agencies other than schools, in-service education is properly targeted to any staff group that is crucial to the effective operation of that agency.

Purposes of improving performance is a phrase with substantial hidden meaning. Improving rather than maintaining is implied, which in turn emphasizes the change process and eliminates monitoring activities. The term "performance" is utilized to emphasize job relatedness and practice. A narrow interpretation of this term would emphasize training activities and skill development. However, knowledge and attitude development are not excluded in this definition so long as they are clearly associated with job performance.

Still another omission is the term "instruction." To be sure, one could argue that in-service education should improve instruction. However, in-service education for noninstructional personnel is included within this definition, even though instructional improvement performances are obviously among the most important ones needed in school settings.

The individual is designated as the focus of in-service education in this definition. Obviously, only individuals can learn. However, the specification of individual performance as the focus for improvement emphasizes the concern for personal development within the school organization. The importance of needs assessment on a personalized basis is suggested. Furthermore, the implications of an individual focus are extensive when we come to consider planning procedures, the proper involvement of participants, and the array of learning alternatives that need to be afforded.

Already assigned positions is a restrictive phrase in this definition of in-service education. This is an essentially arbitrary restriction, which simply excludes a variety of educational endeavors that are directed toward changes in personnel assignments rather than toward improvements in present assignments. Arbitrary as this distinction is, it has the effect of giving emphasis to improving performance in assignment without running the risk of in-service activities being directed toward promotions to new positions or even out-migration from the field or agency being serviced (Edelfeldt 1976).

DIFFERENTIATING STAFF DEVELOPMENT

In a previous section, in-service education has been defined to include only limited aspects of supervision of instruction and program development. Similarly, various aspects of staff development and an array of terms in common use need to be more carefully defined. Throughout this book, staff development is seen as embracing much more than in-service education. Although general agreement does not exist on the meanings of these two terms, it serves educators well to become more precise in their use of them.

A Variety of Terms

The variety of basic titles or terms in current use to refer to in-service education is bewildering. Some are so general in meaning or so broad in scope of meaning that they cannot be useful when referring to in-service education. "Continuing education" undoubtedly is useful as a term referring to a great unspecified diversity of educational endeavor beyond the usual sequences of schools and colleges. "Professional growth" is likewise a term that may be useful in making reference to a very broad unspecified set of events. Neither of these terms can add anything but confusion, however, if utilized as synonyms for in-service education. "Renewal" appears to be one of those curious euphemisms used by some, in an effort to avoid an unfortunate connotation. Unfortunately, this term offers confusing niceties in place of precision in meaning.

Howsam (1977, 10) supports a very precise definition of in-service training and proposes to distinguish among three widely used terms: preservice education, in-service education, and continuing education. Yarger (1976) developed a more detailed five-stage model for describing the time sequence for professional training. The term "continuing professional development" has been utilized as an overarching concept referring to a variety of kinds of training. These various individuals and groups have developed terms that reflect concepts largely associated with teacher certification. When the focus is on the formally organized schools with clearly designated staff groups to be served, a somewhat different perspective seems more useful.

Staff Development

The focus on school operations is important in giving emphasis to the context within which the staff works; the purposes toward which they direct their energies and talents; and the relationships among staff development, in-service education, and other operations. Exhibit 1–2 emphasizes only one side of the school operation—*the change function*. Ignoring unplanned change, five distinctly different approaches to planned change are recognized. Only one of these is *staff development*.

Within this framework, two distinct aspects of staff development are suggested in this exhibit. One aspect of staff development is referred to as "staffing" because it involves an array of endeavors that determines who serves, where, and when. The staffing task is concerned with having the best person in the appropriate assignment at the right time (Harris et al. 1985). Change involves group composition as far as staffing is concerned.

The other side of staff development includes at least two kinds of training. *In-service education* involves training of the kinds defined previously. *Advanced preparation* involves training, too, but is quite different in numerous ways. This kind of staff development involves preparation for new, advanced, different job assignments. It is a very important aspect of staff development because it relates to manpower planning.

Advanced preparation differs from in-service education in deriving its goals and objectives from projected or anticipated future needs and alternative job assignments, creating a whole array of relationships between trainee and trainer that are distinctly different from those involved with in-service education. Manpower projections, selective admissions to training, transfers, promotions, and reassignment are a few of the special problems that come into view for advanced preparation approaches to staff development. Important as this approach is, especially in growth situations, it is not in-service education.

EXHIBIT 1–2. In-Service Education as a Part of Staff Development

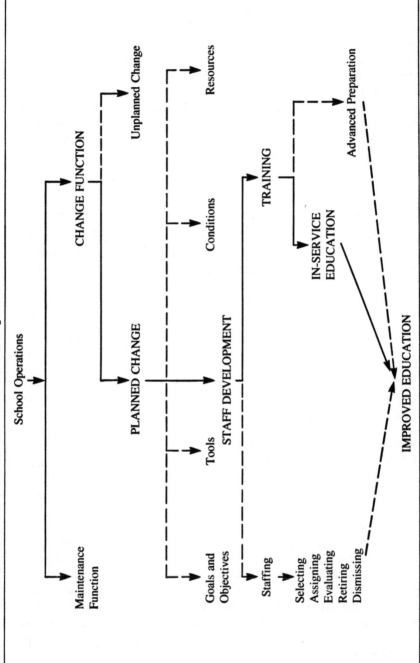

Adapted from *In-Service Education: A Guide to Better Practice* by Ben M. Harris, E. Wailand Bessent, and Kenneth E. McIntyre. (Englewood Cliffs, N.J.: Prentice-Hall, Inc., 1969).

EVOLVING CONCEPTS

The definition of in-service education provided in the previous section is consistent, to a large extent, with current practices and concepts presented in the literature of supervision of instruction, teacher education, and personnel administration. The essential character of the in-service education task as defined has a long tradition in both theory and practice, even though the concepts have been evolving and the terminology is currently in disarray.

Historical Perspective

Historically, in-service education has been reactive rather than proactive. The continuous expansion of the school systems and colleges of an ever expanding nation has necessitated hiring any available person and providing additional training thereafter. The constant loss of well-trained staff to industry and family rearing has created added pressures for the use of "homegrown" personnel with or without recognition of their need for in-service development. The growth of normal schools for preservice training was followed by rapidly developing college preparation programs, but the demand for teachers always seemed to outstrip the capacity of these institutions. The decade of the Great Depression (1929–39) provided one of the few opportunities for teacher supply to catch up to demand. But the World War II era quickly created new shortages that lasted for over thirty years (1945–75).

The past decade has become a short-lived interlude in a century-long struggle for both adequate quantity and high quality in the staff personnel of our schools (Schiffer 1980). It seems unlikely that the years ahead will fully resolve the old dilemma. Persistent shortages in the field of teaching ebb and flow with industrial demands and expanding opportunities for women in other occupations. And now, a new "baby boom" is already upon the land with college of education enrollments at a low level. The 1990s will surely be characterized by enormous shortages of classroom teachers. In-service education can serve to prevent a truly serious decline in educational quality.

The encyclopedic work of Barr, Burton, and Brueckner (1938) was the most influential writing in the 1940s dealing with in-service education as an essential aspect of instructional supervision. These writers emphasized a vast array of "improvement devices." This emphasis on process, procedure, and techniques was magnified by the extensive efforts of social psychologists and educators responding to post–World War II demands for in-service methodology. This was the "group process" era in which discussion leading, the evolution of the work group, group therapy, role playing, brainstorming, and buzz group techniques were being promoted.

Workshops replaced institutes, and action research and consultation became well-conceived ways of working. All of this had to do with in-service
education, even when that term was not explicitly used.

By the late 1950s in-service education had gained sufficient recognition
as a distinctive operation in school programs that the National Society for
the Study of Education devoted one of its yearbooks to the topic. Edmonds, Ogletree, and Wear (1963) were among a small group who were
pioneering studies of in-service education with financing from the Fund for
the Advancement of Education. Unlike earlier efforts that stressed either
helping teachers survive or improving human relations within the school,
Edmonds stressed "professional growth," echoing the earlier pronounce-
ments from the National Education Association (NEA). These writers further emphasized "the reality of the environment in which [the teacher]
teaches" as the basis for in-service experience, clearly breaking with earlier notions about teacher preparation as course work and degree seeking.
They also departed from earlier concepts in stressing "continuous and
constant effort," criticizing "erratic, occasional activities" (Edmonds et
al. 1963, 6). In these respects, these writers of the early 1960s were well
ahead of the practices of that era.

Post-Sputnik Developments

The post-sputnik era was one of new interest in in-service education related
to curriculum revision. The National Science Foundation institutes became
the fad, with $30 million spent in 1959 and $40 million in 1962. These
developments were regressive in the sense that a single approach and only
content learnings were emphasized to the near exclusion of any other concepts or strategies.

The era of institutes and curriculum reform gave educators an opportunity to begin to emphasize program development, innovative programming,
organizational restructuring for learning, materials development, and new
staffing patterns. All of these developmental efforts were stimulated by
various federal programs, including the Education Professions Development Act and the Elementary and Secondary Education Act with various
amendments. Curiously, these acts initiated many changes in instructional
programs in schools and greatly stimulated in-service education activities
for facilitating these specific planned changes in existing programs. However, the emphasis was on program change, not on the needs of personnel
for learning and growth as professional practitioners.

Even so, many federal programs began to serve in-service education
needs at local levels. Even though such in-service programs were often
distorted by compliance with guidelines of funding agencies, there were
opportunities and money for attempting to design new and more imaginative in-service education programs.

The ferment caused by extensive efforts at instructional innovations in schools began to place emphasis upon the concept of design. What had tended to be only fragments of change—a guide, an institute, a learning packet—in the late 1950s and early 1960s became increasingly programmatic in the late 1960s. Individually Prescribed Instruction (IPI), a set of materials, gave way to Individually Guided Education (IGE), an approach to restructuring operations. Team teaching, an organizational arrangement, gave way to open education involving teaming and much more.

Similarly, in-service design began to have meaning in the literature. Bessent edited a monograph in 1967 emphasizing concepts of in-service design. In this document, Michael P. Thomas, Jr., developed a rationale for "organizational learning" as an essential outcome of in-service education where program change is desired (Thomas 1967). This is but one of a whole host of efforts to *design* for in-service education utilizing gaming and simulations (Seidner 1976, 226), laboratory approaches (McIntyre 1967), and assessment/intervention systems among many others.

Current State of Affairs

This chronicle of in-service education as an evolving set of concepts and methodologies from 1940 to 1985 is hardly reassuring. Despite a long history of recognition as an essential part of the ongoing operation of the school program, in-service education seems constantly ensnared or diverted by less fundamental, but seemingly more urgent, development efforts. Most recently, statewide programs and even national commission reports stressing "excellence," "reform," or "school improvement" under other banners have often abandoned in-service education, giving it little or no attention. Instead, the current emphasis of both state and national policy-making seems to be on mandates for monitoring, testing, rewarding, regulating, dismissing, and promoting.

Nonetheless, a clearer notion about the unique character of in-service education as a developmental task of school organizations is emerging. This, in turn, is promoting fuller recognition of the fundamental importance of in-service education to the welfare of all concerned. Translating these new concepts into in-service education operations of better kinds is the substance of this entire book.

SUMMARY OF ESSENTIAL TASKS

This chapter has presented an introduction to in-service education as an approach to improving instruction in school settings. Tasks to be accomplished in mounting high-quality in-service education programs have been suggested but not analyzed in any detail. Much of this chapter has been focused on clarifying ideas, defining terms, looking at issues, and reviewing practices. The vignettes presented earlier were intended to give focus to the people who are in need of in-service learning opportunities. Assumptions about how people grow were briefly presented to provide a rational base for program planning. The different approaches to instructional improvements in schools were presented as a reminder that they are often associated with in-service efforts, yet must be clearly distinguished.

In rather carefully defining in-service education as a limited aspect of staff development, the writer seeks to give realistic, practical focus to all other chapters. There is a great need for better ways of conceptualizing the whole of staff development in education. Manpower planning, career development, selective recruitment, creative assignment, and productive personnel evaluation are all sadly neglected areas of *both* thought and practice in education. However, the focus of this book is not on any of these, because in-service education is more promising than any other aspect of staff development. More importantly, perhaps, it appears to be a cause whose time has come!

The tasks of building quality in-service programs are given detailed attention in subsequent chapters. Policies and other structural arrangements must be put into place at various levels—national, state, local, and individual. Strategies must be developed that can be responsive to a variety of problems, needs, and situations. Program plans are needed for implementing and maintaining ongoing operations offering learning experience of quality, but with strategic importance and continuity clearly recognized. The core of any program will always be the *session,* and the quality of the design for learning cannot be treated lightly. The training of leadership personnel to conceptualize, plan, implement, train, and evaluate for in-service education is perhaps a more serious concern than a chapter of this book can adequately reflect. The evaluation of in-service is a task that must be carefully provided for in order to assure both continuity and improvement in these operations.

Several chapters deal less with distinct tasks of in-service program development and are more illustrative in nature. Case studies, illustrations of instruments, plans, and training materials are provided in several chapters as well as in the Appendixes. It is hoped that these will serve as resource materials from which practitioners will wish to borrow.

STUDY SOURCES

American Association of Colleges for Teacher Education. 1979. "In-Service Education: Opportunities and Options." *Journal of Teacher Education* 30 (January-February).

> An entire issue devoted to in-service education; provides a variety of perspectives. While most of these articles emphasize policy, funding, and issues, a few report on research and promising practices.

Christensen, Judith C. 1985. "Adult Learning and Teacher Career Stage Development." Chap. 8 in *Career-Long Teacher Education*, edited by Peter J. Burke and R. G. Heideman. Springfield, Ill.: Charles C. Thomas, Publishers.
Various theories of adult development are reviewed: maturational, life-age, lifecycle, and developmental stages. Andragogy as contrasted with pedagogy is discussed.

Cropley, A. J., and R. H. Dave. 1978. *Lifelong Education and the Training of Teachers*. Advances in Lifelong Education, Vol. 5. UNESCO Institute for Education. Oxford: Pergamon Press.
A thoughtful treatment relating adult education to teacher education. Both preservice and in-service models of teacher education are discussed. The authors use UNESCO programs and projects in several countries as examples.

Gage, N. L. 1978. *The Scientific Basis of the Art of Teaching*. New York: Teachers College Press.
A brief but very helpful perspective on what is known about good teaching (considerable), balanced by the recognition that much is still not known and may remain more an art than a science. Gage argues for making better use of what we know as a basis for improving practice in very substantial ways.

Grant, Carl A., ed. 1981. "Staff Development: State of the Scene and Possibilities." *Journal of Research and Development in Education* 14 (Winter). Athens, Ga.: University of Georgia, College of Education.
A complete issue devoted to various topics; provides many perspectives. The first article identifies three "domains" of in-service and discusses six guiding principles. Other articles emphasize planning.

Harris, Ben M. 1985. *Supervisory Behavior in Education*. 3d ed. Englewood Cliffs, N.J.: Prentice-Hall, Inc.
As a general reference on instructional supervision, chapters 3, 4, and 5 have general applicability to in-service education. Chapter 11 reports cases of programs in operation. Appendix B details competencies required for directing in-service education programs.

Harris, Ben M., K. E. McIntyre, Vance Littleton, and D. F. Long. 1985. *Personnel Administration in Education*. 2d ed. Boston: Allyn and Bacon, Inc.
The first three chapters provide useful information on educational developments in public schools in the United States over the past century. Chapter 1 stresses change process and emphasizes instructional change. Chapter 2 outlines personnel functions, giving perspective on the broad array of in-service training demands in most schools. Chapter 3 reviews innovations and contrasts them with persistent traditional practices that might well be the focus of in-service training in many situations.

Hasazi, Susan E., Catherine Batsche, Lorella McKinney, Douglas H. Gill, John Langone, and R. Brian Cobb. 1983. *Vocational Education for the Handicapped: Perspectives on Inservice Personnel Development*. Personnel Development Series, Doc. 6. Washington, D.C.: Division of Personnel Preparation, Office of Special Education and Rehabilitation Services. ERIC ED 224 939.
A document dealing essentially with policy and planning concerns for in-service

programming. Chapter 1 reviews current practices. Chapter 2 discusses planning strategies, while chapters 3 and 4 attend to procedures and evaluation.

Joyce, Bruce, and Beverly Showers. 1983. *The Power of Research on Training for Staff Development*. Alexandria, Va.: Association for Supervision and Curriculum Development.

A brief overview of key concepts relating to in-service education and training that clearly affects teaching practice. The authors stress the use of coaching as a strategy for transferring knowledge and skill into practice.

Lieberman, Ann, and Lynne Miller, eds. 1979. *Staff Development: New Demands, New Realities, New Perspectives*. New York: Teachers College Press.

An excellent collection of readings on a variety of topics relating in-service to school change, unionization, teacher centers, and a variety of other topics. This volume presents many points of view and identifies many issues and problems.

Lieberman, Ann, and Lynne Miller. 1984. *Teachers, Their World and Their Work: Implications for School Improvement*. Alexandria, Va.: Association for Supervision and Curriculum Development.

Chapter 5 of this monograph reviews and synthesizes an array of studies on school improvement efforts. The authors emphasize the teacher in the process as one in need of understanding, support, and training, as well as involvement.

Nevi, Charles. 1986. "Against the Grain: Half-Truths That Hinder Staff Development." *Principal* 65 (January): 44–46.

A curriculum director criticizes overly simplified or misapplied principles of in-service. He calls them "half-truths." He calls into question needs assessments, single sessions, reliance on collaboration, and the principal as "leader," among other practices. A good discussion piece!

Peterson, P. L., and H. J. Walberg, eds. 1979. *Research on Teaching*. Berkeley, Calif.: McCutchan Publishing Co.

Discusses complexity of teaching as revealed by research. Argues for a "deliberate orientation" in line with views of Eisner and others. Urges policy initiatives that avoid rigid, mechanistic approaches to improving teaching.

Schiffer, Judith. 1980. *School Renewal through Staff Development*. New York: Teachers College Press.

One of the few sources for reviewing staff development and in-service education in historical perspective. The author stresses teacher development efforts from colonial times to the present. Much of this work emphasizes authority/autonomy relationships in teacher development. The perspective is predominantly that of a New Yorker, emphasizing the rise of teacher unions.

Zumwalt, Karen K., ed. 1986. *Improving Teaching*. ASCD Yearbook. Alexandria, Va.: Association for Supervision and Curriculum Development.

An excellent source of a broad variety of views on the general topic; various chapter authors stress such diverse strategies as technical consultation, self-analysis, peer supervision, collegial support groups, and curriculum development. Curiously, all writers manage *not* to mention the words *in-service education*.

2.
Principles and Strategies

INTRODUCTION

The general overview of the nature of in-service education in the previous chapter is made more explicit here with a focus on the purposes to be served, the principles and guidelines that assure effectiveness, and the strategies available to guide planning.

In-service education is only one of numerous approaches to improving education, hence, the specific purposes best served need to be clearly kept in mind. No developmental task is an answer to all things. Purposes need to be carefully defined so that training is utilized only to the extent and in the ways that produce desired results.

Principles and guidelines for planning and organizing high-quality in-service education are still being debated and studied. However, the research of recent decades plus the successes and failures in past practice have provided a substantial array of principles by which we can function. Principles have their greatest utility in guiding specific practices based on the wisdom of past experience. Without such guidelines we run the risk of reinventing the wheel and reliving past failures.

Strategic considerations are still much neglected in the thinking about quality in-service education. Various groups and individuals are often advocates for policies and programs that imply only simple notions about location, control, relationships, or types of activity sequences. Rarely are these isolated concerns or simple proposals brought together in any unifying manner. This chapter attempts to offer a framework for thinking, at least, about relating purpose, principles, and strategies.

GUIDING PRINCIPLES

Various writers have proposed sets of operating principles as guidelines for in-service planning. A surprising amount of similarity is found in the guidelines suggested by Edelfeldt (1976), Joyce and Showers (1983), Lawrence and Harrison (1980), Lieberman and Miller (1984), and McLendon (1977) and the principles listed here. All workers in this field have a natural tendency to give emphasis to biases and interests. Hence, we rarely give attention to the broader picture. An effort has been made here to synthesize and generate a comprehensive list of reasonably defensible guiding principles.

Clients Served

1. All personnel within a designated target organization or operating unit should be provided opportunities for in-service education.
2. No client should be required to participate in a specific program or session.
3. Different client groups (or individuals) should be recognized within any given program plan.
4. Individuals or groups should be designated as clients on the basis of rational and explicit relationships between needs and goals.
5. Groupings of clients should be developed to facilitate optimum learning.

Timing of Training

6. Time frames normally allocated for in-service programs should be part of the normal work load.
7. Special events, requiring substantial variations in normal work load, should be utilized sparingly.
8. Time allocations should allow for continuity of training experience.
9. Time allocations should allow for flexible use of time as needed.

Involvement

10. Clients should have opportunities to serve as planners, designers, managers, presenters, and evaluators.
11. Clients should be provided opportunities for making choices among alternative activities.
12. All personnel involvement should recognize needed competence.
13. Client perceptions of needs in relation to job realities should be criteria influencing involvement.

Locale(s) for Training

14. The locations selected for training should reflect training requirements rather than preferences.

15. The use of remote locations should be open options.

16. Cost/benefit ratios rather than simple cost figures should be used to justify remote locations.

17. Remote locations should be planned with predeparture and reentry activities to assure effectiveness.

Resources

18. Time should be provided to meet urgent needs and assure quality experiences.

19. Personnel, programs, materials, and other resources should be shared among various institutions providing training.

20. Funds for in-service education should be budgeted through normal channels regardless of source.

21. Costs associated with full participation should be fully defrayed without personal expense to clients.

Locus of Control and Decision

22. Those most directly affected should be most completely involved in decisions.

23. Control over various operations should be retained close to the people responsible.

24. Decision making should involve all who have responsibilities.

Scope of Planning

25. Program plans should be clearly related to larger efforts at improving instruction.

26. Each school district, college, service center, state department, and other educational entity should have a comprehensive plan for ISE.

27. Program schedules and timetables should provide for continuity, both within the program and among related programs.

Systematicness of Planning

28. Program planning should continue as implementation and process evaluation indicate needs for change, refinements, and additions.

29. Program plans should include statements of objectives that are specific in identifying the kinds of performance changes anticipated.

Design for Learning

30. The design of activity sequences and materials for use should provide for differentiated experiences.
31. The activities and materials should be designed to assure active, meaningful, and purposeful experiences.
32. A great variety of activities should be planned that are both task oriented and reality based.

Content for Learning

33. Objectives should be selected to reflect both organizational development needs and those of individuals.
34. Objectives should be identified that relate directly to job expectations of important kinds.

Incentives for Participation

35. Special incentives should be provided whenever activities extend beyond the normal workday or year.
36. Negative incentives should be eliminated.

Leadership

37. Responsibility for each major component of in-service programming should be clearly assigned.
38. Responsibilities for each major component should be assigned on the basis of available time, expertise, commitment, and involvement.

Evaluation

39. A planned, systematic evaluation effort should be part of any major ISE program.
40. Efforts to evaluate ISE should be focused primarily upon identifying strengths, weaknesses, and possible improvements.
41. Objective data, free of bias and error, should be utilized for evaluation purposes.
42. Both short-term and longer-term evaluation efforts should be planned.
43. The scope and complexity of the evaluation effort should be consistent with the extensiveness of the ISE program.

Policies

44. Policy statements should clearly indicate that ISE is both a right and a responsibility of all faculty and staff.

45. Policy should clearly provide for funding, staffing, and standard operating procedures.

46. Policy should provide for cooperative and collaborative relationships with colleges, service centers, and other selected agencies.

System Relationships

47. Program and personnel evaluation data should be utilized as data bases for ISE planning.

48. The unique contribution of ISE to other program and projects should be clearly identified in planning and operating documents.

49. Other developmental programs should be adapted and planned so as to assure coordinated implementation along with ISE programs.

PURPOSES TO BE SERVED

Planning, organizing, and implementing in-service programs must be guided by differentiated individual purposes and needs as well as by fundamental guiding principles as previously stated. This focus on the individual can be promoted via overall operational plans that clearly reflect four different purposes:

> basic, generic competency development
> remediation of inappropriate performance patterns
> specialized competency development
> innovations-related competency development

Any individual staff member may need one or more kinds of in-service training, but any given training experience is *not* likely to serve more than a single purpose. Furthermore, programs of in-service education, planned with one or more of these four purposes in mind, is likely to be more effective if each purpose is clearly designated and appropriate plans developed accordingly.

COMPETENCY DEVELOPMENT. This refers to in-service education and training that relate to the preservice goals of the teaching profession. The development of a common core of generally accepted and widely employed competencies is the purpose. Such programs recognize the limited character of preservice programs; they seek to assure more than survival levels of competence and eliminate deficiencies.

REMEDIATION. This refers to the elimination of undesirable practices. The retraining or behavior-modifying approaches are called for. This is the aspect of in-service education that is necessarily most highly individualized. It is critically important both because of the difficulty of eliminating certain inappropriate behavior patterns that may have been developed over many years and also because these patterns often interfere with basic generic performances.

SPECIALIZED COMPETENCY DEVELOPMENT. This refers to competencies that have importance to only a limited number of staff members because of unique position, role, or problem. Hence, they are sometimes advanced levels of competence of generic kinds or truly different competencies.

INNOVATIONS. This refers to the special sequence of in-service education that must be associated with each systematic effort to introduce a significant change in the operation that also demands substantial changes in people as well as structures. In-service activities supporting systematic adoption of innovations involve awareness training and systematic trials with associated evaluation activities to determine feasibility and relative advantages.

Each purpose will be different for individual trainees who are appropriately involved. Preconditions and needs assessment procedures will be substantially different for each purpose. Furthermore, the staff assigned, the strategies employed, the locale selected, and the time frame utilized may all be affected by the realities of purpose.

To illustrate only a few of these differential implications of purpose for operations and planning, consider a program to implement individualized instructional practices in a given school system. For new teachers, the focus may be *basic, generic skill* development in organizing and operating classrooms with multiple-activity groups. For certain experienced teachers, the focus may be *remedial* in the sense that rigid achievement standards with undifferentiated objectives are eliminated and replaced with at least a limited variety and flexibility in expectations. For primary teachers, the focus may be upon developing *special* competence in the use of diagnostic testing procedures in determining reading deficiencies of selected students. For an entire team and their principal in one school, the focus may be upon the numerous changes in procedures, new knowledge of materials, and the team-planning competencies essential to operating as a team-teaching program in conjunction with a newly developing media resource center.

For each individual or group, the appropriate locale, staffing, and strategy may be quite different. The new teachers may need highly individual assistance with in-class guidance as new room arrangements and lesson plans are tested. The remedial efforts to reduce rigidly enforced standards on students, with no options in content or in learning mode, may require a strategy of carefully designed behavior modification, including the use of peer influence. For the innovative team, the local building where the new facility exists will be the locale for much of the training activity. However, the primary-grade teacher group may attain specialized competence in diagnostic assessment of reading skills on a college campus in summer, with the help of a laboratory that is in operation there.

RELATING PURPOSE TO PRINCIPLE. The four essential and different purposes to be served by in-service education require careful attention in planning programs. Operating principles can better serve as guides for planning when related to the specific purposes to be served. Just as differentiating purposes helps assure that individual needs of trainees will be better served, so relating purposes to principles assures that the latter will be applied so that form follows function. Ritualistic use of guiding principles is neither intended nor desired. Instead, careful planning is required to apply each principle to the extent that it serves well to assure the quality of the in-service program in operation that produces results.

Many of the guiding principles presented here have applicability to an in-service education-planning endeavor regardless of the purpose to be served. However, certain groups or clusters of principles may require special consideration when different purposes are in focus. For instance, special competency development (purpose 3) requires much more critical consideration of principles relating to clients than is likely to be true for generic competency development (purpose 1), since the latter embraces larger portions of the total staff. On the other hand, if a crisis situation prevails, timing principles become especially critical when remedial purposes are being served; but timing is almost always of critical importance when innovative purposes (purpose 4) are being served, because the success of the entire venture may be at stake and the various stages of implementation are sequenced rather explicitly.

Exhibit 2–1 attempts to indicate the *more* critical relationships between clusters of principles and each type of in-service purpose. The symbol (+) is inserted to suggest that a cluster of principles might be more important to consider seriously and systematically when planning in-service programs for a particular purpose. Accordingly, the principles relating to clients— who they are, whether they are required to participate or not, and how a group is designated—are worthy of special review for program planning of any kind. In contrast, the principles relating to timing are designated as of special importance only for remediation and innovation purposes. This is not to suggest that other plans ignore work load, reimbursements, continuity, and flexibility in use of time. However, these principles may not be so clearly important when basic and specialized competency development is being served.

The principles that appear to be most clearly important to all in-service education purposes are those related to clients and design. It seems ines-

EXHIBIT 2–1. More Critical Relationships between Principle Clusters and In-Service Purposes

	PURPOSES			
PRINCIPLE CLUSTERS	1 BASIC, GENERIC	2 REMEDIA- TION	3 SPECIAL- IZED	4 INNOVA- TIONS
Client Served	+	+	+	+
Timing Training		+		+
Involvement			+	+
Locale for Training		+		+
Resources		+	+	+
Locus of Control and Decision		+	+	
Scope of Planning	+			+
Systematicness of Planning		+		+
Designing for Learning	+	+	+	+
Content for Learning		+	+	+
Incentives for Participation	+	+		
Leadership		+		+
Evaluation		+		+
Policies	+	+		
Systems Interrelated	+	+		+
	6	13	6	12

capable in any effort at program planning and implementation, if it is likely to be effective and efficient, that the clients and their experience be given full consideration. However, most clusters of principles may be differentially important according to purposes to be emphasized in program planning. Generic or basic and specialized competency development are shown by this analysis in Exhibit 2–1 to be somewhat less dependent upon the application of a full array of guiding principles. These purposes are quite similar in that only a few highly important clusters of principles are related to each. However, they are different, too. Basic, generic purposes are related to scope of planning, incentives, policies, and interrelatedness of systems. The more specialized purposes give importance to principles related to involvement, content, resources, and control.

Both *remediation* purposes and those related to *innovations* seem to be more fully dependent upon a full array of operating principles. Thirteen out of the fifteen clusters of principles seem quite important for consideration when programs for remediation purposes are being considered. It may well be that since this purpose is based on a "deficient model," has negative connotations, and is often made necessary because of prior neglect, it is an unduly sensitive operation. For quite different reasons, *innovations*-related competency development purposes also require full consideration of twelve out of the fifteen clusters of operating principles. These programs are *sensitive,* too. They often involve heavy commitment to major changes; they involve many unknowns; participants are often on the spot to demonstrate change; and complex systems adaptations may be related to the in-service efforts.

STRATEGIES FOR TRAINING

In-service training programs are properly conceived in great variety. Current practice embraces highly individualized efforts, elaborate "supermarket" operations, and tightly focused courses. It is still common for a faculty meeting or grade-level meeting to pose as "in-service," with or without objectives or design. The planning for and direction of continuing in-service education programs is discussed in detail in other chapters. Here it is more appropriate to review various strategic considerations bearing on the kinds of training provided and the overall quality of the experiences that result.

Focus on Trainee

In-service training of a wide variety of kinds shares a common strategic concern for serving the "needs" of the trainee. Clinical supervision programs, for instance, are highly individualized and give extensive freedom to the trainee to influence the process. Other individualized approaches may offer the structure of a diagnostic analysis system (Harris and Hill 1982), or the personally tailored plan of management by objectives (MBO) (Redfern 1980). Personalized in-service programs as discussed in detail in Chapter 6 attempt to offer a unique service to each individual. Even large programs of supermarket or cafeteria design often serve to address individual trainee needs or interests as they offer choices in topics and alternative schedules.

Small group approaches to in-service training may also be heavily influenced by strategic consideration for the individual participant. Groups that are small allow for more individual expression. Groups organized around common interests, needs, or affiliations emphasize the trainee as an individual. Mouton and Blake (1984) make a new and significant contribution to training in small groups with their notions about *synergogy* and the place of participants as responsible stimulators of their own learning.

Emphasis on Experiences

It has been said that "the medium is the message," and so it may be with in-service programs emphasizing a particular kind of medium or activity as a strategy for training. Computer-assisted training, simulations, games, field trips, laboratory exercises, and even discussion groups all have in common the emphasis on a particular kind of experience. The compelling character of the experience offers in-service participants unique opportunities that are often assumed to transcend individual needs.

Each selected kind of experience or any combination of them has special advantages for training. The computer speeds information processing; simulations encapsulate and simplify reality; field trips show reality in its full complexity. When the strategic emphasis is on selecting particular experiences, it minimizes concern for individual needs or preferences. But rich and varied experiences do accommodate diverse needs.

Emphasis on Outcomes

All in-service education is by definition concerned with learning outcomes; however, the nature of those outcomes and the specificity with which they are emphasized are important elements of strategy. When knowledge outcomes are of primary interest, then the application and use to which such knowledge is put becomes secondary and the strategic demands are simplified. When specific skills command attention as primary outcomes, their application to specific performance changes is likely to be more clearly in focus and strategies are made more complex.

The greatest demands for strategic planning for in-service education are often found when outcomes involve complex changes in many aspects of behavior. Innovative programs succeed or fail for various reasons, but none appears more central than the demand for changes in roles, ways of thinking, self-concept, knowledge, skill, and relationships. Hence, a simple innovation seeking to introduce a few hours a week of television or study-film programming into the classroom has been generally a failure despite a half century of concerted efforts by many agencies. Such massive failures are at least partially explained by training endeavors which were consistently lacking in strategic consideration of the enormous variety of outcomes required.

Relating Trainee to Experience to Outcomes

Each of the three strategic considerations identified here has a place of importance in promoting good in-service education and training. The relationships between each of these that can be reflected in the design of the program will be important in determining overall effectiveness.

In Exhibit 2–2 illustrative relationships between individual needs, the type of experiences planned, and the intended outcomes from the program are presented in highly abbreviated form. Where outcomes are simple and associated with an isolated individual, the experiences needed are limited in scope, number, and type. However, when either the diversity or com-

EXHIBIT 2–2. Relating Trainee to Experience to Outcomes

TRAINEE CONCERNS	TYPES OF EXPERIENCES	INTENDED OUTCOMES
(a) To know about . . .	To read . . .	To understand . . .
(b) To operate . . .	To demonstrate . . . To try . . . To receive correctives . . . To use . . .	To perform as a skilled operator of . . .
(c) To feel confident . . .	To be observed . . . To receive assistance . . . To get positive reinforce- ments . . .	To become more self- confident about . . .

plexity of the need is great, then strategic concerns for the kind of experiences that will be effective must be extended. If both needs and outcomes are diverse and complex, then experience requirements are still further complicated. In Exhibit 2–2, the combination of (a), (b), and (c) might represent a growth plan for an individual. However, if a faculty group is the focus of the training endeavor, then the strategic requirements for serving them are greatly multiplied. The logistics of working with a group instead of an individual are one factor. However, individuals within a group are still very different from one another with respect to their interests, available time, priorities, and prerequisites. Hence, the planning for this simple array of outcomes still necessitates thoughtful consideration of a variety of relationships between individuals, experiences needed, and outcomes desired.

Other Strategic Concerns

Immediate versus *intermediate* versus *long-term* outcomes is an issue of practical import. As busy practitioners, teachers are most eager for training that promises immediate worth. Unfortunately, those outcomes easily and quickly produced are also least likely to be of great consequence. Longer-term outcomes may be more highly valued, if they can indeed be produced. But the experienced teacher knows only too well about the shifting fads of school improvement programs. Teachers tend to be wisely skeptical about long-term commitments that fade away in a year or less. Hence, the "a bird in the hand" attitude prevails in many schools. The strategic problem is to respond to immediate needs and interests, and still sustain commitments to larger accomplishments.

Knowledge versus *technique* versus *practice* is still another issue of strategic importance. The design of training for knowledge acquisition is deceptively simple, and well-known arrangements are available—courses, lectures, videotapes, study groups, and so on. To emphasize technique also has the allure of simple task analysis converted to behavioral objectives. "Tell us what you want and we'll train for it" is the standard slogan. In a larger sense, the strategic problem is to design to avoid neglect of knowledge, avoid mechanistic emphasis on techniques, but to foster change in practice that combines knowledge, understanding, skill, and good judgment. This is akin to the best concepts of *competence* (Harris et al. 1985), but such training calls for very rigorous efforts over extended periods of time (Showers, 1985).

QUALITY CHARACTERISTICS

As suggested at the beginning of this chapter, one can expect high-quality in-service education in a variety of forms. There is no one best model or design, even though the list of principles offers many specific ideas that should guide in planning, implementing, and evaluating programs, as well as delivery systems that offer multiple programming. Still, there is much to be said for trying to conceptualize quality ISE in terms of a limited array of features or characteristics that are independent of specific strategies or techniques.

Two studies have recently been completed that provide convincing evidence regarding at least some quality characteristics. In one study, Hagen (1981) investigated in great detail the features of three distinctly different, yet apparently successful in-service education programs. In another study, Cavender (1986) has analyzed the operations of over seventy school district programs which were nominated by independent judges as truly high in quality.

Unlike so many reported studies of in-service efforts, these two were focusing upon actual in-service education programs as they were operating in public school situations. They were not associated with special research programs, nor with funded projects. They also are studies of operations that have had continuity over time and a reputation for quality.

These two studies approach the question of quality characteristics from very different perspectives, yet both found strong evidence that characteristics do exist that are relatively independent of specific forms of training.

Contrasting Three Delivery Systems

Based on a review of the literature and previous studies by Lawrence et al. (1974), Joyce (1977), Lozano (1980), Yarger (1976), Almanza (1980), Creekmur (1977), and others, Hagen identified 18 widely regarded characteristics or practices. She then selected three operating school programs or "delivery systems" for study. Each selected program was known to be well organized and well supported by staff and funds, and had been in operation for several years. The selections were made with additional attention to *design features*. Each program was dramatically different in design. The names of these programs are at least somewhat descriptive of these differences:

1. *Equivalent Time Program.* This was a rather elaborate program utilizing a "supermarket" or "cafeteria" approach with extensive offerings, freedom of teacher choice, and time-reimbursement features.
2. *Individual Professional Guided Improvement Program.* This was patterned after well-known MBO models, managed at the building level, and provided with staff and fiscal resources. It was implemented with a strong effort to maximize teacher initiative and autonomy.
3. *Professional Development Center Program.* This was a highly structured operation with a team of trainers, a special training facility, a preplanned program involving intensive workshops followed by in-building implementation activities with trainers acting as "coaches" and support staff.

Characteristics were assessed for each of these three programs by the researcher. Classroom teachers and a panel of on-site administrators and supervisors provided data. The researcher conducted in-depth interviews, site visits, and document reviews to construct analytic case studies before making assessments of characteristics. Classroom teachers were asked to assess their program on the eighteen characteristics based on their individual experiences as participants for a year or more. Teacher satisfaction and impact estimates were also obtained from teachers.

Exhibit 2–3 reports on the correlations between teacher satisfaction with their in-service education and the array of characteristics. Strikingly positive correlations were produced for intensity of training experience, active involvement in training, individualization reflecting needs, and certain forms of incentives. Equally interesting were the negative correlations found for a variety of characteristics relating to grouping, content, grade level, incentives, and experience in the program.

Additional analyses of these teacher reports on their in-service experiences showed three clusters of characteristics to be most clearly associated with teacher satisfaction. *Intensity of training* accounted for 39 percent of the satisfaction and was consistently high for all programs. *Degree of involvement* and *individualization* were also related to teacher satisfaction, but with less effect (Hagen 1981, 122–23).

EXHIBIT 2–3. Correlations between Teacher Satisfaction and In-Service Program Characteristics

CHARACTERISTICS OF THE PROGRAM	CORRELATION COEFFICIENTS
Focus	
1. Relating to a specific discipline	−0.097
2. Focused on an instructional process	−0.035
3. Directed toward a product	−0.085
4. Focused on concepts	−0.113
Individualization	
5. Activities tailored to meet needs of individuals	+0.453
Incentives	
6. College credit available	+0.200
7. Stipends paid	−0.011
8. Compensatory time provided	−0.258
9. Assessed needs emphasized	+0.279
10. Evaluation of one's own instruction	+0.268
Grouping for Training	
11. By grade or subject groups	−0.097
12. By levels (elementary and secondary)	−0.167
13. By program (Title I, gifted, etc.)	−0.069
14. By assessed needs	+0.315
15. By individual choice	−0.036
Involvement	
16. Extent to which participants are actively involved	+0.476
Intensity	
17. Extent to which training was dynamic	+0.617
18. Years of experience with this same program	−0.220

Impact estimates of teachers, even in the most satisfying and high-quality programs, were modest. Most teachers for all three programs indicated only moderate effects on their classroom teaching practices. Exhibit 2–4 reports on these impact estimates of teachers by program. It seems that these programs all had some impact on the practice of the vast majority of participants, but the amount of this impact varies substantially for individuals. Nonetheless, 44 percent to 77 percent of the teachers in each program report substantial impact on their teaching from such training.

Similarities among Seventy-four Programs

Cavender's (1986) study included a broad array of ongoing in-service education programs in local school districts. He secured nominations of specific programs from a large number of educational leaders. He then invited program directors of all nominated programs to verify the contin-

EXHIBIT 2–4. Teachers' Estimates of Impact of ISE on Their Classroom Teaching Practices

	IMPACT ESTIMATES (% OF TEACHERS)				
PROGRAMS	NONE	SMALL	MODERATE	LARGE	COMPLETE
1. Equivalent Time Program (n = 200)	18	38	37	7	0
2. Individual Professional Guided Improvement Program (n = 264)	8	33	46	11	2
3. Professional Development Center Program (n = 129)	2	22	54	19	3

Adapted from Hagen (1981, 119).

uing character of the operation, and sought agreements for participation in the study. Seventy-four out of about a hundred programs were then studied.

A survey questionnaire was completed for each program describing its operating characteristics. Follow-up case studies were also undertaken to verify reports and extend findings.

This study focused upon specific characteristics that are seemingly related to the transfer of knowledge and skill into classroom teaching practice. Twenty-five descriptors of operating practices were clustered to produce scores for six characteristics for each program. Exhibit 2–5 summarizes these scores for seventy-four programs. These raw scores have little meaning in themselves, but they do show considerable range among the programs, as might be expected. Total scores summed across the six

EXHIBIT 2–5. Summary of In-Service Education Characteristics for Seventy-four Programs

PROGRAM CHARACTERISTICS	MAXIMUM POSSIBLE SCORE	MEAN SCORE	% SCORE	RANGE
Needs: Teacher needs, relation to program objectives, etc.	8	6.5	81	2–8
Goals: Expectations for teaching outcomes, etc.	32	26.3	82	15–32
Plan: Forecasting of barriers, teacher involvement, etc.	40	26.1	65	5–38
Design: Incentives, time, location, etc.	120	53.4	45	11–90
Experience Impact: Groupings and types of activities, etc.	80	53.9	67	17–75
Follow-up: Frequency, duration, evaluation, etc.	40	27.3	68	12–39

EXHIBIT 2–6. Program Characteristics Associated with Impact and Follow-through

NEEDS & PLANNING   DESIGN & GOALS   IMPACT & FOLLOW-THRU

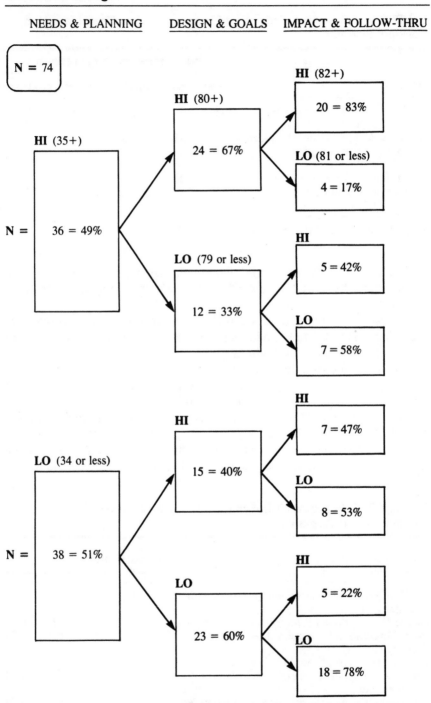

characteristics range from a low of 125 to a high of 355 with no program scoring at the maximum possible level of 460. On these total scores the various programs are surprisingly well distributed following the "normal" curve.

Realizing that these characteristics scores were at least somewhat discriminating, Cavender employed Harris's branching-diagram analysis technique to determine probable relationships among these characteristics. Exhibit 2–6 shows relationships among three sets of characteristics. The programs most highly characterized by attention to individual needs and participant involvement in planning (n = 36), when also characterized by sensitivity to goals and design, are shown to be clearly higher on experience impact and follow-through. Less attention to needs and planning (n = 38), accompanied by less attention to design and goals, resulted in programs generally less powerful in impact and follow-through.

These are hardly surprising relationships. The issue of actual effectiveness is not directly addressed in these findings. However, it is interesting to note that the analysis in Exhibit 2–6 suggests that design and goal setting seem more clearly associated with impact and follow-through than are needs and planning characteristics. Furthermore, as important as attention to individual participant needs may be, along with involvement in planning, these data support Hagen's (1981) finding that the character of the training program itself is most important. Quality characteristics associated with the training endeavor are especially influential in predicting outcomes.

SUMMARY

Principles of good practice are generally widely accepted in the literature. Applying them to the actual operation of ongoing in-service education programs remains a substantial challenge. Much of the remainder of this book deals, in fact, with ways of planning, designing, implementing, and evaluating to assure the fullest use of these principles as guides to action.

Given the great diversity of models for training that can be utilized, strategic choices are offered as one approaches to applying numerous principles while fulfilling specific program requirements.

The literature is prolific regarding involvement, needs assessment, teacher control, and peer relationships. This same body of literature has not addressed the technical design and implementation problems nearly so well. There is still much to be learned about the quality characteristics of in-service education. But preliminary studies from various sources point clearly toward giving more attention to goal setting, design for intensity, high-experience impact, and follow-through.

STUDY SOURCES

Friedman, Myles I., Patricia S. Brinlee, and Patricia B. Dennis Hayes. 1980. *Improving Teacher Education: Resources and Recommendations.* New York: Longman.
Chapter 12 is entitled "Designing In-Service Teacher Training Programs." The authors deal with terminology but also propose five "postulates" as principles to guide model building. Interesting and useful ideas to consider.

Fullan, Michael. 1982. *The Meaning of Educational Change.* New York: Teachers College Press.
A comprehensive review of factors associated with implementation of innovative programs. The author focuses primarily upon federally sponsored programs in the 1970s. Specific chapters analyze various factors, including emphasis on the place of in-service education and related support activities in promoting improvements in education.

Glatthorn, Allan A. 1984. *Differentiated Supervision.* Alexandria, Va.: Association for Supervision and Curriculum Development.
The author uses the term *supervision* to mean *in-service education*—"facilitating the professional growth of a teacher" (p. 2). As such, four differentiated approaches or strategies are proposed: (1) clinical, (2) cooperative group, (3) self-directed, and (4) administrative monitoring. Each approach is discussed in some detail.

House, Richard M. 1983. *Standards of Practice in Continuing Education: A Status Study.* A research report of the Project for the Development of Standards and Criteria for Good Practice in Continuing Education. Silver Spring, Md.: Council on Continuing Education Unit.
As the title and subtitle suggest, this is a report on standards of practice as applied to continuing education programs. They offer useful insights for in-service education. Many of these "standards" are supportive of the principles presented in this chapter.

Hundley, Anna, and Martha Hartzog. 1981. *Characteristics of Effective In-Service Education.* Austin, Tex.: Southwest Educational Development Laboratory.
A literature review reporting on a variety of recent efforts to conceptualize effectiveness in in-service education planning. The wide-ranging sources utilized in this document distinguish it from others which often lack perspective or scope.

Hutson, Harry M., Jr. 1981. "In-Service Best Practices: The Learnings of General Education." *Journal of Research and Development in Education* 14 (Winter): 1–10.
The author details an array of "fifteen best practices." He emphasizes collaboration, incentives, explicit support, and use of outside consultants. He also stresses avoidance of a "deficit model." The author's effort to distinguish among "procedural," "substantive," and "conceptual" domains of planning is an especially valuable contribution.

Mertens, Sally. 1983. "The Basics in In-Service Education: Findings from the Rand and Teacher Studies." *Action Teacher Education* 4 (Spring and Summer): 61–66.

In describing the findings from two major studies of federal projects, the author identifies basic principles: (1) relevance, (2) credibility, (3) accessibility, (4) collegiality, and (5) support.

Mouton, Jane S., and R. R. Blake. 1984. *Synergogy: A New Strategy for Education, Training and Development.* San Francisco: Jossey-Bass.
A fascinating book based on years of executive development training by the authors. In addition to distinguishing among pedagogy, andragogy, and synergogy, the authors describe various training models for working with small adult groups. The early chapters are especially useful in conceptualizing strategic concerns that make training groups synergistic in their effects.

National In-Service Network Task Force. 1980. *Quality Practices Task Force: Final Report.* Bloomington, Ind.: Indiana University, School of Education (July).
As the title suggests, this is another of numerous recent efforts to identify and/or catalog "quality practices." This report draws heavily on federally sponsored project experiences and, hence, is only useful in limited ways.

Nevi, Charles. 1986. "Against the Grain: Half-Truths That Hinder Staff Development." *Principal* 65 (January): 44–46.
A curriculum director criticizes overly simplified and misapplied principles in in-service education. He calls into question needs assessments, single-shot sessions, reliance on collaboration, and the principal as "the leader." An excellent vehicle for class or group discussion.

Showers, Beverly (1985). "Teachers Coaching Teachers." *Educational Leadership* 43 (April): 43–48.
This is one of an array of recent articles emphasizing both the coaching idea and the use of peers as "coaches" for in-service training of teachers.

Showers, Beverly, Bruce Joyce, and Barrie Bennett (1987). "Synthesis of Research on Staff Development: A Framework for Future Study and a State-of-the-Art Analysis." *Educational Leadership* 45 (November): 77–87.
A fairly careful review of a substantial array of studies in non-technical terms provides the reader with some generalizations about training. Little attention is given to studies prior to 1980 except those of Joyce. However, the conclusions, for the most part, are supportive of earlier work from 1945 to the present, and dispell myths about enthusiasm, participation, and locale.

Sprinthall, Norman A. and Lois Thies-Sprinthall (1983). "The Teacher as an Adult Learner: A Cognitive-Developmental View" in *Staff Development,* 82nd Yearbook, Part II, National Society for the Study of Education, edited by Gary A. Griffin. Chicago, Illinois: The University of Chicago Press.
The authors devote the latter part of this chapter to a discussion of real experience in developing complex outcomes. They refer to "significant role-taking experiences" and discuss quality factors associated with the growth potential in such experiences. Factors included are quality experience, discussion/reflection, continuity, and personal support.

3.

Goals and Objectives

INTRODUCTION

The initial phase of planning for any in-service education effort must include concern for what is to be accomplished. This is so obvious that it is often given too little attention, even ignored in practice (Harris et al. 1969, 30). Goal setting is in fact much more complex than generally realized. Goals and objectives for education and training are meaningless except in the context of a situation, problem, or need for change. But training goals relate to people—individuals and groups—and their perceptions of the context as well as their unique needs for learning must be taken into account as goals are selected and objectives specified.

Goal setting is complicated still further by the fact that outcomes desired may be short-range in nature, but are often, in fact, quite long-range. Short-range outcomes are highly desired, of course, because we love to "point with pride" without too much delay. Realistically, only relatively simple attitude, skill, and cognitive outcomes are likely to be forthcoming in short-term training efforts. The truly significant, complex understandings and behavior changes take much time and hence are guided by long-range goals (Joyce and Showers 1983). Imagination, vision, and the courage to "think big" are also much neglected features of goal setting, and this is especially important when planning for the long term.

THE SHORT-, LONG-TERM DILEMMA

A dilemma to be faced by trainees and trainers alike concerns optimizing short- and long-term outcomes. Time, energy, interest, and commitment are not readily sustained over long periods of time unless there is periodic short-term satisfaction. However, short-term outcomes are likely to be trivial, not highly functional and, hence, hardly appreciated for their intrinsic worth. Incentives are sometimes utilized to deal with this dilemma. Released time, extra pay, compensatory time off, and peer recognition can be helpful in sustaining interest and involvement over time to assure significant and worthy outcomes. Supporting services are also helpful (Pedras, 1984), as is the active involvement of trainees in the planning and implementing of programs (Little 1981; Smith 1979).

Goal-setting process can anticipate the dilemma and address needs with both short- and long-term outcomes clearly in view. Ideally, any in-service endeavor should be guided by long-term goals of such clear and large import that they assist in sustaining interest and commitment even beyond the training experiences themselves. However, such long-term goals must also be the frame of reference for intermediate-term and short-term goals and objectives. Hence, participants can take pride in new learnings which are not of great consequence alone, but which have special meaning because they relate to larger, more important goals.

IDEALS, GOALS, AND OBJECTIVES

The terms being utilized here all have one thing in common. They speak about *things to be accomplished.* The ideals we hold are things we strive to accomplish, knowing full well that they are realized only in very limited ways. Long-term goals are outcomes toward which we work, even though their accomplishment may take many years, and often are only partially realized. Intermediate-term goals and major objectives can be more easily managed over a period of a few years, but the full realization of such outcomes is still somewhat risky as time and circumstance take their toll. It is the very short-term objectives, especially the very explicit and simple outcomes, that are truly manageable.

Exhibit 3–1 suggests graphically a way of thinking about these various outcomes as selected for in-service education planning purposes. An ideal or a set of ideals has value for planning purposes as a beacon light has a value for navigation. We don't expect to actually accomplish our ideals, but they give us a long-term sense of direction. They also lend prestige to our efforts.

Many long-term goals could easily be associated with only a single ideal. *Individualization* of teaching and learning as an ideal might be addressed by numerous goals directed toward teachers' learning many things about curriculum design, materials development, diagnostic testing, multisensory experiences, grouping alternatives, and so on. The ideal serves to call into view the full array of related goals, but demands a selection process.

EXHIBIT 3-1. Ideals, Selected Goals, and Specified Objectives

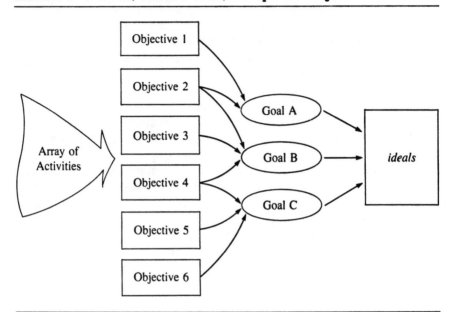

When an ideal and one or more long-term goals have been clearly recognized and selected, intermediate-term goals (subgoals or major objectives) are required to make them manageable, and to facilitate communications about what is to be accomplished over time.

DETERMINING GOALS AND OBJECTIVES

The concepts illustrated above involve a logical, rational, goal-setting process. Such a process offers an ideal for conceptualizing and communicating about outcomes. In the real world, decisions are usually made in a more eclectic fashion. Experienced teachers, administrators, trainers, and planners agree, however, that the objectives must be relevant, feasible, and explicitly defined. Bessent (1967, 6) has proposed a "commandment" in this regard:

"Thou shalt not commit in-service programs unrelated to the genuine needs of staff participants."

Other commandments might include:

Thou shalt not fail to be explicit about what is to be learned.
Thou shalt not specify trivial objectives.
Thou shalt not promise outcomes that are not realizable.
Thou shalt not confuse learning outcomes with activities.

Relating Goals and Objectives

A useful technique for assuring clearly delineated relationships between goals and objectives is to explicate them at three or more levels of specificity. Such a detailed breakdown of goals and objectives is often necessary to assure that long-term goals or complex program developments are addressed by the objectives selected for training.

Exhibit 3–2 illustrates schematically the relationships between goals and objectives for a faculty group in a senior high school.

In this exhibit, it is important to recognize that only a single goal and a *selected* array of objectives are shown in relation to each other. This is the *product* of a planning process in which many goals and objectives were discussed in terms of priorities for the school, needs of individuals, and practical realities. The objectives finally agreed upon were still too general for session-planning purposes. However, the schematic illustrated here is a document that reflects a set of agreements and understandings about what the various sessions will seek to accomplish.

Based on one of the objectives in Exhibit 3–2, a specific set of performance objectives for one or more in-service sessions is shown as follows:

1.2. To communicate better with students.

1.22. To ask open-ended questions. (The teacher will make use of open-ended questions in talking with students on a one-to-one basis or in small informal groups.)

1.221. To differentiate open-ended from closed questions, given a teaching episode containing a variety of questions.

2.222. To identify both open-ended and closed questions on tape recordings of one's own teaching.

2.223. To revise closed questions into open-ended questions.

2.224. To role-play informal conferences with students using predominantly open-ended questions.

2.225. To utilize open-ended questions in an actual classroom situation, avoiding closed questions more than one third of the time.

EXHIBIT 3–2. Goals and Objectives: An Illustration of Relationships

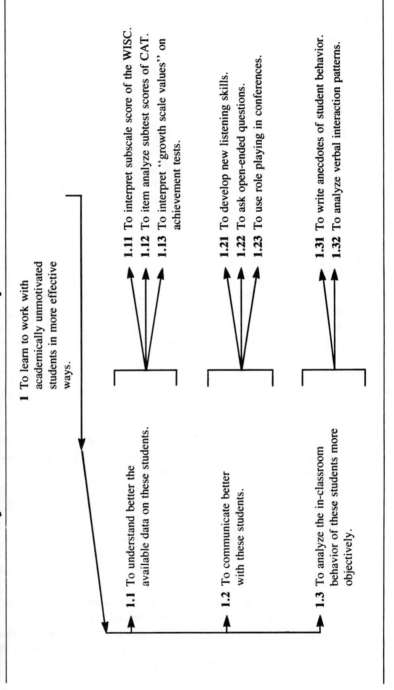

1 To learn to work with academically unmotivated students in more effective ways.

1.1 To understand better the available data on these students.

1.11 To interpret subscale score of the WISC.
1.12 To item analyze subtest scores of CAT.
1.13 To interpret "growth scale values" on achievement tests.

1.2 To communicate better with these students.

1.21 To develop new listening skills.
1.22 To ask open-ended questions.
1.23 To use role playing in conferences.

1.3 To analyze the in-classroom behavior of these students more objectively.

1.31 To write anecdotes of student behavior.
1.32 To analyze verbal interaction patterns.

Making Objectives Explicit

Training objectives should be as explicitly stated as possible, both for purposes of validating them against the needs they are intended to serve and to guide the selection of activities and other design considerations. Mager (1975) has developed a very useful guide to the writing of performance objectives. He argues that objectives are well stated, explicit, and convey maximum meaning with least uncertainty when they clearly express three things: (1) the *performance* sought in behavioral terms, (2) the *conditions* under which the behavior will be demonstrated, and (3) the *standard* of acceptability of the performance. These guidelines for writing performance objectives are certainly useful in session planning. However, they have limitations that must be recognized:

1. Certain learning outcomes (performances) cannot be so clearly specified in advance.
2. Such explicit statements of outcomes tend to encourage preoccupation with fragments of a larger, more complex performance.

Defining Realistic Objectives

The problem of assuring that objectives are realistic as well as relevant cannot be overestimated. It is easy to be overly ambitious, to specify idealized outcomes that cannot possibly be accomplished within a given time frame or with available clients, materials, leadership capability, or resources. It is often necessary to complete a preliminary session plan before the realistic character of the objectives can be determined. Specifically, once a set of objectives is specified, one or more activities are selected and associated with each objective; materials, facilities, and personnel are designated; and events are sequenced (see Exhibit 3–3). Then the following questions need to be asked:

1. Do all activities as sequenced (including consideration of procedures required) fit into a realistic time frame?
2. Does each activity or set of activities associated with each objective seem thoroughly adequate for accomplishing that performance for nearly all of the participants?
3. Can we secure the materials, facilities, personnel, and time as specified in the plan?
4. Are the personnel we can secure to lead participants in these activities competent to do so?
5. Are the participants as we know them going to participate in these activities willingly?

EXHIBIT 3–3. Illustration of a Sequence of Activities Related to Objectives

GENERAL
OBJECTIVE

1.22   To ask open-ended questions.

TIME OBJECTIVE	ACTIVITY DESCRIPTION	MATERIALS/ARRANGEMENTS
(min.)		
0 1.2	Visualized Lecture. Present via a transparency a review of the several concerns expressed (i.e., communicating with students, understanding test data, and analyzing classroom behavior). Identify communicating	Overhead projector, screen. Extension cord. Three-pronged male adapter. Transparencies 1 and 2.
3 1.22	with students and open-ended questioning as focus of session.	
1.221 4	Reading. Distribute a teaching episode. Ask participants to read it quickly.	Teaching episode reproduced for all. Leader's copy of episode already analyzed.
6	Guided Practice. Present on screen via transparency the first question from the episode. Ask, "Is it an open or closed question?" Say, "It is closed if the student response is restricted in some way. It is open if the student has a variety of	Transparency 3.
7	optional ways of answering."	
8	Present on the screen the next question from the episode. Repeat the question: "Is this open or closed?"	Transparency 4.
	Reading. Direct participants to study each question and mark each "open" or "closed" in the margin. Circulate about the room to give individual assis-	Allow silence.
12	tance as needed.	
14	Buzz Groups. Ask each group of 5 to 11 participants to discuss their decisions and see if all	
35	can agree.	
	Visual Lecture. Call participants to attention. Present a key via transparency, allowing each to check his or her decisions. Ask "How many agreed 100 percent?" Count hands raised.	Use natural groupings at library tables, or have every other row turn about to face the one behind. Transparency 5. Overhead projector.

EXHIBIT 3–3 (continued)

TIME OBJECTIVE	ACTIVITY DESCRIPTION	MATERIALS/ARRANGEMENTS
(min.)		

Praise. Ask if there are disagreements. "Do we need to discuss some?" Respond to questions with clarifying points. In any case, review.
(1) Open-ended questions give students response options—optional content and optional format for response.
(2) Closed questions tend to restrict *both* content and form of response.

TIME OBJECTIVE	ACTIVITY DESCRIPTION	MATERIALS/ARRANGEMENTS
40 1.222	Tape Listening.	Tape recorder, tape of classroom dialogue. Pre-analyzed examples of questions.

Tape Listening. Ask participants to see if they can differentiate open-ended from closed questions when listening to a tape; start recorder. Stop after first question and student response. "Bill, do you think this is an example of stereotyping?" Student: "No, I don't think so."
Guided practice. Repeat the question. Ask participants, "Open or closed?" Reinforce: "Yes—closed. The yes-or-no response was dictated and the 'I don't think so' was about as much as was asked for."
Tape Listening. Proceed to play another tape segment. Stop after one question.
Guided Practice. Repeat above.
Tape Listening. Proceed to repeat several times until no problems seem evident. Stop before interest begins to wane.

Lecture. Suggest next steps. Ask each participant to prepare a 10 to 30 minute recording of his or her talking with students using questions, etc.

60

Adjourn.

If *any one* of these questions is answered with a no, then changes in objectives may be in order from the point of view of feasibility. Of course, these questions may help in identifying other weaknesses in the selection of activities, materials, and so on. However, a logically developed session plan emerges from its objectives; hence, any weaknesses in these statements of intended purposes must be detected as soon as possible to assure a well-developed plan.

In answering question 1 in the list presented near the beginning of this section, those developing the session plan must mentally "walk through" the procedures proposed for each activity. A time estimate must be made for each activity with allowances made for passing materials, late arrivals, answering unanticipated questions, and special difficulties. The more experienced trainer-designer knows how to estimate the time consumed by any given activity within close tolerances. The inexperienced will have to allow for errors in estimates. When a new or unfamiliar activity or set of materials or situation is involved, it may be wise to be more cautious, allowing more than a minimum amount of time. A trial run of an activity is always helpful, of course. When time estimates are summed for an entire series of activities for a session, the planners can readily see whether the total amount of time exceeds that available in the time frame provided. If the time required exceeds the length of the available frame, alternatives are open for corrections: (1) extend the time frame; (2) eliminate certain activities; (3) change the objectives. It is this last alternative that needs very serious consideration in the *early stages* of planning.

Too many objectives, or objectives that are too complex, cannot be adequately dealt with by a longer session or by abbreviating activity sequences. To resort to these solutions courts failure. It is important to look at objectives with a critical, realistic eye and to revise them as drastically as necessary before the plan becomes fully developed. The cardinal principle here might be: *better do a little well than a lot poorly!*

Selecting the Important Objectives

When objectives have been selected for relevance by relating them to larger goals and needs, specified clearly, and tested for feasibility, they may still *not* be very important. The rigorous processes of narrowing, limiting, selecting, and specifying can lead to choosing the least important ones of all. This is not likely, given a thoughtful set of sequences as suggested above, but it surely can happen. How does one avoid this (Tom 1984)?

A simple technique for testing the importance of a carefully selected objective is to allow a few days to pass before finalizing decisions about objectives for a session. Still another technique is to compare and contrast selected objectives with a representative group of those objectives that were cast aside in the planning process. A still more elaborate but very promising technique involves asking participants and others concerned to review and react to a set of proposed objectives.

NEEDS ASSESSMENTS

Selecting goals and objectives presumes that some needs assessment has been undertaken, formally or informally. Assessing needs is a part of the goal-setting process. As commonly used, however, this term refers to the *needs* of individuals or groups of specific individuals. But needs can and perhaps should be defined in a variety of ways (Naumann-Etienne and Todd 1976).

Individual and Group Needs

Mager and Pipes (1970) tend to view needs as "performance discrepancies" that reflect some systematic assessment of actual performance compared to expectations. But individuals have needs that reflect interests, aspirations, and alternatives. Surely these should not be neglected, for they are the growing edge of educational practice. On the other hand, individual needs that reflect whim, bias, or rationalization can hardly command the same influence on goals and objectives as those defined in more rigorous ways.

Group needs are hardly the same as individual needs. Even when a survey has been conducted and "needs" are identified as the objectives, goals, or topics most frequently chosen, individual needs are inevitably neglected. There are many differences between a needs assessment process that attends to diagnosing and prioritizing needs for an individual (Harris and Hill 1982) and those procedures utilized which are in effect an opinion survey. Opinions tend to be unstable, influenced by various extraneous events, and should not be presumed to be based on diagnostic processes. In fact, public opinion polling techniques tend to encourage "off-the-top-of-the-head" responses.

Institutional Needs

Needs of schools, programs, and students may deserve much more consideration than they tend to receive. A school with a serious problem of poor staff morale, deficient library skills, or an inappropriate science program may have needs for training of teachers that are substantially at odds with those of individual teachers or teacher groups. A program that has not been adequately developed, or is nonexistent across a district or even in a state, may suggest needs for in-service education at odds with those that individuals identify. Changes in student populations—economic, social, educational—may also command attention as having implications for in-service education, and these may not "track" with the needs perceived by teachers or other staff members.

I am not suggesting that *needs* of trainees should be mandated by institutional or societal expectations. There is, in effect, already too much dictating and mandating of in-service goals. It is important, however, to see goal setting as a process which includes a variety of perspectives on needs assessments. Collaborative planning should strive to find common bases for giving priority to selected goals without neglect of individual priorities.

WRITING USEFUL OBJECTIVES

In-service training objectives like any kind of instructional objectives need to communicate intended training outcomes. Generally, it is agreed that they should describe the behaviors or performances that the training experiences are expected to produce. However, objectives are most useful when they clearly relate to the training situation itself. Furthermore, they should not be confused with *operational* objectives that describe training activities rather than outcomes.

Exhibit 3–2 can be used to illustrate. The long-term goal, "1. To learn to work with academically unmotivated students . . . ," provides only a general statement of intent; however, it is made more explicit by goal statements 1.1, 1.2, and 1.3. When we focus on one of these, 1.2 for instance, the intended outcomes are still in need of definition. Objective statement 1.22 provides a fairly clear indication, for the first time, regarding what the teacher will be trained to do: "To ask open-ended questions when talking with students in the classroom. . . ." The usefulness of such an objective is still limited, however, by the frame of reference used, "in the classroom." Hence, it is of limited use in designing a training session for developing various related knowledges and skills.

In Exhibit 3–3 highly explicit objectives are utilized to indicate the activities for training. For instance, if we believe that teachers need to know the difference between open and closed questions, and we decide to train for that knowledge outcome, then an objective should reflect that intent: "1.221. To differentiate open-ended from closed questions. . . ." However, this statement of outcome is made even more useful by relating it specifically to training plans: "given a teaching episode [script] containing a variety of questions."

The usefulness of objectives is greatly enhanced when they are explicated in sufficient detail, indicating *both* the specific knowledge or skill intended and the nature of the training activity required. It sounds more exciting to be less explicit: "Our objective is to improve your power of

EXHIBIT 3–4. Examples of Operational and Instructional Objectives

REVISED AS OPERATIONAL OBJECTIVE	CONFUSED, UNCLEAR STATEMENT	REVISED AS INSTRUCTIONAL OBJECTIVE
To verbalize personal experiences connected with readiness problems. To write a set of anecdotes, briefly reporting experiences. To use a list of readiness principles and concepts as the basis for discussing anecdotes.	"To analyze a personal experience as a basis for discussing readiness."	Given a set of readiness principles or concepts, will analyze anecdotes to match principles and concepts to events described, to concur with peers 85 percent of the time.
To meet with a specialist following a lesson that is tape-recorded to apply guidelines and check agreements.	"To evaluate own performance during a lesson applying guidelines."	To analyze a tape-recorded lesson applying performance guidelines so as to agree with a specialist on 80 percent of the items.

communication." But the hard work of designing meaningful training is not enhanced.

Confusion over Operational and Learning Objectives

Instructional or learning objectives specify intents for change in performances. *Operational* objectives are a very different kind of statement. They too can be very useful in planning documents, but they should not be confused with objectives for learning.

Some examples of objectives that are not clearly stated and hence are quite confusing are shown in Exhibit 3–4. This exhibit also illustrates how either instructional objectives or operational objectives can be specified using some of the presumed intents of the original, confusing statements. The important distinction is that an operational objective describes the process or procedure that is intended. An instructional objective describes the behavior change (learning) that is intended as a consequence of certain instruction.

Obviously, operational and instructional objectives can *both* be utilized in in-service plans. In Exhibit 3–4, the operational statements on the left-hand column could be the intended activities leading to the outcomes described in the right-hand column. Mager (1975) has provided rather useful guidelines for using operational objectives in planning instruction. Generally, they seem to be more widely used in specifying project operations of noninstructional kinds.

In evading responsibility for being rather explicit about the intended outcomes of a session or program, some planners resort to an array of vague and curious phrases. For instance:

"Specifically, this conference aims to provide opportunities to study the way in which . . ."

". . . the focus is on an exploration of how attitudes . . . influence and the ways in which men and women exercise authority and leadership."

The training planning document from which these vagaries were taken also assures participants that their several days and hundreds of dollars will not include an "attempt to prescribe what anyone shall learn. The focus, however, is upon the problems encountered in the exercise of authority and leadership." This dedication to lack of prescriptiveness is likely to be more appreciated than the lack of specificity about what might be taught. Plans such as these, without objectives, cannot be criticized so long as participants are willing, recognize that no specific learning outcomes have been designed for, and have pretty explicit information about the character of the activities planned. These conditions don't often hold in training situations. Participants have needs and interests, and the designers have a responsibility for trying to arrange relevant experiences. If objectives cannot be specified, how do we validate the experiences? The foregoing quotation, along with many years of experience with such group relations sessions, leads this author to conclude that the objectives are, in fact, clearly specified but not shared with the participants. That possibility raises many new issues.

Withheld Objectives

The illustrations given of confusing, vague, and even evasive statements of objectives may bring to the mind of the reader questions about discovery approaches where the design calls for participants, in effect, to discover what the objective was. Certainly, this is a legitimate approach. It represents one of a number of circumstances that justifies either withholding objectives (even though they have been made explicit in the plan) or even failing to specify objectives at all.

In those instances when the design is such that a carefully sequenced series of activities is planned to lead the participant to discover, deduce, or synthesize, the objectives must still be clearly specified. They are withheld from participants to heighten curiosity, maximize initiative, stimulate creativity, challenge for involvement, and the like. Similarly, the objectives are used at a later point in the sequence as a way of helping participants check their accomplishments and organize the learning.

In-service sessions involving cases, simulations, and games (Heyman 1975), or the laboratory approach (McIntyre 1967) often call for withholding objectives. They rely instead on the stimulating nature of the activity itself, the face validity of the material, and the confidence or trust in the trainer to motivate participants and make the session meaningful from the beginning.

There are, of course, experiences that are so real, so involving, so satisfying *in the doing,* and so potentially productive of a broad range of learning outcomes that they can be utilized without carefully specified objectives. Examples of such in-service activities include demonstrations of teaching, visits to other classrooms, field trips, internships, a powerful dramatic production, or a social-recreational event. Unfortunately, the outcomes from such experiences tend to be more potential than assured. To be sure, all of these experiences have been productive for some individuals under some sets of conditions, but when they are quite expensive in terms of time and other costs, their use without specified objectives must be questioned. In fact, using these same experiences with carefully formulated, even if general, objectives seems to add to their effectiveness.

SUMMARY

Goals, objectives, and needs have a variety of meanings as utilized in the literature and in practice. They have a commonness of meaning as they all relate to projected outcomes of some kind. In this chapter, the term *ideals* is added to the above list to represent the concept of long-term, idealized outcomes.

Much of this chapter has emphasized fairly standard notions about the nature of goals and objectives and their uses in guiding plans for in-service education. Relationships among ideals, goals, and objectives and the special utility of each are of practical value. In-service education must be guided by ideals and longer-term goals to avoid trivialization. However, in-service education must produce tangible results, largely in terms of specific behavior changes. Such outcomes are guided by explicitness of intentions.

STUDY SOURCES

Bloom, Benjamin S. 1956. *Taxonomy of Educational Objectives. Handbook I: The Cognitive Domain.* New York: David McKay.

One of three volumes on objectives for instruction. A classic in the field of education for its influence on curriculum planning as well as in-service education and testing. The emphasis on objectives and the various levels of performance anticipated by objectives of different kinds is fundamental to effective goal setting as discussed in this chapter.

Brookover, Wilbur B., chairman. 1980. *Measuring and Attaining Goals of Education*. A document of the ASCD Committee on Research and Theory. Alexandria, Va.: Association for Supervision and Curriculum Development.

Chapter 2 presents a very useful discussion of goal-objective-teaching relationships. Major goals and subgoals are discussed for various kinds of learnings. This same chapter explores ways of seeing interrelationships among goals that is very useful.

Harris, Ben M., E. Wailand Bessent, and Kenneth E. McIntyre. 1969. *In-Service Education: A Guide to Better Practice*. Englewood Cliffs, N.J.: Prentice-Hall, Inc.

Chapter 3 discusses ways of thinking about designs for in-service programs. Relationships between ideals, goals, and objectives are analyzed. Activities in relation to goals and objectives are also considered.

Hasazi, Susan E., Catherine Batsche, Lorella McKinney, Douglas H. Gill, John Langone, and R. Brian Cobb. 1983. *Vocational Education for the Handicapped: Perspectives on In-Service Personnel Development*. Personnel Development Series, Doc. 6. Washington, D.C.: Division of Personnel Preparation, Office of Special Education and Rehabilitative Services. ERIC ED 224 939.

Chapter 2 addresses procedural concerns for planning using a model that emphasizes awareness, readiness, and commitment in planning for specific activities.

Kibler, Robert J., L. L. Barker, and D. T. Miles. 1970. *Behavioral Objectives and Instruction*. Boston, Mass.: Allyn and Bacon, Inc.

A fairly elementary overview of the use of behaviorally defined objectives in instructional planning. Various kinds of objectives, ways of specifying them, and many practical illustrations are provided. Bloom's taxonomy is the basis for most of the illustrations presented. The writers also draw heavily on the UCLA objectives exchange for illustrations.

Mager, Robert F. 1975. *Preparing Instructional Objectives*. Palo Alto, Calif.: Fearon-Pitman Publishers.

Another old one, but still one of the best. This book offers a simple-to-use reference on techniques for writing objectives that communicate.

Mager, Robert F., and Peter Pipes. 1970. "Is Non-Performance Rewarding?" In *Analyzing Performance Problems or "You Really Oughta Wanna."* Palo Alto, Calif.: Fearon Publishers.

Another classic of practical ideas about analyzing performance problems to avoid unrealistic selection of objective and strategies. These authors alert the reader to be cautious not to regard all performance problems as needs for training.

Marshall, Jon C., and S. D. Caldwell. 1984. "How Valid Are Formal Needs Assessments?" *NASSP Bulletin* 68 (November): 24–30.

Both informal and formal needs assessment practices are studied and compared. They are reported as "equally valid" in providing information for planning. The authors express many fundamental concerns regarding widespread reliance on these assessment practices.

Nadler, Leonard. 1982. *Designing Training Programs: The Critical Events Model.* Reading, Mass.: Addison-Wesley Publishing Co.
A comprehensive treatment of nearly all aspects of design, the book emphasizes industrial situations. Early chapters give a great deal of attention to analyzing organizational needs. Chapters 7 and 9 provide substantial detail on curriculum and resources, even though activities are somewhat neglected.

Naumann-Etienne, M., and J. W. Todd. 1976. "Applying Organizational Development Techniques to In-Service Education." A paper presented to the American Educational Research Association at San Francisco, Calif. (April). ERIC ED 122 357
A report on a Midwest school-system effort presents a 5-step sequence to analyze "needs" from various perspectives. System needs, teacher concerns, and program priorities of teachers are among the perspectives surveyed. Feedback on these needs was provided emphasizing data rather than opinions.

Tom, Alan R. 1984. *Teaching as a Moral Craft.* New York: Longman, Inc.
A look at teaching from a variety of perspectives. The author raises very critical questions about the efforts to define teaching in simple, mechanical, behavioral ways. He suggests that the tendency to specify teaching behaviors in simple terms may also mean ignoring the most important features of the "craft."

4.

Designing Training Sessions

INTRODUCTION

Sooner or later, in-service education takes the form of a *training session* in which one or more individuals engage in activities for purposes of improving individual performance. A session may be part of a larger program; it may be of short or long duration; or it may involve an individual, a small group, or a mass. It may be highly structured with carefully detailed activity sequences, or it may be fairly freewheeling. Whatever its form, certain preplanning and instructional designing are essential to success.

THE CONCEPT OF SESSION

The session is a basic unit of training in several respects. A designated client or group, one or more objectives, and a time frame are the essential minimum requirements for planning and designing. Without at least some solid information regarding each of these three factors, a design for instruction is not feasible. Other kinds of planning are undertaken for in-service education when clients are only nebulously defined (i.e., teachers, staff, aides), but session planning that provides some assurance of an effective learning experience for clients requires information about their numbers, their past experiences, their perceptions of need, their job responsibilities, and the like. These data provide the designer with at least a starting base upon which to determine objectives for training, specify an appropriate time frame, and proceed to develop a session plan.

A Time Frame

A time frame is a specified period of time, designated as to date and time, during which a given client or client group engages in planned activities, for specified purposes, without significant interruption. Ordinarily, a time frame for training will be no less than thirty minutes and not exceed four hours in length. The specified minimum length of a session is based on the belief that shorter time frames are not likely to be productive of discernible outcomes. The specified upper limit for a time frame is based simply on the physiological need for food and rest. Obviously, it is conceivable that an effective session of shorter or longer duration could be designed under special circumstances. However, the more important design problem is that of tailoring objectives and activities to time available and adapting time allocations to essential requirements of selected activities and objectives.

Objectives and Client Needs

The focus of a session plan upon objectives that are explicit and directed toward needs of a specified client or group, however determined, gives a unity to the learning experiences that result. A session is designed, therefore, to assure the accomplishment of the objective(s) for the client(s) at the conclusion of the designated time frame. Still another session might follow, of course, utilizing another time frame. Similarly, other objectives might be pursued with the same client(s), or with a different client or group.

The importance of the *session* as a distinct and basic unit of training is that it assures a focus on the who, what, and when in planning for in-service education. Still other important design considerations remain, but clients, objectives, and time are the minimum essential bases upon which to begin designing for learning. Once these are clearly known, activities can be selected, objectives refined, events sequenced, described materials developed, and logistical arrangements made.

Planning Distinctions

A set of distinctions in terms will assist the reader in understanding the details to be presented in this chapter regarding designing in-service training sessions. One of these distinctions is that of *a session* versus *a session plan*. A second distinction is that of a *plan* versus *planning*. Finally, let's distinguish between *design* and *plan*. A session is an operating reality. It involves real people, using time, engaging in activities for purposes of learning. In contrast, a session plan is a physical thing, a document or set of materials that precedes a session and guides the events of the session.

This thing referred to as a session plan may be developed and utilized in a variety of ways, and the planning process is often regarded as of great importance (Berman and McLaughlin 1975, 19). This chapter is not primarily concerned with planning processes, as important as these are. Design is our concern here. A design can be distinguished from a plan only with considerable difficulty. A plan is a physical thing while a design is a quality or set of qualities reflected in the plan.

In studies of innovative programs closely associated with in-service education, Berman and McLaughlin (1975, 19) reported that the "*amount* of planning was not . . . related to project outcomes." However, they found that "the quality" of the planning was important. In part, at least, the concept of the *quality* of a plan is one of process. We hold, however, that a grand and glorious process that lacks design will not suffice. The frequently observed, teacher-planned, grade-level meetings tend to be rather poor in-service education even when participants report positively about them. Planning process that leads to a high-quality design for in-service education is essential. In this chapter, our concern will be with such design.

THE SESSION PLAN

The *plan* referred to here is a document or set of documents and materials that guides the implementation of session activities in operation. Session plans are sometimes retained in the head of the person in charge, but this is not a *plan* as referred to here because of the serious defects associated with such tangible planning. While it is conceivable that an individual with great skill and experience can direct an effective in-service session with no planning document in existence, this is highly unlikely in most instances. Carefully detailed plans are important in order to assure the following:

1. That the best possible design has been developed.
2. That all materials and arrangements have been provided for.
3. That the design can be communicated to others who need to be involved.
4. That the session leaders will be guided to implement the session designed.
5. That the design can be reused with minor variations with another client or group.

A session plan may be a relatively simple document when only a few activities or persons are involved or when the design is highly standardized, as in the case of programmed materials. As a greater variety of materials, activities, and persons become actively involved in the session events, the planning document and support materials are necessarily more elaborate. A plan in its most simple format may consist of a two- or three-page outline, as shown in Appendix B. This outline provides details regarding the theme or topic, date(s), place, phone contact, sponsoring organization, and characteristics of participant group. A major goal and specific objectives are given. A detailed agenda includes a timetable for activities as sequenced. Activities are described and keyed to an objective. Responsibilities are designated. A checklist of the equipment and materials needed is provided and responsibility designated.

Basic Parts of a Plan

Much more elaborate plans are most often required, because the limited detail provided in the outline described above leaves too much for further development. Exhibit 4–1 outlines eight parts of a more complete session plan. Each part presents essential information for assuring a well-designed, readily implementable in-service session. A checklist for use in reviewing a completed plan is provided in Appendix C.

The various parts of the plan will take different forms dictated by the need for each part to guide the implementation process readily. Hence, the statement of the problem and need may be just a written narrative, but it may also include tables, charts, or graphs to communicate more vividly. Similarly, the client group and goals and objectives may be described in both narrative and graphic forms. Goals and objectives may need to be clearly prioritized or categorized to show their relevance to certain clients and needs. The schedule of events is often just a simple schedule, detailing time allocations and sequences. However, it may be important for more complex designs to be depicted, using flowcharts and a PERT (Program Evaluation and Review Technique) (Cook 1966) network, as well as simple schedules.

An often neglected portion of a session plan is the description of procedures. When the session leader is also the designer, the process of carefully describing, in narrative form, the detailed procedures to be used helps to detect flaws and refine other portions of the plan. When the leader and designer are different people, then details of procedures are truly indispensable for communicating about intended events. The dangers in assuming that a few sketchy notes on procedures will suffice are very great. Notice the difference in the following procedures:

Abbreviated Procedures
Introduce the session briefly. Have communicator describe the message (Form A). Instruct receivers to estimate their confidence.

Fully Described Procedures
Introduce the session by telling the group that they are going to take part in a demonstration concerning communicating with people. Specifically, announce "We will focus on how to have your directions understood."

EXHIBIT 4–1. Guidelines for Preparing an In-Service Session Plan

I. *Statement of the Problem*
   A. The educational problem to which the session is related is clearly identified.
   B. The problem is described in concrete terms related to real situations. The problem is documented as real and its importance to the organization made clear.
   C. The problem is defined in terms that make it at least partially responsive to in-service education or training, as distinguished from curriculum development, staffing, funding, and so on.
   D. The problem is translated into needs for improved performance of staff members.

II. *Client Specified*
   E. The individuals or groups toward which the activities will be directed are clearly specified. Clients are described in terms of background of training, experience, prior involvement with the problem, and the like.
   F. The relationship of these clients to the problem is indicated. Similarities and differences in attitudes, skills, and knowledges related to the problem are described or estimated.
   G. The rationale for focusing upon these clients instead of others is presented.

III. *Goals and Objectives*
   H. The major outcome(s) anticipated from the session(s) is (are) specified. Major outcomes specified are clearly in observable terms. Major outcomes specified are related directly to the problem and needs described in item I. Portions of the problems or needs *not* addressed are clearly designated.
   I. The specific objectives anticipated as outcomes are specified. Specific objectives are each clearly designated as relating to a major outcome. Specific objectives are expressed in performance terms. Specific objectives reflect differentiated needs of participants.
   J. The goals and objectives selected are the most important as well as realistic ones. Specific objectives are selected to deal with the problem in a truly significant way.

IV. *Schedule of Events*
   K. A master calendar of events indicates dates for preplanning, implementing, and follow-up.
   L. An agenda for the session clearly indicates the timetable of activities. Careful, realistic allocations of time are designated for each activity.
   M. Sequences, allocations, activities, and relationships among them are shown.

EXHIBIT 4-1 (continued)

V. *Description of Procedures*
    N.   Each activity specified in the session agenda (item L) is fully described, as to what happens, the objective(s) in focus, the sequence, the materials used, the special arrangements, persons involved, simultaneous events, and special problems to consider.
    O.   The selection of each activity is justified in terms of the specific objective focus, and special conditions limiting activity selection.
    P.   Illustrations of materials, displays, room arrangements, and so on are included to clarify procedures of special kinds.
    Q.   Alternative procedures or variations that might be required are described.

VI. *Evaluation*
    R.   A set of evaluation procedures is clearly described. Evaluation of outcomes related to objectives is provided for. Evaluation of affective, skill, and cognitive outcomes is included where appropriate. Processes as well as outcomes are evaluated.
    S.   Carefully developed instruments are selected and/or prepared for each aspect of the evaluation. Instruments are objective, pretested, appropriate to objectives and activities. Instruments are simple enough for practical administration.
    T.   Analytical procedures to be used in the evaluation are clearly shown. Tables to be used are prestructured. Analytical procedures are described.

VII. *Follow-up Plans*
    U.   Follow-up plans are outlined and/or described in sufficient detail to show continuity toward full resolution of the problem.
    V.   Immediate *next steps* are carefully detailed to guide *both* clients and leaders.

VIII. *Exhibits*
    W.   Materials to be used in the session are illustrated. Handouts, advanced information, name tags, tests, work sheets, tapes, transparencies, questionnaires, instruments, bibliographies, and lists of materials are included.
    X.   Equipment and special physical facilities arrangements are listed with sources clearly designated.
    Y.   Resource persons are clearly designated including all pertinent communications relating to each: curriculum vitae, address, phone, letters of invitation and follow-up letters, assignment sheets, and so on.
    Z.   A budget is prepared showing all expenses and clearly detailing cash outlay costs.

Introduce the communicator and say "There has been no coaching of our communicator; he has been instructed in the rules we are all to follow. You are to receive the message; he will communicate. Here's how it works. . . ." (Rules explained. Procedures presented. Materials distributed.)

As the communicator begins, the group leader reminds him to record the time. The session continues without interruption until the communicator is finished. If necessary, remind the group of any rules not being followed.

When the communicator has finished, participants are instructed as follows: "Estimate the number of items you *think* you got correct." The leader circulates among the participants and assists them if they need help. "Record your estimate of the number you think are correct in the space designated for your C score."

While this is going on, the communicator can relax. He is then given the new set of directions to study.

Evaluation plans need to go well beyond the preparation of some kind of instrument. Questions to be answered need to be selected and specified. Product and process questions both need attention. Instrumentation needs to be pretested, and analytical procedures should be worked out in advance. Although more careful attention is given to procedures for evaluating in-service sessions in Chapter 11, it is important to recognize here that evaluation can rarely be successful as an afterthought. Planning for evaluating must be a part of session planning.

A session plan is called upon to give at least passing attention to follow-up activities. A session planned without considering necessary follow-up events is very likely to be unrealistic in trying to accomplish too much. Furthermore, the realities associated with possible follow-up events may influence the very nature of the session plan. In any event, follow-up is nearly always desirable, if not essential, and should be reflected in the plan itself.

A unique and most practical part of a plan is the collection of exhibits. These are detailed in Exhibit 4–1. The plan at this point may take the form of a box, suitcase, or even a trunk, as each item of material (or a facsimile) is prepared or selected and physically made a part of the plan.

The Planning Documents

The character of the plan under discussion and outlined in detail in Exhibit 4–1 makes it clear that a variety of documents will be contained in any well-developed plan. Curiously, few documents have become *standard*. Only in the instance of independent, self-instructional modules has any standardizing of format been accepted. It may well be that the great variety of potential forms of in-service training sessions defies any effort to adopt common forms of documentation. The experienced observer, however, noticing the almost complete absence of formal plans for in-service sessions, is inclined to suspect that the art of plan making is simply quite primitive among most school and college staffs.

Certainly, a few basic documents are clearly suggested by Exhibit 4–1 that go beyond efforts at narrative presentation. These *basic* documents include:

1. *A Session Agenda.* This supplies basic supporting information on the time, place, group, and materials needed (see Appendix B).
2. *A Checklist of Presession Arrangements.* A working instrument for use during planning and final preparations phases to assure that no detail is overlooked (see Exhibit 4–1).
3. *A Flowchart of Events or a PERT Network.* This provides a graphic overview of events, their sequences, and relationships (see Exhibits 4–2 and 4–3).
4. *A Checklist of Materials.* The checklist indicates each item of material and equipment in the sequence in which it will be utilized.
5. *One or More Evaluation Instruments.* Refer to Chapter 11 for illustrations.

Flowcharting Events

One document that has special utility when a session plan is rather complex and involves subgroups and a diversity of activities is the flowchart. Flowcharts can be rather simple, giving only limited information, but they can also be more detailed, using an array of symbols for easy visual communications. Exhibit 4–2 illustrates a flowchart with an array of details for a teaching demonstration session. This flowchart depicts three simultaneous sets of events that provide groups of forty to sixty viewers with carefully planned demonstrations of exemplary teaching practices on closed-circuit television screens.

Three strands of events are shown. The topmost series depicts the sequence of events planned with teacher and students. This series constitutes not just the demonstration but prior and subsequent events that are crucial to the demonstration and related activities for viewers. The second sequence of events is numbered from 2 through 8. These represent the actual experiences of the participants from arrival at the demonstration center to follow-up. The third strand or sequence of events simply indicates technical support activities x and y. These are related to the use of closed-circuit television, multiple monitors, remote-operated cameras, and various kinds of sound equipment, the proper and coordinated operation of which was essential to the session.

While each of these three *strands* of events was quite distinct from each other, they illustrate dramatically the importance of coordination of events during a session. The flowchart shows approximate time relationships be-

EXHIBIT 4–2. Illustration of a Flowchart for an In-Service Session

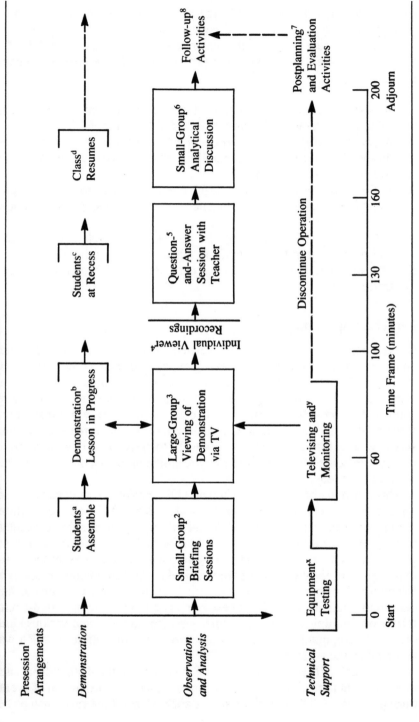

tween events in the three strands. More detailed plans for each strand were, of course, developed. This illustration suggests the utility of the flow-chart in showing such relationships and providing an overall view of all essential events while avoiding minor details.

PERTing Events

The PERT network is another document for inclusion in an in-service plan. This document generally provides more detail about specific events than the flowchart and concentrates on careful timing and the coordination of simultaneous activities that must be associated with each other.

Exhibit 4–3 illustrates a PERT network that depicts events.

Pacing Events

Both the flowchart and the PERT network, illustrated in the exhibits as planning documents for in-service education, give special attention to time-event relationships. They can also be employed so as to give systematic attention to the problems of pacing events.

Pacing involves planning for events so that activities as sequenced in the plan are completed in a reasonable amount of time, so that idle time periods are not needlessly lengthy, and so that the next scheduled event follows without delay. Of course, such pacing requires that planned events be sequenced, but it also requires that the time required for each event be accurately estimated. The big problems in such planning for pacing involve the following:

allowing for individual differences in completion rates of participants
allowing for interruptions, diversions, or unforeseen difficulties
allowing for reasonable amounts of time for rest and contemplation be-
    tween events

The problems of pacing that relate to individual differences can be dealt with in part by allowing the fast workers to take extra time to relax and contemplate the implications of the activity. In this way, the first problem can help alleviate the third one. However, for the slower participants, the pacing problem is severe. If the session is planned for an individual, of course, a simple change in time frame may suffice. Thus, another use may be found for the fast workers in group sessions; they may be utilized as tutors to move slower ones along. Activities may be planned to allow for more and less involvement of participants, depending on the rate of progress of individuals. Whatever the specific approaches selected are, this first problem of pacing is crucial and must be given careful planning consideration.

EXHIBIT 4–3. Illustration of a PERT Network for an In-Service Session

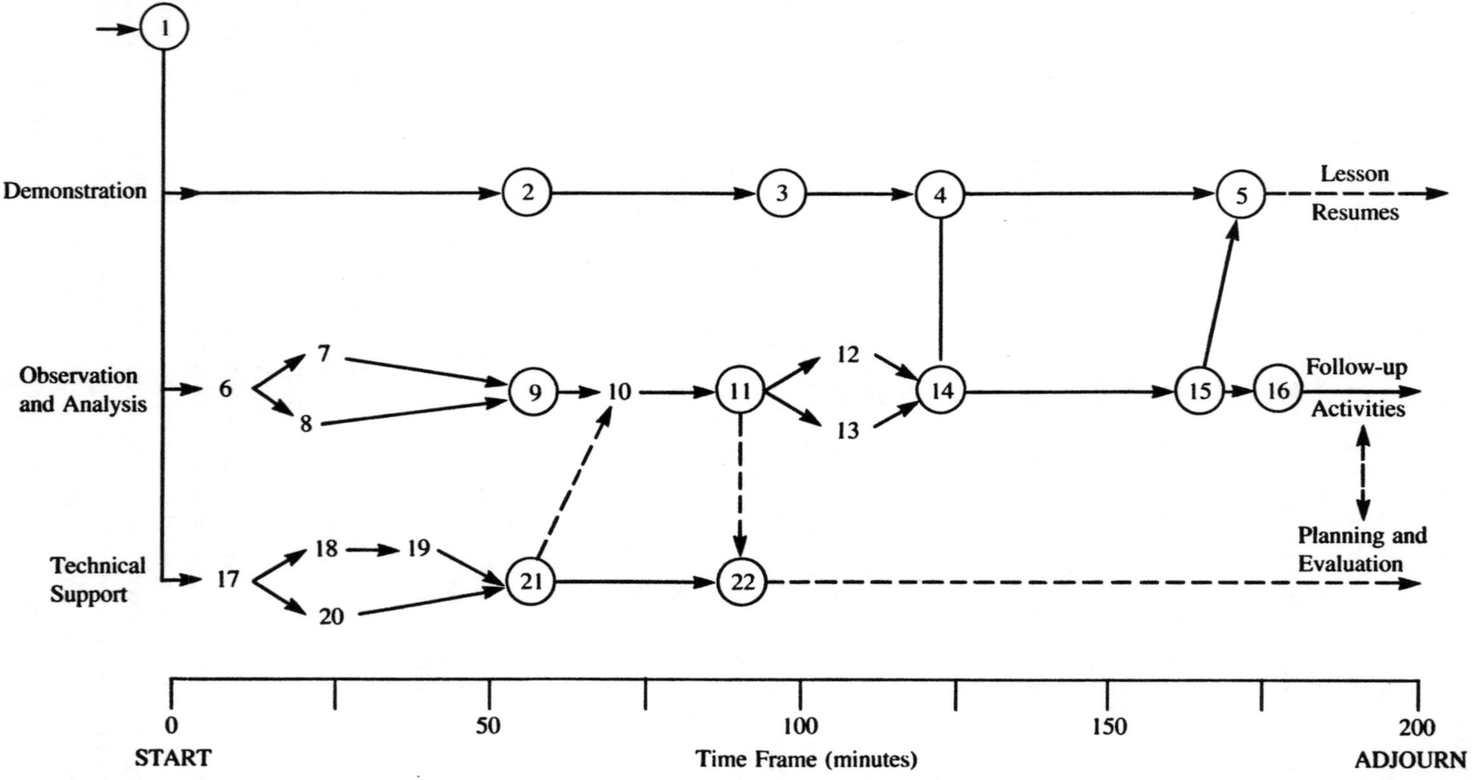

EXHIBIT 4-3 (continued)

TIME		DESCRIPTION OF EVENTS
(0)	1.	All arrangements completed.
(60)	2.	Students, aide, and teacher all assembled ready for lesson to begin.
(110)	3.	Demonstration lesson terminated.
(120)	4.	Students leave for recess with aide. Teacher goes to demonstration viewing center.
(160)	5.	Teacher returns to classroom; students return from recess.
(15)	6.	Viewers arrive at designated briefing session rooms.
(35)	7.	Materials distributed.
(40)	8.	Coffee serving ended.
(55)	9.	End of briefing session for teacher viewers.
(60)	10.	Viewers assemble in viewing room.
(110)	11.	End of observation for viewers.
(111)	12.	Lights turned on.
(112)	13.	Viewers reminded of recording procedures.
(125)	14.	Completion of writing period during which teacher viewers complete observation and evaluation reports.
(155)	15.	End of question-and-answer period with demonstrating teacher.
(200)	16.	End of discussion of observed demonstration and recorded notations.
(15)	17.	Power switch on.
(35)	18.	Camera testing completed.
(4)	19.	Sound testing completed.
(45)	20.	Television monitor testing completed.
(50)	21.	Coordinator notified of technical readiness.
(115)	22.	Television system turned off. Operations discontinued.

The problem of allowing for interruptions, diversions, and unexpected difficulties cannot be planned for so much as handled *in progress*. If plans provide too much slack to allow for the unexpected, then other pacing problems are aggravated. It is better to alert and caution session leaders regarding the sources of such problems within the design, and leave it to those leaders to make adjustments. For instance, an activity that is likely to generate a great deal of chatter or confusion among some (e.g., the non-mathematical) can be scheduled with only minimum time allowances for these diversions. However, the schedule of events can allow for shortening a discussion or buzz session to allow for errors in such allowances.

Time for rest, relaxation, or contemplation is partially provided for when some finish ahead of schedule. However, the slower participants may be neglected if this is the only opportunity provided. Short *stretch breaks* can be planned to allow relaxation without losing the pace of events. Short *buzz sessions* can be scheduled to assure opportunities for sharing. Coffee breaks are scheduled, of course, at appropriate intervals, and these must be timed to offer rest and relaxation without destroying continuity of activity. The use of such formal breaks—coffee, lunch, adjournment, and the like—

scheduled on the basis of "take a break when you are finished" can greatly assist in dealing with the fast-working participants previously discussed.

SELECTING RELEVANT ACTIVITIES

Activities are the building blocks of the training session. Much has been written over the years about activities for training—brainstorming (Taylor et al. 1958), discussing (Gall and Gall 1976), role playing (Shaftel and Shaftel 1967), demonstrating (Harris 1966, 1985). Harris has developed and refined on several occasions lists of activities and detailed descriptions of their unique characteristics (Harris 1985, 70–86). While it is not possible to exhaust the possibilities open to selection by in-service designers, those presented in Exhibit 4–6 are relatively comprehensive.

The design problems to be resolved when selecting activities for an in-service education session include:

1. What activity or activities are most likely to stimulate learning toward the objective(s)?
2. Will more than one activity be required? If so, which ones?
3. What sequence of activities is likely to be most effective?
4. How feasible are the chosen activities, given the time frame, size and composition of the client group, leadership competencies, materials, and other resources available?

Each of these questions needs to be carefully answered for an effective design to emerge. If any cannot be answered with reasonable certainty, then the probable effectiveness of the session *in operation* must be questioned. In fact, of course, the designer is always faced with uncertainty and hence must be both creative and analytical in approach.

Activity-Impact Relationships

Every activity in use is presumed to have some influence for learning. The influence potential of an activity as distinguished from the actual influence of an experience on an individual has been the focus of interest for in-service designers as well as researchers for many years (Andros and Freeman 1981; Sparks 1983). Activity selection has tended to be a by-product of other interests rather than the central focus of concern for design. Hence, learning theory has dictated interest in drill, sequence, task analysis, reinforcement, and other principles. The various technological developments of photography, electronics, and computers have each emphasized unique applications of machines to training (Strother and Klus 1982). Psychiatry and clinical counseling are examples of other specialized fields of inquiry that have spawned methodologies, which in turn have been advocated for adaptation to training. The influence of Carl Rogers and many others, emphasizing nondirectiveness in relationships among staff personnel, is widely represented in the literature on in-service education by persistent references to teacher involvement, self-renewal, joint decision-making outcomes, self-evaluation, free choices from among many alternatives (Yeatts 1976), respect for preferences, and even "staff liberation" (Beegle and Edelfeldt 1977). Whatever the merits of this thrust toward client-centered in-service education may be, it leaves questions about selection of activities in the design of training experiences confused and uninformed.

Advocates of coaching and peer observations (Joyce and Showers 1983), synergogy (Mouton and Blake 1984), and "action learning" (Pedler 1983), as well as "double-loop learning" as advocated by Argyris (1982), all emphasize structure for training of kinds not previously advocated. They argue for client-centered approaches, but for much more than nondirectiveness. They argue for a focus on reality but not the imposition of the institutional definition of the problem or solution. The design grid presented in Exhibit 4–4 offers one way of relating experience impact, type of activity, and type of objectives to each other so as to identify three different design categories.

The types of objectives shown on this design grid are based on Bloom's (1956) taxonomy of educational objectives. The specific training objective,

EXHIBIT 4–4. In-Service Design Grid

TYPE OF ACTIVITY (EXAMPLES)	LEVEL EXPERIENCE IMPACT*	TYPE OF OBJECTIVE					
		KNOWLEDGE	COMPREHENSION	APPLICATIONS	SYNTHESIS	VALUES	ADJUSTMENT
Lecture	7						
Demonstration	12						
Observation	13						
Interviewing	12						
Problem Solving	14						
Brainstorming	12						
Discussion	10						
Buzz Session	14						
Role Playing (Structured)	15						
Guided Practice	19						

Design I — Cognitive Outcomes

Design III — A Broad Spectrum of Outcomes

Design II — Affective Outcomes

*Based on estimates of potential influence for learning inferred from specific criteria.

if clearly specified, can usually be located along the horizontal dimension of the grid; when objectives are specified, they can be designated as appropriately belonging in one or more columns of the grid. As activities are selected for any given objective, an intersection between type of objective and activity is produced. A cell, in effect, is designated by the relationship between activity and objective.

Such intersections, on inspection, can be determined to fall within or outside one of the three designated areas—Design I, II, or III—on the grid. When within one of these areas, appropriateness of match can be inferred between activity and objectivity. When *outside,* inappropriateness of match can be inferred and the selection of activities reexamined.

To illustrate the utility of this simple procedure for selecting activities, the objectives specified below show how both appropriate and inappropriate activity selections can be designated.

CHOSEN SPECIFIED OBJECTIVES	ALTERNATE ACTIVITY SELECTIONS	APPROPRIATE
"To increase the variety of praising terms used three or more times during a lesson."		
1. To recall from memory at least ten *praising* terms.	Lecture	Yes
	Demonstration	Yes
	Role playing	No
2. To substitute for commonly used terms one of the others, when editing a lesson transcript or tape.	Interviewing	Yes
	Group discussion	Yes
	Lecture	No
3. To use spontaneously at least seven different *praising* terms in a practice session.	Role playing	Yes
	Guided practice	Yes
	Lecture	No

The table illustrates three objectives at three levels of outcome: knowledge, comprehension, and application. While lecture or demonstration activities might have sufficient experience impact to produce the recall of terms, higher levels of impact are needed when comprehension involving substituting one term for another is required. However, at the application level, higher impact activity is required such as that provided by role playing or guided practice.

It should be noted that while the lecture is completely inappropriate for objectives 2 and 3 specified above, role playing is not so completely inappropriate for objective 1. In fact, role playing might indeed be utilized to assist participants in recalling *praising* terms. The rejection of this activity is based on the criterion of inefficiency. That is, there are more efficient (less elaborate and/or more direct) ways of accomplishing this simple knowledge-type objective. Even demonstration activity might be criticized as needlessly elaborate for presenting a set of *praising* terms that could form the basis for demonstrating knowledge. Reading a list, underlining such terms in a typescript, or writing such terms as observed in use are relatively direct, simple activities for accomplishing objective 1.

This illustration of the in-service design grid as a useful tool for selecting activities is based on the assumption that the designer is aware of the numerous in-service activities and their *levels of experience impact*. Only a few examples of activities are shown in Exhibit 4–4, and they are already arranged in order of impact from lowest to highest. A more complete list of activities is shown in Exhibit 4–6 and is discussed later in this chapter.

More about Experience Impact

This notion that an activity, by its very nature, has either more or less potential to influence learning of various kinds needs to be considered carefully. First of all, it is important to realize that the *quality of use* of the activity is not involved in this concept of experience impact. Obviously, an activity of any kind that is poorly utilized, improperly implemented, disrupted, or distorted cannot be expected to have a positive influence for learning toward any kind of objective. However, when a distinctive set of events referred to as an *activity* is utilized with reasonable procedures, skillful leadership, and appropriate conditions, *only* certain types of outcomes are likely to emerge. A lecture, no matter how skillfully delivered, is highly unlikely to produce new skills in listeners. A demonstration, if well organized, planned, and presented, is more likely to help participant-observers comprehend relationships between teaching materials and techniques for their use than reading about them will do. Role playing is more likely to give one a sense of spontaneous application of skills and knowledge to a given context than a writing exercise about such applications.

The critical dimension we refer to as experience impact seems to be one associated with each distinctive activity type, making each one more or less appropriate for use in accomplishing objectives. The characteristics of an activity that seem associated with experience impact are not surprising. Since activities vary widely on a number of characteristics that make a difference in impact, it is not surprising that impact levels are also quite different. At least some of these are listed as follows:

1. *Senses involved:* extent of involvement of the various senses called upon.
2. *Interactions multiple:* extent to which communication flow is two-way or three-way or multichanneled.
3. *Controlled experience:* extent to which character of the experience is under control—has structure.

4. *Focus:* extent to which the experience is given a focus, has unity, internal consistency.
5. *Activeness:* extent to which the experience calls for active use of inputs.
6. *Originality:* extent to which inputs are original in content, form, or relationships.
7. *Reality:* extent to which realities rather than abstractions are utilized as frames of reference.

A few highly contrasting activities will serve to illustrate the distinct differences in experience impact among them, based on these seven characteristics. Exhibit 4–5 shows impact estimations based on ratings applied to each of the activities for each of the seven characteristics listed. Using an arbitrary three-point scale, the highest impact level would be twenty-one while the very lowest would be seven. Harris previously made similar estimates for a set of twenty-four activities, using a more limited number of characteristics. In Chapter 11, these impact-level estimates are used in evaluating session plans.

Other Features of Activities

The designer of training sessions cannot overlook the fact that selection of activity considerations may extend beyond experience impact. As important as this concept might be, other possibilities should not be ignored. McCleary and McIntyre (1972) distinguished types of skills to be learned. They indicated that activities may be differentially appropriate for technical, conceptual, and human skills. Their scheme involved relevance to these three types of skills. In contrast, Mouton and Blake (1984, 9) emphasize four important features of training sessions that are "synergogic" in their effects on learners: "(1) replacing authority figures . . . , (2) enabling learners to become proactive . . . , (3) applying the concept of synergy . . . from teamwork . . . , (4) using learners' colleague affiliations to provide motivation."

Another important way of thinking about activities and their usefulness in a training session involves relating type of outcome to type of involvement. Verbal involvement may well generate verbal learning; psychomotor involvement is most likely to generate psychomotor learning; emotional involvement may be essential to attitudinal and value changes. This is such a simple, self-evident way of viewing designs for learning that it seems needless to develop it in detail. However, the practice of ignoring such simple guidelines is all too common. We are tempted to settle for a simple discussion in hope that skills will emerge, rather than plan the more complex activities needed. Conversely, having decided to settle for the simple-

EXHIBIT 4–5. Experience Impact Estimates for Four Selected Activities*

SELECTED ACTIVITIES	1 SENSES INVOLVED	2 MULTIPLE INTER-ACTIONS	3 EXPERI-ENCE CONTROL	4 FOCUS	5 ACTIVE-NESS	6 ORIGI-NALITY	7 REALITY	IMPACT TOTAL
Demonstration (A presentation of a prearranged series of events to a group for their observation)	1	1	3	1	1	2	3	12
Brainstorming (A structured inventory of ideas orally expressed in a group setting so as to stimulate maximum numbers of ideas and contributions by all)	1	1	3	2	1	2	2	12
Buzz Session (A small-group verbal interaction session, limited to a particular time, topic, and purpose to assure maximum verbal interaction with full involvement)	2	3	2	1	2	2	2	14
Guided Practice (A guided individualized experience in a real situation modified only by close direction)	3	3	3	2	3	2	3	19

*Rating criteria: 1 = low; 3 = high.

to-implement activity, it is tempting to revise our objectives to conform to the simple outcomes that can be expected.

Faced with the need to train for complex patterns of performance, the designer cannot seek comfort in inappropriate activities or in unimportant objectives. A variety of activities must be selected and put together as a sequence of experiences, much as a tailor puts together different garments for different clients and purposes. The basic problems of design are always present, but the fabrics must be carefully chosen to fit each unique garment.

An Array of Activities

Selecting activities for inclusion and sequencing in a training session relies heavily upon the designer's understanding of each of the many activities at his or her disposal. Exhibit 4–6 provides a list of activities described and differentiated with respect to sensory involvement, group size, experience impact, and type of objectives to be served.

Ideally, designers should have firsthand experience with each of these activities in order to use them discriminatingly in designing sessions. The preoccupation of individuals with a pet activity, previously criticized, does often offer the advantage of producing numerous descriptions in books, monographs, and journal articles regarding these techniques. Hence, the designer of training sessions will do well to turn to the references provided here and elsewhere to read about each of the many activities available.

The principle of variety provides the designer with a highly trustworthy if not very sophisticated way of approaching the problem of activity selection. When all is said and done, any session is likely to be better with activities of a substantial variety than with only a single activity or two that are very much alike. This principle of variety, simply stated, holds that a variety of activities, other things being equal, is likely to be more effective than any given activity. Unfortunately, the danger in applying this principle lies in selecting for variety while ignoring the question of appropriateness. Inappropriate activities will not produce results, no matter how diverse. However, less *efficient* activities can often be included in a session to add variety and strengthen impact characteristics of the experience, even if such activities may be more costly than necessary.

The selected descriptors shown in Exhibit 4–6 for each activity listed are more carefully defined here:

(1) *Sensory involvement* refers to the physiological senses utilized by the participant. Only those clearly used in the activity are included. Each of the senses is listed in order of importance for learning. For instance, "Panel presenting—Audio, visual" indicates listening is most important, while visual involvement with the several panelists is less important for participant learning.

EXHIBIT 4–6. Basic Activities for In-Service Education Session Design

ACTIVITY	SENSORY INVOLVEMENT	GROUP SIZE	EXPERIENCE IMPACT	TYPE OF OBJECTIVE
(1) Analyzing and calculating	Visual, kinesthetic	Ind.	16	Cognitive
(2) Brainstorming	Audio, visual, oral	Med.	13	Cognitive
(3) Buzz session	Audio, oral	Sml.	14	Cognitive, affective
(4) Demonstrating	Visual, audio	Med.	12	Cognitive
(5) Discussing, leaderless	Audio, oral, visual	Sml.	10	Cognitive
(6) Discussing, leader facilitated	Audio, oral, visual	Sml.	11	Cognitive, affective
(7) Film, television, filmstrip viewing	Visual, audio	Med.	10	Cognitive, affective
(8) Firsthand experience	Audio, oral, visual, kinesthetic	Ind.	21	Skill, cognitive, affective
(9) Group therapy	Audio, oral, visual	Sml.	16	Affective
(10) Guided practice	Kinesthetic, visual, audio	Ind.	19	Skill, cognitive
(11) Interviewing, informative	Audio, oral	Ind.	9	Cognitive
(12) Interviewing, problem solving	Audio, visual, oral, kinesthetic	Ind.	15	Cognitive
(13) Interviewing, therapeutic	Audio, oral, visual	Ind.	17	Affective
(14) Lecturing	Audio	Lrg.	7	Cognitive
(15) Material, equipment viewing	Visual, kinesthetic	Med.	12	Cognitive
(16) Meditating	Kinesthetic	Ind.	12	Affective, cognitive
(17) Microteaching	Audio, visual, oral	Sml.	18	Skill, affective
(18) Observing systematically in classroom	Visual, audio	Sml.	13	Cognitive, affective
(19) Panel presenting	Audio, visual	Lrg.	8	Cognitive
(20) Reading	Visual	Ind.	14	Cognitive, affecuive
(21) Role playing, spontaneous	Audio, visual, oral	Sml.	16	Affective
(22) Role playing, structured	Audio, visual, oral	Sml.	18	Cognitive, skill
(23) Social interaction	Audio, visual, oral	Sml.– Med.	13	Affective, cognitive
(24) Tape, radio, record listening	Audio	Lrg.	7	Cognitive, affective
(25) Testing	Audio, kinesthetic	Med.	16	Cognitive
(26) Videotaping or photographing	Visual, kinesthetic	Ind.	16	Cognitive
(27) Visualizing	Visual	Lrg.	9	Cognitive
(28) Writing or drawing	Visual, kinesthetic	Ind.	12	Cognitive

This activities list is adapted from Ben M. Harris, *Supervisory Behavior in Education,* 3d ed. (Englewood Cliffs, N.J.: Prentice-Hall, Inc., 1985), p. 72. Detailed descriptions of each activity are found in Harris's work, pp. 72–87.

(2) *Group size* indicates the group that probably represents optimum use of the activity. For many activities, *both* larger and small groups are feasible, but effectiveness may be sacrificed or special arrangements may be required.

(3) *Experience impact* is estimated for each activity, utilizing the scale of assigned values illustrated with selected activities in Exhibit 4–5.

(4) *Type of objective* refers to the outcomes that are most probable and clearly possible under normal conditions of use of the activity. Other objects are always *potentially* possible, of course. For instance, a lecture could be so dramatically presented as to have affective outcomes. Testing could be employed under special circumstances to produce affective outcomes. The interview could relate to problem solving in ways that model and hence produce problem-solving skills.

Group Size–Activity Relationships

The number of participants involved in a particular session has a bearing on the kinds of activities selected. The characteristics of each activity impose some limits on group size, ranging from those activities that are essentially individual in nature to those that are capable of accommodating large masses of participants. Some activities can be used with various-sized groups, depending upon special arrangements.

Exhibit 4–6 indicates for each of the activities listed a single group size. This is designated as the size that is most appropriate, offering optimum conditions for each activity to be well utilized. Generally, low experience impact activities—for example, lecture, visualization, panel presentation—have unique advantages in that large groups can be accommodated. However, these can readily be adapted for use in much smaller group situations. Middle-range experience impact activities tend to be most readily useful with small or medium-sized groups. Hence, discussing and buzz session activities are often utilized in groups ranging from five or six to a dozen or more persons. Obviously, somewhat larger numbers of participants can be accommodated by procedures that provide for multiples of the buzz groups or discussion groups in operation simultaneously. Demonstrations and classroom observations represent middle-range experience impact activities that can accommodate larger groups only with special logistics but can readily be utilized on an individual or small-group basis. Obviously, their use on an individual basis would be rather costly.

Exhibit 4–7 provides a graphic view of the relationships among the group size, experience impact, and complexity of objectives in any session design situation. These three variables enter into selection of activity decisions as shown. Lower experience impact activities can be chosen as less complex outcomes are sought, and larger groups can be utilized. As objectives become increasingly complex, increased experience impact is

EXHIBIT 4–7. Relationships among Impact, Objective, and Group-Size Variables

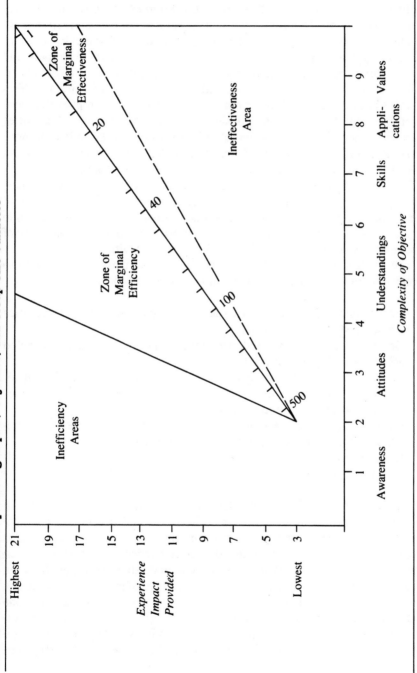

required of selected activities, and small groups must be utilized. High experience impact activities selected for less complex outcomes with smaller groups lead to inefficiency. Low experience impact activities directed toward more complex outcomes with larger groups lead to ineffectiveness.

The areas on each side of the group-size diagonal indicate *zones of marginality* where activity selection to serve a range of objectives and group sizes is possible without undue loss in effectiveness or efficiency. It is important to note, however, the rather narrow zone of marginal effectiveness compared with that for marginal efficiency. This implies that considerable latitude is allowed a designer in using higher impact activities than necessary. Costs are just increased. However, less latitude is allowed in using lower impact activities for more complex objectives because of the risk of having no resulting outcomes or even negative consequences.

Similarly, it is important to note the narrowing of *both* zones of marginality as the group size is increased. In practical terms, this means that the designer must select lower experience impact activities as the group size increases and hence must be very hardheaded about the complexity of objectives to be served in such groups by such activities.

The general principles governing the selection of activities as related to group size and experience impact can be stated as follows:

1. Group size can increase as experience impact of selected activities decreases (inverse relationship).
2. Group size can decrease independent of experience impact of selected activities (independent relationship).
3. Larger numbers of participants can sometimes be served by higher experience impact activities by arranging for multiples of smaller groups operating simultaneously.
4. Middle-range experience impact activities tend to provide most flexibility in being adapted to a wide range of group sizes.
5. Highest levels of experience impact are persistently provided by small-group or individual activities.

These principles offer useful guidelines for session designers not only in selecting activities but also in making logistical and procedural arrangements. The ideal sequence or pattern of session activities provides precisely the amount of experience impact needed to accomplish each objective at the lowest possible cost in time and other resources. Such an ideal is rarely realized, because the art and science of instructional design is not yet very advanced. However, in seeking to design in-service sessions that will produce optimum conditions for both *effective* and *efficient* learning, consideration of the relationships noted above should prove most useful. Larger groups *should,* of course, be used to increase efficiency, but higher experience impact activities should *not* be rejected to accommodate large groups if objectives require greater impact. Conversely, the efficiency gained in serving larger numbers of participants should *not* be sacrificed whenever low experience impact activities will in fact suffice. Finally, high experience impact activities should be utilized as needed, but larger numbers of participants can be served, if necessary, by adapting activities and procedures for handling medium or large groups.

A case illustration making use of some of the principles discussed above may be clarifying at this point.

An in-service session was designed for teachers involving cognitive objectives relating to the importance of two-way communications rather than one-way communications with students, faculty, and parents. The objectives were at the comprehension and applications level (see Exhibit 4–4) and hence required some middle-range experience impact activities.

A laboratory-type training session was designed, utilizing a simulated communications problem in which all participants were to engage actively and individually in trying to show accurate reception of a message being delivered orally to all.* The sequence of activities was as follows:

1. *Lecture.* A very brief introductory statement was followed by an *oral, no-feedback* message, to which all participants were asked to react by listening.
   1a. *Writing and drawing.* A work sheet was used to determine participants' understanding of the message.
2. *Lecture.* The procedures above were repeated except that a new message was used and procedures changed so participants could
   2a. *discuss* the information being presented, ask for clarification, react, and reinterpret.
   2b. *write and draw* on a second work sheet simultaneously with listening and discussion activities.
3. *Analyzing and calculating.* Participants were guided in scoring their two work sheets on accuracy of perception of the messages.
   3a. *visualizing* the correction key that participants were to use was presented on two transparencies, along with oral directions.
4. *Social Interaction.* Coffee break.
5. *Visualization.* During the break, a team of tabulators proceeded to collect and tabulate scores for individual participants. Transparencies were prepared and presented at this time showing comparisons between *no feedback* and *free feedback* in communication.
6. *Brainstorming.* Participants were asked to use data presented showing that a message presented with verbal interaction (free feedback) from

---

*The laboratory exercise referred to here is described in detail in *In-Service Education: A Guide to Better Practice* by Ben M. Harris, E. W. Bessent, and K. E. McIntyre (Englewood Cliffs, N.J.: Prentice-Hall, Inc., 1969).

presenter to receiver was more accurately received, better understood, and more confidently understood. Ideas from brainstorming were to be focused on "implications of these data for our practices in school."

Session ended with indications of follow-up activities for individual faculty groups.

The session just described could readily be utilized with a group of ten to fifteen participants. All activities selected were appropriate for small- or medium-sized groups (see Exhibit 4–6) *except* writing or drawing and analyzing and calculating. These are individual activities. However, any group can be restructured so as to become a set of individuals. In this instance, an individual work sheet on which to write and draw and a structured scoring procedure allowing each individual to score his or her own work sheet facilitate use of individual activities. Without such logistical arrangements, participants might or might *not* function as individual *writers* and *analyzers*. If they failed to do so, much of the impact of the activity could be lost and the integrity of the whole session jeopardized.

What about utilizing this laboratory session with a large group? This writer has, in fact, followed almost identical procedures with a group of over five hundred participants from many different schools. But adaptations and special arrangements were essential for *discussion, analyzing* and *calculating,* and *brainstorming* activities. In such a large mass situation, discussing was feasible only because the session leader had five assistants, each with a microphone on a long cable, who circulated among participants. As questions or comments were to be expressed by participants, an assistant passed the microphone to each individual so that all could hear. The message presenter was also equipped with a microphone so that his or her words were clearly heard by all. A similar arrangement permitted brainstorming comments to be expressed by over one hundred individuals, and heard by all. Three recorders using separate screens and overhead projectors permitted all participants a ready view of ideas generated in the brainstorming.

The above case illustrates logistical problems associated with the use of small-group and individual activities with large numbers of participants. Structuring of individual activities to assure that they will be actively experienced as intended, even within the context of a mass situation, was essential. Providing special sound and video equipment to assure that a large group could hear, speak, and see was prerequisite. Having a carefully coordinated team of leaders handling different aspects of the session was facilitating. As the total number of participants to be served increases, logistical requirements become increasingly complex. Therein lies the danger! Larger numbers to be served tend to promote large-group activity selection regardless of the experience impact required. The replication of a session designed for small- or medium-sized groups is not always feasible.

The alternative described above involves the very careful adaptation of a session involving small-group and individual activities to larger numbers of participants.

SUMMARY

This has been a lengthy chapter attempting to develop the concept of session as the basic training unit. The design of sessions has been stressed in an effort to be both practical and challenging. The relationship of objectives to goals and to activities was developed in an effort to promote design of sessions that are related to larger programs of in-service education and yet to attend to specific needs for learning. Considerable attention was devoted to the concept of experience impact as the main tool for design. The selection of activities does not follow directly from a consideration of either objectives or group size, as important as they are. Hence, experience impact considerations have been emphasized to promote *both* efficient and effective designs for sessions.

This chapter has presented numerous illustrations for use in assisting with session planning. It is the planning process that counts most, of course, and the design concepts are central to that. However, a carefully developed planning document has been proposed and illustrated as a prerequisite to effective implementation.

STUDY SOURCES

Argyris, Chris. 1982. *Reasoning, Learning, and Action: Individual and Organizational*. San Francisco, Calif.: Jossey-Bass Publishers.
    An organization theorist's perspective is provided on the importance of individual and group learning as an essential core element in the effort to solve problems of organizations. This author makes an interesting case for what he calls "double loop learning" as something dramatically different. He argues for interventions that assist individuals and groups to understand their reasoning processes, overcoming "massive unawareness."

Bedient, D., and M. Rosenberg. 1981. "Designing Instruction for Adult Learners: A Four-Stage Model." *Educational Technology* 21 (November): 25–27.
    This article explores the differences between adult learners and traditional college students. The authors propose a four-stage model for presenting material. Preassessment, guided practice, sharing experiences, and evaluation are the essential elements in this model.

Cook, Desmond. 1966. *Program Evaluation and Review Technique: Applications in Education*. Washington, D.C.: U.S. Department of Health, Education, and Welfare, U.S. Government Printing Office.

Although this is an old document, it continues to be a very useful guide to the application of PERT in educational planning. It is sufficiently detailed that the reader can learn to construct a network for a specific effort.

Engel, Herbert M. 1973. *Handbook of Creative Learning Exercises.* Houston, Tex.: Gulf Publishing Company.
A very practical book emphasizing case studies, role playing, and in-basketry. Several chapters on systematic use of role playing goes well beyond most sources.

Freeman, Robert E. 1983. "Effective Workshop Processes for Global Education." *California Journal of Teacher Education* 10 (Winter): 40–56.
Basic workshop processes and procedures which lead to successful training are outlined. Although the focus is on "global education," the processes are widely applicable. Objectives, teamwork, postsession follow-up, and use of resources are all given attention.

Gage, N. L., John Crawford, Nicholas Stayrook, Jane Stallings. 1978. "An Experiment on Teacher Effectiveness and Parent-Assisted Instruction in the Third Grade." Stanford, Calif.: Center for Educational Research at Stanford University (May). ERIC ED 160 648.
An elaborate study of two modes of training for in-service teachers is reported in this and a series of other documents. The special usefulness of this report is in the distinctions made between "minimal" and "maximal" training designs utilized and tested. Maximal training involved discussions, role playing, film viewing, reading, and testing. Minimal training was much less elaborate but utilized much more initiative and self-direction.

Harris, Ben M. 1985. *Supervisory Behavior in Education.* 3d ed. Englewood Cliffs, N.J.: Prentice-Hall, Inc.
Chapter 4 provides brief descriptions of each of 21 training activities. This provides a useful source of quick reference information on many of the activities that might be considered for a session design.

Harris, Ben M., E. Wailand Bessent, and Kenneth E. McIntyre. 1969. *In-Service Education: A Guide to Better Practice.* Englewood Cliffs, N.J.: Prentice-Hall, Inc.
An old but unique source of illustrations and discussion of the laboratory design for training sessions. Introductory chapters are general, but most of the volume provides detailed directions for guiding a variety of specific in-service sessions. Each of the various sessions reflects a different application of the laboratory design.

Hart, Louis B., and J. Gordon Schliecher. 1979. *A Conference and Workshop Planner's Manual.* New York: ANACOM.
This guide is a basic "do-it-yourself" type of publication. Forms are provided, ready for use or adaptation. There are several checklists included to assist planners in reviewing the components of their plans.

Mouton, Jane S., and R. R. Blake. 1984. *Synergogy: A New Strategy for Education, Training, and Development.* San Francisco: Jossey-Bass.
Synergogy is conceived by these two trainers as "systematic . . . learning . . .

[by] small teams . . . through structured interactions" (p. xii). This is a fascinating book with much to offer to in-service education. Chapters 3, 4, 5, and 6 present descriptions of specific designs for training. While all of them are based on the concept of synergogy, each has interesting and unique features.

Pedler, Mike, ed. 1983. *Action Learning in Practice.* Aldershot, Hants, England: Gower Publishing Company Limited.

This book offers numerous perspectives on "action learning" as conceived and promoted in management circles in England. The concept has much in common with organization development and quality circles. A variety of case descriptions are reported in Part II; however, Part I describes the unique design features and assumptions of the approach. Chapters in Part III give detailed attention to the components of action learning and elaborate on the notion of a "set adviser."

Sparks, Georgea M. 1983. "Synthesis of Research on Staff Development for Effective Teaching." *Educational Leadership* (November): 65–72.

A variety of studies on both teaching and in-service training are reviewed to draw conclusions about the improvement process. The main emphasis of this synthesis is on the activities that are consistently reported as effecting outcomes. Unlike so many reports on effective practices, this writer is quite specific about diagnosing, demonstrating, practice feedback, discussing, role playing, microteaching, observing, and coaching.

Sprinthall, Norman A., and Lois Thies-Sprinthall. 1983. "The Teacher as an Adult Learner: A Cognitive-Developmental View." In *Staff Development,* 82d Yearbook, Part II, National Society for the Study of Education, ed. Gary Griffin. Chicago: The University of Chicago Press.

These authors focus on experiences that influence growth of more complex types. They stress the concept of "role-taking" experiences, but also emphasize the quality of experience and continuous guided reflection.

Tracey, William R. 1984. *Designing Training and Development Systems.* Rev. ed. New York: American Management Association.

This volume is a comprehensive sourcebook for nearly all aspects of planning and design from a business management perspective. The author gives much attention to measurement and evaluation, but chapters on selecting and sequencing content, using various training strategies and materials are especially useful.

5.

Presentations and Logistics

INTRODUCTION

While all in-service education does not necessarily involve presentations in a formal sense, there are logistical problems associated with all in-service—time, schedules, facilities, funds, communications, materials, etc.—regardless of strategies or design. This chapter surveys a variety of the more commonly encountered logistics problems and attempts to suggest ways of dealing with them. Simple arrangements for meetings, the use of visiting presenters, refreshments, and materials handling are a few of the topics addressed.

These topics are rarely researched in formal ways, hence we rely on experience and the professional wisdom of practitioners. There are many ideas offered in the literature, primarily to business and industrial trainers. These are not always fully applicable to in-service education in public school settings. However, they add significantly to our "tools for training" when adapted thoughtfully.

LOGISTICAL ARRANGEMENTS

Much of what needs to be done to assure an effective in-service training session amounts to good communication and careful organization. These are matters of logistics rather than design, but they influence the character of the training that emerges. Physical facilities are among the most important arrangements that directly influence design.

However, transportation, schedules, and communications among all of those involved are important to both planning and implementing for success.

Physical Facilities

The right spaces, furnished properly and with necessary special equipment, are crucial to the success of an in-service education session. Such simple arrangements as reserving a room large enough to accommodate all participants seated at tables when writing or manipulative activities are planned assures comfort for participants and makes certain activities feasible. If the appropriate space or the tables were not available, changes in the session plan would be required.

Consider the foolishness of planning for the use of a colored 16-millimeter film in a room with trilateral lighting and no drapes. Even plans to utilize the overhead projector can be full of frustration for want of a three-prong adapter for the power cable or an extension cord. But much more subtle influences of physical facilities need attention during the time planning is in progress (Finkel 1986).

Space for subgroups. Any session, regardless of the number of participants, may call for subdividing into several smaller groups. Role playing may require simultaneous involvement by several two- or three-person teams. Buzz sessions or discussions may require subgroupings. Being sure that appropriate physical spaces are available is essential to the success of such subgroups. If a very large room is available, each of the four corners can serve for a subgroup, but tables, chairs, screens, chalkboards, and other necessary equipment need to be arranged in advance so that movement from total group to subgroup can take place without waste of time and without confusion. The noise from one subgroup may distract another, so such problems need to be anticipated in advance and separate rooms provided nearby.

Materials distribution with ease, speed, and a minimum of confusion becomes a problem when groups become large. A schedule of distributions should be developed if numerous handouts are involved. Generally, handouts should be passed directly to each individual, *not* passed along from one person to another. However, in auditorium situations, rows may be too narrow to allow for passing handouts to each person individually. This situation requires careful counting of materials for each row and, if possible, passing from *both* ends of the row.

Obviously, if the group exceeds a very small number or more than a few handouts are involved, the leader should make advance arrangements for participants to assist with distributions, and the procedures they employ should be planned prior to the beginning of the session. In addition to expediting distributions, arranging for handouts to be timed properly is very important. Materials should not be allowed to distract from the focus of attention on a presenter, nor should they disrupt participant activity.

Seating arrangements must vary for different activities. Changes in seating can be time-consuming and confusing, however, unless advance arrangements are carefully planned. Brainstorming, films, visual presentations, panel presentations, and lectures all require an auditorium arrangement in the sense that participants must be facing in a specific direction to focus on the screen or presenter(s). This is a simple arrangement, but if such activities are preceded or followed by buzz groups, role playing, discussing, writing, interviewing, and the like, then changes in facilities are demanded. One approach is to have alternate spaces as mentioned above, so that participants simply leave the "audience" setting and go to another location. Another approach involves a "conference arrangement," with rows of tables instead of just chairs. This permits regrouping *around* tables with only limited movements of furniture. Buzz groups are sometimes organized by having every other row of participants turn their chairs about to face those behind them.

Assigning participants to subgroups can be arranged well in advance to avoid confusion and loss of time. This is especially desirable when participants will frequently form subgroups, when a variety of regroupings is required, and when control is needed over who is assigned to which group. On-the-spot assignments can be made, of course, but this can be time-consuming. Name tags or plaques that are prepared in advance for participants can include assignment information to buzz groups, teams, rooms, and so on.

Transportation and Schedules

Participants as well as leaders of in-service sessions need to be well informed in advance regarding the schedule of events. When people come from great distances, transportation becomes a factor in planning the starting and adjournment times. Furthermore, if the site selected for the session is not thoroughly familiar to all, special instructions are in order.

Provide everyone with an advance schedule of events, even if all the details are not included. Suggest early arrival times if hotel registrations, travel from an air terminal, or just walking distances are likely to be time-consuming. If the time for adjournment is set to allow for some uncertainty in scheduled activities, be sure that the session will not extend beyond the specified time.

Transportation grows increasingly costly and always requires some special arrangements. When several participants are coming from the same school or town, aiding them in sharing a ride can be helpful, and it can also pay dividends in learning outcomes as they share ideas in follow-up travel.

On the other hand, transport availability can dictate attendance. "Cafeteria" type programs have been less successful than they might be when teachers choose a session simply because friends are attending and a ride is readily available. Arranging for transportation relieves participants' minds and permits grouping individuals for maximum opportunity to learn.

Communications and Clearances

Any in-service training session that has more than routine activities built into it will demand close attention to be sure that all who need to be involved and informed are. As various individuals share responsibilities for physical arrangements, refreshments, name tags, presentations, equipment, materials reproduction, or any other part of the operation, someone needs to ensure that they are all fully informed. Appendix B shows a basic planning document that helps to assure that the person in charge has communicated well. However, those who share responsibility need general information; they need specific guidelines; and they need personal contact to provide them opportunities for questions, counterproposals, reassurance, and reinforcement. While the person in charge is well advised to put in writing his or her directions to each responsible person, this hardly takes the place of face-to-face contacts.

Miscellaneous Arrangements

It goes without saying that certain other arrangements should be made. Name tags should be provided if even a few participants do not know each other. Place cards with names indicated in large letters are especially important when verbal interaction of any kind is desired. Serving refreshments at a break in the session activities has become so universal in practice that it seems unwise to omit arrangements to do this.

Flow pens and extra acetate sheets, marking pencils, a cloth for cleaning, and a pointer should all be standard equipment, along with an overhead projector, screen, and prepared transparencies. When any kind of audiovisual equipment is to be used, extension cords, extra projector lamps, and three-prong adapters will save many a session plan from early disaster. Even if pencils, notepads, and drinking water are not provided for every participant, it is a good idea to have them on hand for those who need them.

THE VISITING PRESENTER

The use of visiting experts or practitioners to serve as lecturers, consultants, workshop presenters, or demonstrators is widespread practice. When handled well, such visitors can greatly enhance in-service education efforts. But there are many problems, mostly logistical in nature, associated with the use of visitors with special assignments. Expectations must be clear; travel arrangements are crucial; and communications of special kinds are called for (Tracey 1984).

Selecting the Right Person

A strategic consideration that has implications for design is finding the appropriate visiting presenter. There is nothing magical or automatic about the contribution of a visitor. Inviting a visiting presenter involves great risks, unless the individual is well known and fits the design of the program or session.

When the plans call for a particular kind of expertise that is clearly not available locally, then a visiting presenter should be sought. A visitor should be contacted only after careful *search* and *verification* procedures have been completed. Ask for the names of potential visiting presenters from persons who know what you need, and consider nominations only if they are based on direct, personal experience. Ignore nominations if they are based on hearsay or on a reputation that is unrelated to your need. A writer or researcher of great renown may not be an effective presenter.

Once a promising person is identified, try to get verification from someone else as to how well that person really does "fit." You are then ready for direct contacts. Since truly capable visiting consultants and presenters are in great demand, always try to verify more than one possible alternative. Complete search and verification procedures as early as possible, and make contacts months in advance, even for limited assignments.

Clarifying Expectations

The success of a visiting presenter or other consulting assignment requires that the person be highly competent, but even a very competent person has to know what is required. Clarifying expectations involves informing the visitor of program goals and objectives, outlining for that person the overall plans that have already been completed, and designating the specific objectives and type of activities you wish the visiting presenter to employ.

Most visiting presenters who have considerable experience can offer more than a single address, workshop, or presentation. Hence, it is important to make clear the requirements of your design and the needs of the participants. On the other hand, it is not appropriate to dictate specific techniques, procedures, and elements of content. Any knowledgeable presenter wants some freedom in these matters.

Visitors are often frustrated by nebulous assignments. It is hardly helpful to such a visitor to request that he or she make a presentation on "discipline management," for example. Such a topical assignment is very broad and an expert in the field probably has numerous presentations at hand within this general area of content. Equally frustrating is an invitation to: "Choose your own topic. We can give you about forty minutes." The designated length of time is informative, but the invitation appears to call for an entertainer rather than for someone to fill a serious need. Most educators do not need such assignments.

Confirming and Reconfirming

Once a visiting presenter has agreed to an assignment, planning with that individual has only just begun. The specific assignment should be confirmed in writing. Fees, travel arrangements, housing, dates, times, and locations should all be communicated clearly in writing.

Beyond the written confirmation of details it is important to follow up on goals, objectives, and plans in written form also. Much of what is said in a telephone conversation or a preliminary letter of inquiry may not communicate well. Hence, any visiting presenter should be supplied with as much of the written plan as is needed to communicate the context within which the special presentation is to be made. Who the participants are, what presentations will precede, what will follow, what the rationale is for this presentation, and how it relates to others are all helpful to a visitor. Of course, the specific objectives previously discussed should be provided in writing as well.

Once these kinds of confirming endeavors have been engaged in, the visiting presenter is likely to want to negotiate some changes. Objectives may need some revisions. Time frames may need altering. Facilities and materials requirements may need attention. These plan modifications are exactly what is needed for success. They result in the fine tuning that avoids problems. Even small inconsistencies can have serious consequences. Recently I experienced such an event. Careful communications somehow failed to make clear that I was using a 16-millimeter film when the local planners presumed I was using a videotape. No projector was available, and we found ourselves in an emergency situation.

Reconfirmation involves a last minute check on dates, times, places, and crucial arrangements. Usually it involves a phone call and is only a simple courtesy to the visitor. Occasionally it uncovers errors of omission or commission. In either case, last minute corrections can be undertaken.

THE USE OF PEERS (BEYOND COACHING)

The involvement of peers in any and all aspects of the in-service program operations is widely advocated and is gradually occurring more and more frequently (Bang-Jensen 1986; Luke 1980; Ryor, Shankee, and Sandefur 1979; Showers 1985). Several fundamental principles of design support the use of one's peers in a variety of roles—planner, presenter, facilitator, demonstrator, observer, and evaluator. Some of these roles are strongly supported by the principles of *involvement, locus of control,* and *leadership* as detailed in Chapter 2. From a logical point of view, these general principles calling for the use of peers require careful implementation.

Peer Advantages

The general rule to follow is to utilize the most readily available resources to the fullest extent possible. Peers are generally quite available. They are on-the-job; they are close at hand; they are familiar with the problems of their colleagues. And, in the case of teachers serving other teachers, it is relatively inexpensive to release them from other duties to use them for in-service education.

These advantages are so clear and numerous that we need to be careful not to go overboard on the use of peers. No individual, and no one group, has a monopoly on talent, know-how, skills, or competencies. The widely espoused notion that teachers know best is one of those half truths that create serious logical as well as design problems if we act as though they are, in fact, whole truths (Nevi 1986).

Harris et al. (1985, 132) have suggested one way of viewing some restrictions on the general principle of involvement:

> "All . . . people should be involved, as nearly as possible, who have the interest and are willing to participate, if they also have some responsibility for the consequences that follow, are directly affected by the consequences, or have special expertise that will enhance the process."

Pros and Cons

From a logical point of view, peer teacher involvement has its greatest potential in operationalizing, especially at the local building level. Teachers are available on-site. They tend to be interested in the same kinds of problems in-service training programs deal with. However, they have numerous limitations that should not be ignored.

Teachers are:

very busy with classroom teaching responsibilities.
often not experienced or trained to work effectively with adults.
often less than expert in program design, observation, and program evaluation.

One of the common arguments for using peers in highly personalized in-service programs is the notion that teachers are less threatening to other teachers than are "outsiders." This may be true in some instances, but it should not be accepted as generally true. There appear to be many causes of perceived "threat," and using peers is not clearly a guarantee of threat reduction (Andros and Freeman 1981). In fact, it may be that successful working relationships are outcomes based on a process of collaboration (Bang-Jensen 1986, 60) rather than preconceptions about roles and relationships (Hutson 1981).

Another potential disadvantage to be considered when relying heavily upon peers to plan, implement, or evaluate in-service education derives from the insular effects that can result. Teachers tend to be insulated from the cross-fertilization of ideas by virtue of their restricted operations within the classroom. While getting involved in in-service education activities as a leader can be job enriching, it is more so if the teachers work in collaboration with people from other walks of life, other specializations, and different levels of the bureaucracy. When teachers are encouraged to virtually take control of their own in-service education, as sometimes happened in the teacher center projects, a new organizational entity emerges. The net effect can be to accentuate separatism within the school and, hence, to diminish collaborative efforts.

In fact, strong commitment to full-scale collaboration among all interested parties is good assurance that peers will be utilized without the many negative consequences noted above. Furthermore, peer involvement should be utilized in ways that emphasize the importance of in-service education *as an integral part* of the school operation.

NUTRITION, REST, AND RELIEF

Training sessions or programs that extend beyond a few hours require thoughtful provisions for rest, relief, and even nutritional needs. Appropriate timing of rest periods, avoidance of wasted time, and the provision of food and drink are important parts of a plan. When overnight sessions or extended periods of time are involved, rather careful arrangements for sleeping accommodations, meals, and recreation are in order.

Scheduling Session Breaks

Brief interruptions in the activities of a training session are commonly scheduled at one and a quarter to one and a half hour intervals. It is useful to schedule time breaks each morning, afternoon, and evening so that only one is required for each half-day. Breaks of ten to twelve minutes are often adequate for relaxation, stretching, and toileting. However, about twenty minutes may be required if refreshments are served. Extended breaks have unfortunate effects on the continuity of the activities and should be limited in number and frequency.

Serving food and drink need not take a long time. Even if a long break is provided, participants are not pleased to spend that time standing in a long line. When provided, food and drink should be close at hand. Food, coffee, soft drinks, tea, sugar, and cream should all be in separate locations. The common practice of putting all refreshments at one spot is simply time-wasting. The person who wants tea stands in a long line of coffee drinkers while the tea server is unused. Those using cream and sugar keep others from being served when those who take it without could be moving along.

Pouring service is an arrangement that makes serving drinks without waiting in lines a simple matter. One person can pour five to ten cups of coffee or tea for others in the time that it takes for an individual to serve himself. Hence, plans should call for someone to serve as a pourer whenever the group exceeds six to eight persons. If several cups are poured by the time the group is dismissed, hardly anyone will need to stand in line.

Stretch breaks can serve to allow for relaxation and release of tensions. A stretch should not replace a regular break. However, when participants have been sitting without much physically active involvement for an hour, and a full break must be delayed, then a stretch break is very useful. Directions for these must be very explicit, otherwise participants begin to leave their seats and an unscheduled break interrupts the flow of events.

Working breaks can often be utilized to excellent advantage. When the activities of a session call for regrouping, that process of getting up and forming a new group can be combined with a scheduled break to conserve time and avoid discontinuity. This works especially well when buzz groups, discussions, or team activities are scheduled to follow a break. Participants can be instructed to "get refreshed" and take drinks and food directly to the assigned group. Some time must still be allowed for toileting, but these work breaks can be shortened considerably.

Other forms of breaks that conserve time and enhance the continuity of activities are also utilized. When individual assignments such as tests are being used, the amount of time required for completing varies among participants. Some who finish quickly can be invited to leave and take a break while others remain to complete the assignment. Luncheon or dinner meetings are a long-established form utilized by business and professional people in their daily routines. These can also be employed for in-service training purposes. Instead of a long luncheon break, groups can be formed with training activities included on the menu. A luncheon or dinner group can be a small buzz group, a discussion group, or a work team. However, luncheons or dinners can also be used for brainstorming, lectures, or other large group activities.

Socialization

A delicate balance should be maintained whenever possible between tasks and diversions. In-service training sessions and programs should be as intensive as possible, making optimum use of people's time and gaining as much training impact as possible for the costs involved (Hagen 1981). However, people get tired, need to relax, and often gain significant value from socializing in one way or another with other participants.

Recreation activities should be offered participants when a program extends over long hours or days. Hence, a two- or three-day workshop might be planned to include a cocktail party, some musical entertainment, swimming, cards, dancing, or other diversions. These should generally be voluntary and other options should be provided. But participation in such recreation has special advantages when trainees are to be working together at other times. Relationships can be developed that enhance the application of the skills developed and promote subsequent collaboration.

Socializing during breaks and luncheons and between sessions has both positive and negative effects. To the extent that participants have time and opportunity to meet each other, share experiences, and check out the reactions of others, the objectives of the training are enhanced. However, socializing becomes nonproductive in many instances. The objectives of the training session can be cast aside and the unrelated "business" of individuals or groups can, in effect, take over. Gossiping is another common form of less than fully productive activity. Whenever socialization occurs, it tends to break the continuity of the training efforts and, hence, requires some special attention.

"Icebreaking" activities are still another form of socialization that should be used with caution. Every group at some point in time may need a chance to release tensions, to laugh and joke. However, the use of jokes or warm-up activities at the beginning of each session is of doubtful value. In fact, serious-minded participants may resent having their time wasted.

MATERIALS PREPARATION AND HANDLING

Materials in various forms are nearly always useful for in-service education purposes. Sometimes they are the crucial element in implementing successful activities. Each type of material—transparency, videotape, film, handout, disk, poster, or realia—has special requirements for effective use. Preparations for using the materials, their handling, and the techniques for their utilization need attention in nearly all instances.

Preparation of Visual Materials

When materials are to be prepared, their use and the situation need to be carefully reviewed. A videotape needs to be *prepared* in the sense of its selection: be sure it is appropriate, and check on time requirements as well. However, equally crucial considerations relate to whether a selected tape is really usable and what arrangements are required. Is the group too large for a single monitor? Can multiple monitors be utilized? Can lights be controlled adequately? Do we have the correct machine? Are tables or stands tall enough for clear viewing?

Similar concerns are generally of crucial importance when transparencies, 16-millimeter films, slides, or other visual aids are being utilized. Is material really suitable; is it available; can it be seen; and will equipment and facilities be appropriate?

Transparency preparation often involves a unique set of considerations. Transparencies are often not commercially available, hence their technical preparation offers both opportunities and potential problems. Visual aids are intended to interpret in visual terms, hence ordinary written material should generally be provided on paper, not on a screen. When we do present words on transparencies, they should be few in number and written in large neat letters. Adding colors for emphasis is also useful. Typewritten copy should rarely be used unless it is enlarged. Computer graphics are now available to provide many large, clear captions and symbols for transparencies.

Transparency production is made simple and more professional with readily available equipment. Thermal and photographic copying machines can transfer paper copy to transparent film in bold black images. Pens as well as colored film are available for making attractive transparencies. Some copying machines allow for enlarging a sketch or other image to make it suitably large for visual projection. Small lettering and other minute details are common complaints of viewers. They can be avoided by using computers or Kroy lettering.

Projector and screen arrangements are as crucial as the preparation of materials for their use. A projector that is clean, in good working condition, and properly placed for easy viewing by trainees is a minimum requirement. A screen or other reflecting surface should be large enough to ensure an image that the viewer seated farthest away can see with ease. Even those without twenty-twenty vision should be served. Large screens are often unavailable, so a smooth, white wall may be the better choice. Projecting and enlarging computer screen images is now possible with special equipment, adding new dimensions to presentations.

Light and glare control can affect a presentation using transparencies. If bright sunlight penetrates a meeting room, participants should have their backs to that glare. However, the projection screen may then catch the glare, making images faint and unclear. Generally, every effort should be made to control light. Drapes and blinds help to control outside light, but overhead fixtures can also pose problems. Projection screens can be placed in a shaded corner while fixtures directly over the screen can be disconnected or shaded. Some day school architects may provide for more than one light switch per room in our multimillion-dollar buildings, but in the meantime, trainers must improvise. Keep a large roll of brown wrapping paper with masking tape handy at all meetings.

Power cords, outlets, and spare bulbs are small but crucially important items when projectors are to be used. Wherever they go, some trainers carry an emergency supply kit consisting of a projection bulb, a three-prong adapter, and an extension cord. Such a kit is a simple solution to the numerous and common problems of using electrical equipment. Properly stocked, the same kit can protect against problems in the use of tape recorders, video players, 16-millimeter projectors, and slide projectors.

Handouts

Materials in printed or typewritten forms continue to be more commonly and extensively utilized than any other material for in-service education. The preparation, packaging, and handling of these materials are important considerations, especially when a substantial number of sheets are used during a session or a workshop.

Preparation of handouts should be planned carefully and plenty of "lead time" allowed for typing, proofing, and reproducing and assembling the material. Photocopy machines are now so widely used that there is little tolerance for sloppy or unclear copy.

Packaging materials involves several decisions. When many handouts are to be used in a single session or a series of sessions, it may be desirable to assemble them in some logical order in a loose-leaf binder or other secure packet. This is especially appropriate when the material will be utilized more than once and will be referred to at a later time. However, the spontaneity and attention-getting effects of handing materials to participants as they are first being discussed has many inherent advantages.

Distributing handouts during an activity should be done in ways that avoid loss of time and, if possible, stimulate interest and attention. This is a crucial problem with large groups. With most groups the most efficient distribution mode is to hand a copy to each individual, *one by one!* The presenter can use this passing of papers as a chance to establish eye contact and make things seem a bit more personal. But, most importantly, lost time is minimized. When handouts are passed down long rows or around tables, delays are nearly always encountered, and trainees and presenters have to wait.

With large groups it may be necessary to recruit one or more assistants to pass materials. They too should be instructed to pass materials individually to each participant. If such a mode of distribution is not possible because of close auditorium-type seating in long rows, then a modified plan may be required, but the problem of delays is still very real. The best approach for handling long rows involves counting out the correct number of copies and passing them down each row from *both* ends. With handouts being passed along from both ends of a row, participants in the middle are alert to expect a copy from one end or the other.

SUMMARY

Presentations may have less overall impact on participants than is commonly supposed, but they are important parts of most in-service education programs. Logistical arrangements of many kinds are unusually important when large group presentations are involved. They can make or break any kind of training effort, however. Visiting presenters, the use of peers, and provisions for nutrition, rest, and relaxation are all of special importance and hence require thoughtful planning.

Materials are given a special place in this chapter, since they are almost universally used in one or more forms. They too can be much more effectively utilized with only small attention to details.

STUDY SOURCES

Finkel, Coleman. 1986. "Pick a Place, But Not Any Place." *Training and Development Journal* 40 (February): 51–53.
   The author discusses the importance of environmental factors in the success of a meeting or workshop. The need for multiple spaces is discussed in terms of differentiated training purposes. Also mentioned are such considerations as noise, color, lighting, chairs, glare, and power outlets. The article is brief but a practical review of numerous environmental concerns.

Maidment, Robert, and William Bullock, Jr. 1985. *Meetings: Accomplishing More with Better and Fewer.* Reston, Va.: National Association of Secondary School Principals.
   A booklet focusing on principals' meetings primarily, but with practical implications for any group endeavor. The authors present 40 "rules" for improving meetings. A worthy set of admonitions for in-service leaders.

Munson, Lawrence S. 1984. *How to Conduct Training Seminars.* New York: McGraw-Hill Book Company.
   One of the few sources that focuses specifically on implementation process as well as on planning and design. Chapters 9 and 10 are especially valuable for suggestions on specific implementing procedures. In other chapters a variety of logistical concerns are given specific attention. Details on "breaks," evening assignments, icebreakers, participant materials, and visual aids are among the numerous topics.

Sauer, Stephen F., and R. E. Holland. 1981. *Planning In-House Training: A Personal System with an Organizational Perspective.* San Diego, Calif.: University Associates, Inc.

A brief practical overview of ideas on planning for training from needs to evaluation. Each chapter has unique displays and a planning work sheet to give clarity to the ideas presented. Each chapter addresses one aspect of planning in practical detail. Although the approach is a bit mechanistic, it is a fine source of ideas.

Tracey, William R. 1984. *Designing Training and Development Systems.* Rev. ed. New York: American Management Association.

This volume is a comprehensive sourcebook for nearly all aspects of planning and design from a business management perspective. The author gives much attention to measurement and evaluation techniques, but other chapters focus on sequencing content, using various training strategies, and materials preparation.

Zemke, Ron, and John Gunkler. 1985. "28 Techniques for Transforming Training into Performance." *Training* 22 (April): 56–63.

Specific techniques are discussed with emphasis on self-assessment, the use of "life-like situations," and posttraining activities.

6.
Personalized Training

INTRODUCTION

This chapter and Chapters 7 and 8 are intended to assist the in-service planner in considering the proper uses and limitations of several widely varying approaches to in-service education. Clinical supervision, independent study, peer supervision, consultation, individual growth planning, self-paced instruction, and diagnostic/prescriptive systems of in-service education are among the numerous variations emphasizing the individual staff member and the personalizing of in-service education. However, equally strong and promising developments in in-service education emphasize simulations, gaming, laboratory training, study groups, organization development, and other group approaches. These latter approaches are considered in subsequent chapters.

FOCUS ON THE INDIVIDUAL

As suggested, there are numerous ways to approach in-service education with a focus on the individual as distinguished from focusing on a problem, a program, or an institutional need. Clinical supervision, as promoted by the work of Cogan (1973), Goldhammer (1969), Boyan and Copeland (1978), and others, has provided carefully developed and highly structured approaches to consider. In contrast, interest in independent study remains high, especially among college and university staffs where the tradition of the sabbatical and self-directed learning is strong. Increasingly, however, more highly structured approaches to self-directed learning have emerged in the form of learning packets, programmed material, computer-assisted instruction, and individual growth planning (Harris and Hill 1982; Matthews 1984; and Wolf 1981).

Some of the oldest approaches to training are highly personalized and tend to be neglected even though they are among the most carefully validated approaches. Some of these include intervisitation (Harris 1985, 83–84), field trips, internships, and on-the-job training involving directed practice. Hence, when we think about personalized training for in-service staff development, it is important to consider a rather broad array of alternatives.

Learning Is Always Personal

There are strengths and limitations inherent in any approach to training. One of the most obvious realities that makes personalization so promising is a fact about learning: it is always a highly personal thing. It occurs within the individual—nowhere else. It occurs in highly individual ways with unique sequence, timing, and processes involved.

The focus on the individual and the identification of those unique learnings that need to be facilitated are greatly complicated by consideration of the person within a situational context. Mager and Pipes (1970) have emphasized motivational constraints that must be recognized. There is the need for relating teacher concerns, stated needs, and community and institutional needs in programs of in-service training. However, these may all be quite inconsistent one with another. Personalizing is further complicated by contrasting the "public" versus the "performance platform" of the individual. Simon (1977) points out that what teachers espouse as appropriate performance and believe they are doing may in fact be very different from what they can demonstrate to others.

The view of learning, via in-service education, as a very personal phenomenon is not in dispute. The problem for planners of training is to avoid the overly simple conclusion that personalization equates with complete freedom—even license—to make in-service education a completely personal operation. In fact, as personal as the learning outcome must be, the inputs are social and institutional as well as personal. The same must be recognized for process. The challenge is to provide experiences for learning that are not just productive, since all experience will result in some learning. The character of the in-service education must be shaped to provide the most learning, of the most appropriate kinds, as determined by a congruence of personal and institutional needs. Exhibit 6–1 suggests ways of utilizing as many as four distinctly different perceptions that reflect both personal and institutional priorities.

The four perceived needs include two that focus on the individual and two that focus on the organization. One of each utilizes an *internal* frame of

EXHIBIT 6–1. Needs for In-Service Education Prioritized via Congruence of Perceptions

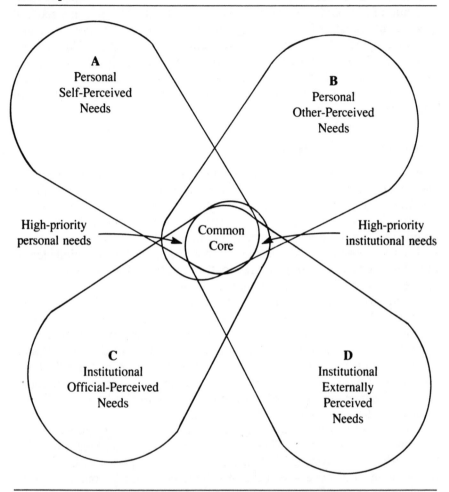

Based on discussions with Dr. N. Grant Tubbs and other staff members of the Virginia State Department of Education, Richmond, Virginia, September 7, 1978.

reference, and one of each employs an *external* frame of reference. Where three or four of these perceptions are congruent, an obvious priority can be presumed.

Change and the Individual

In-service education in whatever form is uniquely associated with change process. By definition, all the purposes of in-service education are related to promoting change in the individual. However, Chapter 1 discusses at length the importance of recognizing change process as multifaceted, and not exclusively a matter of education or training. Furthermore, in-service education in its most effective forms inevitably relates to the larger context of the school or program in which the individual staff member performs.

The reader may wish to refer to Chapter 1 for the discussion of in-service education assumptions (see Exhibit 1–1) and also to Vignette 3, which describes the high school language arts team. Ann, the reading specialist, as a member of that team was off at a seminar or conference, pursuing her need and interests in the teaching of reading. If she returns with new performance capabilities, how will she put them to work? Will her teammates encourage, discourage, or frustrate her efforts? If she is able to *change* her performance in some ways that are desirable from her *personal* point of view, will those changes be compatible with practices of others on her team? Is it possible that her learning resulting in new performance could conceivably even reduce the effectiveness or cohesion of the team?

Change process has been widely studied as an organizational phenomenon. But organizations are people, and much too little attention is given to the problem of making an array of individual personal changes add up to an innovation or improvement of substance in program. Berman and McLaughlin (1975), in a report on federal program outcomes, emphasize that "the amount of planning seemed less important than whether the quality of planning matched the needs of the project *and its participants*" (italics mine). Similarly, Fullan and Pomfret (1977) review a variety of studies indicating the close relationship between amount of training and the fidelity of implementation of new programs and their effects on student learning.

In a nutshell, we have strong reason to personalize and individualize training, but we cannot lose sight of the organizational context to which the training applies as offering constraining, but also facilitating, influences. Gordon Lawrence and his colleagues at the University of Florida summarize their findings from an analysis of ninety-seven separate, well-evaluated studies of in-service education (1974). They found that:

1. Programs that have differentiated training experience for different teachers are more effective.

2. Programs offering teachers opportunities to choose goals and activities are more effective.
3. Self-directed training activities, while rare, tend to be successful.

However, they also found that:

4. Programs that linked the individual activities to a larger organizational effort were also more effective.

Hagen's study (1981) of both individualized and structured group program designs suggests that structure, impact, and relevance are crucial to effective individualizing.

Individual Designs

Several designs for personalized training are discussed in subsequent sections of this chapter. Some are highly individual oriented, and others provide for individualization even though the activities are not essentially individual in nature.

Clinical supervision programs are generally designed to be highly individual oriented. They begin with an individual and are controlled and/or guided on an individual basis. Independent study programs, study or travel leaves, intervisitations, internships, and related field study programs are often designed as highly individual undertakings. In such programs the client is an individual, the goals and objectives may be highly idiosyncratic, and the activities and sequences are tailored to the individual, with minor variations. Even the level and amount of active involvement of the client tends to be a highly personal matter.

Of the various highly individual approaches, programmed instruction in the form of programmed packets or computer-assisted instruction tend to give less freedom to the individual client. However, they remain individualistic in nature, requiring a careful match between the unique needs of the individual and the programmed objectives and activities that are designed.

Some designs for in-service programs allow for highly personalized training but do not call for isolating the individual so completely as those just mentioned. Cooperatively developed and collaboratively implemented individual growth programs can be designed to respond to individual needs in ways that bring the individual into a variety of interactions with others. Field trips, demonstrations, field study projects, and even study leaves can be designed as group experiences in which personal needs in congruence with those of others, and in congruence with institutional priorities, can be addressed. Coaching as advocated by Showers (1985) and others stresses feedback, interaction, and collaboration as well.

CLINICAL SUPERVISION

Clinical approaches to in-service education are becoming widely utilized. This type of program has its origins in some very old concepts of supervision. A single supervisor observes teaching and then sits down with the individual teacher to help with rethinking and replanning the lessons for the next day.

To overcome some of the abuses and inconsistencies that developed as rural programs were moved into urban settings, Goldhammer, Anderson, and Krajewski (1980) and Cogan (1973) were responsible for the early testing and more careful formulation of a "clinical cycle." Their work represented a synthesis of techniques drawn from nondirective counseling, studies of interviewing, and analysis of instruction technologies being developed during the 1960s.

In his early work and writing about clinical supervision, Cogan was concerned primarily with interning teachers and the kind of supervision "master teachers" could provide. Four "levels of supervision" were distinguished as: (1) the inventory of events, (2) the anecdotal account, (3) the pattern of events, and (4) the constructive program. The emphasis of this approach was on observation of performance and a follow-up conference focusing on "the objective facts . . . as the base line." In their later writings, both Goldhammer and Cogan formalized the clinical process while moving toward a less directive approach as far as interpersonal relationships are concerned. Boyan and Copeland (1978) have given emphasis to analyzing patterns of events while others, in recent years, stress counseling more.

The Basic Model

Various programs and plans for clinical supervision have much in common. They tend to be uniformly represented by a prescribed set of steps, stages, or processes, which are represented as follows with only minor variations in detail:

> Preobservation Conference
> Observation and Data Collection
> Analysis and Strategy Session
> Follow-up Conference
> Postconference Analysis

Various writers specify events to be included in each of these five stages somewhat differently, but each step tends to be a fairly distinct part of the total process.

The preobservation conference is a time for planning and establishing agreements on the focus of the observation. Reavis (1976) argues for the preconference as an opportunity to establish or reestablish rapport, to receive information, and to develop a contract of agreement.

The observation and data-gathering process may range from rather systematic, well-instrumented procedures to relatively casual note taking. Audiotape or videotape recording along with notes, a verbatim "script," or systematically sequenced sets of descriptive notations are among the recording techniques sometimes utilized.

The analysis and strategy stage in the commonly accepted cycle is generally not well defined by writers in this field. Obviously, the kind of data gathered will influence the analysis techniques selected. Furthermore, data and analysis procedures will greatly influence strategies that can be employed. The search for recurring patterns is stressed by Cogan, and he has urged such formal systems of analysis as those developed by Flanders (1970) for use in verbal interaction analysis. When sequential narratives of events are employed, only the most demanding forms of content analysis are likely to be particularly useful.

The follow-up conference has been carefully detailed as a twelve-step sequence:

1. Specifying objectives.
2. Reviewing data related to objectives.
3. Selecting a focus.
4. Agreeing on the need for change.
5. Reinforcing some aspect of current practice.
6. Suggesting alternative practices.
7. Selecting an alternative practice.
8. Planning for implementing selected change.
9. Practicing new behaviors or procedures.
10. Agreeing on criteria of success for the new practice.
11. Getting feedback from the client regarding the conference.
12. Reviewing plans and commitments.

These steps or stages provide a useful guide emphasizing the importance attached to the postobservation conference by those advocating clinical supervision. Obviously, this may be a rather protracted conference. In fact, several sessions may well be required and the "practicing" prescribed in step 9 may well occur in a different place and context from those utilized for the other conference activities.

Postconference analysis is incorporated as step 12. This is a "postmortem" and appears to be an effort to convey to the client that critical analysis of performance is appropriate for all—not just for teachers.

Recent Refinements

The clinical cycle described here has made its greatest contribution to in-service education by providing for a systematic, sequential, and logical pattern of experience for the client trainee. While much is written about rapport, nondirectiveness, acceptance, and a helping relationship in the clinical process, these do not give it a unique place among approaches to in-service education. It is the systematic sequence of events that is unique. In Cogan's words, it is "a system of supervision with enough weight to have impact and with the precision to hit the target" (1973, ix).

Boyan and Copeland (1978), Melnik and Sheehan (1976), and Harris (1985) have all proposed substantial variations to the more commonly accepted clinical cycle discussed above. Each of these writers has attempted to add still further to the "impact" and the "precision" of the earlier models.

The Boyan-Copeland Scheme departs very little from the traditional. Instead of five stages, eight steps are specified, however:

I. Preobservation Conference.
 1. Behaviorally define area of concern.
 2. Decide to obtain a base rate
  or
  Set a performance criterion.
 3. Select an observation instrument.
II. Observation.
 4. Observe the specified behaviors.
III. Analysis and Identification of Change.
 5. Analyze the observation results.
 6. Identify behaviors needing maintenance or change.
IV. Postobservation Conference.
 7. Feed back the results.
 8. Determine strategies.
Recycle.

While this set of procedures is not basically different, it does give greater emphasis to formal observation (step 3) and tends to be more explicit about the leader's responsibility for diagnosis, based on data analysis (step 6).

Harris's three-loop clinical model emphasizes complementary activities to be related to the "basic cycle" without any effort to change the latter (1985, 99). This model proposes additional steps or stages in somewhat independent activity loops, as follows:

0. Preconference planning.
1. Teaching.
2. Observing.
3. Analyzing————→ 3a. Securing other related data.
4. Feedback ←———— 3b. Analyzing other data.
5. Interpreting and diagnosing——→ 5a. Providing training experiences.
6. Planning for implementing change. ←——
7. Trial.
Recycle.

The inclusion of other kinds of data is advocated to provide a better basis for interpretation and diagnosis than a single observation is likely to provide. The limited reliability of any single observation makes reliance on such data unwise. However, if prior observation data, student report data, teacher self-report data, or even student achievement scores or grades have any relevance, they could be utilized to great advantage.

The other significant contribution in Harris's model may be found in the expectation that specific training experiences will be provided *in addition* to those of the clinical cycle itself. A severe limitation is imposed upon the clinical model when only conferencing activities are experienced by the client. When new skills or concepts or attitudes need to be developed, other training activities may well be essential. This is especially urgent in psychomotor learning where guided practice is very important, especially in the initial stages of learning to utilize a new technique or procedure (Showers 1985, 44).

The Teaching Improvement Process designed by Melnik and Sheehan (1976) may well be the most promising of the clinical models to date. Exhibit 6–2 represents an adaptation of a sequence of events with many more options for dealing realistically with the complexities faced in improving teaching practices. As complex as the flowchart makes the process appear, it is not fundamental departure from the basic clinical model. However, the data collection is more realistic in attending to an array of possible data sources. The design of a specific improvement plan is seen as a process that often requires inputs from consultants and others who may not have been involved previously. Steps 7a and 7b give recognition to the fact that certain improvements may well be self-initiated while others require training or guided practices.

Strengths and Weaknesses

The strengths of the clinical approaches are substantial. The focus on the individual; the use of classroom reality as a point of departure; the utilization of counseling, observing, problem-solving, and evaluating techniques in a carefully sequenced design promise a great deal of experience impact

EXHIBIT 6-2. Flowchart of the Teaching Improvement Process

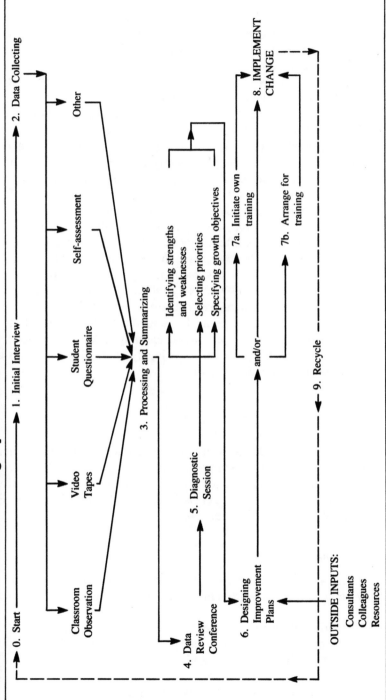

Adapted from Michael A. Melnik and Daniel S. Sheehan, "Clinic to Improve University Teaching," *Journal of Research and Development in Education,* vol. 9, no. 2 (1976): 68.

for learning. Several weaknesses include those of economy, efficiency, and effectiveness. Undoubtedly, the clinical approach in any form—old or refined—demands large amounts of time by highly skilled clinicians. Those who argue that sensitive, competent teachers with limited training can guide clinical supervision processes are engaging in wishful thinking. Because of its potential impact, it may be that the costs are not prohibitive, but they certainly must be viewed as a limitation.

The inefficiencies inherent in the traditional clinical models might be overcome, in part, by incorporating group training activities as suggested by Harris (1985) and Melnik and Sheehan (1976). However, it seems entirely probable that much training for changing individual practices can be quite readily accomplished in small-group situations using approaches discussed in the next two chapters without resorting to clinical modes. Such group endeavors would certainly be more efficient in many instances.

The effectiveness question still needs to be addressed. Clinical approaches have demonstrated effectiveness with young, inexperienced personnel. They undoubtedly have promise for more seasoned teachers, too. However, it would be foolish to assume that all persons or all performance improvement needs can be effectively dealt with by this one approach (Glatthorn 1984). When teachers are unaware of, or unwilling to enter into, a contractual arrangement for clinical encounters, other approaches are surely required. When teachers are facing learning tasks that call for relatively unknown alternative practices—the highly innovative—it seems unlikely that clinical approaches will work.

INDIVIDUAL GROWTH PLANS

The use of collaborative diagnosis and planning models for individualizing in-service experiences has shown promise in recent years. Unlike the clinical models discussed in the last section, much more reliance is placed on independent activity, guided by a *growth plan* (Wolf 1981; Harris and Hill 1982; Matthews 1984; and Sullivan 1983).

Growth-planning Sequence

The approach to individual growth planning takes various forms but can generally be described as a sequence of events as follows:

gathering of performance data
collaborative analysis and interpretation of data
identifying both strengths and weaknesses
selecting growth objectives
identifying appropriate, feasible learning activities

sequencing selected activities
deciding on a target date for completion of each activity
designating shared responsibilities
deciding on a review date
initiating the plan of action
making necessary arrangements
providing materials and resources
monitoring progress and reviewing outcomes
replanning
recycling

Unique Features

The growth-planning process is highly personal and individual. It calls for close collaboration between the client and principal, supervisor, team leader, or facilitator. Performance data are also utilized. However, the learning experiences are not restricted to either the classroom setting or the conference. Classroom observation data are crucially important when the client is a teacher; however, various other kinds of data can also be utilized.

In this *individual growth-planning* model, it is not necessary to secure agreement on a problem or a need *in advance* of observing. The observation data are utilized as the basis for *collaboratively* diagnosing needs. This approach has several advantages over the clinical approach. For one thing, the entire process begins on an objective data base. Second, analysis, interpretation, and diagnosis are collaboratively accomplished. Diagnosis focuses on *both* strengths and weaknesses. A final advantage is found in the fact that strengths and weaknesses *both* emerge from the data rather than from opinions (Harris 1986, 200).

The Planning Document

Appendix E includes illustrations of an individual professional growth plan as a formal planning document. The use of some kind of document has advantages over planning that relies on memory. The planning document serves to bring the data together in summary form, as the basis for the plan of action. It also clearly documents strengths and weaknesses or limitations in performances that usually extend beyond the plan of action itself. This is to say that, while strengths are not in need of in-service training, they do need to be recognized, reinforced, and documented for various reasons. Similarly, an ample array of data regarding performances will yield many needs for improvement when thoroughly analyzed. It is rarely practical to plan for improvements of many kinds simultaneously. When a few specific needs have been selected for individual growth planning, the document should provide a record of those growth needs *not* selected. This permits recycling of the growth planning process without necessarily gathering new data or engaging in new analysis and diagnosis.

Growth-planning Illustration

Remember Bill Thompson, sixth-grade "core" teacher at the end of his first year? (See Chapter 1, Vignette 1.) Had his principal been observing systematically in his classroom or utilizing any self-assessment or student report instruments with Bill, the *end-of-the-year* conference could have been the *beginning* of a growth plan for better teaching and more satisfaction as a teacher. Here is a scenario to depict such a process:

March 15: Principal confers with Bill Thompson on contract renewal. Bill brings his self-assessment report. The principal has already reviewed his observation records for the past three observations in Bill's classroom. The principal also has a set of student descriptions of classroom practices that match the self-assessment report.

In their conference, the main activity is *studying* the three kinds of information—looking for agreements, consistencies, patterns, and discrepancies. Prior to this, the principal has made clear to Bill his intention to recommend his reemployment; hence, that is not an issue. However, as the full range of data are shared, analyzed, interpreted, and discussed for possible *growth implications,* the principal adjourns the conference without any decision making. "Let's get school closed now. Keep all of this under your hat. I'll turn in my recommendation for reemployment on the assumption that you can do even better next year. When you get your new contract in April or May, let's sit down together again. We'll work out a *growth plan* to guide us both for the next year."

May 15: The principal sees Bill in the office and asks if his contract came through from the personnel office. Since he gets an affirmative answer, they set a date for a growth-planning conference. A sample of a well-developed growth plan is sent to Bill the next day with a note attached: "Bill: Look this over along with your notes from our previous conference. Come in and use the data in your file if you want to. Don't try to make decisions; just consider possibilities. See you four to five o'clock, June 3."

June 3, 4:00 p.m.: Bill Thompson and his principal review the data summary prepared previously. Agreements are readily reached on "essential and desirable aspects" of teaching reflected in the data. These agreements are *recorded* very explicitly:

"Shows enthusiasm for the subject and for his work with students by frequent smiling, highly energetic presenting, and helping. Withholds negative reactions, is accepting of students' ideas, and incorporates them into the lesson."

Describing practices "most in need of modification" is more difficult. Bill volunteers several possibilities: "I need to find better room arrangements.

Also, I need to make more library assignments." The principal listens, nods, and suggests another look at the data. He asks about the fact that relatively little evidence from any source (observer, students, or self) indicates "use of a variety of activities that give students multisensory experience or active involvement opportunities." Bill agrees. "Yeh. That's a problem, all right. But, gosh! That's going to take some doing."

The principal nods. "Sure. But maybe there are some small parts of that important cluster of practices that might be worthy of attention this coming year."

"What do you suggest?" Bill asks.

"Well, what makes sense to you?" He pauses. Bill looks perplexed.

"One approach to a variety of activities involves using role playing. Another is using media—16-millimeter films, tapes, and so on—especially on an individual or small-group basis. Still other possibilities include class discussions, peer-tutoring arrangements, small-group projects that are action oriented, independent study projects, and using games."

"Wow! Now I'm confused. There is so much to be learned. I need to be doing all those things, don't I!" exclaims Bill.

"Well, not necessarily, but they are a few practices many teachers have found highly useful," the principal responds.

"Let me get started on the use of media. That's concrete and practical. I think I can handle that and would like to try," Bill proposes.

"That makes sense, Bill," the principal says, encouragingly. "How do you see your growth there? Can you describe several specific practices you think you could learn to incorporate into your teaching?"

"Well, I'd start using films. I haven't made use of more than one or two this year," Bill replies.

"Are you saying your *growth* would consist of making use of more 16-millimeter films in the coming year?" asks the principal.

"That doesn't seem very ambitious, does it?" Bill responds in a contemplative way.

"Well, more is not necessarily better, I suspect," the principal answers. "Let me try a statement of an objective out on you, to see what you think. Let's write it out on scratch paper to consider." The principal takes a pad and writes:

1. To improve and extend the variety of audiovisual media utilized regularly in the classroom, by:
   a. Making use of at least three different kinds of AV materials.
   b. Making use of AV materials on an individual or small-group basis.
   c. Using each media item as an integral part of a lesson involving introductory activities, student participation, and follow-up activities.

"Can you visualize yourself doing these kinds of things next year, with some assistance in the form of training?" the principal asks.

Bill furrows his brow. He doesn't respond for a few seconds. Then he says, "I'd need some help. I'm not quite sure how to do some of those things." He continues to look a bit worried.

The principal smiles, leans back in his chair, and says, "Of course you'll need help! If you knew how to do these things, I'd be worried about your *not* doing them. That's what *growth planning* and in-service education are all about—to help you learn to do things better or differently is the name of the game.''

Bill laughs. The principal looks at his watch. "Bill, it's getting late. You need to go home, and I do too. Let me suggest one more objective for you, and then we'll get together to review, revise, and add others if appropriate. We also need to make plans for giving you that help.

"Another objective that would be closely related to the one we are considering might be expressed as follows." The principal writes it out on the scratch paper:

2. To lead total class and small-group discussions, using an array of questioning and other leadership skills to facilitate full participation and student-to-student interaction, with a high degree of task orientation.

"Don't try to react to this one at this time. Let's both think about it and see if we can make plans that are realistic in providing you with the help you'll need. How about June 8? School will be over. We could spend nine to eleven that morning on this. Okay?''

These episodes reflect at least some of the processes and steps required to generate a fully developed individual growth plan like the one illustrated in Appendix E. Of course, even after the data review conference is completed, the review process outlined in step 5 of Exhibit 6–2 requires still another series of conferences or interviews.

Strengths and Weaknesses

Individual growth planning has strengths not unlike those of clinical supervision. A careful sequence of events is logically prescribed. A cooperative, collaborative relationship is maintained. Objective performance, not opinions, is the focus. In addition, the individual growth-planning approach appears to have strengths in securing fuller involvement of the client in various aspects of the data analysis, interpretation, and diagnosis processes. This approach offers much flexibility in the variety and kinds of data utilized and in the training activities that can be incorporated into the plan of action.

Weaknesses include some that are shared with clinical approaches. A willingness to participate on the part of the client may not always be a reality. Heavy reliance is placed on both client and leader to be objective analysts and diagnosticians, and this is difficult to bring into being. The cost of this approach is still quite high in terms of staff time. Furthermore, only highly skilled consultants are likely to be very effective in this process involving data analysis, diagnostic interpretations, and detailed planning.

The DeTEK system (Harris and Hill 1982) offers a diagnostic process which is relatively simple and surprisingly powerful, making possible diagnostic-based growth plans for a limited array of specific teaching skills.

DIAGNOSTIC/PRESCRIPTIVE MODELS

Along with the growing interest in clinical and individual growth planning, concerns have emerged about the diagnostic processes inevitably required. A spin-off of this interest in diagnostic analysis has been the development of diagnostic/prescriptive models. Diagnosis can be separated from prescription, but linking these processes to each other logically and operationally has been an intriguing possibility. Individualized reading programs, individually prescribed programs in arithmetic, and diagnostic/prescriptive efforts for handicapped children all have given encouragement to similar approaches in in-service education. Competency-based teacher education programs have also been struggling with diagnostic/prescriptive models.

Since none of these efforts, working with relatively simple diagnosis of tasks, has been singularly successful, in-service program leaders should be cautious in employing such approaches. Furthermore, situational variables, including teacher characteristics, seem to be very influential in determining outcomes (Hall and Loucks 1978; Glatthorn 1984). The several interesting diagnostic/prescriptive models provide, nonetheless, some logical ways of thinking about the problems of focusing, in genuinely relevant ways, on the unique training needs of individuals.

Early Diagnostic Efforts

Flanders's (1970) matrix analysis technique for diagnosing verbal interaction patterns in classrooms was among the first efforts to be genuinely diagnostic. The *matrix* became a highly effective method for diagnosing behaviors worthy of improvement. This technique remains, after all these years, the most flexible, precise, truly diagnostic process available. Still, it has serious limitations.

Mager and Pipes (1970) developed an analytical schema for differentiating "performance discrepancies" by type—skill deficiency or nontraining problems. This analytical scheme provides prescriptions of general kinds, but is not truly diagnostic. One starts with a selected discrepancy, but the analytical process does not provide that diagnosis. In short, it is long on prescription and short on diagnostic power, a common failing of management by objective improvement plans (Redfern 1980).

The De Kalb County supportive supervision model (1975) was an early effort at truly data-based diagnostic analysis of teaching for in-service training purposes. This system has since been adapted for the new teacher evaluation and certification program of Georgia. It makes rather elaborate use of a variety of data forms and involves specialized personnel (Georgia State Department of Education 1983).

Diagnostic/prescriptive models continue to be crudely defined. They tend to be limited in scope, or rather costly, or both. The importance of this problem is such that continuing efforts are clearly justified. *Coaching* is the latest effort to prescribe a model with diagnostic power. As advocated by Joyce and Showers (1980, 1982, 1983), the focus is on use of peers to observe and give feedback to each other, in efforts directed toward "acquiring new teaching skills and strategies" (Showers 1985, 44). Three purposes of coaching as specified by Showers emphasize diagnostic analysis if not prescription: (1) "engage in study of their craft," (2) "collegial study of new knowledge and skills," and (3) "provide[s] a structure for the follow-up to training that is essential for acquiring new teaching skills and strategies."

Coaching

Coaching is promoted as "a cyclical process designed as an extension of training." Initially, observation and feedback sessions are required for "checking performance against expert models of behavior." Checklists are utilized to record the presence (or absence) of specific behaviors. As in any diagnostic process, data gathered with these checklists form the basis for feedback which is "accurate, specific, and non-evaluative" (Showers 1985). Later stages of coaching seem to take on the forms of action research. "Team members . . . begin to operate in a spirit of exploration." Problem-solving sessions are proposed. New lessons are planned and implemented with "hypothesis-forming and testing" procedures being called into use.

The DeTEK Diagnostic Process

Formal diagnosis of *both* accomplishments and probable needs for improvement within the context of a multiplicity of known good teaching practices remains an important focus for in-service education. Teacher-effectiveness studies and research reviews over more than a generation clearly indicate many good teaching practices that are simply not widely known or used by classroom teachers. The Harris-Hill DeTEK system (1982) was developed to address this problem in a unique way.

Initially, 101 specific teaching techniques were identified and verified in terms of both research and theory on teaching effectiveness. These criteria or techniques were adopted as the guidance system for diagnosis of both strengths and needs for improvement. Growth planning is utilized as the vehicle for prescribing training activities following a two-phase analysis process.

A survey of the current status of the teacher's practices comprises the first phase of a collaborative data-gathering process. Collaboration and objective use of data are established with teacher self-assessment and classroom observation procedures that are purely descriptive in nature.

The second phase involves the "Focused Diagnostic Analysis" process. Again, collaboration and objective data gathering are stressed. A specific set of techniques is selected for focused analysis from among the array of 101. Three observer estimates are obtained for each specific technique. Teacher self-report, a classroom observer report, and a student inventory provide these data. Congruence analysis techniques are used in highly simplified form to permit the teacher and the observer to derive diagnoses of both accomplishments and needs. Details of these procedures and a rationale are to be found in Chapter 8 of Harris's (1986) volume. See Appendix E for an illustration of the DeTEK growth plan.

CONSULTATION, CONFRONTATION, AND ADVICE

Despite the long history of independent study and self-directed learning (Knowles 1975), some form of intervention is nearly always associated with these efforts. The character of the interventions ranges widely, from text material in programmed format to various styles of interviewing and consultation. The various advocates of some human intervenor are often highly apologetic and urge cautious approaches. The literature is full of references to self-supervision, peer supervision, collegiality, and other notions as substitutes for someone who knows something but might be perceived as an intruder. Obviously, teachers rarely have need for authoritarian and coercive interventions in their efforts in the classroom (Manolakes 1975, 52). However, it seems strange to argue for excessive autonomy in a field of practice still struggling to operate on a truly scientific basis (Gage 1978) and engaged in overwhelmingly complex responsibilities. In any case the relative effects of various forms of feedback and their associated intervention are still not fully understood (Andros and Freeman 1981).

Self-analysis, in contrast with nondirective feedback, seems less than fully effective. Feedback from another individual is an important part of the process of improving instruction (Showers 1985; Sullivan 1983). Various studies of systematic versus unsystematic feedback indicate that the former are more influential in producing results. Feedback presumes something to "feed" and skill and understanding in one or more modes of communication. These and numerous other studies that might be cited seem consistently to point toward the use of interviews, consultations, and advisory relationships in promoting individual performance changes.

The Interview as Feedback Technique

The interview is most widely referred to as the *conference* in educational circles. Clinical supervision, individual growth planning, and diagnostic/ prescriptive models all call upon the face-to-face interaction of the interview. Interviewing is a technique for communicating both verbally and nonverbally. The heavy influence of counseling therapy on the thinking of educators has emphasized two-way interaction and nondirective techniques in interviewing.

The use of interviewing in other behavioral sciences often calls for *information-gathering* as well as *information-giving* interviews that may not be highly interactive in nature. Even when nondirective techniques are most appropriate to our purposes of in-service education, it may well be useful to recognize that Rogerian techniques were developed and tested primarily for therapeutic purposes where the content was essentially that of feelings. Substantial departures from these techniques may be quite appropriate when information sharing, analyzing objective data, describing events, planning, and decision making are in progress.

The basic skills of interviewing, regardless of the particular approach, include questioning, listening, and nonverbal interacting. Still other techniques are of special use in lesson analysis with a teacher. They include *restating* an idea or question, making a *clarifying* statement, *reflecting* feelings, *summarizing,* and *suggesting.* Obviously, the problem of utilizing these various techniques in a patterned form of behavior that guides a productive interview is of special importance.

This problem of pattern and sequence is made more complex when still other interviewer skills are recognized. Some of these include providing data in usable forms, eliciting feelings and opinions, asking for clarification, listening attentively and expressing acceptance even when not in agreement, responding to the substance of the teachers' ideas, avoiding premature advice, and providing specific reinforcement and corrective feedback. Still further skill requirements may include offering comparisons, contrasts, and illustration; and guiding careful consideration of alternative explanations or approaches. While a variety of these skills might be essential to the success of an interview, it is not to be assumed that all of them are needed or that they are useful in any particular sequence.

Schemes for considering verbal interaction skills and sequences have been developed by various researchers and practitioners (Bales 1950; Flanders 1970; Ober 1969; and Acevedo, Elliott, and Valverde 1976). The systems developed by Bales and Ober were employed for use with classroom and discussion groups, but might still be useful for analyzing conferences or interviews.

Bales's Interaction System

The information categories used by Bales were of four types with three specific categories within each type. Type I was positive reactions including: (a) expressions of solidarity, (b) expressions of tension release, and (c) expressions of simple agreement. Type II relates to attempted answers including: (d) expressing suggestions, (e) expressing opinions, and (f) expressing information (orienting). Type III was questioning including: (g) asking for information, (h) asking for opinions, and (i) asking for suggestions. The last type was negative reactions including: (j) expressions of disagreement, (k) expressions of tension, and (l) expressions of antagonism.

In considering the appropriateness and the utility of each category of verbalization, pairs of categories, as well as types, receive special attention. Asking for opinions can be contrasted with giving opinions. Giving suggestions can be contrasted with asking for suggestions. Agreeing can be contrasted with disagreeing. While all categories of events are likely to occur, efforts to emphasize positive reactions and to balance questions and answers might be worthy alternatives to excessive reliance on any cluster or type of verbal endeavor. Similarly, certain sequences of categories might be worth considering.

The Reciprocal Category System

Ober developed a modification of the Flanders system of classroom verbal interaction analysis. Each verbal event is coded differently depending on who is talking as shown below:

Interviewer Talk	Category of Verbal Behavior	Interviewee Talk
1	Accepts feelings	11
2	Praises or encourages	12
3	Uses others' ideas	13
4	Asks questions	14
5	Presents opinions, ideas, suggestions, or information	15
6	Gives directions or instructions to be followed	16
7	Criticizes, disagrees, corrects, or defends position	17
8	Responds directly to a question or suggestion	18
9	Initiates ideas or point of view	19
10	Silence or confusion	20

When conferences or interviews are analyzed using these categories, patterns of interaction are revealed. A matrix analysis technique is most effective in helping to understand what the pattern of complex interactions reflects.

The Advisory/Helping Relationship

The "advisory system" is the term utilized by Manolakes (1975) in describing the various consulting or advisory "functions." He describes the advisor as "seed planter," "technical helper," "personal support person," "expediter," and "informant and communication stimulator." The consultative relationship is always multifaceted and conditioned, if not controlled, by the problem, situation, and personalities involved. Three ways of distinguishing roles of consultants are suggested by the terms *expert, process* specialist, and *resource* specialist. The role of expert is often deprecated, but is nonetheless clearly appropriate in limited areas. When factual information, experience, or technical competence is clearly available in one individual and not in another, then judicious use of that expertise may be extremely helpful.

Consulting as process facilitation is a special kind of expertise. The process specialist utilizes skills in helping people interact, analyze, plan, or otherwise approach their problems in more effective ways (Silverblank 1979). Such process-oriented helping has been widely utilized in group situations, but is, of course, applicable to consultation on an individual basis. Caution needs to be exercised to be sure that facilitation of problem-solving process does not become manipulation of people toward predetermined decisions or actions.

The resource specialist's role is still somewhat different from the other two discussed above. The resource person emphasizes facilitating access to and use of materials and resources of various kinds. Central staff supervisors and outside consultants are often unusually well qualified resource specialists simply because they have greater freedom of movement which brings them into contact with diverse resources. The principal as instructional leader gains much of his or her competence from knowing resources both within and without the individual building. Classroom teachers often have, or can develop, great expertise regarding the specifics of their own operation within the classroom, but they are less likely to gain expertise as resource specialists, given the very restricted locus of operations they command.

A set of consultation stages has been described by Alpert (1982, 312–16). This offers still another way of thinking systematically about the advisory relationships that can be developed in personalizing in-service education. Four fairly distinct stages proposed and illustrated in case studies by Alpert and her associates include entry, diagnosis, intervention, and evaluation. This view of consultation argues for the advisor to be rather versatile in stimulating and guiding the individual through these four stages. They are, of course, related to well-known problem-solving processes, and place high priority on the consultant as a process person. These four stages also have close parallels with the four phases of the DeTEK system reviewed above.

DIRECT FIELD EXPERIENCE

It would seem neglectful in any review of individualized or personalized approaches to in-service education to fail to briefly consider well-recognized field-based alternatives. Intervisitations, field trips and studies, "shadow" studies, and internships or job reassignments are all reputable though seldom-used approaches.

Intervisitations

The practice of providing opportunities for teachers and other staff members to visit other school organizations to observe others at work is one of the oldest supervisory activities. When well organized and planned to serve the specific interests and needs of an individual staff member, such visitations are apparently valuable experiences.

Harris (1985) defined intervisitation with emphasis on the selection of "a person who can skillfully do these things that the observer wants and needs to see." In describing intervisitation in more complete detail, Harris emphasized distinctions between field trips and demonstrations and intervisiting. Compared with demonstrating, intervisiting is more highly individualized and more real. It may also be more economical, and offers flexibility in timing and variety that is not practical via demonstrations.

While it is possible to think of intervisiting as simply a single experience that might be part of an individual growth plan, it could be much more. With a consultant making prior arrangements; observing with the visitor; leading a discussion with the staff members observed; perusing materials in use; analyzing lesson plans, schedules, and other documents, it could become a distinctive approach to guiding improved performances.

Field Trips and Studies

The field trip is usually employed for children. That is an unfortunate association, for staff members can gain from a variety of field trip experiences. The literature on the field trip as it relates to student learnings is readily available and should not need review here. However, short and extended trips into field environments different from those of the school may well be essential for certain attitudinal changes in staff personnel. They may also be essential if the knowledge base of the teacher, administrator, or curriculum specialist is to become broad enough to deal with problems of social relevance.

Trips to factories, laboratories, and mines, even if not accessible for student use, can provide science, mathematics, and vocational teachers with new concepts and knowledge for use in better teaching. Trips to a foreign country, to a black ghetto or a "barrio," and to a remote village or reservation can provide teachers and other staff personnel with both insights and empathy.

The field trip is, like many approaches, suitable for both individuals and groups. However, as an unguided, passive experience it is not likely to have much value. Plans for such trips should be carefully detailed in advance, as with any other in-service program. Objectives should be specified, activities designated, and responsibilities for follow-up return clearly recognized.

Field studies are variations on field trips in that they take the form of some systematic mode of inquiry. Sometimes community opinion surveys can provide information about opinions and also provide firsthand experiences with people of different kinds. Living with a family in another country to systematically study the language, customs, and culture can have an enormous impact on the visiting staff person.

The VISTA- and Peace Corps-type experiences suggest models for future use of field experience for in-service education that need development and testing. The impact of such extended live-in and work-with experiences has been fully recognized. The impact of modifications of these crudely designed programs, to focus on learning for participants, may be very great.

Shadowing Technique

The technique of following another person around, acting much like that person's shadow, has been usefully employed for both training and research. It has been most useful in understanding performance patterns of those staff persons who do not work in one specific observable location. While the classroom teacher's performance is easily studied using observation techniques, the busy principal, school social worker, nurse, supervisor, personnel director, and others move about to do their work. Their performance patterns may change drastically from one location to another. Accordingly, the "shadow" learns simply by following along, watching, recording events, and then having periodic discussions with the staff person being shadowed.

The strengths and weaknesses of this approach as in-service experience are not easily assessed. Undoubtedly, it will have greatest impact in combination with other related activities. It may well be that its utility is restricted to awareness levels of learning. Studies of the effects are needed.

Internships and Reassignments

Internships and other forms of planned assignment to new job situations have long been advocated as among the most useful forms of in-service education. Unfortunately, they are not widely utilized as carefully planned training in education. When utilized, they are rarely evaluated for effect.

Internships can be distinguished from job reassignments by the circumstances that surround each. Internships are assignments to real job situations without expectation that the responsibilities of a *regular position* will be fulfilled. In contrast, job reassignments are real in the sense that the former incumbent is *not* present and the *intern* or *trainee* must assume full responsibilities.

Both internship and job reassignment approaches have the education and training of the individual as a primary purpose. The internship promotes training objectives of open-ended kinds, however. The intern can model the incumbent but can also create new roles and assignments for himself. The intern can enter into the real job situation and become deeply involved, but can also extricate himself when necessary. The intern can analyze, criticize, and make mistakes (within limits).

The reassignee on a new job for in-service training purposes enjoys few of the luxuries for learning that the intern does. However, assuming prerequisite skills and knowledge, or assistance in transferring and adapting old skills to the new situation, the trainee gains new experience, practices new or adapted skills, and develops broad understandings.

The internship is an expensive approach to training but can hardly be equaled by any other approach for effectiveness in developing complex performance patterns not previously exhibited. The internship probably is, therefore, most suitable for pretraining of those moving into new positions. Job reassignment, on the other hand, is relatively inexpensive and perhaps most effective in helping experienced staff members gain new understanding regarding the work of others and the relationships between staff assignments.

SUMMARY

Individual, personalized approaches to in-service education are numerous, currently very popular, and full of interesting potential. These same approaches are full of problems, with many unanswered questions. The problem of high cost for nearly all such in-service approaches demands careful selecting prior to use. Conversely, however, whenever approaches can demonstrate unusual experience impact for important changes in performance, cost factors should not hinder their use. Certainly, clinical supervision, growth planning, and consultation programs under expert direction have demonstrated considerable promise.

New and more finely tuned approaches to individualized in-service education can and will be developed in the years ahead. What needs to be developed simultaneously is a better understanding of the unique and differentiated powers of each approach. Such understanding will make it possible to design programs for in-service education that incorporate a variety of individual and group approaches.

STUDY SOURCES

Alpert, Judith L., and Associates. 1982. *Psychological Consultation in Educational Settings*. San Francisco: Jossey-Bass Publishers.
A valuable book of case reports that provides useful insights into the various ways of utilizing consultants to assist in solving school problems. The first and last chapters are uniquely valuable as they offer ways of conceptualizing the roles and strategies of the professional consultant. A valuable antidote to the naive notion that anyone can be an effective advisor.

Bailey, Gerald D. 1983. "Implementing a Self-Directed Staff Development with a District-Based Leadership Model." ERIC ED 238 848
This article describes a district-based leadership program which has been developed to train teachers in self-assessment so they can improve their instructional skills more independently. Training in self-assessment procedures is provided, utilizing the services of a staff development director, steering committee, and building administrators, as well as classroom teachers.

Barell, John. 1981. "Developing Professional Improvement Plans: A Strategy for Staff Development." ERIC ED 211 449
A plan for individualized staff development for teachers which involves teachers working with an outside consultant. Teacher support groups are also utilized in this plan. Training in observation and other evaluation techniques are provided under the direction of the consultant.

Good, Thomas L., and R. S. Weinstein. 1986. "Teacher Expectations: A Framework for Exploring Classrooms." Chap. 6 in *Improving Teaching*, ed. Karen K. Zumwalt. Alexandria, Va.: Association for Supervision and Curriculum Development.
The authors present the Brophy-Good model describing teacher expectations and their influence on student behavior. The model is illustrated with two classroom observation reports—first grade and an upper grade. The upper grade situation is used to discuss hypothetical ways of using feedback conferences to influence the teacher's conceptions about students.

Grant, Carl A., and Kenneth M. Zeichner. 1981. "In-Service Support for First Year Teachers: The State of the Scene." *Journal of Research and Development in Education* 14 (Winter): 99–111.
A survey of first-year teachers about the types of "induction" programs they experienced. Only 17 percent reported being provided with a formal "buddy system." Informal interactions with peers were most common and also perceived as the most useful way of "learning the ropes." However, mixed reactions to buddy systems and the limited scope and depth of informal interactions give emphasis to limitations inherent in these approaches.

Harris, Ben M. 1985. *Supervisory Behavior in Education*. 3d ed. Englewood Cliffs, N.J.: Prentice-Hall, Inc.
Clinical supervision is discussed briefly as a "basic approach." A three-loop clinical model is presented (pp. 98–101) as a way of making clinical sequences more powerfully responsive to specific problems. The author argues that observation may not provide adequate data and conferences may not be sufficient assistance.

Harris, Ben M. 1986. *Developmental Teacher Evaluation*. Newton, Mass.: Allyn and Bacon, Inc.
Chapter 9 includes sections on the use of collaborative procedures as related to feedback and growth planning. Chapter 8 also gives detailed illustrations of diagnostic techniques.

Harris, Ben M., and Jane Hill. 1982. *Developmental Teacher Evaluation Kit*. Austin, Tex.: Southwest Educational Development Laboratory.
A completely instrumented system for diagnostic analysis and growth planning for individual teachers is provided in this *Kit*. The authors provide a *criteria list* of 101 specific teaching practices related to 22 *behavior* patterns derived from research on teacher effectiveness. The unique features include a user's handbook, complete instrumentation for diagnostic analysis purposes, plus a training manual and resource guide.

Iwanicki, Edward F., and Lucille McEachern. 1983. "Teacher Self-Improvement: A Promising Approach to Professional Development and School Improvement." *Journal of Staff Development* 4 (May): 62–77.
This article approaches staff development from the viewpoint that a self-improvement process is essential. Emphasis is given to distinguishing between the self-improvement process and the teacher evaluation efforts that might also be involved. Self-improvement is urged on a continuous basis.

Manolakes, Theodore. 1975. "The Advisory System and Supervision." In *Professional Supervision for Professional Teachers*, ed. Thomas J. Sergiovanni. Washington, D.C.: Association for Supervision and Curriculum Development.
A systematic way of viewing supervisory practice as an advisory system is presented in very interesting and concrete ways. The author builds on basic knowledge regarding consultation but adds the dimensions of a system.

Matthews, Doris B., Howard Hill, and Jim Frank Casteel. 1984. *Staff Development: A Matter of Survival*. A paper presented at the annual conference of the

Association for Supervision and Curriculum Development. New York (March). ERIC ED 241 510

A report on the use of in-service education in a small rural school district with limited resources. The study findings emphasize systematic long-term planning utilizing need assessment and careful evaluation. Design features stress reduction in structure of experiences over time using classroom follow-up and self-improvement plans.

Miller, Gerald V. 1979. "Individualizing Learning Objectives." *Training and Development Journal* 35 (July): 40–42.

The author discusses the problem of relating individual needs to programs with "preset learning objectives." An instrument is presented and discussed for use in facilitating planning individually within a framework of preset objectives. It is another approach to individual growth planning.

Showers, Beverly. 1985. "Teachers Coaching Teachers." *Educational Leadership* 43 (April): 43–48.

The author defines and describes coaching as a peer group process, among teachers, to improve the transfer of newly learned teaching skills into the classroom. The effects of coaching are discussed, as is the relationship between school administration and teams of coaching teachers.

Sullivan, Cheryl Granade. 1980. *Clinical Supervision: A State of the Art Review.* Alexandria, Va.: Association for Supervision and Curriculum Development.

A brief but comprehensive pamphlet which defines and reviews the history, tenets, and steps of clinical supervision. The author cites research which supports the process as a valuable tool in supervision of teachers.

Sullivan, Debra K., and Joseph C. Basile II. 1983. "Implementation of the Stallings Classroom Management Staff Development Demonstration Project in Putnam County, West Virginia." Charleston, W. Va.: Appalachia Educational Laboratory. ERIC ED 225 976

The operation of a seven-phase model emphasizing classroom observation, direct training, and feedback is described. The Stallings Model utilizes a structured classroom observation instrument with systematic recording, analyzing, and feedback to teachers.

Wircenski, Jerry, and David Just. 1984. "An In-Service Staff Development Program for Vocational Teachers Working with Disadvantaged Students." *Research in Education* (June). ERIC ED 239 068

Resource team reported working with vocational teachers in Pennsylvania school districts. Observations utilized as basis for determining "eight general services" needed by forty-two teachers in six schools. Emphasis on "instructional strategies" and "improving the quality of teaching" was reported as successful over a 10-week period by 99 percent of teachers.

Wolf, Steven. 1981. "The Alaska Special Education In-Service Training Center." *Journal of Staff Development* 2 (November): 2–18.

A model is described utilizing individualized, field-based procedures. Cooperative planning and implementation utilize a growth plan that is also utilized for follow-up assessment purposes.

7.

Simulations, Games, and Structured Reality

INTRODUCTION

Learning by experience always implies experiences that are real or at least clearly associated with a concrete reality, in contrast with an abstraction or fragmentation only remotely related to reality. Just as beauty is in the eye of the beholder, reality is in the mind of the perceiver. What seems real, concrete, and relevant to one trainee may not be for another. Even so, much interest in recent years has been focused on real or highly realistic, simulated experience as the heart of in-service education. Accordingly, the Teacher Corps (Smith 1978) emphasizes school and community involvement, almost to the neglect of on-campus training of teacher interns. The Harvard-Newton summer programs, directed by Robert Anderson for many years, were largely focused upon in-classroom experiences for in-service trainees. Butts (1967) developed and tested in extensive fashion a "classroom experience model" of in-service training in implementing teaching strategies. The microteaching programs initiated for preservice training at Stanford University were later extensively utilized for in-service education (Meier 1968). The medical training of military personnel has included intensive simulated field hospital training activities (Cloutier 1986).

The development of entirely simulated school systems by the University Council for Educational Administration has affected administrator training in many universities. That initiative is gradually being extended to other collegiate-level programs. For example, Henderson (1987) reports on the use of a simulated business operation, utilized for the teaching of accounting. The extensive use of videotape in recording and analyzing classroom practices, but also the broader use of classroom observation practices for in-service purposes under the influence of Flanders (1970), Amidon and

Hunter (1966), and Harris, Bessent, and McIntyre (1969, 131–62) has all been based on the notion that interacting with reality in some systematic, structured way is useful for training purposes.

On-the-job training is an old and respected concept and has long been a standard practice in some nonacademic fields. Plumbing and electrical workers' unions have been among those utilizing apprenticeship training programs of very systematic kinds, even providing for in-service training of instructors to assure their being updated (NACEPD 1973, 150–53). Use of OJT programs for training of military personnel has been extensive. There appears to be growing interest in employee development in many fields of business and industry that emphasizes not only on-the-job methods but also "vestibule" training as a related kind of guided practice not unlike that advocated and described by Harris (1975, 86–87).

Professionals have also made extensive use of reality as experience for in-service training. The medical residency is perhaps the classic example of intensive field experience utilized for training beyond the terminal degree. Administrator and supervisor training at the University of Texas at Austin has involved a full-time semester of interning for experienced teachers since 1962. There have been numerous recent efforts to provide new skills for staff by direct, guided experiences in a school setting.

The long traditions and obvious utility of experience in real settings for training should not blind us to serious limitations in the use of experiential learning. The layman tends to have blind faith in the worth of firsthand experience, whereas the academician disdains it for any but trivial learnings. Both are apparently in serious error. This chapter will try to suggest the promising possibilities for building on past uses of reality both for more effective in-service education and for a broader array of in-service education outcomes. The various ways to use *structured reality* to assure both predictable and efficient learning will be reviewed. *Simulations* as specially designed facsimiles of reality will be discussed and described to emphasize one of the most promising of the less costly approaches. *Games and gaming* will be touched upon lightly as still another cousin of experiential learning with some special promise.

SIMULATIONS AND REALITY

The term "simulation" is utilized to encompass a great variety of both training and other kinds of operations and materials. Role playing, gaming, sociodrama, laboratory training, and various computer-assisted programs are all simulations of a kind. Without serious distortion, novels, plays, case studies, scenarios, and films could be included as simulations in the way they utilize some medium for depicting reality as vividly as possible. A map or globe or any miniaturized model, diorama, or display can be thought of as simulated material in the sense that each one represents some real thing or event.

It may be useful for our purposes to recognize the rather broad concept of simulation of "an imitation or simplification of some aspect of reality," as described by Heyman (1975, 11). Still further, it may be useful to recognize simulation as a *process* for in-service training and to distinguish this from the various materials involved.

The Meaning of Simulation

The reference by Heyman to simulation as imitation or simplification provides a very broad and useful framework for thinking about simulations. Stadsklev (1974, 4–8) emphasizes "autotelic techniques" and experiential learning as the unique and important aspects of simulation. He argues for "experience in which the activities of the student are self-directed toward a meaningful end." He also advocates the combining of the peculiar features of the game with the "social" modeling and "role-taking" of the simulation, to produce "simulation games" as the most sophisticated of forms.

Several scholars have developed schemes for analyzing simulations on a continuum from experiential or reality-oriented to nonexperiential, passive or abstract. Heyman (1978) suggests three levels on a continuum, with simulations, games, role playing, and mock trials at the most experiential level; placing lectures, films, and slides at the nonexperiential end of the continuum; and placing discussion at the semiexperiential level. What this arrangement does, in effect, is to focus on passive versus active involvement in much the same way that experience impact was considered in Chapter 2. What is lost is the special attention to simulation as some *representation of reality* regardless of other important processes.

McCleary and McIntyre (1972) defined a continuum of "methods of instruction" of greater variety, ranging from reading, lecture, and discussion on the one extreme to gaming, simulation, clinical study, team research, and internship on the other. In defining each of these methods, these authors differentiate a much larger variety of reality-oriented training alternatives. They also inadvertently demonstrate that while the medium may well dictate the character of the message (to paraphrase Marshall McLuhan), the same medium can be utilized in strikingly different ways. For instance, reading and lecture are seen as very low in reality orientation and hence are not highly associated with the simulation concept. However, a novel, scenario, or case study does call for reading, and each one can in fact be a powerful vehicle for simulation and training. Similarly, a tutorial relationship or a programmed self-instructional module may deal with such abstract content as to reflect reality not at all, but they can also reflect vividly real forms.

The essential and distinguishing feature of a simulation is its imitativeness of reality, with sufficient simplification for use in training. Obviously, the importance of involvement and other characteristics of design should not be neglected. However, only the imitative and simplifying features are unique to simulations.

Why Simulate?

If real experience has so much merit, why simulate? This is an important question because it is a reminder that simulations may be used as a fad or to add frills when real experience of greater worth for training is close at hand. The special conditions favoring the use of simulation *instead of* real experience include the following:

1. To simplify the very complex for better understanding.
2. To provide training experiences that would be too dangerous in the real situation.
3. To provide training experiences with a common situational and problem context for all.
4. To provide training experiences that would be excessively expensive in the real situation.
5. To provide training experiences with more control, structure, feedback, and related experience than is possible in a real situation.

When the reality to be studied is very complex, as it often is, a simulation can screen out the least important elements and assist the trainee in dealing with the more limited phenomenon. Hence, microteaching, utilizing a small group of children and a very short time frame for the minilesson, eliminates a vast array of complex events in the real classroom. No bells ring and no hall monitors arrive delivering messages. There is no roll call to take. Even behavior problems can be screened out if the focus is on a particular skill in questioning, discussing, or presenting.

Many real situations will not tolerate the risks of a trainee not being successful in applying new skills and concepts. The costs associated with failure may be too great (or perceived as too great). Hence, untrained riveters are not allowed to work on high-rise beams. Unskilled counselors are not allowed to engage in therapeutic work with the severely disturbed, and inexperienced teachers are not asked to present the new grade-reporting system to a hostile parent group. When the trainee is likely to be unsuccessful and the consequences would be severe, then simulation offers the *safer* vehicle for training.

The need for a common set of situational and problem realities for training purposes has been widely neglected in many training programs that rely on group process. When trainees come together in a group, they bring a vast array of experiences with them. These experiences assure much of the prerequisite learning needed for extending in-service growth. However, the tendency of practitioners to particularize their own experiences, to see every individual's problem as essentially unique, creates serious barriers to new learning, especially in group settings. In-service programs based largely on sharing are not likely to produce either new or higher levels of understanding. Simulations present a common imaginary reality with which all trainees are asked to affiliate. In doing so, they share common experiences but differentiate their learning in transferring it to individual situations at a later point in time.

The expense of real experience can be quite excessive. The long-practiced use of the sabbatical leave represents an example of an extremely high-cost operation. Even if we are to assume that professional leave experiences are truly effective forms of in-service education (and they often are not), the cost is very great. When a person is on leave, the costs include travel, release from productive activity and from individualized supervision, plus the replacement of the trainee by another person. Any such arrangement is likely to be expensive indeed. Simulation may also be quite expensive. However, to the extent that travel costs, released time, and replacement costs are limited, simulations may be among the more economical ways of providing intensive experiences for in-service education.

Perhaps our faith in raw experience is most obviously reflected in the 1945–75 teacher shortage in the United States. This was an era extending over a full generation during which vast numbers of untrained, unqualified teachers were induced to learn by doing, simply because all willing adults were invited to teach in an era of extreme shortage and population growth. Many problems still persist to warn against such simple faith in unstructured experience.

The greatest advantage of simulation over real experience is most likely found in assuring a design for learning with structure, feedback, and reality orientation, giving sufficient impact and focus to produce predictable outcomes. Reality as training experience lacks structure for learning. Sequence is very difficult to impose on the real world. As trainees become immersed in the activities of a real operation, it is difficult to interrupt those events to assure the timely feedback and the critical analysis necessary for optimum learning. In the absence of such feedback, inappropriate learnings may well occur. Then, too, one has no assurance in advance that involvement in the real events will include experiences of the kinds most urgently needed. One can be sure that something will be learned, but to predict what it will be is very difficult indeed.

The Original War Games

Both simulation and gaming are perhaps most widely recognized as used for military training purposes. War games have been utilized in modern army, navy, and air force training to assure that skills and knowledges of individuals are learned at the application, transfer, and synthesis levels (Skinner 1984). Mock wars or battles are actually staged, and as many of the real elements of war are brought into action as possible. Such games are often *simplified* by restricting the use of real ammunition, hence reducing the anxieties associated with real casualties and reducing costs, most importantly in terms of human life, and also in terms of ammunition.

Such a simulation retains, however, as many elements of a real war as possible. Actual aggressor and defender roles and missions are assigned. Strategies are actually implemented according to plans. Planes fly and drop imitation bombs; tanks roll and shoot. Soldiers on foot are "wounded and killed" in simulated fashion. The action of the "war" may last only days or may continue for weeks, depending upon the extent of training planned. *Safe* hardships are experienced with K rations, sleeping in the rain, running out of supplies, and so on.

Obviously, there are the nonreal aspects of such a simulation. Participants receive reports on the results of their efforts from neutral officials who would not normally be involved. There are times during the "war" for pauses to analyze performances and take corrective measures. Hence, the negative consequences of reality are minimized while the opportunities for learning are maximized (Cloutier 1986).

The Collective-Bargaining Simulation

A highly simplified example of a simulation is found in the collective-bargaining simulation. To a degree, this is quite comparable with war games. Trainees are divided into "labor" and "management" teams. Each individual is given a position or role. The situation is vividly described with case material, exhibits, and documents giving all trainees the appropriate information needed to engage in the bargaining activities as realistically as possible. Having studied the materials, all trainees get instructions on the task at hand:

> To engage in a series of bargaining sessions to produce an agreement or contract that both sides will accept while avoiding, if at all possible, the alternatives of a *strike* or forced *arbitration*.

As the two teams get under way they argue, caucus, propose, reject, and worry. After awhile a halt is called, and trainees step out of role to discuss what has been happening (Heyman 1975, 24–25). Questions arise on legal points that require study or access to a lawyer. Techniques are discussed and alternative strategies considered.

A recess over lunch or until the next day provides time for informal conversations among trainees, for thoughtful individual introspection, or for reading and study to be better prepared. As the training resumes, reality is simulated by taking up where the bargaining sessions ended. Roles are more expertly assumed, and participants feel more at ease but also more responsible.

Several cycles of simulation activity may be scheduled during a single day or over a prolonged period of time. Unexpected new information or new elements in the situation may be added by those in charge. For instance, a telegram or telephone call may inform bargainers that the board president has publicly threatened to jail any teacher who fails to show up for class, regardless of the progress in the bargaining sessions. The announcement of a heart attack suffered by the mother of one of the bargainers may be injected into the situation. New sources of funds may be revealed unexpectedly. Such injections of new information or new situational elements are carefully planned to retain the flavor of reality but to create demands for action by participants that will generate new learning.

The two simulations just described are both rather elaborate in several ways. Both rely heavily on lengthy, extended time frames for role taking to become fully developed. Such long hours and a sequence of episodes also assures that the many facets of the real problem situation are fully experienced. These simulations are relatively unstructured, allowing individuals and groups to be spontaneous and even creative in coming to grips with the problem situation. In the case of the war games simulations, the materials, equipment, and plans for use in the training activities are also elaborately arrayed. The collective-bargaining simulation requires much less elaborate material, equipment, and planning. However, in each instance the situational factors and the problems to be addressed are carefully prestructured.

Some simulations are more highly structured, almost programmed. In-baskets represent such structured simulations quite well. The *Shady Acres Elementary School In-Basket,* for instance, was designed by McIntyre to represent the basket of memorandums, letters, phone messages, and reports on the desk of the elementary principal. This set of materials provides the full set of stimuli for trainee response. Additional structure is added in providing each trainee with rather explicit directions for proceeding through the in-basket of materials and dealing with each item. The trainee has substantial freedom in taking the role of the principal to make decisions, procrastinate, or delegate. However, at the end of a limited period of role taking, the trainees step out of role and discuss and analyze their diverse responses to a common set of problems (McIntyre et al. 1970).

Computer-assisted simulations may also be rather highly structured. Examples of these include *Exper Sim* by Dana Main (1975) and an instructional decision-making module by E. Wailand Bessent (1974). Both are designed to guide and direct trainees in applying rather complex technical skills. One deals with experimental designing; the other, with rational decision making. In both instances the computer programs give structure to the kind of problems, the ways of dealing with the problem, and the kind of information that is made available (Bunderson and Faust 1975, 47). The advantages of computer simulation over real problem solving of similar kinds goes beyond the structure offered to guide learning, however. The immediacy of feedback, the easy access to information, and the opportunity to gain "years of experience" in a matter of hours make such simulations potentially powerful in simulation designs.

TYPES OF SIMULATION

Because simulation is such a wide-open concept of imitation and simplification of reality for training, the variety of forms is almost limitless. This variety is both a challenge and a problem for the planner of in-service training. On the one hand, an endless array of alternatives may be considered, and new creations are not to be ignored. On the other hand, how to select according to need poses a problem of overabundance (Ellington 1981).

A suitable typology for simulations does not seem readily available. Extent of structure as described in the last section is a useful way of thinking about different simulations, but the extent to which simulations provide for various kinds of experiences, the extent to which they utilize an array of media, and the group size and time allocations required may all be important, too!

Role Playing

While virtually all simulations call for role taking, the use of simple role plays or sociodramas represents one of the very simple, unstructured types of simulation. Any problem situation shared by two or more individuals can lead to almost spontaneous role playing. The time required can range from a few minutes upward. If a common problem is not already at hand, one can be provided by using a vignette such as those presented in Chapter 1 or by storytelling.

To illustrate the simple and relatively unstructured character of this type of simulation, let's assume that several of us have just read about the new principal, Ms. Jane Hunt. The group leader says, "Okay. Now let's talk about how you might have handled that situation when the irate mother arrived." The discussion will probably generate a variety of points of view. Gradually, two quite different *positions* may emerge. These positions are characterized and put into focus by the leader.

> "I think I hear rather different approaches being suggested, but two strategies seem to emerge from your comments. On the one hand, I hear some of you

saying in various ways, *take a firm stand*. But others of you are proposing a *conciliatory, therapeutic approach" (pause)*. "Now, why not try these out on each other? Who'd like to try the *firm stand?" (Hands.)* "Okay, let's role-play."

With just this much structure, a whole series of role plays of two to five minutes each can give trainees opportunities to become involved, to try various techniques, to feel anger and frustration, and so forth. Periodically, role playing can be interrupted and discussions interjected to assist trainees in analyzing their feelings, actions, and the consequences of these. The entire session, from reading the vignette through discussion, role playing, discussions, and summary wrap-up by the leader, might extend over a two-hour period. (See Chapter 8 for further directions on techniques for using role playing.)

Role playing can, of course, be employed in more elaborate and structured ways in connection with games and simulations. Even microteaching is a form of role playing with simulated lessons, but also with adults serving as simulated students. In another professional area, Kintsfather (1985) describes an interesting example of the use of role playing in communications of broadcast journalists.

When role playing is utilized in rather formal ways, the purposes to be served need thoughtful attention. Different purposes require different structures. Milroy (1982) discusses eight purposes including applying theory, practicing skills, stimulating discussion, clarifying ideas, and so on. Regardless of purpose, role playing nearly always demands three elements of structure: (1) Briefing about roles, (2) the interactions of role taking, and (3) follow-up discussions and analysis.

Situational Simulations

A number of simulations provide a set of materials that describe situations but offer only general suggestions or guidelines for role taking. The problems are not specified but are *in context,* to be discovered and selected by trainees. The various simulations developed and distributed by the University Council for Educational Administration (UCEA) tend to be of this situational kind. A school system, a school, or a program is described, using films, simulated handbooks, policy manuals, legal documents, and cases. The task of the leader or trainer is to expose participants to the materials, discuss implications, identify problems, role-play situations, suggest courses of action, draft proposals, appear before a board, or do anything else that assures purposeful interaction with the realities of the simulated situation.

The Teaching Problems Laboratory by Donald Cruickshank and his colleagues (1977) was also a relatively unstructured simulation, relying primarily on stimulus materials to focus attention. However, "critical teaching problems" were presented on sound film or in written form as critical incidents. Role-playing cards were provided to suggest roles for some of the incidents. A director's guide provided background information on the "Longacre Elementary School" in which the incidents were supposed to have occurred. The guide also suggested ways in which the leader or trainer might use the material. For the most part, the simulation was unstructured, however. Lots of thought-provoking problems were presented, but their use was left almost entirely to the leader and participants. Old as this simulation is, it remains one of a kind.

The Case Study

The case study has gained renown as a form of simulated training material as utilized by the Harvard School of Business. Other graduate education programs have made extensive use of "case" discussion and analysis. A case is a simulation in the sense that reality is very carefully depicted in narrative form and documentation provided. Such cases can stimulate student discussion, but they are invaluable in providing organized information and in focusing attention upon aspects of a problem that might be ignored in open, unstructured discussions. To date, very little use has been made of case materials for the in-service training of teachers. However, Harris (1986) makes extensive use of case materials in the form of lesson scripts, interview scripts, and narrative cases relating to classroom problems.

The Laboratory Approach

The science laboratory of the secondary school was originally a facility for simulating the work of the scientist. While much of that early concept has been lost in current practice, it has been more fully developed in other fields of training. The industrial arts or vocational shops of secondary schools are sometimes excellent simulations of their counterparts in the real world of business and industry.

Various efforts have been made over the years to adapt the basic notion of the laboratory as simulated research to the many problems of training personnel. The work of Harris, Bessent, and McIntyre (1969) in the 1960s resulted in the development and testing of a uniquely designed hybrid version of the simulated research laboratory. This so-called laboratory approach can be described in five general steps or "elements of design":

1. A problem is simulated and presented for trainee consideration.
2. The trainees are guided in actively dealing with (resolving) the problem.

3. The active, problem-solving involvement of each trainee is recorded in some predetermined way.
4. The recorded information from each trainee is analyzed and feedback provided.
5. The leader guides trainees in drawing interpretations, seeing implications, and generalizing from the feedback data.

These five steps appear to be very similar to those discussed by McKibbin et al. for simulations in general (1977, 48).

Numerous laboratory sessions are presented and discussed in detail in the volume by Harris, Bessent, and McIntyre (1969). A single illustration of the five design elements follows:

Evaluating Pupil Performance: Long Division*

1. Introduce the *"problem"* very briefly as "How to properly evaluate student performance?"
   Distribute a sheet of paper containing a single long division *problem,* and showing the work of a student in solving the problem.

   Arithmetic Test
   Directions: Work the following problems and show your steps in arriving at the solutions:
   #1. If 3 apples cost 13¢, how much will 7 apples cost?

$$
\begin{array}{r}
4.56 \\
3\overline{)13.00} \\
12 \\
\hline
1\,0 \\
8 \\
\hline
20
\end{array}
\qquad
\begin{array}{r}
4.56 \\
\times\,7 \\
\hline
31.92
\end{array}
$$

   Answer: 31.92

2. Give directions for *actively* evaluating the performance of the student. Emphasize that each participant should consider himself the teacher of this student. Call attention to the directions to the student.
3. Distribute a score sheet and ask each participant to *record* the score s/he thinks is most appropriate for the quality of the work shown on the paper. Score sheets provide simply for assigning a single value ranging from 0 to 10.
4. Collect the score sheets. Let participants get into "buzz groups" and discuss their evaluations while scores are being tabulated. Completed tabulations tend to look as follows for a group of 28 participants.

Scores Assigned

	0	1	2	3	4	5	6	7	8	9	10	
Frequency of Scores	///	/	//	/	////	ʬ	////	///	ʬ	//	—	
	3	1	2	1	4	5	4	3	5	2	0	

Present the analysis as shown above to the participants on a transparency or on a wall chart.

5. *Lead participants* in the interpretation of the data. Note the following:
   a. "We are not in agreement apparently on the proper scores to assign this performance."
   b. "Some of us think it quite 'good' while others think it quite 'poor.'"
   c. "There is some tendency for a substantial number of us to agree that it is middle-range performance."
   d. "No one seems to think it is perfect performance."

Now, ask participants to explain. "How can we disagree so over a simple, objective, long-division problem? Isn't it either right or wrong?" (Smile)

Participants generally get very much involved in *explaining* their scores. Some say they scored low because of "careless errors." Some retort that "process is more important" and point out that s/he did indeed seem to know how to proceed. Others take different positions, mention different rational, logical ways of arriving at quite diverse evaluations.

Shift the discussion by asking: "What does this tell us, if anything, about our responsibilities as student evaluators?" Some probing may be needed to get participants to verbalize the implications they recognize. Put them on the board or on a transparency as they become well articulated. For instance:

1. Student evaluation tends to be subjective even when it seems objective.
2. Students have reason to be concerned about how the teacher is evaluating.
3. Teachers should be clear about their evaluative criteria and be sure students are too.

The structure imposed by the five design elements as illustrated here is not sufficient to inhibit involvement or direct thinking. However, it does assure an orderly sequence of experiences in which all participants have freedom of independent thought and response but are expected to consider the data generated in the group in drawing interpretations.

The power and impact of the laboratory approach has been most clearly demonstrated in the *Homogeneous Grouping Exercise* (Harris, Bessent and McIntyre 1969, 95–106). Here the problem to be simulated is an emotionally charged one. What does homogeneous grouping accomplish? Is it effective? Participants become laboratory analysts in this exercise. They take "real data" on one hundred students and try various grouping procedures. They work in teams of two or three participants to promote discussion about each "experimental" grouping effort. They *record* the results from each grouping plan, and these are put on transparencies for discussion and interpretation. When such an exercise comes to an end, after two and a half or three hours, emotions have greatly subsided and factual concerns are much stronger. It is difficult for participants to disagree with their own findings—the data they generate themselves.

Games

Simulations become games when they are structured for competition and scoring in some form. The collective-bargaining simulation described earlier could be organized as a game if a scoring system were developed to clearly decide on a winning side of the bargaining table.

Simulations in game format have been most imaginatively developed by several groups concerned with training in government and politics. The *Napoli* game published by the Western Behavioral Sciences Institute (1965) is one of several games that deal with problems of political-governmental affairs via the game. The Foreign Policy Association has a school services division devoted to promoting uses of games in high schools and colleges. The Society for Academic Gaming and Simulation in Education and Training is active in promoting game development (Race and Brook 1980).

Napoli simulates the politics of the House of Representatives. Each member of the group is assigned a political party affiliation and a region. The group operates as a legislative body considering eleven different bills involving various social, economic, and political issues. Party platforms are described in simplified form. Survey data on public opinion are provided, region by region and issue by issue, for each party. Several sessions are conducted, and the game director scores legislators after each session, based on a formula that indicates the chances of being reelected. Each participant plays the role of a legislator as he or she desires; however, the goal is clearly that of being reelected. At the end, the director "conducts elections" to see who is reelected and who is defeated. Obviously, the excitement and struggle (and learning) are produced as individual legislators try to vote their convictions without being defeated at the polls.

*Queskno** is a very simple game that illustrates the use of game format with only limited verisimilitude. Pictures are used to stimulate responses. However, teams of players roll dice and select a picture at random. The

*This description of *Queskno* is based on an unpublished paper. The game is credited to the work of Lewis B. Smith, Virginia M. Rogers, Marcella Kysilka, Caroline Gillan, and Geneva Winterrose.

player's task is to write a test question based on the picture, but one that is *also* at the appropriate level in Bloom's taxonomy of educational objectives. Hence, if a trainee rolls a one and turns up a picture of a rabbit eating lettuce in a garden patch, the question to be written would be simple knowledge or recall question about the picture. Since several groups are working simultaneously, the competition is between groups to produce the most *points*. The higher the level of the question on the Bloom taxonomy, the more points a team earns, but only if the proper form of a question is written.

What is being simulated, in a way, is the problem of developing a test. Obviously, the features of a game tend to predominate more than the simulation of a real test design or construction situation. This illustration emphasizes that games are not always related to simulations (Shubik 1975, 3). How much is lost in the process of emphasizing gaming at the expense of verisimilitude is not clearly known. It seems probable, however, that participants in work settings will be more responsive to the most realistic and challenging games. However, De Vries's study (1976) on the effects of "nonsimulation" games on elementary-age children found that *team competition* made for significant results.

The *Napoli* game obviously would have little merit for many groups of school personnel, at least as far as contributing to their on-the-job performances is concerned. *Conflict,* however, is a game that deals with basic problems of human relations and might be widely useful. A rather extensive "register" of games is included in Gibbs's volume (1974). Another sourcebook with descriptions of over six hundred games and simulations has been compiled by Horn (1977). Megarry (1977) provides a four-volume anthology of simulations and games. The recent work by Hyman (1986) includes detailed illustrations and directions for using a variety of training exercises, many of which are games or simulations that have been widely acclaimed for use in school settings with adults.

Other Simulations

The concept of simulation is sometimes best applied to in-service training needs by utilizing actual *reality* with sufficient structure to simplify rather than to imitate. This is illustrated by a device developed by the U.S. Air Force for training B-52 crews to repair defects in the hydraulic system in flight. An *actual, working* hydraulic system of the aircraft was mounted in a room in a simulated frame of the plane. Training experiences of elaborate kinds were designed utilizing this training facility. Defects were planted in the system, and trainees were guided in locating and correcting them.

This hydraulic system training device illustrates several of the great advantages of the simulations under discussion. Although the device cost over $3 million to develop, this was a small amount in terms of the lives that might be saved and of the cost of the plane that might also be saved by effective training. However, the cost of training in simulation over use of real flight-line situations was very great. Furthermore, since the hydraulic system was removed from the actual plane, it was much easier to use for training purposes and greatly improved the amount and rate of learning. Finally, in a few hours this simulation provided trainees with experiences in handling problems that might take years to acquire in flight. Obviously, the risks of in-flight learning were greatly reduced.

An illustration of adapting reality to simulated use for training is provided through classroom observation. The use of an observation instrument of a comprehensive kind requires the development of an array of complex knowledges and skills (Harris and Hill 1982). Although preliminary training can be accomplished in a laboratory context using films and videotapes, the full range of skills and knowledges is rarely developed except on application in *actual classroom* settings. Unfortunately, when observers who are unskilled go to real classrooms for training purposes, the complexities of the situation create confusion, and frustration is experienced by the trainee-observer. Abandonment rates are very high.

The simulated approach to this training problem is relatively simple and effective (Harris 1986, 242–46). The outline of procedures presented in the following list guides each in-classroom observation training session following introductory sessions in a laboratory or workshop format:

1. Arrange with the teacher to be observed.
2. Assemble as a group at the school in advance of the scheduled observation for a briefing.
3. Observe as a group in the prearranged classroom for a full period (ordinarily forty to sixty minutes).
4. Leave the classroom and reconvene immediately in a quiet place for writing and rewriting of observation reports.
5. Compute interobserver reliability coefficients (or percent of agreement) between trainees or between trainer and trainees.
6. Discuss and analyze observation procedures, evidences recorded, problems incurred, and so on.

In following these procedures the classroom reality is retained with only small variations. Arrangements with the teacher of the class are directed mainly toward reassuring him or her, and clarifying expectations. The teacher is asked to proceed as naturally as possible and to ignore observers.

The briefing of the observer-trainee group is directed toward informing them about the lesson, the students, and the location of the classroom and other facilities to be utilized.

The observation period in the classroom is a practice session, but trainees are urged to proceed just as though it were real. Using procedures and techniques previously presented, each trainee attempts to produce a full and complete observation record of the kind that could be utilized for teacher improvement purposes. Two trainers are utilized whenever possible in this classroom, along with three to seven trainees. One trainer uses all observation procedures to produce a model observation report at the end of the period. The other trainer quietly circulates among the trainees, watching their recording techniques, suggesting modifications, reassuring, and reinforcing. Hence, trainees receive some limited feedback in the midst of observing.

On leaving the classroom, all trainees and trainers assemble in a quiet work area. They delay any discussion until each individual observer completes the observation record, including an analysis of data required. Then comparisons are made between and among observers in the form of computing interobserver reliability coefficients or calculating simple percentages of agreement. Finally, careful discussion follows. The entire sequence requires approximately three hours.

COMPUTERS AND INTERACTIVE VIDEO

Computerized simulations, like computer games, are rapidly being developed and used for training purposes. Bunderson pioneered a variety of efforts to link computers and visual displays to produce realistic situations for computer-assisted instruction. Bessent et al. (1974) demonstrated the feasibility of training elementary principals in decision making, using the computer for instantaneous feedback. The more recent development of microcomputers, video cassettes, and videodiscs has greatly enhanced these earlier efforts. It is now more practical and economical to use video simulations of problems and simulations linking microcomputers to provide for rapid response and feedback. Apple Computers has recently announced a new model that offers sound as well as visual displays, including various kinds of graphics (Ingber 1987).

Computer-assisted Observation Training

A very simple example of video-computer linking for training is found in the analysis of classroom teaching events. Teachers and supervisors, already trained in Flanders's techniques for interaction analysis (1970), watch a videotape of a teaching episode while seated at microcomputers. They simply "punch-in" each code number to represent each observed unit of verbal interaction. When a tape ends, preprogrammed analyses are produced in minutes. The interaction matrix is displayed on each observer's screen. Alongside is the "key" providing feedback on accuracy. Discussion follows on interpretations and possible ways of helping the "video teacher" improve his or her lesson.

A variety of portable "lap computers" are now being marketed, some with battery packs. These units are gradually being utilized for classroom observation, using narrative descriptive techniques, codings, or frequency counts. The use of a quiet keyboard by an observer who can type fairly well produces a lesson script (Harris 1986), or other record of events in neat, legible, ready-to-be-printed form.

The Interactive Videodisc Technology

The development of videodiscs, video cassettes, and computer links for training purposes is among the most promising innovations in many decades. Applications of videodiscs and computers to training are among the most exciting of future developments. While costs have been prohibitive in the past, the flexibility, speed, and versatility of the computer linked to the videodisc or video cassette player now offer possibilities of simulated training of immensely important kinds. Schroeder (1983) reports on a U.S. Army program of interpersonal skills training using videodisc simulations with instantaneous feedback being one outstanding feature. Ulmer (1986) reports on a training system for vocational-technical education using interactive video techniques and equipment.

Various manufacturers are now marketing reasonably priced equipment and new training discs are becoming available. A recently funded project is now underway in the Fort Worth area to develop a science curriculum using interactive videodiscs which will also include teacher retraining using this technology.

The ultimate promise of any new technology is not easily projected. It does seem fairly certain, however, that the linking of the computer, with its capacity for rapid and versatile information processing, to the laser-operated videodisc player, provides opportunities limited only by our imagination and persistence.

Computers linked to various video players and to projection equipment are now in use in a variety of settings (Marx 1982). The interactive use of a videodisc with a computer link permits presentation of both moving visuals and still frames. The use of such technology with nearly instantaneous random access to any of thousands of pieces of information is unique and promising for many varieties of training activities. Teaching episodes can be viewed, analyzed, and re-viewed for focused discussion or confirmation. Presentations of information can be manipulated with both sound and visuals. Moving images can be stopped, and sequences can be varied.

The potential for interactive technology is still in the research and development stages. Bork (1987) stresses the need for extensive development of a variety of training designs, before research and evaluation efforts make clear the full promise of such technology. Marx (1982, 56–57) analyzes videodisc applications in comparison with more traditional media—print, slide, film, and computer-assisted video—used for training. His analysis reveals enormous advantages for interactive use of videodiscs. However, he clearly recognizes two major limitations: the cost of both hardware and software, and the fact that the discs must be produced at the factory (Marx 1982, 61). Both of these problems may be resolved with new developments in the future, but for now, they are limiting factors to consider.

SUMMARY

The design of in-service education programs is inherently related to the questions of applications to on-the-job expectations. However, realities as influences for training and learning can have even wider application. Reality should always be consciously considered in planning and implementing ISE; however, overly simplistic notions must be avoided. Experience may be the best teacher, but not without purpose. Raw experience may be frustrating or satisfying, depending on the way it is utilized. Experience may be highly meaningful or confusing, depending on the structure for interaction that is provided.

Simulations and games offer a vast array of ways of manipulating experiences for learning. When reality is too expensive, not available, too dangerous, or too unpredictable, then simulations have greater promise for ISE. Games, too, may be more or less useful. They are not necessarily simulations but are sometimes contrived for entertainment rather than for learning. When games employ reality simulation, they have a uniqueness about them that may well prove especially useful as planners become more skilled in their application to ISE program design.

Computer and video technology offers a wide range of potentially powerful approaches to design for training in ways that combine reality and structure. Computer-assisted presentations of visuals, video cassettes that reflect real or simulated events, and interactive video technology that is designed to combine the visual/auditory presentation capability with programming, promise powerful training options ahead.

STUDY SOURCES

Arwady, Joseph W. 1984. "Improving Training Results through Behavior Modeling." *Performance and Instruction* 23 (March): 23–25.
   The author describes sales training techniques, giving emphasis to those promoting more active involvement for transfer. Video presentation techniques are given most emphasis. Ideas are drawn by the author based primarily upon the training programs utilized by Monroe calculator relating to equipment sales.

Ellington, Henry, Eric Addinall, and Fred Percival. 1981. *Games and Simulations in Science Education*. London: Kogan Page Ltd.
This book deals only with games and simulations related to science teaching; however, several chapters are especially interesting to trainers with other interests. Chapter 6 is instructive in detailing practical ideas about selecting and adapting exercises. Chapter 7 offers details on designing exercises. The introduction to games and simulations in chapter 1 is also quite useful. Board games, card games, computer simulations, case studies, and other "manual" exercises are distinguished.

Greenblat, C. S., and R. D. Duke, eds. 1975. *Gaming-Simulation: Rationale, Design, and Applications: A Text with Parallel Readings for Social Scientists, Educators, and Community Workers*. New York: Sage Publications.
As the elaborate title suggests, a series of essays is presented in this volume with supplementary readings provided. The readings address specific topics of design and application. An extensive bibliography is also provided.

Harris, Ben M., E. Wailand Bessent, and Kenneth E. McIntyre. 1969. *In-Service Education: A Guide to Better Practice and Laboratory Materials*. Englewood Cliffs, N.J.: Prentice-Hall, Inc.
This two-volume work introduces the concept of laboratory training as simulation for classroom teachers. Detailed leaders' guides are provided for a variety of highly developed laboratory exercises. The second volume consists of consumable materials for use by trainees.
These volumes, while nearly 20 years old, offer interesting guides to simulated training regarding perennial problems of schools and classrooms.

Heitzmann, William Ray. 1983. *Educational Games and Simulations*. 2d ed. What Research Says to the Teacher. Washington, D.C.: National Education Association.
This document is a general overview of basic concepts and a historical review of games. It also provides systematic, but brief, reviews of research on practices and effects. An excellent bibliography of sources and selected research references is provided.
Although the emphasis is on games in school classrooms, the implications for in-service training are quite clear.

Horn, R. E., ed. 1977. *The Guide to Simulation/Games for Education and Training*. Cranford, N.J.: Didactic Systems, Inc.
The authors describe over 600 simulations and games in some detail. Several essays are also provided on topics related to design of such training materials.

Hyman, Ronald T. 1986. *School Administrators' Staff Development Activities Manual*. Englewood Cliffs, N.J.: Prentice-Hall, Inc.
This is a paperback volume detailing a variety of training exercises. While most are well known, they have been thoroughly tested and proven to be useful. Each chapter gives sufficient detail on a single exercise so that a trainer can use it with minimum preparation.

Jones, K. 1980. *Simulations: A Handbook for Teachers*. London: Kogan Page Ltd.
This book focuses on practical aspects of choosing and using simulations in

classrooms. Actual simulations are included to illustrate matching objectives to simulations. Pitfalls are discussed.

Marx, Raymond J. 1982. "Videodisc-Based Training: Does It Make Economic Sense?" *Training/HRD* 19 (March): 56–65.
This article discusses cost factors associated with the use of interactive videodisc technology compared to other media for training. The objective and detailed descriptions of both strengths and limitations are most useful. Videodiscs are compared with other media on seventeen criteria.

Megarry, Jacquetta. 1977. *Aspects of Simulation and Gaming: An Anthology of SAGSET Journal, Volumes 1–4*. London: Kogan Page Ltd.
As the title indicates, this is an anthology with brief reviews of a wide variety of presentations relating to simulations and gaming. Various well-developed games and simulations are discussed. Some relate to schools, others to industry and government. Each item presented is a small piece of the field.

Pareek, Udai, and T. V. Rao. 1982. *Developing Motivation through Experiencing: A Trainer's Guide for Behaviour Simulation in Motivation Training*. New Delhi: Oxford and IBH Publishing Co.
Various forms of games and simulations are reviewed. Emphasis is given to the pedagogy of simulations as well as the variety of designs. This is one of the best sources for stimulating one's thinking about simulation as a broad array of ways of using structured reality or "experiencing" for training purposes.

Race, Philip, and David Brook, eds. 1980. *Perspectives on Academic Gaming and Simulations 5*. The proceedings of the 1979 Conference of the Society for Academic Gaming and Simulation in Education and Training. London: Kogan Page Ltd.
A set of papers presented at the conference covers many aspects of gaming and simulation. Chapter 1 is of special interest in dealing with technical concerns for "replication." Chapter 3 in Part 4 deals with adapting games. Although many of the presentations describe very specific designs, they do stimulate ideas for original designs, adaptation, and utilization.

Schroeder, James E. 1983. "A Pedagogical Mode of Instruction for Interactive Videodisc." *Journal of Educational Technology*, vol. 12, pp. 311–17.
This article describes videodisc utilization for training in the U.S. Army relating to interpersonal skills development. The use of standardized roles in role playing is described with the videodisc providing instantaneous feedback.

Sculli, Domenic, and Wing Cheong Ng. 1985. "Designing Business Games for Service Industries." *Simulation/Games for Learning* 5 (March): 16–27.
The authors analyze game design using the concept of "service" as the output of games. Three separate systems are discussed relating to the design process. The systems discussed are the physical, financial, and external environment systems. They are illustrated using the hotel management game.

Skinner, Michael. 1984. *Red-Flag: Air Combat for the '80s*. Novato, Calif.: Presidio Press.
An interesting discussion of military use of sophisticated simulation training.

Sowden, Susette, and Ronald Harden. 1984. "The Use of Two Innovation Games in a Staff Development Programme." *Simulation/Games for Learning* 14 (August): 113–21.

Games of diffusion strategies and on the "printing press" are discussed as they are used for medical staff development in Scotland. The authors detail events as they transpired in using these games.

Taylor, John L., and Rex Walford. 1978. *Learning and the Simulation Game.* Beverly Hills, Calif.: Sage Publications, Inc.

A very basic and useful introduction to instructional simulations is provided in this volume. Part I is largely basic information for the beginner. Part II presents brief reviews of seven simulations or games with illustrations from each.

Ulmer, Dale. 1986. "Interactive Video for the Electronics Age." *Workplace Education* 4 (March–April): 6–7.

This article describes a training system using interactive videodisc technology for vocational-technical education in electronics, semiconductors, and other applied fields. Various examples of such sophisticated simulated training are provided. The reader gets some insights into possible future applications of the videodisc to a broad array of training objectives.

8.

Working in Groups

INTRODUCTION

The group as a unit for implementing in-service education outcomes is so
universal that its critical, essential contributions can be readily taken for
granted and even neglected. The era of group dynamics, group process
analysis, and group relations training was at its height in the 1940s through
the 1960s. The era emerged out of the urgent demands of new and unbeliev-
ably complex military undertakings. Group techniques were fostered by
educators and social scientists alike as tools for developing a better, more
democratic, and more humane society. The resurgence of authoritarianism
was a predictable consequence of the social and political upheavals of the
1960s; but that, too, will pass, and the lessons of previous decades need
renewed attention by in-service planners. Small groups continue to appear
to be among the most natural of all social phenomena known to man.
Hence, organizational development specialists continue their efforts to reform bureaucracies, and auto manufacturers search for small-group approaches to the assembly line.

In viewing the essential group as both natural phenomenon and working
tool for in-service education, the relationship of individualization to group
process needs to be considered. As interest in group techniques and processes began to wane, interest in all forms of individualization reached new
heights. There is some tendency to treat these two concepts as antithetical.
This writer's cautions about individualized approaches to training, as expressed in Chapter 6, are intended to seek resolutions between highly
personalistic in-service education and that which is more fully anchored in
group relationships (Schmuck et al. 1975).

It is our view that just as man lives not by bread alone, his training cannot be a solitary thing. Personal needs, like bread, are essential and must be addressed, but the group context for personalized ventures in in-service education is also essential, though not prerequisite. In the two previous chapters the focus has been on the individual as client and on reality as context and content. This chapter directs your attention to basic ways of working in groups to facilitate optimum interactions of clients with both context and content for in-service growth.

WAYS OF WORKING IN GROUPS

An enormous array of group forms is available to consider. The family is a natural and ancient small group only recently threatened by social pollutants. The hunting group is another of ancient vintage that survives to this day in many cultures, if only for social purposes. Social groups of diverse kinds are developed by various cultures. Card playing, prayer meetings, happy hour drinking, Sunday picnicking, and Little League baseball illustrate a few of the diverse activities and forms. Groups organized for economic, political, and production purposes are also highly diverse.

Our interest, of course, is in groups designed to promote learning and especially adult, job-relevant learning. All groups, interestingly, promote learning; and some (the family, for instance) may well be among the most powerful in influencing learning, if not directly producing specific outcomes. Learning-oriented groups include therapy groups, study groups, discussion groups, action research teams, workshop groups, and a host of other special-purpose groups.

A Variety of Purposes

Groups are as different in form as they are in purpose. When groups are purely social and recreational, commonness of interests and values tends to influence their formation, and personal satisfaction and a sense of unity and allegiance among group members is important to its survival and functioning. When groups are task oriented or production groups, common interests may be very limited and a sense of satisfaction and unity may come more from recognition of differences than from the homogeneity of group members.

Learning groups have much in common with social groups, but they are also task oriented. Common interests in anticipated learning outcomes help build the unity and allegiances that may be necessary when trainees are being made uncomfortable, even threatened by insights into their own behavior. On the other hand, personal satisfaction is not an adequate reason for affiliation in a learning group. The purposes of the undertaking both reflect and contrast with individual participant needs as perceived. The inevitable diversity within the group may need to be accentuated to produce the dynamic experiences needed. The group is always client but is to a large extent simultaneously the determiner of process. A group is never a passive thing—void, vessel, or sponge.

Choice, Structure, and Variety

The various forms of learning groups give the in-service education planner a problem of choice. Without attempting to provide details regarding the more widely known group forms, some direct relationships can be suggested. For instance, *therapy* groups are intended for use in helping people learn to deal with feelings, attitudes, and values. *Discussion* groups stimulate knowledge- and opinion-level learning outcomes most readily. Higher-level cognitive learning outcomes may well be more appropriately stimulated by a *study* group format.

These distinctions among therapy, discussion, and study may not be easily maintained when a group continues in association for learning over prolonged periods of time. Hence, a workshop or intensive course extending over a period of a week or more may incorporate a broad variety of group and solitary activities. A study group may be thought of as a series of discussions focused by study materials and sequenced for learning purposes. A discussion group may become highly therapeutic from time to time.

Clear or not as these distinctions may be, they can serve to suggest differentiation in structures and leadership style, given different learning expectations. The emphasis in therapy groups on permissive, accepting nondirectiveness on the part of the leader calls for specialized training and self-discipline (Rogers 1969). On the other hand, study groups have purposes that call for setting limits, agreeing upon outcomes, and stimulating disagreements. Discussion groups employ leadership and structures that assure maximum levels of sharing and interacting (Gall and Gall 1976). As such, a facilitating kind of leadership becomes essential.

The emphasis on three group forms should not cause us to neglect a larger variety of activity that groups engage in for learning purposes. We do, of course, have *viewing* groups, *listening* groups, *role-playing* groups, *manipulating* groups, *planning* groups, *analyzing* groups, and *deciding* groups. Nearly every event associated with in-service education involves group activity. Here of course we are most concerned with group activity as the primary experience of learning. Even highly structured clinical or simulated ISE involves group activity in many ways. The essence of group work, however, is making human interactions productive of learning outcomes.

A FEW ESSENTIAL ACTIVITIES

Certain activities have emerged over the years as especially stimulating and adaptable ways of working with groups regardless of purpose. Just as interviewing was stressed in a prior chapter as essential to individual approaches, so the following might be considered as essential to work with groups. Brainstorming, buzz sessions, discussions, and role playing were identified in previous chapters as important activities for in-service education and design. In the following pages, each of these is defined, described, illustrated, and analyzed.

Brainstorming*

DEFINITION. Brainstorming is an activity in a group session in which ideas held by participants are orally expressed, with special procedures employed to avoid any discussion, criticism, or analysis. Some record or report of all ideas is maintained for later use. It is essentially an oral inventory of ideas.

PURPOSES
1. To inform all participants of ideas held by others.
2. To stimulate the development of ideas.
3. To provide an inventory of ideas for later use.
4. To suggest a variety of alternative approaches to problems.
5. To influence opinions or attitudes regarding the state of thinking of the group.
6. To cultivate positive attitudes toward alternative approaches to problems.

PROCEDURE. Orientation is given to the group of participants on brainstorming. A problem, topic, or issue is selected as the focus for the brainstorming activity. The selected focus is clearly described to the group to assure unity in the frame of reference employed by each brainstormer. The ground rules or special procedures are made explicit, as follows:

1. All ideas related to the focus in any direct way are desired.
2. A maximum number of related ideas is desired.
3. One idea may be modified or adapted and expressed as another idea (sometimes called "hitchhiking" on ideas).

*A. F. Osborn is generally credited with having originated this term and formalized the activity itself.

4. Ideas should be expressed as clearly and concisely as possible.
5. No discussion of ideas should be attempted.
6. No criticism of ideas should be attempted.

A time period is established for the brainstorming to fit the situation, type of problem in focus, size of group, and so on. Ordinarily, twenty to thirty minutes is minimal. Often, brainstorming can continue effectively for an hour or more. When ideas run out and interest seems to wane, the leader should terminate the session.

Ideas are permitted to flow without formality. In a large group, the leader may recognize individuals. In a small group, spontaneous expressions may be more desirable without formal recognition.

Each idea is recorded by a person designated as recorder. The ideas may be slightly abbreviated but should not be changed in context or terminology any more than is absolutely necessary. Ideas are recorded on a chalkboard, transparency, or large chart so that participants can refer to them during the brainstorming session.

The group leader might want to repeat ideas as expressed to indicate acceptance of each and to make sure others hear each idea. In very large groups, the leader can use a microphone on a long cord and move around among participants to assure that every contribution is heard. The leader encourages rapid-fire expression of ideas, restricts his comments, repeats ideas if necessary, and avoids any criticism by word, facial expression, or tone of voice. He receives every idea with enthusiasm and acceptance as something worthy of expression and future consideration. If ideas begin to flow that are distinctly irrelevant, the leader should briefly restate the focus and ask for ideas related to it without being critical of specific ideas.

The leader allows silence to prevail after a round of expressions. Silent periods provide time for thought. New ideas may be generating. A period of silence lasting thirty seconds seems long, but it is often essential to idea production. When silence is no longer productive of new ideas, when the same ideas are being repeated, when interest seems to wane, or when available time has been exhausted, the leader terminates the session.

A brief feedback session on the many ideas recorded should be provided to let participants see how productive they have been.

Recorded ideas, slightly edited, should be made available for whatever follow-up uses have been planned.

SUGGESTED FOLLOW-UP ACTIVITIES
1. Buzz sessions can be used for analysis and criticism of ideas.
2. Group discussion can be undertaken for analysis, criticism, assigning priorities, proposing revisions, combining ideas, and so on.

3. Committee sessions can be held for editing, revising, and suggesting ways of implementing ideas.
4. Panel discussion of ideas can be used for the purpose of suggesting combinations, challenging, or suggesting implementation procedures.

ILLUSTRATION. A new videotape recorder had been purchased by the West Valley schools in connection with an in-service training project and a demonstration center. As the in-service project was nearing completion, the superintendent felt the need for ideas about future uses for the recorder. He wanted ideas for use by a planning committee, and he wanted to involve his school principals and supervisory staff as much as possible.

A dinner meeting was planned, and all principals and supervisors were invited. After dinner the superintendent briefly described his purpose in bringing the group together. He then introduced a college consultant who had been working in the West Valley schools. The consultant reviewed the procedures for brainstorming, set a time limit of forty minutes, and assured the group that follow-up on their ideas was planned by the special committee. He then asked for all ideas.

The ideas came slowly at first. The consultant used a chalkboard to record ideas himself while asking an elementary supervisor in the group to act as official recorder. Soon the ideas began to flow more rapidly:

"We should involve other grade levels."

"Can we get beyond language arts into other subject areas?"

"Let's turn attention to special education."

"Videotaping in real classroom situations would be worthwhile."

"Can you get videotape presentations of units—for example, physical education?"

"How about using tapes to inform the public of plans?"

"How much of this can be assumed by our own staff? How much additional staff is needed?"

As several of the ideas seemed somewhat irrelevant, the consultant reviewed the focus: "Remember, we're trying to get any and every idea on how we might use the videotape recorder for in-service purposes." The group resumed without further interruption:

"Let's get teachers involved in planning for demonstrations."

"Develop narrowly focused demonstrations involving specific skills."

"Homogeneous groups of observers should be tried."

"Can't we involve certain teachers according to their needs or interests?"

"Use the recorder for demonstrations of model faculty meetings."

"Let's plan for specific needs of teachers—beginning teachers as well as experienced teachers."

"Use the tapes to help the teacher see her own progress."

"Explore possibilities of bringing in specialists to demonstrate."

"A mobile unit to operate in classrooms would be helpful."

"Teachers need to have information on what to look for in demonstrations."

After the forty minutes came to an end, the consultant asked the recorder to report: "Tell us how many ideas you have listed, and read them in abbreviated form for our review." The elementary supervisor took about five minutes to read some sixty ideas. The consultant turned the meeting back to the superintendent, suggesting that he comment on next steps in making use of these very interesting ideas.

CAUTIONS AND LIMITATIONS. Brainstorming should not be used without follow-up. Participants enjoy brainstorming, but they also expect something to be done with their ideas.

Brainstorming should not be used unless there is a real need for a look at all available ideas or the production of new ideas, or both, by a group. Obviously, this implies that the group has some knowledge about, or interest in, the topic or problem in focus. It would be useless to brainstorm with a group lacking either knowledge or interest. On the other hand, when a problem can be solved by consultation with an expert, brainstorming is hardly in order despite the group's interest. When only one or two alternative solutions are feasible, brainstorming is inappropriate.

Participants should be cautioned that not all ideas can be implemented, that critical analysis must follow, and that not all ideas should be expected to survive the process.

SUMMARY. Brainstorming is an activity for stimulating idea expression and production. It can be used to inform, stimulate, and develop understanding and attitudes relating to a problem and a group. The special procedures that are employed make this activity unique, and it is usable with a wide range of group sizes. Extra precautions should be observed to plan appropriate follow-up activities and to avoid use of brainstorming for inappropriate purposes.

Buzz Sessions

DEFINITION. The buzz session is a small-group activity in which groups are temporarily formed to discuss a specific topic with minimum structure, maximum emphasis upon interaction, and full opportunity to express ideas related to the topic. An optimum amount of critical analysis of ideas related to the topic is encouraged in a permissive topic-centered situation.

PURPOSES
1. To facilitate maximum verbal interaction among participants.
2. To promote understanding of all points of view held by participants.
3. To determine the possibility of arriving at consensus on certain points.
4. To identify points of view that are distinctly at issue.
5. To stimulate interest in, and commitment to, working on a project or problem.

PROCEDURE. A group that has focused its attention on a topic or problem issue is divided into subgroups referred to as buzz groups.

Each buzz group is assigned a specific location in which it is to work. Usually this is around a table, but in a large auditorium setting it may be simply an identified section of the available space or a cluster of chairs.

Buzz groups are asked to focus specifically upon a given topic. This topic is identified, defined, and described in advance by the leader so that all will be tuned in on it.

Buzz groups are given a definite time limit during which they are expected to discuss, analyze, and maximize their expression of ideas about the topic. Ordinarily, a minimum of ten to fifteen minutes is provided. A topic of some complexity may require forty minutes to an hour and a half.

A recorder is designated for each buzz group, with instructions to record the highlights of ideas expressed, including main points of view, agreements, disagreements, and suggestions.

Buzz groups are informed that completely free interaction with full expression of all ideas is being sought. In buzz sessions, unlike in brainstorming, participants should feel free to discuss, agree, disagree, or suggest alternatives. The interaction should be spirited, free flowing, and unrestricted. On the other hand, participants should be cautioned against making long-winded speeches or dominating the discussion.

A discussion leader is usually appointed, simply to facilitate interaction. Leaders should be selected who will not dominate or overstructure but simply encourage full, fair, and well-distributed participation. Sometimes no discussion leader is appointed, in which case the groups are clearly informed that there will be none. In such instances, each buzz group may be instructed to select its own leader, or a leaderless group discussion procedure may be followed in which each individual is expected not only to be a fully participating discussant but also to facilitate the participation of others.

Recorders should turn notes over to appropriate officials for follow-up activity planning.

Leaders should circulate among buzz groups, "eavesdropping" but not verbally participating in the interaction. This gives the leaders a feel for the quality of the thinking and of the ideas emerging. It also eliminates any notion on the part of participants that they have been abandoned by their leaders.

SUGGESTED FOLLOW-UP ACTIVITIES

1. A panel or symposium of recorders or selected participants and consultants analyze ideas expressed.
2. Recorders' notes are analyzed, and study groups, committees, lectures, or discussion groups are organized.
3. A tentative draft of a written document may be developed by a representative committee to synthesize ideas as a policy statement or in other appropriate form for review by all participants.

ILLUSTRATION. The Georgetown High School building was a shining new monument to educational progress. It was the first school building constructed in Georgetown in many years, and it served the people on "the other side of the tracks." Superintendent James Ramey took real pride in promoting this new building for the "poor kiddos." His assistant, Bill Holdsworth, had worked closely with the architect and selected staff members to be sure that instructional facilities were designed for flexibility and modern methods.

As the fall semester began in the new building, painters and electricians were still finishing their work. Trouble with the air-conditioning system caused some difficulty in September, and projection screens were still not installed in October. Despite these inconveniences, the staff members carried on as best they could. Everyone was enthusiastic about the new building. The students seemed to reflect their pride in both conduct and appearance.

By late October, Bill Holdsworth was able to turn from mechanical details to instructional concerns. He was commissioned by the superintendent to work with the high school principal and staff in developing an outstanding instructional program. Here was a fine facility, an eager and able teaching staff, and a waiting community. The new language lab could accommodate foreign language, drama, speech, and regular English classes. Some classrooms had folding walls for large-group instruction. Windowless construction made extensive use of visual aids practical. A beautiful library was available, and no study halls cluttered the facility. Bill decided to move before the holiday season to stimulate the faculty group and to get plans developed for improving instructional practices.

In consultation with the principal, Holdsworth arranged for school to be dismissed a bit early on the following Wednesday, October 27. The principal announced to his faculty that a special program-planning meeting would be held on that day, in the library, from 2:45 P.M. until 4:30 P.M. Holdsworth got in touch with a university professor who was familiar with the building and willing to serve as a consultant to the faculty. He agreed to attend this meeting and make a few introductory remarks.

As the faculty group assembled at about 2:40, coffee and cookies were served. The principal called the meeting to order at 2:50, introduced the visiting consultant, and briefly stated the purpose of the meeting. Holdsworth then reviewed the plan of action.

"We want to begin thinking seriously about ways of using this building so as to provide the best possible instructional program. Superintendent Ramey has assured me that we can have just as much freedom as we need to try new ideas. We've had a couple of months now to get school started and become familiar with the building. These have been trying months for all of you, but things are now under control. We'd like to move with you in the direction of identifying promising new ways of working at teaching. If you can come up with some promising ideas, we'll work with you in developing project plans and trying these ideas this spring and next year.

"Now, to get to work today, we'd like to have you break into buzz groups. We will break into four groups of eight and nine persons each. The purpose of all of the groups will be the same. You are to concentrate on suggesting new teaching practices that might be worth trying in this school. Each group should try to identify a few practices someone in that group finds promising. Each practice suggested should be discussed and analyzed freely. When the session is over in about forty minutes, you should have one or more new teaching practices to propose in fairly well developed form. Your group does not need to agree on the value of the practice. You are not committing yourself or anyone else to adopting any practices. You are simply developing some promising ideas for further serious consideration.

"Now, are you ready to go to work?"

At this point, Holdsworth made quick buzz group assignments, getting clusters of teachers into four corners of the library where large tables had already been arranged. Group leaders were not designated, but a recorder had been assigned to each buzz group and instructed in note-taking procedures.

Holdsworth, the visiting consultant, and the principal circulated from group to group. They did not enter into the discussion. Instead, they listened for a few moments, sitting at the edge of the circle of participants. After about five minutes of "eavesdropping," the three men changed buzz groups. This was repeated at intervals until all three had listened to each group twice and had a feeling for the thinking in progress.

After thirty-five minutes, Holdsworth interrupted with an announcement. "Will you try to pull your thoughts together in the next five minutes, please? Your recorder has been taking notes. Let that person review the highlights of those notes and then spend the remaining time getting your suggestions formalized. We'll ask recorders to report suggestions of each buzz group to the total group at three forty-five.''

As Bill stopped talking, the buzz of interaction reached a high pitch. Each group was now under pressure to pull its diverse ideas together. By 3:40, three groups were breaking up. By 3:45, the recorder in the last group made final notes, and Bill called for attention, directing all participants to be seated again in the center of the library. Recorders reported their suggestions after being cautioned to take only one minute each. The visiting consultant wrote brief phrases on a transparency as the recorders mentioned each major suggestion. When the reporting was over, Holdsworth asked the visiting consultant to discuss the suggestions that were made. He did so, using the visual he had prepared based on the reports. He focused attention upon similarities in suggestions, commenting on uses of facilities for implementing suggestions and emphasizing the need for attention to what was known about good teaching before any suggestions would be selected for development into project plans.

The principal concluded the meeting with a request: ''I hope each of you will give some further thought to these teaching ideas in the next week. We will be asking for volunteer groups to do further planning on some of these ideas with the expectation that several new things will be in progress by early spring. Meeting adjourned.''

CAUTIONS AND LIMITATIONS. Buzz sessions, like most other in-service activities, do not suffice without follow-up activities. Unlike brainstorming, buzz sessions are rarely used as introductory activities; they presume some prior events. For each session to be effective, participants must have a concern for the problem or an interest in the topic, some knowledge about the problem or topic, and opinions, attitudes, or feelings to express.

Buzz sessions should be avoided when attitudes, opinions, and feelings of the participants are not of crucial importance in approaching the problem. Teachers might appropriately engage in a buzz session when the topic is how to allocate library funds to various categories of instructional materials. A buzz session on the format of the purchase order, on the other hand, is probably not worthwhile.

Similarly, when a problem is such that expert advice is required, such advice should either precede or substitute for a buzz session. When a problem has only one feasible solution, a buzz session is inappropriate except as a way of testing the hypothesis that no other solution is feasible.

SUMMARY. The buzz session is an activity that permits maximum face-to-face interaction in small groups even when large numbers of participants need to be involved. This activity has been used for a variety of purposes. It serves especially well when interest, stimulation, and consideration of diverse points of view are required. As temporary groups, buzz groups can be organized with maximum flexibility and can function with a minimum of structure. Lead-up activities are important to the success of a buzz session, and follow-up activities are essential.

Group Discussions

DEFINITION. A group discussion is a small-group activity usually extending over a prolonged period of time in which systematic verbal interaction on a given topic (or problem) leads to consensus, decisions, recommendations, or clearly recognized disagreement. An extended life span assures the development of a genuine group with clearly defined group purposes, as distinguished from an aggregation of individuals sharing independent ideas.

PURPOSES
1. To share the knowledge of individuals with others in the group.
2. To develop understanding about complex problems.
3. To analyze proposals for dealing with problems.
4. To stimulate the development of new attitudes and opinions.
5. To arrive at carefully considered decisions for dealing with complex problems.

PROCEDURES. Group discussion activities of a variety of kinds have been developed in recent years. The buzz session is a striking variation described in the last section. Case analysis and leaderless group discussion are briefly described as well. The procedures described here are those that apply to most discussion situations as defined. They would be modified somewhat, of course, as variations are employed.

Analyze the selected problem (or topic) to be sure that it is one that is important enough to justify the time required and is suitable for discussion as contrasted with the use of the lecture, buzz session, or other activity.

Check to see that an appropriate group of discussants is available. Discussants are appropriate when they have:

a real interest in the topic or problem
a need to discuss the topic or problem
some pertinent information, opinions, or feelings concerning the topic or problem

Select an appropriate discussion leader. It is not essential that the leader be an expert on the topic or problem in focus. In fact, expertness of that kind can complicate efforts toward efficient group action. The leader must have other characteristics, however. He should be interested in the problem, be reasonably knowledgeable about the various ramifications of the problem, have the respect of the group members, be open-minded regarding approaches to the problem, and have skill in discussion-leading techniques.

Provide training in discussion-leading techniques for the leader. Massey (1979) suggests that "skillful" leaders will initiate, provide information, encourage participation, and summarize. In addition, "harmonizing differences" is a special requirement for the leader, who must deal openly and directly with divergent views, yet avoid disruptive effects. Skillful leaders also help groups see relationships between different sets of information as they emerge from the discussion. Unless the leader is already highly skilled, he usually welcomes an opportunity to receive training.

Brief discussion sessions focusing upon vignettes of problem situations serve as effective training experiences when followed by critical analysis by a skilled discussion leader. Tape recordings of brief discussion sessions can be analyzed to help leaders employ techniques more skillfully.

Organize the initial discussion session by informing prospective discussants of the problem and the nature of the group being formed; suggest a tentative schedule and specify possible outcomes.

Conduct the initial discussion sessions with emphasis on getting acquainted, exploring the problem area, and reviewing and revising plans. It is not necessary or even desirable that procedural decisions be made at this point. Too much eagerness to "decide what to do and get it done" can lead to confusion and frustrate group cohesion.

Conduct subsequent sessions with a focus upon the identification of the basic elements or specific problems within the larger problem area. Relevant questions include: (1) What concerns participants most? (2) What is most important? (3) What may be resolved?

A group may have to wander verbally about the problem area without much direction for several sessions before basic elements or specific problems can be identified. Don't become discouraged with the group. Don't let the group become discouraged with itself. Expect some anxiety and discontent to be expressed, and accept it.

Provide resources for gaining more knowledge relevant to the problem area. This may involve use of films, books, pamphlets, visiting consultants, tape recordings, and similar resources. These should not be imposed on the group but made available and their use encouraged by individuals and the group as a whole when appropriate.

Encourage the group to make decisions or otherwise achieve bench marks of its progress by consensus. (These may be agreements, conclusions, disagreements, suggestions, and so forth.) Avoid formalities like voting or recording conclusions in very carefully worded language, but stimulate participants to consider progress and then move on.

Encourage open-mindedness in considering all ideas relevant to the basic problem or topic. Encourage participants to assume the attitude of the trial judge who withholds judgment and considers all relevant evidence before rendering a verdict. In promoting this attitude among participants, the discussion leader sets the example and uses a variety of techniques:

1. Ask open-ended questions that stimulate a variety of responses.
2. Restate unpopular points of view with the suggestion that discussants might want to react.
3. Encourage the less active discussants to express themselves.
4. Encourage discussants to search out new information and report it to the group at appropriate times.
5. Invite resource persons to share relevant information with the group at appropriate times.
6. Accept all ideas expressed as worthy of consideration by the group.
7. Avoid ignoring or criticizing ideas that seem least acceptable.
8. Avoid promoting certain ideas over others.
9. Summarize main ideas, information, or points of view relevant to a basic element in the discussion to encourage full consideration.
10. Suggest postponement of decisions when consensus has not really been achieved or information is lacking.
11. Encourage the decision to agree or to disagree when consensus does not seem possible.

Encourage the group to project its own plan and timetable for accomplishing its purposes and dissolving itself.

Arrange for the recording of group outcomes. This should not be a stenographic record but an abstract of ideas, agreements, disagreements, decisions, and plans. These notes should be maintained by one or more designated persons. The responsibility can be a rotating assignment among discussants, or an assistant to the group can serve as permanent recorder. A copy of the recorder's notes should go to each discussant prior to the session.

CASE DISCUSSION. The case method in group discussion has been developed to provide for a more highly structured discussion situation. In this form a carefully developed case is presented to all discussants. A case is an objective report of a real situation in which many aspects of a complex problem are presented as information. This is usually a narrative description of a real situation that illustrates in very specific terms a problem or problems worthy of discussion. The case, then, not only stimulates meaningful participation but also contains much relevant information for use by discussants. The simulation of reality is discussed in Chapter 7 as a unique feature of cases.

In case discussions, the basic style and most techniques of discussion leading still apply. Certain procedures are significantly different.

Since the case is not the actual problem of the participants, and information is readily available, less time is required for analysis, and the interest span of the participants is likely to be relatively short. Such discussions are rarely extended over more than two or three sessions. Often a single two-hour session is the limit of time profitably spent.

Since the problem situation is described in narrative form with a minimum of irrelevant information included, discussants are led to analysis with a minimum of exploratory discussion.

A certain amount of interpretation has entered into the case writing as the writer selected information to include or omit. This places the leader in the position of being one who stimulates participants to discover the interpretations that are possible. This places him in the role of one who already knows many of the alternatives. This may or may not be true in real problem-centered discussion groups. The case discussion leader, therefore, structures the discussion to some degree. It can be quite structured when used to illustrate only a specific theory, concept, or pattern of events, but leaders should take care not to overstructure the discussion and lose spontaneity. Furthermore, a well-written case has potential for illustrating a variety of concepts, and speculation can be freely stimulated regarding the consequences that might follow from alternative events to those reported in the case. For such uses, the discussion technique must be much less structured.

LEADERLESS DISCUSSION. This variation of group discussion activity calls upon participants to share the leadership responsibilities described previously. The advantage offered by having no designated leader derives from the greater feeling of responsibility and involvement on the part of the discussants. Disadvantages include the possibility that leadership responsibilities will not be adequately assumed by participants. When leadership development and group assumption of responsibility are more important outcomes than problem solving, leaderless discussions have much to offer. Leaderless group discussions tend to require the following procedures.

1. The group is oriented regarding the absence of an assigned leader and the reasons for this, unless the situation requires no such explanation. Each group member is encouraged to exercise responsibilities as both discussant and leader. Formal selection of a leader is discouraged, and the group is urged to guard against letting any one person exercise leadership for an extended period.
2. Leaderless groups are carefully observed by those responsible for organizing them. Should a group completely fall apart, a skilled leader may be assigned to the group just long enough to assist discussants in analyzing progress, setting new directions, and overcoming obstacles.

This technique provides each group member with an opportunity to try his hand again at exercising leadership.

SUGGESTED FOLLOW-UP ACTIVITIES. Frequently, a discussion group will have purposes that can be relatively well accomplished in the group without other follow-up activities. This is likely to be the case when development of attitudes, opinions, and understanding are the purposes selected. When decisions, suggestions, or recommendations for action come from a discussion group, the follow-up activities are important.

1. Publish a brief report on the conclusions of the group for dissemination to others interested in the same problem or topic.
2. Organize a committee or study group to formulate plans and make arrangements as suggested by the discussion group.
3. Undertake an action research or pilot project to develop and evaluate ideas generated in the group.

ILLUSTRATION. The Austin schools, like many, were confronted with the problem of securing public acceptance and support for changes in the mathematics program under the label of "The New Math." Teacher attitudes posed a problem in some instances, too, but interest was highest in meeting the need for a program of parent information.

The mathematics supervisor developed plans for a discussion group to face this problem. Each junior and senior high school was asked to send one mathematics teacher, which made a total of fifteen teachers. Most of these people were acquainted with one another and with the supervisor.

The discussions were scheduled in the conference room of School A, a new and modern school that was centrally located in the city. In the conference room, a large round table was available to seat up to twenty people.

A series of four sessions was tentatively planned. The sessions lasted from 3:00 P.M. to 5:00 P.M., with the teachers released from teaching duties during the last period of the school day. Coffee was served at the beginning of each session, and ten to fifteen minutes were used for social interaction at this time.

Since the group was formed for a special problem, the leader initiated the first session by a brief statement of the purpose and suggested that discussants share their experiences related to the problem. Several discussants began to ask about their responsibilities as related to the problem. The leader suggested that they might be able to clarify the problem and attempt to develop some recommendations for improving public relations in this field. The leader asked that each of the participants discuss the problem with his colleagues.

As a stimulus for the first discussion period, the leader used a tape recording obtained when a parent came to him for an interview. In the recording, the parent told about a back-to-school night experience with his child's math teacher. The child was taking geometry, and the teacher left the parent feeling that modern mathematics would make this course completely obsolete. Consequently, the parent felt that the child was wasting his time. The interview graphically illustrated a misunderstanding and the need for better public information. The discussion followed from this in a free and spontaneous manner, with the leader acting almost as a participant.

Sometimes group members engaged in side conversations in their eagerness to express views or feelings. These continued briefly, but the leader encouraged all members to share their thoughts with the total group when such a side conversation continued. The leader interrupted occasionally to ask for clarification of some point or to summarize briefly, and this usually stimulated still more discussion.

The discussion was scheduled to stop at 5:00 P.M., and the schedule was followed. In terminating the discussion, the supervisory leader briefly summarized major points and promised to provide a written review discussants could refer to at the beginning of the next discussion period. The leader suggested some possible next steps for the group to consider, including an attempt to identify several of the more serious public relations problems. With that the session was adjourned.

CAUTIONS AND LIMITATIONS. Do not assume that any informed, personable, or eager person can lead a group discussion effectively. The most highly informed person may inhibit discussion, and specific skills are required for discussion leading in any case. Training of a discussion leader is essential in most situations.

Avoid a discussion group in which opinions, attitudes, and knowledge of participants are highly similar. Diversity among group members is important.

Avoid the temptation to make critical decisions for the group when consensus cannot be reached. Similarly, avoid taking a vote. If consensus has not been reached and the decision is critical, the group is not ready for decision making.

Avoid letting a discussion become a recitation in which the leader asks questions and responds to everything that is said. The leader should generally be silent, and he should make his few questions as open-ended as possible to stimulate a variety of responses.

Avoid the tendency to get everyone to participate by calling upon each participant in some systematic way. A good discussion leader gets everyone involved by stimulating free interaction, being sparing with his own remarks, and keeping others from dominating the discussion.

Do not be afraid of silence. Sometimes a group needs a chance just to sit and contemplate an idea or a problem. The silence will be broken when someone feels the need. In fact, most adults feel so uncomfortable with silence that a group discussion leader might have to encourage it occasionally.

Do not involve a discussion group in your problem unless it is also the group's problem in some significant way. Most people are too busy to deal with a problem for the time required in a discussion group unless they are interested and concerned. Leaders who organize discussion groups to make themselves feel less insecure with a problem are not likely to meet with success.

Do not organize a discussion group to support what you or some authority have already decided. Participants are very quick to sense that they are discussing a problem that the leader has already solved in his own mind. A reasonably intelligent group sees through manipulation by the leader very quickly. Even the most skilled manipulator is less than successful in that his discussion group senses that something is not quite right and hence functions inefficiently and tends to lack creativity.

SUMMARY. The group discussion is an activity facilitating extended group interaction with focus upon a problem or idea of common interest and concern. Such an activity under skillful leadership serves well in stimulating ideas, sharing information, developing understanding, and influencing attitudes and opinions. Discussion groups are not usually action groups except in that they can make decisions, recommendations, or express consensus and disagreement. They often provide the basis of understanding upon which action groups can operate.

In several modified forms, group discussions serve special purposes. The case method of discussion provides a unique approach to stimulating thinking about complex situations. The leaderless group discussion provides for maximum involvement and is a valuable approach to leader identification and training.

Role Playing

DEFINITION. Role playing may be defined as a spontaneous dramatization involving one or more persons assuming designated roles in relation to a specified problem in a given situation. The drama is structured by the problem and the situation but is unrehearsed and not preplanned. The objective is to encourage the fullest possible assumption of roles by the players so that they act and feel as they might in a real situation.

PURPOSES
1. To provide concrete examples of behavior as a basis for discussion.
2. To stimulate new attitude formation.

3. To develop skill in interviewing and questioning, or other skills needed in spontaneous verbal interaction.
4. To develop understanding of feelings and attitudes of other people.

PROCEDURES. Role playing has been widely used to stimulate learning associated with problems of human interaction. The terms "sociodrama" and "psychodrama" have been used in describing role-playing activities of various kinds. The specific procedures vary, depending upon the purposes, the size of the group, and the extent of involvement required. Essential procedures for role playing under nearly any conditions seem to include establishing rapport, identifying a specific problem, assigning roles, adhering to roles, and terminating the activity at an appropriate time.

Participants should feel comfortable with each other if role playing is to be for real. Initial experiences with role playing are often resisted, but a group readily learns to accept this kind of activity once it comes into use. Often a group leader can begin role playing by assuming roles and inviting one or more self-assured individuals to join him. Role playing can be more comfortably experienced by some participants if two or three people are all involved and no audience is observing. Above all, leaders need to display a friendly, permissive, and constructive attitude toward all role players as they become involved for the first few times.

Role players must be directed toward a very specific problem to which all participants can relate. Roles must be played in terms of individuals interacting with others in a very concrete situation. A critical incident, a case, a lesson can be the basis for role playing, but the players must act in terms of a specific time and place as well as having the problem clearly in mind. A lesson protocol or vignette might be used for this purpose, with the role playing built upon this lesson involving this teacher, class, and period. However, each role-playing session should begin with a specific instance in the lesson with the leader suggesting, for instance, "Let's role-play that portion that starts with item number sixty-eight and see how we would try to get expressions of pupil attitudes."

Roles need to be specifically assigned so each person knows what is expected of him. It is not wise to tell participants how to act, for spontaneity is essential. However, teacher, parent, pupil, principal, and other persons involved in the specific situation should be designated in advance. When one role is not too complimentary or flattering, it may be wise to ask a very well liked participant to assume it. Roles do not need to match the people playing them. One of the characteristics that makes role playing a very useful activity is the ease with which participants can assume a role and then return to reality and discuss it objectively.

Role players should be urged to adhere to assigned roles. This is not always possible, but when roles are abandoned, the action should stop. Anxiety may cause role players to find themselves unable to adhere to the role assigned. However, participants can learn to adhere to roles with a bit of coaching and encouragement. Leaders should be alert to keep participants from getting into the habit of dropping out of a role when it becomes a bit awkward. Some self-discipline can be cultivated.

Leaders should terminate role-playing sessions at an appropriate time. Ordinarily, a few minutes of involvement in a role provides a lot of experience for discussion. If a role player remains in his role too long, he may get emotionally involved to the point of embarrassment.

SUGGESTED FOLLOW-UP ACTIVITIES
1. Ask observers to react to the role playing they saw.
2. Ask each role player to describe his or her feelings as he or she became involved.
3. Discuss alternative ways of dealing with the situation.
4. Have an observer-analyst report on his analysis of the interaction.
5. Switch roles among the role players and have the same situation played again.

ILLUSTRATION. Role playing is involved in most of the laboratory-type sessions discussed in Chapter 7. An interesting illustration of role playing involved Dr. Laurine Johnson, the new director of special education in the Wakeville City schools. As she met for the second time with the new screening committee, she decided to role-play a situation in which a pupil had been designated for possible placement in a special class for the brain-injured. In a previous meeting with the committee she was concerned that they seemed to want her to make the decisions for them to accept. Their discussion of the responsibilities of the committee to "review all relevant information and make the best educational placement" seemed to worry several of the committee members. One elementary school principal had said to her following the meeting, "I don't know too much about this kind of problem, but I'll go along with what you recommend." A sixth-grade teacher had asked, "Are there some materials we should read to guide our decisions?" A counselor had been overheard commenting to a supervisor during the last committee meeting, "I hope we can get a lot of new classes organized for these kids who can't make it in the seventh and eighth grades."

With these comments and questions in mind, Dr. Johnson carefully planned her second meeting of the committee as an in-service session. On the arrival of the committee members, she briefly introduced her plan to have a practice session. She distributed folders containing information on a single pupil. "Now, this is not for real. We don't need to make a decision on this boy at this time. It is a real case, however, and we could well have this or another just like it at out next meeting. Let's role-play our approach to this problem. This boy is not doing at all well in school."

After this introduction, each committee member read the material carefully. Finally, when all seemed to have finished, Dr. Johnson asked, "Well, what do you think?" A discussion followed. Opinions were given; additional information was requested; suggestions were made. When specific kinds of additional information were requested, Dr. Johnson provided it, since she had a much more complete case record than had been provided for the committee members.

After nearly forty minutes, one member said, "Let's make a decision. We have other cases to review today!" Dr. Johnson said, "All right. Will you make a specific recommendation?" Another committee member volunteered, "I move we ask the parents for permission to place him in a special class for the emotionally disturbed." A flurry of discussion followed this motion. Some agreed strongly. Others were not sure. Some thought a class for minimally brain-injured would be better.

After awhile, Dr. Johnson asked, "Do we have a second to this motion for placement?" Several volunteered to second the motion. "Are we ready for a decision?" Heads nodded. "All in favor?" Most assented. "Those opposed?" One or two weak negative responses were heard.

It was now 5:05 P.M. Dr. Johnson glanced at her watch and acknowledged the lateness of the hour. "I know we must leave promptly. Before we go, however, I want to share some additional information with you about this boy and set a date for another meeting." As she talked, Dr. Johnson distributed a mimeographed sheet. "This contains physical examination data, a report from the school social worker on a home visit, and a quotation from the psychologist. Most of this is new information in the sense that you did not ask for it so I did not give it to you."

As the participants glanced at the new information, there was a flurry of comments. They saw almost immediately that some of this information might have changed their decision. Some complained, "Why didn't you give us this information, even without our asking?"

CAUTIONS AND LIMITATIONS. Many of the cautions in using role playing have already been mentioned. Players must be encouraged to become involved for the first time and then be protected from embarrassment. Leaders must be alert to terminate role playing before emotional involvement becomes excessive.

Role playing is an activity uniquely suited for in-service education sessions designed to deal with human relations problems. The depth of involvement in simulated reality provides high experience impact for attitude and insight development as well as for building certain verbal interaction skills. While groups may need some coaching and encouragement in the use of role playing, it is readily accepted by most people in a comfortable group situation and stimulates much interest.

INNOVATIVE APPROACHES

In addition to the relatively well-known ways of working with groups for education and training discussed above, new approaches emerge from time to time. Some are fads while others seem worthy of further testing in use. In this latter category are laboratory-training exercises, quality circle groups, and several techniques described by Mouton and Blake (1984) as "synergogic exercises."

The *laboratory approach* has been utilized in a variety of forms over the past twenty years. Many of these exercises are closely related to simulations (Bessent 1967). Harris, Bessent, and McIntyre (1969) formalized the concept of "laboratory approach," identified some unique contributions for such activities, and illustrated a variety of applications as well as providing materials for specific exercises.

The *synergogic exercises* advocated by Mouton and Blake are illustrated with four variations. Like the laboratory approach, these exercises build on techniques formerly developed. They have much in common with case method and utilize group discussions, but they emerge as unique in a variety of important ways.

Quality circles have been popularized in both educational and business circles as an approach to grass-roots problem solving (Ouchi 1981). While the emphasis of the procedures for quality circles is on problem solving, there is obviously much group learning required in the process. Hence, adaptation of this approach to working with groups seems to have potential for in-service education purposes.

The Laboratory Approach

The laboratory exercise represents a special form of training in which simulation is utilized in a fairly highly structured way, yet it is not gaming. Laboratory sessions generally have the following design:

1. Participants are presented, in a group, with a *bit of simulated reality* directly related to a specific problem of general concern (grading, grouping, discipline, testing, and so on). See Chapter 7 on types of simulations.
2. Participants *respond* individually to the simulation, in some personal way, being asked only to exercise good professional judgment.
3. Participants *record* their reactions individually in a standardized way that permits easy analysis of responses while assuring individuals that they can remain anonymous.
4. Recorded responses of all participants are *analyzed.*

5. *Feedback* is presented to the entire group, showing similarities, differences, special approaches, and diversities.
6. Interpretations, generalizations, and implications are drawn using a combination of the recorded information, the simulated reality, and the problem being addressed.

This six-step process is fairly rigidly followed in designing laboratory exercises even though the problems and simulated content vary widely. To illustrate one simple exercise, the problem of evaluating student arithmetic performance may be instructive:

Simulation—A single example of an arithmetic test item is provided, showing teacher directions and the work of one student.

Response—Each individual participant is asked to pretend to be "the teacher," to study the student's work on this test item, and to assign a grade.

Recording—A response form is provided to each participant to be collected when completed. Each participant is instructed to report a "grade" in the form of a score for the student of 0, 1, 2, . , . up to a maximum of 10.

Analysis—While participants discuss their "grading" of this student's work using either buzz groups or another activity, an assistant tabulates responses, showing the distribution of numerical "grades" from 0 to 10. A transparency is prepared showing the distribution of grades.

Feedback—The transparency showing the analyzed scores assigned by different individuals is shown. The facts are pointed out. "Different teachers assign different grades to the same student, viewing identical work."

Interpretations—The participants discuss their interpretations of their own responses in relation to those of the group. Many "good" reasons are mentioned: "We didn't know this student personally." "Well, he/she did understand process. That's worth something." "Yes, but he/she didn't get the correct answer." "No, but he/she showed understanding in the approach to the problem." "I think the student was just careless." "I agree and gave him/her a zero." "Oh, you can't do that. After all, much of the work was correct." The discussion can go on and on.

Generalizations—The leader tries to synthesize the many diverse points of view about evaluating pupil academic performance. For instance: "Can we try to generalize on this exercise?" (1) Equally competent teachers may not agree on the worth of identical student performance. (2) Different values and instructional purposes will make for different evaluations. (3) Different evaluations can be justified in rational ways. (4) Grades are only symbols that have diverse meanings. (5) Others.

Implications—The participants form buzz groups to interact and attempt to share at least one practical suggestion for improving grading based on this exercise.

Other laboratory exercises have been designed using the same six-step format, but addressing an array of problems. In the "Homogeneous Grouping" exercise (Harris, Bessent, and McIntyre 1969, 95), teacher teams try various methods of grouping students into three class-sections. Record folders are provided to help create the simulated reality and make actual test scores available for influencing decisions.

In a classroom observation exercise, participants watch a teaching film and "evaluate" the teacher's performance. One subgroup uses *judgmental ratings* and is provided with biasing information about the film teacher. Another subgroup of participants makes *descriptive estimates* of practices observed without biasing information. Ratings and estimates of the two subgroups are then analyzed and compared in a feedback session.

These and other exercises designed according to the laboratory approach have several apparent strengths. They are highly stimulating to those who can relate to the simulated problem. They get participants actively and personally involved. They protect the anonymity of each participant, yet focus attention on a personal basis, encouraging critical self-analysis. These exercises do not solve problems, but they do promote understandings on which to build.

Quality Circles

Quality circles were originally developed as formally organized ways of getting working groups, sharing common concerns, to voluntarily develop proposals for improving their performance and/or getting other changes made in the workplace. In educational settings, the same basic approaches have been used (Ladwig 1983). Quality circle groups are expected to follow a structured pattern of activities as they approach the problem. It is this pattern of activities which makes this approach so promising as in-service education or training. The activities, if followed, assure that the individuals in the group become informed participants. Hence, group decisions and recommendations for action are based more on rational analysis than shared ignorance, expediency, or preconception (Ouchi 1981).

The essential steps in the quality circle process can be generally described as follows (Harris 1985, 104–07):

1. *A problem* is chosen and defined using discussion and systematic voting as needed to formalize agreements.

2. *Information* is gathered systematically to assure the fullest practical understanding about the dynamics of the problem. Participants brainstorm, interview experts, make systematic observations, and delve into the available records.
3. *Analytical processes* of a variety of kinds are utilized in an effort to clearly determine causes of the problem. Statistical checksheets, Pareto analyses, and Fishbone analyses are described by Gryna (1981, 62). Other analytical techniques can be used as are appropriate to the character of the problem. Harris's "Branching Diagram Analysis Technique" (1985, 200) and "Congruence Analysis Technique" have been highly useful (1986, 175).
4. *Decisions* are made regarding solutions to be implemented or recommended. Brainstorming, buzz groups, discussions, and voting are all applied for this purpose.
5. A *plan of action* is developed for implementing agreed upon solutions.
6. Plans are *implemented*.
7. *The problem is reviewed.*

The quality circle design for problem solving can readily be adapted for use in in-service planning and has direct in-service learning outcomes when applied to any realistic situation. It offers unusually good opportunities to combine efforts at curriculum development, discipline management, or program evaluation with in-service education. Even when problems addressed can be solved only in limited ways, the substantial learning outcomes produced by the quality circle process make the approach worth using. Like any structured design for training, leadership training is prerequisite for successful implementation (Metz 1982). Group leaders need training in the specialized techniques and sequences even when standard, known activities are also employed.

Synergogic Approaches

Synergogic training is described by Mouton and Blake (1984, 10) as unique in several ways, while sharing a variety of strengths with other "learner-centered" approaches. Three principles that these authors stress are: (1) meaningful directions for participants, (2) teamwork, and (3) synergy. Advantages are described for this approach because of the broad applicability to various groups and purposes and the limited array of materials and other resources required. But, most importantly, greater learning is claimed because of the effects of synergy.

Four designs using the synergogic approach are described and illustrated. The "Team Effectiveness Design" stresses factual learning. The "Team-Member Design" also stresses knowledge acquisition, but relies on peer presentations. The "Performance Judging Design" is used for skill building while the "Clarifying Attitudes Design" is just that.

The character of all of these designs is reflected in the active involvement of individuals, working as members of a group or team, but utilizing very carefully structured materials and procedures which guide learning. Hence, Mouton and Blake show their genius for combining structure and freedom to enhance human development.

The *Team-Member Design* divides responsibility for presenting the content materials among the members of a team. Text material is provided to each team member in three to five parts that comprise the whole presentation. Each team member studies only his/her portion of the text and prepares a plan for teaching the material to all members of the team, but without using the original text. This assures that an effort is made to be creative in presenting to others. The session proceeds as follows:

1. Teamwork with each person presenting a portion of the material.
2. Testing over the entire text material.
3. Scoring of the tests.
4. Interpretations of test scores for both individuals and the team as a whole.
5. Reviewing the teamwork to promote better procedures.

The *Performance Judging Design* is proposed for developing skills. Instead of judging behavior in the traditional ways or relying on modeling with no explicit use of criteria, Mouton and Blake (1984, 74–75) develop and apply criteria of performance as an integral part of the training process. The sequence of activities for this design includes the following:

1. Individuals complete an initial task to pretest their own skill levels.
2. Team members meet to discuss criteria that could be applied to such tasks. They compare their criteria against external expectations and then finalize a set of criteria all can live with.
3. Each individual completes a "sample performance" and submits it to the team for evaluation. Anonymity is maintained as far as possible until the team's critiques are completed. Then they are returned to the individual and discussed openly.
4. A second performance assignment is completed by each individual and subsequently evaluated by the team as in step 3 above.
5. Finally, when all performance samples have been completed, the teams meet to review their teamwork.

Each of the designs briefly reviewed here is illustrative of approaches to working with groups in creative, imaginative ways. These groups are not only actively involved, but purposefully as well. Furthermore, the team-work structure of all of these designs, including two not described here, maximizes learning opportunities beyond the *lowest common denominator* level that tends to characterize many group approaches.

OTHER USEFUL ACTIVITIES

Working with groups offers special challenges to trainers and leaders to assure the effective and efficient use of the time and efforts of participants. While individualized approaches (see Chapter 6) are very expensive in terms of the time and efforts of leaders, groups are very expensive in terms of the time and efforts of the participants.

In Chapter 4, Exhibit 4–6 lists and analyzes twenty-eight different activities in terms of experience impact, complexity of objectives, and group size. Approximately half of these activities are suggested as suitable for groups—large, medium, or small. Buzz sessions, brainstorming, group discussions, and role playing are described above as more or less *essential* to nearly all of our efforts to work with a group of any size. Here descriptions and suggestions for using some other activities with groups are presented.

Visualizations

The lecture is one of the oldest forms of presentation to groups. It is still widely used in formal courses, conventions, sermons, and political campaigns as well as in in-service education. By utilizing various visualizing techniques the essential features of the lecture may be enhanced dramatically. The lecturer may use slides, transparencies, chalkboard drawings, charts, films, and even dramatic techniques to transform the lecture into a more powerful mode of presentation, offering information and stimulating understandings, attitudes, and feelings (Gite 1983).

Visualization techniques add visual sensations to the listening effects provided by a simple lecture. Futhermore, visualizations can be developed in ways that sharpen the focus of attention of participants. Concepts not readily presented via words alone can be handled effectively when visual techniques are utilized.

Transparencies utilizing overhead projection are now among the most widely used supplements to the simple lecture (Friant 1983). The potential impact of well-designed, well-utilized transparencies is enormous, but rarely realized. Most transparencies simply present words for participants to read on a glaring screen. As such, the technique adds a bit of focus, but few other advantages are realized. The communicating still depends upon words that can just as easily be spoken or read. Effectiveness in the use of transparencies depends upon visualizing concepts, showing relationships, focusing on key terms, adding color to attract attention, and guiding participants as they put ideas into relationship, as well as reinforcing and supplementing the spoken or written word. Ideally, a visual should call for fewer words than the traditional lecture form, hence saving time and improving learning.

Specific techniques for preparing and using overhead transparencies are fully presented in various publications (Davis and McCallon 1974; Friant 1983; and Lynch 1979). A few general rules guide trainer/presenters and have special importance.

1. Minimize words on the transparency while emphasizing visualizations.
2. Avoid crowding too much detail on a single transparency.
3. Use color to underline, highlight, reduce glare, and focus attention, but avoid a splash of many colors that add nothing to the message.
4. Assure large, clear, bold letters and other details, avoiding the use of typewritten or hastily drawn material.
5. Sequence transparencies carefully in relation to the spoken presentation and other activities (Lynch 1979).
6. Avoid talking about the visualized content any more than is absolutely necessary.
7. Use a pointer to focus attention on specific details, and point at the film, not at the screen.
8. Turn the projection lamp off when not in immediate use.
9. Have a water-soluble flow pen handy and use it as a marker for underlining, circling, or adding information.
10. Keep a spare bulb handy, and check your machine. Clean and focus the lenses well in advance of your presentation.

Films and videotapes are increasingly available media for use in visualizing presentations. Unlike the overhead projection of transparencies that are aids to the lecturer or presenter in supplementing the oral presentation, films and videotapes *take over* from the presenter and replace him or her for a specific period of time. Hence, a photoelectronic robot becomes the presenter. If well designed and produced, such visualizations along with prerecorded narrations can make for powerful presentations. However, the use of such *canned* presentations must be carefully planned. The contents of the presentation must be carefully reviewed for determining appropriateness to the situation (Friedlander 1972). When quite appropriate, plans for the presentation of a film or videotape should be based on answers to the following questions:

1. Where does it (film or tape) fit best into the overall plan for the in-service session or program?

2. Is the entire film or videotape worthwhile, or should only a portion of it be used?
3. What introductory and follow-up activities will make the visual presentation most meaningful?
4. Should other materials be used with the film or tape (handouts providing viewing questions, discussion points, an outline of contents, or a quiz)?
5. Should the film or tape be presented from start to finish or interrupted periodically for discussion or elaboration?

Additional, ever-present concerns need to be addressed, of course, regarding the readiness of the equipment, the visibility of the images, and what to do if there is equipment failure. (See Chapter 5.)

Charts, chalkboard displays, and slide presentations continue to be important ways of presenting for visualization. Each has its own unique contributions to make. Hence, they are utilized or not with thoughtful preplanning. Slides provide many of the advantages of transparencies, but are especially advantageous when an extensive amount of primarily visual information is to be presented. Slides lend themselves especially well to presenting photographic material. The chalkboard has none of the unique advantages of slides, but is still among the most versatile of visualizing media. When the extemporaneous display of visual material is needed, when erasure and revision is needed, when dynamic interaction between the presenter and the participants calls for visual clarification of relationships, then the chalkboard becomes nearly indispensable.

Charts too have unique contributions to make in visualization. Charts prepared in advance can be displayed in a series accompanying the lecture or other presentational activity. Used in this way, charts have much in common with transparencies and slides. Charts can serve as a cumulative chalkboard however. The amount of material that can be displayed on a chalkboard is quite limited, but the flip-chart provides nearly unlimited display capacity. Especially unique are techniques for using the chart and chalkboard in tandem, with chalkboard information being transferred to charts for later use as the chalkboard is erased.

Demonstrations

This type of activity involves the presentation of a series of events, usually prearranged, for group viewing. Demonstrations are preplanned to be very realistic, yet details of special importance are accentuated (Bessent 1967; Harris 1985, 75).

Planning for effective demonstrations focuses on both physical arrangements and the structure of the demonstration activity itself. Ideally the demonstration sequence is rehearsed with the persons involved (Coody

1967). The unique contributions of demonstrations relate to offering fairly large groups opportunities to see model practices or procedures in actual operation. The staging and rehearsing should not destroy the verisimilitude of the demonstration, but a variety of simplifications and special arrangements can be made to maximize the understanding gained by the viewers (Butts 1967).

Demonstrations often present teaching practices and make use of students as part of the demonstrating team. This provides viewers opportunities to use a specific time period and be assured that specific practices will be observed. Such assurances cannot be given when visiting "live" classrooms.

Demonstrations that do not involve students are often easier to arrange but need detailed planning and rehearsal just the same. For instance, a demonstration of techniques for using the overhead projector seems simple until the numerous specific skills and knowledge components are analyzed:

1. Plugging the projector into a power outlet.
   length of cord
   extension cord needed
   three-prong adapter
2. Switching the projector on and off.
   location of switch
   type of switches
   fan switch
   high-low brightness settings
3. Positioning the projection screen.
   wall-mounted screens
   tripod screens
   glare on the screen
   adjusting room lights

These notations refer to numerous specific components of knowledge and skill which are essential to the successful operation of this simple machine. The three designated tasks are, of course, not a complete listing because the projector must still be positioned, focused, and used. Obviously, what appears to be a simple, single demonstration becomes in fact an extended workshop with a series of demonstrations and other related activities.

Demonstrations of any kind will be more effective if those viewing the activity know what to watch for, have a checklist or observers' guide, and have opportunities to ask questions.

Observations

The use of systematic classroom observations has at long last been recognized as an in-service training activity. Traditionally, to observe in classrooms has been equated with evaluating the teacher (Goldstein 1982). Observations by student teachers of "master" teachers has become common practice in many preservice teacher-training programs (Good and Brophy 1978). The value of observing, recording objectively what is observed, and systematically analyzing, interpreting, and discussing such observations with the individual teacher, has been advocated for many years as "clinical supervision" (see Chapter 6). However, studying teaching *in the act* through group observations is practiced in some in-service training programs for both administrators and classroom teachers (Harris 1963, 511–15; Harris, Bessent, and McIntyre 1969, 131–62; and Harris 1980, 370–75).

Group classroom observing to be truly effective must be systematic. Our experience dictates that a specific *focus* is essential. Observers should consciously search for *events* related to the designated focus. Related events should be *recorded* in some objective fashion. Then, of course, the observers individually and as a group need to analyze, interpret, discuss, and draw implications for practice in their own classroom.

The power of group observations of classroom teaching in its natural forms derives from the unique situation most teachers and administrators face living busy lives in schools. Curiously, the main business of the school—teaching—is for the most part carried on privately. Teachers rarely see other teachers at work. Administrators and supervisors see problem teachers at work and "evaluate" teachers using observations, but these circumstances do not allow for group sharing, thoughtful analysis, or creative thinking. When a small group of five to seven teachers with an administrator or supervisor observes a classroom with *learning about teaching* as their purpose, a highly stimulating experience can be provided for all.

Classroom observation as experience in understanding teaching involves the following procedures:

1. Get approval from a very secure teacher for an observation on a specific day and hour.
2. Preplan with the selected teacher to assure that normalcy is maintained. "We'll take whatever would be the normal routine for that lesson."
3. Preplan with the observing group to be sure they know the when, where, what, and why of the observation.
4. Pretraining in objective recording of events and in suspending value judgments needs to be provided for observers.
5. Observers gather in a conference room near the classroom to be observed. In a thirty-minute orientation session the focus for the observation is reviewed (questioning, verbal interaction, use of media, individual assistance, or other). The recording techniques are re-

viewed. The teacher's lesson plan is distributed, as well as an agenda for the follow-up activities.

6. The observation group enters the classroom at an agreed upon time, selected for minimizing disruptions. The teacher ignores the observers and proceeds with the lesson as planned. Observers take chairs provided for them and immediately begin recording. They remain for an entire lesson—thirty to fifty minutes—and then leave without formalities.

7. On reassembling in the conference room, observers are instructed to review their observation recordings rather than begin a discussion. This assures time for reflection and focuses on events as recorded rather than on impressions.

8. Once each observer has had time to review and analyze the individual observation record, the leader opens the sharing session using one or more activities structured to emphasize interpretations of events while avoiding judging. Brainstorming is often useful. "Let's brainstorm for a few minutes to be sure we have a comprehensive picture of the critical events." (Brainstorming rules may need to be reviewed.) "OK, what did you see that is worthy of attention because it appeared to be a critical element in the teaching/learning process and relates to our focus?" (See Harris and Hill 1982: "Trainers Manual," pp. 24–25, for other suggested techniques.)

9. Following brainstorming and discussion, implications for good teaching are discussed. Lead questions might include: What practices best reflect research on effective teaching? What model or theory of teaching was being implemented? What practices observed could be added to your repertory? What adaptations of observed practices might be useful? Why?

10. The session should end without any final conclusions. No value judgments are accepted. Plans for follow-up bring the session to a close.

Debates and Panels

Panel discussions are widely employed with fairly large groups to present information much as a lecturer might. A set of three to five panel members makes it possible to provide listeners with a variety of points of view or a more diverse range of expertise than is generally available from a single presenter. However, the unique feature of a panel is the potential for rather spontaneous interaction among panel members as they comment on each other's ideas or on questions from a moderator and the participants.

The *debate* is a formally structured form of the panel which is especially useful when controversial issues are being studied. The debate involves selecting one or more presenters to take each side of an issue, to systematically present arguments supporting a position, and to engage in rebutting the positions of the other side. The structure takes advantage of the unique character of issues, namely, that there are no right and wrong positions clearly known. Hence, the debate calls for sharing information and stimulating participants to consider more than one position.

The "Conpar method" developed by Moran (n.d.) for General Motors executive training is an approach to using panelists as expert presenters with maximum emphasis on participation. Moran refers to Conpar as "stimulating and controlling participation in panel discussions." The problems often encountered in panel presentations include a series of short speeches with little interaction between panelists and little opportunity for participants to get actively involved. The Conpar method tries to overcome these problems with a structure as follows:

1. A leader, recorder, and timekeeper are designated.
2. Speakers and participants are closely timed, using a clearly visible and audible timer.
3. The general topic is determined in advance, but participants, in buzz groups, give specific focus to the session.
4. A panelist introduces the topic in a five-minute time period. (Timer is used.)
5. Buzz groups discuss for five minutes preparing questions.
6. Buzz group questions are submitted on 3" × 5" cards for panel members to consider.
7. The leader reads a question from a card to the panelists, asking for a *bid* to respond. Panelists bid for a chance to answer. The question goes to the panelist with the lowest *bid in minutes*. (Timer is set. Panelist responds to question.)
8. The leader invites another panelist to respond to the same question. (Timer set for the same amount of time used in step 7.)
9. The buzz group secretary who wrote the card is asked to react to the responses by the panelists. (Timer: one minute.)
10. If the buzz group secretary raises supplementary questions or asks for clarification, the leader invites responses from panelists, allowing not more than one minute each.
11. The leader repeats the process (steps 7, 8, 9, and 10) for each card from each buzz group until all groups have had at least one question or concern addressed. The process (steps 4 through 10) can be repeated as often as time permits and additional questions are available.
12. The recorder summarizes the entire session for the participants before adjournment.

The Conpar method uses time economically, paces events quickly, and allows for participant involvement from the very beginning. If leader and timekeeper do their jobs well, a single round from the introduction of the topic (step 4) to completion (step 10) can be completed in twenty to thirty minutes. Hence, a session of less than two hours can thoroughly deal with a topic.

SUMMARY

Working in groups for in-service education is basic. Group planning, evaluating, and implementing are inescapable, even in highly personalized program operations. The natural advantages of group endeavors are enticing. Furthermore, an extensive knowledge based on the use of group processes is readily available for in-service planners to draw upon. Unfortunately, the extensive body of literature reporting on research and development in group processes is now somewhat old. It is not, however, outmoded. It should be studied and put to good use.

Much of this chapter has been devoted to a careful explication of four basic group techniques or activities. These are only four of a much larger variety. They are basic, however, in the sense that they alone can enormously enrich and diversify group experiences for in-service education. Furthermore, without the use of such basic techniques group endeavors are likely to be less fruitful than they might otherwise be.

In addition to brainstorming, buzz-group sessions, group discussions, and role playing, a few innovative or non-traditional approaches to working with groups have been described here. The laboratory approach, often using buzz sessions, role playing or discussions, offers some unique ways to design for active involvement and high-experience impact in a group context. Quality circles are discussed here in brief as a promising approach to *both* problem-solving and training. The unique contribution of the synergogic designs for cooperative group learning is described very briefly as perhaps the most promising of recent developments in giving group training more structure and impact.

The final section of this chapter reviews the obvious importance of various tools for working with groups. Visual tools such as transparencies, films, videotapes, charts and even the chalkboard are discussed, with emphasis on selective use with clear concern for purpose, and on avoiding common problems that detract from their effectiveness. Demonstrations and associated classroom observation techniques are presented here as reminders that these need not be restricted to use in a clinical mode. These activities can serve whole groups with special advantages.

STUDY SOURCES

Fever, Dale. 1986. "Training by Committee at Good Samaritan Hospital." *Training* 23 (March): 73–76.

A low-budget management training program, in which the managers use volunteer time to serve as trainers, is described. However, the program is managed by a committee. Furthermore, team teaching arrangements are utilized with three-person teams offering lectures, role playing, case studies, and group discussions.

Friant, Ray J., Jr. 1983. *Preparing Effective Presentations: How to Make Presentations Pay Off.* Babylon, N.Y.: Pilot Industries, Inc.
A guide that offers many concrete illustrations and suggestions on presentational techniques. Much attention is given to transparencies. Other display and presentation modes are also discussed and illustrated.

Gall, Meredith D., and Joyce P. Gall. 1976. "The Discussion Method." In *Psychology of Teaching Methods,* 75th Yearbook, Part I, ed. N. L. Gage. Chicago: National Society for the Study of Education.
A systematic review of research on group discussion over a period of some thirty years.

Glickman, Carl D. 1985. *Supervision of Instruction: A Developmental Approach.* Newton, Mass.: Allyn and Bacon, Inc.
The chapter on "Group Development" (pp. 330–57) offers a review of a wide variety of concepts related to working with groups. Roles, leadership styles, resolving conflicts, and group development are all briefly discussed. The author also provides a set of practical guidelines for discussion leaders to use.

Gryna, Frank M., Jr. 1981. *Quality Circles: A Team Approach to Problem Solving.* New York: AMACOM, A Division of American Management Association.
This document represents a major effort to adapt the quality circles approach for use in the United States. Although industrial uses are emphasized, the techniques are clearly adaptable to schools.

Janis, Irving L. 1972. *Victims of Groupthink: A Psychological Study of Foreign-Policy Decisions and Fiascoes.* Boston: Houghton Mifflin.
Case studies support the notion that group processes can be malfunctioning, produce poor answers, and make unwise decisions. Janis describes "groupthink" as a common problem at the highest levels. Problem diagnosis includes the following: (1) Limited alternatives considered, (2) failure to reexamine, (3) ignoring advantages of other ideas, (4) using little or no outside expertise, etc.

Lynch, Pat. 1979. "Prompt Cards End Those Transparency Fumbles." *Training/ HRD* 16 (June): 34, 36.
This brief article details using transparencies in presenting to a group. Prompt cards are illustrated for easy use in discussing material as it is being projected. The cards are designed for easy manipulation and use right alongside the transparency instead of relying on separate text.

Margolis, Fredric H., and C. R. Bell. 1985. "How to Break the News That You're Breaking Them into Small Groups." *Training* 22 (March): 81–85, 88–89.
The authors urge leaders of groups to follow a standard sequence for forming small groups. They recommend that the leader give the rationale, explain the task, define the context, and explain what is to be reported. They also discuss each point in some detail.

Massey, Sara R. 1979. "Staff Development: Teaching Adult Professionals." *NCSIE Inservice* (April): 18–20. National Council of States on Inservice Education, Syracuse University, Syracuse, N.Y.
The techniques used by skillful moderators of group discussions are identified. Seven key points are initiating, informing, encouraging, setting norms, harmonizing differences, coordinating, and summarizing.

Milroy, Ellice. 1982. *Role-Play: A Practical Guide.* Aberdeen, Scotland: Aberdeen University Press.
The author gives brief but specific instructions on the techniques for using role playing in educational settings. Part I, section 1 is especially useful. It deals with "the technique." Examples are provided and sequences outlined.

Munson, Lawrence S. 1984. *How to Conduct Training Seminars.* New York: McGraw-Hill Book Company.
One of the few sources that focuses on implementation, as well as planning and design. Chapters 9 and 10 are uniquely valuable.

Ouchi, William G. 1981. *Theory Z: How American Business Can Meet the Japanese Challenge.* Reading, Mass.: Addison-Wesley.
This is a major effort to analyze Japanese business management practices in search of their implications for American society. Appendix 2 provides considerable detail on the use of quality circle techniques in Japan.

Pareek, Udai, and T. V. Rao. 1982. "Role Playing: The Basic Tool of Behaviour Simulation." In *Developing Motivation through Experiencing.* New Delhi: Oxford and IBH Publishing.
A rather detailed analysis of role playing rationale, procedures, and variations is provided with specific exercises. Case illustrations describing fairly elaborate applications are also provided.

Pollack, Gertrude K. 1975. *Leadership of Discussion Groups: Case Material and Theory.* Holliswood, N.Y.: Spectrum Publications, Inc.
This is a simple treatment of some basic ideas about organizing and leading adult groups. Extensive case material makes this valuable. Most cases report on women lay groups.

Rodriguez, Sam, and Kathy Johnstone. 1986. "Staff Development through a Collegial Support Group Model." Chap. 7 in *Improving Teaching,* ed. Karen K. Zumwalt. Alexandria, Va.: Association for Supervision and Curriculum Development.
The authors use observation reports on two very different teachers to illustrate professional development plans which reflect the individuality of each teacher. Monthly meetings are proposed as the means for sharing and supporting each other as they pursue different plans.

9.

Programmatic Planning

INTRODUCTION

High-quality in-service education requires more than specific sessions, utilizing a variety of activities, materials, and arrangements. Program structures must be designed, plans implemented, organizations formed and related efforts given leadership and direction. Without long-range and intermediate-range plans for training, the creative and exciting experiences offered in sessions cannot be assured of follow-up toward lasting improvements in performance. Without organizational structures providing for continuing planning, funding, staffing, and coordinating of training activities to meet the needs of school personnel, they will be too little too late, and inadequate in a variety of ways. Without leadership personnel assuming responsibility for planning, organizing, and directing training as an integral part of the larger school operation, little improvement of instruction can be realized.

Programs of in-service training can be planned and organized at school, local district, regional, state, national, or even international levels. There is no one best way to organize for the continuing professional development of the millions of diverse practitioners in the schools of the United States. Different organizational structures will respond to different needs. But organization is essential and often lacking. A major challenge for the public schools as delivery systems for in-service education will be to improve both efficiency and quality while meeting demands for enormous quantities and varieties of training.

In this chapter program planning for both intermediate- and longer-range training will be considered in some detail. Briefer consideration will be given to staffing delivery systems, assuring collaboration, and establishing policies and priorities. A set of guiding principles is also reviewed.

PLANNING PROGRAMS

When more than a single person is involved in any operation, some means of communication about what is to occur becomes important. If only a few individuals are involved, the operation is a simple set of routines, and the individuals can interact about the operation face to face, no further medium of communication may be needed. Why, then, are plans required? They are media of communications, guides to actions and their coordination. Plans also provide reference materials for monitoring and evaluating operations (Cunningham 1982). For in-service education, as with virtually all human operations, plans are indispensable under the following condition or conditions:

1. Operations are to continue over sustained time periods or are periodic rather than continuous.
2. An array of persons is involved in nonroutine, differentiated ways.
3. When face-to-face communications cannot be consistently provided before and during the operation.
4. Events comprising the operation must be sequenced and coordinated with others.
5. Approvals, allocations, or commitments of resources are required that are not routinely available.
6. Creative, original, unique contributions of individuals are desired as part of the operation.
7. Evaluation of the operation and/or its products is an important undertaking.

Plans are media for communication about future intended operations. They take some physical form—written document, graphic display, mathematical formula, or visualization. As media of communications, they are best when multisensory in nature. As communications, they must take differentiated forms, depending upon the persons who are to use them and the purposes for which they are intended.

Plans are guides to actions and the coordination of such actions. As such, a plan should clearly indicate what people should do; what they should do it with; when, where, in what sequence; and in what ways. These are simple requirements for a plan, but they become elaborate when many persons are involved or a variety of whats, whens, and wheres makes for great complexity.

Plans are reference works for use in implementing, monitoring, and evaluating operations. As such the who, what, when, where, and how provisions of the plan must be sufficiently specific that all concerned may know when compliance and deviations are occurring. For evaluation of outcomes, the plan must be explicit about goals and objectives. But for more comprehensive evaluation purposes, the plan must indicate relationships among resources, operational events, and anticipated outcomes.

Systematic Planning

Planning is essential to all efforts at directing organizational endeavors in a goal-oriented fashion. Many views of planning as process have been developed stressing sequence, resources, and interpersonal dynamics. Nearly all approaches to planning presume that a plan of some kind will be the product of planning as process (Cunningham 1982). Furthermore, it is often assumed that either the process of planning, the product (the plan), or both will somehow guide and facilitate implementation and evaluation of actual operations. In fact, this latter assumption might well be challenged. The emergence of "management systems" or techniques such as systems analysis (Gay 1980), PERTing (Cook 1966), and Gantt (Strother and Klus 1982), chart analysis and program budgeting all direct attention, in part, toward the fact that "the best-laid plans" are often not realized in operation (Lozano 1980).

Despite the serious problems inherent in operationalizing or implementing any plan, its existence is a prerequisite for ordered change, and the physical character of the plan as well as the processes employed probably make a difference in the consequences likely to follow (Lozano 1980; Cunningham 1982). Haskew* utilizes the term "plan-making" to refer to a systematic planning operation with a set of clearly delineated tasks with a plan as a tangible end product. He conceptualizes a set of technical procedures utilized to produce an operations design in the form of a plan. While not a sequence of events, such procedures can be viewed as two sets in relation to each other (see Exhibit 9–1). These sets of procedures in plan-making do no more than suggest what needs doing to produce a plan and how the various procedures relate to each other. The upper set all tend to involve choice making growing out of logical, analytical, interactive processes. The lower set of procedures all tend to involve information processing essential to choice making that is realistic. Communications among related subsystems assures that the planning process makes use of available resources, secures needed information, and assures that the larger organization is aware of the intents of the emerging ISE plan.

Two procedures of highly creative kinds are required as outgrowths of choice making, information processing, and communicating. One of these involves *synthesizing an operational design.* The other is *transforming the operational design* into tangible materials that can facilitate communications about intents in the form of a plan. In the real world of plan-making

---

*Adapted from lecture notes developed by L. D. Haskew and utilized in his teaching of plan-making at the University of Texas at Austin, 1976–78.

EXHIBIT 9–1. Plan-making as Informed Choosing, Communicating, and Designing

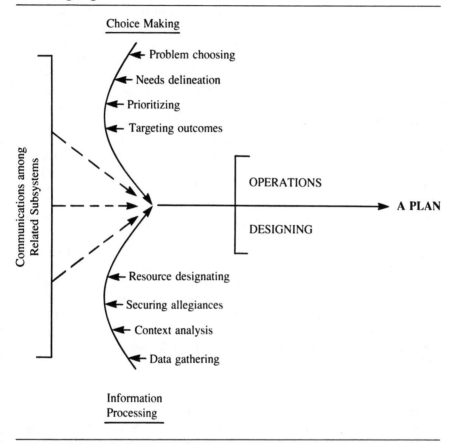

for in-service education, operational designing and plan producing are closely interrelated. They overlap one another in sequence and evolve as a paper representation of future operational reality that does not yet exist. Hence, operational designing is largely a conceptualizing, imagining process. As the planners complete the choice making, information processing, and interacting, the *creative tasks* are undertaken in an effort to imagine what the new training operation will be like if fully implemented and what the various events will be like. To the extent that the planners have vivid and detailed images of these new operations, they can be transferred to paper in the form of performance statements, operational descriptions, scenarios, vignettes, systems diagrams, PERT networks, program budgets, and illustrations (Cunningham 1982; Gay 1980; Hite and McIntyre 1980; and Strother and Klus 1982).

Planning models tailored specifically to in-service education have received considerable attention in recent years. The experiences of the Teacher Corps are utilized by various observers in stressing the need for "comprehensive" planning based on needs assessments, the use of problem-solving processes, and a "governance structure" that assures teacher collaboration (Hite and McIntyre 1980). Specific steps in a planning process advocated for vocational education are illustrative. The steps include: (1) creating awareness, (2) assuring readiness, (3) getting commitment, (4) planning, (5) implementing, and (6) maintaining (Hasazi et al. 1983). This practitioner, among others, finds such logical, sequential, step-by-step planning less than fully realistic. In fact, good planning in a context of ongoing school operations demands much more flexibility in the process. Nonetheless, these "steps" appear to have substantial support in both the literature and research. Lozano's (1980) study of the relationships between quality of plans and the planning processes used and the quality of the programs that evolved indicates support for more systematic planning as well as for better documentation of such plans.

Systematic and comprehensive planning is given wide support by both scholars and practitioners. Reports from Clark County Community College (Pedras 1984), the Virginia Department of Education (1978), and the Georgia Department of Education (1980) are but a few that stress both systematic approaches and relatively comprehensive views. Conrad et al. (1973), Lutz (1976), and Cunningham (1982) also offer carefully considered guidelines for practitioners in approaching such difficult tasks.

Plan-making Problems

The tendency to *substitute* planning documents for operational designing may be the most common and most serious flaw in plan-making. We often find plans that consist largely of long lists of objectives, detailed schedules, and budgets with little description of events. This derives from the inability to conceptualize, to create mental images of alternative forms of training. This is a very difficult part of plan-making, of course; but it is also an absolutely essential part, unless a plan is to be merely a description of current operations and hence not a plan at all. Plan-making as discussed here involves actions undertaken in response to some kind of discrepancy between what is and what ought to be. If already known and currently operating systems were adequate to respond to the problem, then planning, of this kind at least, would not be called for.

One of the sources of confusion about the kind of planning needed for operationalizing high-quality in-service education is the failure to clearly define different kinds of operations being planned for and the different operational levels at which planning is required. In Chapter 4 the designing and the planning of training sessions are considered in considerable detail. The operations in focus are called sessions and the planning level is clearly at the *level of direct delivery of training services*. However, planning as discussed in this chapter is at a more remote level, at least one planning stage away from session-training plans. At least three levels of planning are needed in most school districts: (1) the overall or master plan (2) the project or program plan, and (3) the session plan. We need to be explicit in differentiating direct training plans from indirect plans even though they have much in common. Conrad (1973) refers to "strategic," "tactical," and "operational" planning as three such levels of plans.

The kind of operation being planned for is also important to distinguish. The distinction between maintenance operations and change operations is presented in Chapter 1. Harris (1985, 20–23) develops in greater detail elsewhere the notion that operations can range from being highly *tractive* to highly *dynamic* in their orientations. From a plan-making point of view, only the more clearly dynamic in-service education operations require detailed, creative planning with an elaborate plan as the product. Conversely, dynamic efforts to improve, depart, upgrade, and innovate cannot be realistic if routine, standard operating procedures are used.

Design Formats and Elements

Operations designing can be conceptualized as a two-dimensional problem. A plan for an ISE operation has both a format and a set of elements. The more tractive, less dynamic designs require little operations designing because standard (well-known and accepted) formats are utilized, and the elements are equally well known. The highly dynamic designs require much more elaborate and detailed plan-making because new formats and elements are being put together in a creative process. A new and different, unfamiliar operating reality is being projected for implementation. This involves more elaborate planning procedures for choosing, information processing, and designing. It also involves attending to the very difficult problems of communicating about the image of operations that has emerged to those not involved in its creation. Obviously, a broad base of involvement and continuous communications in the process of such planning would be well advised (Luke 1980).

A format is a structure for operating that clearly indicates sequences, responsibilities, and groupings as well as space, time, and material utilization. The "clinical supervision" cycles of Cogan (1973) and Anderson and Snyder (1981) illustrate a standard design. Such a format calls for the following:

1. *Preconference.* The teacher and supervisor confer to establish rapport, discuss concerns, and agree to an observation with appropriate, limited focus.

2. *Teaching and Classroom Observation.* The supervisor observes and records according to the agreed-upon focus. The teacher strives to teach as well as possible.
3. *Postobservation Analysis.* The supervisor analyzes observed and recorded data to provide more easily understood information for interpretation.
4. *Postobservation Conference.* The teacher and the supervisor confer. They study the analyzed observation data. They discuss possible interpretations. The teacher is encouraged to draw conclusions regarding the successful and not so successful elements in his or her teaching performance as observed.
5. *Replanning Session.* The teacher does this alone or meets with the supervisor again for teaching to secure further improvements. They agree on changes to be attempted as the focus for further observation.
6. *Reteaching and Observation.* New elements are introduced in terms of special concerns of the individual teacher, the unique set of interpersonal relationships involved between clinician and teacher, and situational elements within the context of the school. However, the format is standardized and requires little imaginative effort for its design.

Microteaching as described by Allen and Ryan (1969) and others offers another illustration of a format for in-service education that is not unlike that used for clinical supervision. The highly standard format includes use of minilessons, focused on a specific technique, videotape recording and collaborative observation and analysis of the lesson via the replay of the videotape. Even though objectives, content, and interpersonal elements may be unique in every situation, this too is a highly standard operation for in-service education. (See Chapter 6 for more detail on clinical and other individualized designs.)

Still a different format for in-service training is illustrated by what might be called cafeteria-type programs. Variations are found in many school systems. The format is usually sequenced and specified as follows:

1. A large diverse target population is designated.
2. A survey of interests in training topics, objectives, or activities is conducted.
3. An array of discrete training sessions is planned to match the most frequently identified interests.
4. The training sessions are scheduled, publicized, and arranged.
5. Individuals within the target population elect to attend and participate in one or more of the sessions.
6. The sequence is repeated periodically.

All the formats outlined above are cyclical in nature. They provide for a sequence that is relatively easy to replicate. Hence, if such training programs seem effective, replications permit serving other needs or increasing the size of the operation with only minor variations in plans. The simplicity and replicability of such standard cyclical formats undoubtedly accounts for their popularity. Unfortunately, such simplistic designs also may account for the ineffectiveness of many ISE programs, especially when used repetitively and indiscriminatingly for all kinds of purposes.

The elements of design are all of the numerous materials, activities, time frames, spaces, group arrangements, locations, facilities, and people that are brought together within a format to give character to the operation. An analogy from architectural design would distinguish the structural character of a house from the materials, appliances, and special features that make a house functionally what it is.

The format outlined for cafeteria-type programs retains the same structural features regardless of many elements that might greatly affect the quality of training experiences produced. For instance, outstanding leaders directing many of the sessions in contrast with amateurs' show-and-tell presentations would make a major difference. Many sessions linked to each other to provide for a set of skills in progression with schedules that promote the selection and use of such a training series would make for a different quality operation. Sufficient numbers of appropriate sessions to assure small groups when needed could make a difference in quality. A diagnostically powerful needs assessment process with incentives provided to encourage participants to select sessions in terms of carefully prioritized needs would enhance the productivity of the operation. Even a timing element that would assure session activities within the morning hours of a regular workday rather than in afternoons, evenings, or Saturdays when participants are tired or inconvenienced can substantially influence program quality.

The design of in-service education programs goes beyond the normal procedures of planning. Design involves creating structural formats that set the stage for more meaningful, purposeful, and satisfying experiences for participants. But attention to structure alone is rarely adequate. The creative, selective use of an array of elements—time, people, materials, groupings, spaces—that provide the best set of conditions for session activity is also essential.

Standardizing the Plan

The arguments for careful plan-making that give special attention to *operational designing* procedures are also strengthened at times by arguments for standardized practices. A plan that has been well developed, implemented, and evaluated can be *adapted* for use in other situations or on similar occasions. The heavy expenditures required for high-quality plan-making with creative designs are much more readily justified when the plan itself is so carefully developed as a set of documents and materials that others can use it for replicating the in-service programs without undertaking such extensive planning.

Simulations and games provide some of the best examples of detailed, carefully designed planning documents. In these particular kinds of training programs, a format is often developed that is extremely complex. Furthermore, elements in the form of playing materials, visuals, tests, scorecards, and many others are often developed with highly specialized purposes in mind. The whole game or simulation represents a creative endeavor that should be preserved and reemployed by many others. To facilitate such diffusion of plans, carefully developed manuals are provided along with a full array of materials for implementation.

Hence, the most exciting plan-making can contribute best, perhaps, to implementation of in-service programs in somewhat standardized ways. (See Chapter 7 for more detail on simulations and games.)

Self-instructional packets and other well-designed training kits are becoming increasingly common as products of special programs or projects. Like well-designed simulations and games, these packets and kits usually contain materials for participants to use that are of a variety of kinds—films, tapes, transparencies, and tests, for instance. These richly varied, often professionally produced elements are an integral part of a larger format of procedures and sequences carefully detailed in manuals or guides. Such kits offer opportunities for extended use of predesigned program plans with formats and elements that could not be readily developed in most school settings.

THE PHYSICAL FORMS OF PLANS

The physical forms and the essential parts of a program plan cannot be well represented in printed form. Unfortunately, any effort to illustrate a plan of complexity requires not only many pages but also numerous visual displays. Portions of an incomplete plan are included in this chapter and in Appendix B. In the pages that follow, some planning documents will be described in greater detail and illustrated, but the reader is cautioned that full understanding is likely to develop only as a result of participating in and using plans that have been developed by others. Unfortunately, only the commercially distributed kits, packets, games, and simulations are generally available. The other work of many creative designer-planners is not often reproduced. Most plans contain a narrative document including the usual list of objectives, schedules, budgets, and staffing plans. When they are master plans or strategic plans (Conrad, Brooks, and Fisher 1973), the documentation may be devoted largely to defining goals, specifying operational components, designating responsibilities, indicating strategies to be implemented, specifying target populations, setting schedules, and estimating costs in terms of time and money. Tactical or program plans usually include the same kind of narrative and tabular material. However, considerable additional detail is usually provided in terms of specifying objectives related to goals, describing the operating events, and detailing anticipated expenditures.

Both strategic and tactical plans specify some arrangements for evaluation. Again, the master plan of long-range character should clearly specify the outcomes to be used for evaluation and may leave details of instrumentation and data handling to be planned by others. Program plans, on the other hand, should clearly indicate outcomes and processes that are to be evaluated. Furthermore, at least a general description of instrumentation, data-gathering procedures, and feedback schedules should be included.

Depending on the specific format, the array of elements included, and the comprehensiveness of a plan, the physical document can vary from a small pamphlet to an enormous box of materials.

The Essential Parts

Most writers describe the essential steps of a planning process in such ways as to at least suggest the documentation. Steps or phases of planning are typically listed as: (1) identify needs; (2) determine specific target(s); (3) determine basic resources; (4) determine effective grouping or format; (5) present specific program plans; (6) complete preparation activities; (7) perform implementation; and (8) conduct evaluation. The first three of these eight steps can be translated fairly readily into a list of needs; a description of participants to be served; and some kind of tabulations or listings of time, space, staff, equipment, and money required. The specific forms in which the other steps are to appear in a plan are not so easily recognized.

Both Cunningham (1982) and Strother and Klus (1982) suggest some additional forms for documentation. They stress developing the data needed, which suggests that data displays showing needs-targets-objectives relationships might be useful. They suggest both establishing goals and clearly describing plans for achieving goals.

Certainly, the minimum essential features of a document representing a plan for in-service education should include the following:

1. A statement of the reason for undertaking the training (the problem or the need).
2. A description of the specific goal(s) and objectives selected as outcomes.

3. A detailing of the participants to be served and how or why they (groups or individuals) are related to goals and objectives.
4. A calendar of major events showing their relationship to objectives and participants.
5. A designation of the responsible person or group assigned to each major event.
6. A description of the operating characteristics—format and elements or strategy or approach—that is anticipated for each major event.
7. A list of resource requirements for each major event and one for overall coordination.
8. A description of the procedures for evaluating the plan providing timely feedback on the operation.
9. A schedule and list of procedures for monitoring the total program.

The challenge in documentation is not in getting these nine kinds of decisions made or ideas developed but in getting them on paper, chart, or other form so that the total plan clearly communicates, guides, and facilitates. An extensive narrative may be necessary to make certain parts of the plan explicit and clear, but such narratives tend not to be much used in the implementing. Outlines, charts, graphs, tables, checklists, and other graphics with sufficient narration to assure clarity of meaning and intended use are often desirable. (See Appendix C for programming criteria in detail.)

Dilemma: Too Much or Too Little Detail

An alert reader might easily react to the ideas and illustrations presented here as calling for too much structure. Still another alert reader might complain of too little specific detail. Both concerns are real and legitimate. To be sure, most planning documentation suffers from one or both of these ailments. Within the same plan, objectives may be specified with almost ridiculous detail, while staff assignments, activity descriptions, or grouping arrangements are nebulous or nonexistent. Planners tend, of course, to present vividly what they know best and to neglect other details. Unfortunately, this often leads to plans that are not very useful.

Robert F. Mager (1968) is well known for making complex things simple to learn. He suggests that a plan needs to answer only three questions:

1. Where are we going?
2. How shall we get there?
3. How will we know we've arrived?

Obviously, these are the very *core* questions a plan must address, but they are only a beginning.

It is popular to represent a plan by the display of a systems diagram with elaborate sequences of rectangles neatly labeled "steps," including: 1.0, identify problem; 2.0, determine alternatives; 3.0, select strategy; 4.0, implement; and so on. Each of these rectangles is logically related to every other one. But the dilemma for the planner-designer-user is that little detail is provided regarding *within rectangle* events.

There appears to this writer to be no acceptable substitute for *maximizing detail*. The details should avoid verbosity. Flexibility should be provided for by detailing alternatives and backup systems. The awesomeness of a bulky, voluminous document with a variety of media and separate component plans can be overcome by properly structured introductory material. When plans are sketchy, there is reason to believe that the planning was also limited.

BRIDGING FROM PLAN TO OPERATIONS

Implementation is widely viewed as so simple and so automatic that it will follow from planning without being planned. Such is rarely the case with high-quality in-service education. As we deal with the implementation of plans for creating highly stimulating learning experiences for mature personnel, that is no routine affair (Petrosky 1986).

A well-developed in-service education plan will clearly and explicitly guide implementation. This is a notion closely related to the problem of *teaching for transfer*. We cannot assume that new knowledge and skill learned in one context will transfer to another. Similarly, we cannot assume that a carefully detailed set of abstract representations of training will in fact become translated into operating reality. The intellectual power that is applied to create images of events that might be tends to blind planners to the fact that images are not reality. Translations are required.

A planning document must include very specific suggestions and/or directions on who is to do what, with whom, using what procedures or materials in what sequence, and within what time frame. The PERT procedures applied to education by Cook (1966) have great utility in this portion of the plan. The Gantt chart is one of the oldest management tools for guiding implementations of programs. (It is illustrated in Exhibit 9–4.) It is of special utility when time allocations are critical and an array of related components need coordination.

The more fascinating management tools should not blind planners to the indispensable use of a master schedule with carefully determined target dates. For in-service planning purposes, the kind of schedule that reflects time, space, and personnel relationships can be especially useful to avoid confusion and assure the smooth flow of activities over time, with flexibility for participants to make individual decisions.

Flowcharts are sometimes utilized to graphically depict the flow of major events. Since they lack time-line designations, flowcharts are not too helpful in monitoring. Most flowcharts are a simple series of rectangles and arrows that show sequences of major events but little more. They look impressive to the neophyte, but they add little detail. They may assist with communication in an overview fashion. (See Exhibit 9–3.)

A Planning Checklist

Plans for implementation can include more than detailed assignments, schedules, and graphic aids. Specific provisions for monitoring ongoing events should be included in plans for implementation. Such a monitoring plan should identify *critical events* associated with each major goal or objective and/or training components. Such critical events can become the basis for constructing a checklist for observers to use in monitoring. Furthermore, these critical events can be focused upon as items in process evaluation instruments for use during the operation of a program.

The checklist for plan review shown in Exhibit 9–2 provides a convenient listing of important components of a plan. When properly documented, in whatever form, the formal plan should provide clear evidence that each kind of information is included. Such a checklist can be useful as a guide in reviewing a plan prior to final preparation. It can also be useful as a guide to planners in the preparation process. Such detailed analysis might be especially important when plans are being selected on a competitive basis. However, for those attempting to refine their skill in plan-making, the more detailed criteria can be used diagnostically as well. (See Appendix C.)

The Flowchart

An illustrative flowchart is included here as Exhibit 9–3. It belongs as a part of one of the displays in a comprehensive plan. This is a flowchart for a single major component of a larger in-service plan. It represents only one year of a five-year plan.

This chart reads from top to bottom. Some charts read from left to right. The events or classes of events are shown as rectangles and are roughly sequenced from top to bottom as shown by the connecting arrows. The approximate sequence of events is further emphasized by the letters assigned to each rectangle. Actually, the letters add to the chart primarily by providing a symbol to identify each rectangle of events.

Parallel rectangles indicate simultaneous classes or sets of events. For instance, while d, e, f, g, and h follow each other, i, j, k, and p are clearly shown as events or sets of events that are in progress during the same time span. Arrows from i to k, from j to l, and from o to p all denote sequential

EXHIBIT 9–2. Checklist for Reviewing an In-Service Education Program Plan

I. *Goal Specification*
_____ A. A problem of importance is clearly described.
_____ B. A need for training is clearly designated.
_____ C. Long-range outcomes are defined.
_____ D. Specific goals and related major objectives are specified.

II. *Strategy*
_____ E. The overall training strategy is clearly developed.
_____ F. Influences or conditions conducive to (or inhibiting) the strategy are indicated.
_____ G. Cautions and limitations of the strategy are made explicit.

III. *Design*
_____ H. A series of clearly designated sessions is sequenced.
_____ I. The various sessions are clearly related to specific goals and/or major objectives.
_____ J. The various sessions are related to clients to differentiate experiences.
_____ K. Resources required for each session are designated.
_____ L. Logistics relating time, space, people, and materials to each other have been described.

IV. *Implementation*
_____ M. Responsibilities for each major component of the program have been assigned.
_____ N. Schedules of events and their coordinate relationships have been carefully detailed.
_____ O. Procedures for monitoring and providing corrective feedback are described.
_____ P. Provisions have been made for detailed planning, training, and orientation activities for leadership personnel.
_____ Q. Communications have been prepared to use in informing all persons involved.

V. *Evaluation*
_____ R. Instrumentation and procedures for gathering data on the program in operation are available.
_____ S. Analytical procedures have been described for processing data.
_____ T. Procedures for utilizing evaluation findings are designated.

VI. *Material*
_____ U. Materials to be utilized throughout the program are fully developed and ready for use.
_____ V. Facilities and equipment to be required are listed and/or described.
_____ W. Resource lists of materials and equipment that might be useful are provided.
_____ X. Facilities arrangements that are to be required (or are desirable) are described.

VII. *Other*
_____ Y.
_____ Z.

EXHIBIT 9-3. Flowchart for Component I: In-Service Education for Observing and Analyzing Classroom Practices

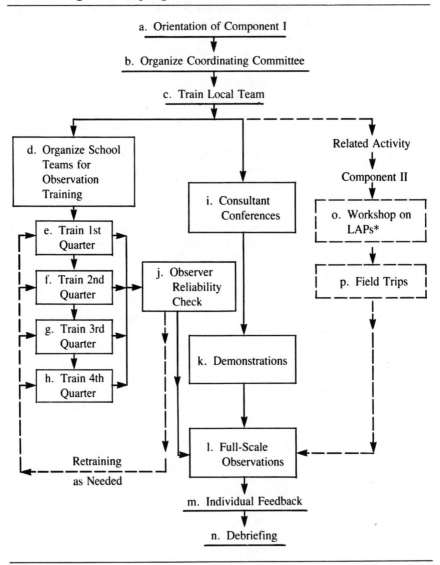

*Learning activity packets.

relationships even though the timing is only crudely indicated on the chart and the specific character of the relationship is not indicated.

A series of *arrows* as shown from e, f, g and h to j can be interpreted in various ways. It is intended to mean that the reliability checking of trainees (j) occurs following each of the other four sets of events. It could, of course, mean that j is continuously in operation, but that was not intended.

Dotted lines are used on this flowchart to indicate two different relationships, so they are labeled for explanatory purposes. Dotted lines from j to e, and f, g and h indicate that the reliability check may lead to retraining or more training that would dictate repeated or continued events in the training rectangles (e through h). Dotted lines leading to o and p are used to indicate that these are events that are associated with, or related to, another in-service component but are significantly related to this one and hence are being shown.

A flowchart of this type is quite informative. It does indicate the main sets or classes of events that are to be implemented. It indicates the sequences and some of the relationships planned. What such a flowchart *does not* communicate is also important to consider. Sequences are roughly shown, but specfic time frames or target dates are *not* shown. Relationships between classes of events (rectangles) are only suggested; they are not clearly specified. For instance, an arrow from e to j, if specified more explicitly, is intended to mean that only after a full series of training activities should the first group of trainees be checked for interobserver reliability. However, the arrow from i to k means something quite different. Reference to the details of the plans reveals that this arrow simply means that pre- and post-observation conferences with observer trainees and those being observed is desirable at an early stage in the operation so that ideas from those conferences can be used to plan and guide field trips and demonstrations.

As the foregoing explanation of meanings of arrows indicates, a flowchart's greatest limitation is its lack of specificity about the relationships, sequences, and events within rectangles. This is a limitation of all flowcharts and also of systems diagrams as used, for instance, in Chapter 10. If the plan-maker tries to add details, include a time line, and show sequences more precisely, what emerges is a very complex chart that loses its graphic simplicity. If we try to extend a chart like this to include a second or third year, it becomes a large display and requires special handling as a wall chart or foldout exhibit.

The distinctions between a flowchart and a *systems diagram* should be carefully *noted*. The two look much alike and are sometimes confused with each other. In fact, a most confusing practice is to corrupt a systems diagram so it is not clearly in either form. Systems diagrams employ very explicit symbols and rules regarding arrows, lines, and rectangle placements. Silvern (1972) offers the reader a very useful guide to these techniques. These rules do not apply to flowcharts; hence, the latter is a less precise tool in some ways but is perhaps more useful in providing a vivid overview of major events in an operation, especially when sequencing is important.

The Gantt Chart

One of the early graphic display tools for planning was developed for industrial production operations. In a rather old book, Wallace Clark reviews the origins of the Gantt chart, named after its originator, and provides detailed illustrations for using the chart in business and industry. In educational planning, the Gantt chart has had a rebirth of use, but in a corrupted form that greatly limits the utility of the technique.

In Exhibit 9–4, a Gantt chart is presented from a plan. The Gantt illustrates the careful plan for sequencing and timing each of an array of specific operations. While only two out of four components of a total in-service education plan are shown, the utility and the unique character of the Gantt chart can be appreciated if the reader will study this exhibit carefully.

The Gantt chart is not a record of what *was* done. The main purposes have to do with making a plan and guiding actions for implementation. Every distinctive operation is represented as a planned and explict time frame. Each operation appears as a simple bracket on a time line. Since all brackets are shown on the same chart with the same time line, a set of time relationships between all operations is graphically and precisely shown. In studying Exhibit 9–4, the plan-maker begins to appreciate the unique and explicit contributions the Gantt chart can make both to plan-making and to implementing.

The symbols for the Gantt chart are very important. The simple bracket is the basic symbol. It shows the time frame for each operation, indicating start-and-stop times *according to plan*. A symbol is superimposed on the bracket to show when the operation *actually* started. *Progress* toward completion of the operation is shown by a heavy line along the top of each bracket. This heavy line is simply extended periodically to show progress at any given *checkpoint* along the time line. The *termination* of an operation is shown by a special symbol superimposed on the bracket at the point on the time line when the operation *actually ended*.

To illustrate the communications power of the Gantt chart, the numbered reference points on Exhibit 9–4 have been added. Notice the bracket on line ID opposite the operation "Full-scale observations and feedback." This is the original plan for a time frame for this operation. It indicates a starting date of March 10 and an ending date of April 25. Notice now the (1) below the bracket for operation IA. This bracket has been darkened to show starting on time in August, continuing in operation through to

EXHIBIT 9–4. Gantt Chart for In-Service Education: Individualizing Instruction Program

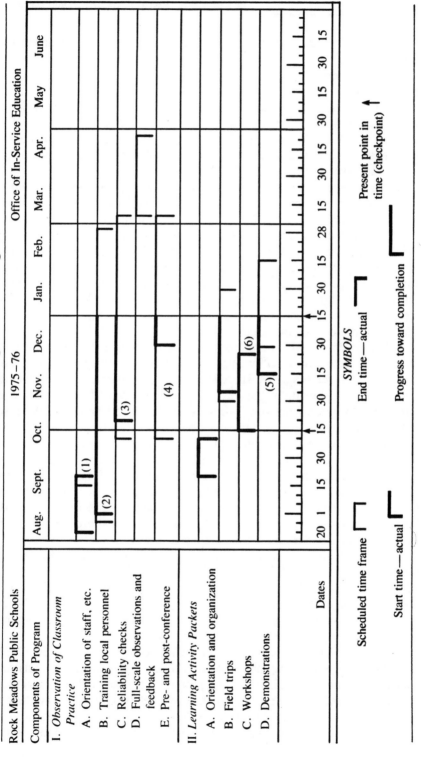

Rock Meadows Public Schools · 1975–76 · Office of In-Service Education

Components of Program	Dates
I. *Observation of Classroom Practice*	
A. Orientation of staff, etc.	(1)
B. Training local personnel	(2)
C. Reliability checks	(3)
D. Full-scale observations and feedback	(4)
E. Pre- and post-conference	
II. *Learning Activity Packets*	
A. Orientation and organization	
B. Field trips	
C. Workshops	(6)
D. Demonstrations	(5)

Dates: Aug. 20 1 — Sept. 15 30 — Oct. 15 30 — Nov. 15 30 — Dec. 15 30 — Jan. 15 30 — Feb. 15 28 — Mar. 15 30 — Apr. 15 30 — May 15 30 — June 15

SYMBOLS

Scheduled time frame

Start time—actual

End time—actual

Progress toward completion

Present point in time (checkpoint)

207

about September 20, somewhat past the September 15 date planned for completion.

Another interpretation is illustrated by reference (2). Notice that the planned start was about August 25, but the actual start was delayed until September 1. A similar delay is shown by reference (3) and a longer delay by reference (4). In contrast, notice that operation IIA started and ended right on schedule. But look at IIC; reference (6) indicates that this operation began on time and ended *early*, ahead of plan. Conversely, operation IID started ahead of schedule.

The uniqueness of the Gantt chart for use in implementing operations according to plan is emphasized by the use of symbols that clearly show progress toward scheduled target dates. Implementation is also emphasized by this technique because the chart is developed as part of the plan, but then must be utilized periodically *during* implementation. In effect, it is a monitoring device and encourages *action* related to plans, but it also encourages use of the plan to guide and coordinate different operations. The fact that all brackets are unchanged from December 15 forward simply means that the last periodic review was on that date, shown by the last triangle at the bottom on the time line.

Relationships among operations are shown by the display of all symbols on a single time line. Relationships are shown only with respect to time, however. Staff relationships, shared resources, or other interdependencies are clearly not shown. In this respect, the Gantt chart fails to offer one advantage the PERT network provides as shown in Chapter 4. Because only time-sequence relationships are shown by the Gantt, it has its greatest utility when several operations (1) are highly independent of each other, (2) need to be sequenced in relation to each other, and (3) are in need of very careful timing. Such conditions do not prevail in all in-service program-planning situations. The Gantt chart may not be superior to a carefully developed schedule if only sequencing is a concern. The PERT network has advantages over Gantt if completion dates are most crucial and inter-dependencies are more numerous among operations.

Time and timing are always critical considerations in in-service education program planning. Therefore, the Gantt chart has potential as one of several kinds of displays. For instance, in a training series in which participants are sequenced from one session and space to another and staff have shared responsibilities, plans for careful timing and sequencing are so important that the Gantt chart could be most helpful.

The illustrations of flowcharts and the Gantt chart, along with the PERT network and systems diagrams shown in other chapters, should assist in-service education planners in selecting a variety of graphic displays. A plan must, of course, contain narrations depicting needs, objectives, activities, people, and other resources. Even extended narratives in the form of scenarios are often quite useful. But graphic displays are especially useful in allowing for alternative ways of conveying meaning to planners, implementers, participants, and evaluators alike. Obviously, no one display can do a complete job. An array of displays is often advisable, and using different kinds is undoubtedly to be desired.

SUMMARY

Programmatic planning is discussed here as systematic process resulting in documents that give form to and guide implementation. Systematic planning is stressed to assure clear and realistic projections, as well as to allow for a fully participatory process.

Some critics of planning may argue that it destroys creative efforts and depresses spontaneity. Due caution should be exercised to prevent such effects. The dynamics of the planning process can maximize the creative contributions of those involved. Since planning is essentially a creative, imagining process, procedures should be highly stimulating and emphasize more than just pedestrian problem solving.

This chapter has stressed some of the physical forms which plans may take. Process cannot be all. A set of documents should emerge that clearly communicates what the planners have as their vision. Schedules, scenarios, checklists, flowcharts, and so on are but alternative ways of conveying intentions.

STUDY SOURCES

Cline, Daniel. 1984. "Achieving Quality and Relevance in In-Service Teacher Education: Where Are We?" *Teacher Education and Special Education* 7 (Fall): 199–208.
  Case studies of 97 federally funded regular education ISE training projects were studied. The author reports on key findings regarding local/state planning and collaboration, and emphasizes field-based programs.

Cunningham, William G. 1982. *Systematic Planning for Educational Change.* Palo Alto, Calif.: Mayfield Publishing Company.
  A very practical yet thoughtful treatment of the relationships between planning and change process in schools. The two initial chapters focus on planning process, and distinguish between operational and strategic planning. Part 2 presents 9 chapters dealing in considerable detail with specific tools and techniques for use in planning documentation.

Gay, Geneva. 1980. "Conceptual Models of the Curriculum-Planning Process." Chap. 7 in *Considered Action for Curriculum Improvement,* ed. A. W. Foshay. Alexandria, Va.: Association for Supervision and Curriculum Development.

While the focus of the monograph is curriculum planning, it relates to in-service education in a variety of ways. Gay identifies and discusses various planning models—academic, experiential, technical, and pragmatic. In her detailed description of the technical model (pp. 131–36), she reviews a variety of techniques associated with systems approaches. Needs assessment, goal setting, and operationalization are clarified.

Georgia Department of Education. 1980. *Planning Education Improvement*. Atlanta, Ga.: Research and Development Utilization Project, Department of Education.
A kit for promoting improved planning contains detailed instructions, checklists, charts, and other materials for local use in project planning.

Harris, Ben M. 1985. *Supervisory Behavior in Education*. 3d ed. Englewood Cliffs, N.J.: Prentice-Hall, Inc.
Chapters 2, 3, and 5 provide insightful discussions of various problems and approaches to improving instruction. Chapter 2, "Dynamics of Supervisory Behavior," emphasizes approaches to change, the importance of planning, leadership, and the dynamics of the change process. Chapter 3 details systems models for organizing for a variety of services. Chapter 5, "Program Implementing Strategies," is useful in discussing various training strategies that imply diverse organizational and planning requirements.

Hasazi, Susan E. 1983. *Vocational Education for the Handicapped: Perspectives on In-Service Personnel Development*. Personnel Development Series, Doc. 6. Washington, D.C.: Division of Personnel Preparation, Office of Special Education and Rehabilitative Services. ERIC ED 224 939
A monograph covering a wide array of issues relating to policy, delivery systems, and planning. Chapter 2 discusses specific planning models. Chapter 3 focuses on implementation.

Hite, Herbert, and Pat McIntyre. 1980. *Planning for In-Service Education (Revised): A Resource Guide*. Washington, D.C.: Office of Education, Teacher Corps. ERIC ED 185 031
A resource guide based on Teacher Corps pilot projects. Guidelines for developing comprehensive plans are proposed. Governance structures are advocated. Management plan illustrations are given along with sample forms for needs assessments.

Hutson, Harry M., Jr. 1981. "In-Service Best Practices: The Learnings of General Education." *Journal of Research and Development in Education* 14 (Winter): 1–10.
While emphasizing 15 "best" practices, the author identifies collaboration, incentives, and the support and use of outside consultants. The distinctions between "procedural," "substantive," and conceptual domains related to planning offer worthwhile insights. The author also warns against programs that reflect assumptions of the "deficit model," and against trying to substitute "democratic" process for logic and expertise.

Mertens, S. K., and S. J. Yarger. 1981. *Teacher Centers in Action*. New York: Syracuse Area Teacher Center.

A report on the systematic study of 37 nationally sponsored teacher centers. While basic concepts underlying these organizations were not seriously challenged, the study does give further support to many principles that seem generally applicable to any in-service education delivery system.

Performance Learning Systems. 1986. *We Can Show You the Secrets of Creating a Championship Teaching Staff.* Emerson, N.J.: Performance Learning Systems, Inc.

This is a commercial brochure depicting one of many in-service program delivery services offered by private consulting firms. In this instance, an array of workshops and programs is offered.

Strother, George B., and John P. Klus. 1982. *Administration of Continuing Education.* Belmont, Calif.: Wadsworth Publishing Company.

A comprehensive sourcebook that gives special attention to program planning in chapter 3. Tools for effective planning are discussed, including the use of committees, delphi technique, Gantt charts, and the critical path method.

Wood, Fred H., S. R. Thompson, and Frances Russell. 1981. "Designing Effective Staff Development Programs." In *Staff Development/Organization Development,* ed. Betty Dillon-Peterson. Alexandria, Va.: Association for Supervision and Curriculum Development.

A carefully detailed statement of design considerations related to program planning. The authors avoid promoting a particular model or technique, offering instead a useful discussion of widely varying perspectives.

10.

Operating Systems

INTRODUCTION

The operation of a system or systems providing for the diverse in-service training needs of a school requires more than plans, guiding principles, and good intentions. As suggested in the previous chapter, a plan must lead to effective implementation that in fact *delivers* appropriate training experiences, according to needs, in a timely and ongoing fashion. This chapter focuses on both design and implementation procedures within a policy framework.

The importance of policy to give status, direction, and support to continuing efforts has been neglected and needs more attention. Christian's (1981) study of thirty-one school improvement programs has demonstrated the importance of board and superintendent commitments as instrumental to success. Within policy guidelines, delivery systems must be designed that provide training according to plan. System design relates general principles to the realities of assuring effective kinds and varieties of training activities (Almanza 1980; Cavender 1986; Hagen 1981; and Lozano 1980).

Last, but surely not least, this chapter addresses staffing and organizing for delivery. It is curious how many state and local school jurisdictions, giving vocal and even legal support to in-service education, find no need to consider staff requirements or ways of organizing the systems (Dillon 1976).

STATE POLICY

The design and strategic planning of in-service education calls into operation a major set of tasks that must be guided by policy provisions. Because ISE intervenes in people's lives, it is a sensitive area of policy. Because

ISE is concerned with changing the operation of schools, it is a crucial area of policy. Because ISE is costly, it cannot command resources without policy commitment.

Prior to 1980 there was little policy in most school settings guiding in-service education (Geffert et al. 1976). Supporting legal structures for ISE are present in nearly every state in the United States in one form or another; however, they tend to vary widely among states (Washington State Department of Education 1981; Smith 1981; Florida State Department of Education 1987). Certain practices and related operating structures have evolved and become established within many educational organizations, simply because of the obvious need and the freedom of action permitted by law or policy. Ideally, a clear mandate for in-service programs will be provided by state law, legal precedents, traditions, local policy statements, and implementing regulations, including contract provisions with individual staff members (and bargaining units, if such are officially recognized).

In addition to a clear mandate for in-service education as a part of the educational operation, resources should be clearly designated. Staff, money, and time for training are resources that need to be routinely provided as the basis for program organizing and directing. However, in many situations, such conditions do not prevail, and important tasks of organizing and directing involve policy developing, budget revising, and staffing for support of in-service programs.

The four parts specified in these suggestions for state law are illustrative of the appropriate *functions* of the state as distinguished from local-level responsibilities. The four parts include comprehensive state planning; creating supplementary educational service organizations; facilitating training programs and innovations; and funding local, regional, and other operations. These are hardly all-inclusive possibilities for state law, but they do reflect a fairly comprehensive view of the state function that allows for leadership through initiation, coordination, facilitation, and evaluation without resorting to control as the primary element of state influence.

The program development and improvement fund proposed under part D of Exhibit 10–1 is of crucial importance for a variety of reasons. The creation of a *fund* from which in-service education programs can be financed is, of course, essential to the kind of ISE program development being advocated throughout this book. Other provisions of part D are uniquely important, too! The level of funding is expressed as 5 percent of total personnel costs rather than as a dollar amount. This has the obvious advantage of allowing for inflationary effects and for growth or decline in personnel to be served. Less obvious is the fact that such a provision eliminates the need for repeated, frequent adjustments that could threaten the entire program from time to time. Another important feature of such provisions includes flexible rather than rigid allocations, so that the purpose of equal educational opportunity can in fact be served. Still another feature is the permissive allocation of monies from this fund for curriculum development, evaluation, and other staff development in recognition that these developmental tasks must often be integrated or closely associated with each other for improvements to come about.

State Legal Framework

There is a growing and urgent need for a legal framework for in-service education in many states that is more comprehensive and more internally consistent than the present statutes. Some states already having a variety of provisions for funding, recertification, accreditation, and teacher evaluation still fail to deal with in-service education as a total program of major importance. The complexity and diversity of the organizational arrangements required for high-quality delivery of ISE on a continuous basis are simply neither clearly recognized nor well reflected in many state statutes. The Washington (1981) and California (1981) state efforts to provide coordination services are, however, promising developments in this regard. Florida, a leader in state-level innovations relating to in-service education, has recently added provisions for using in-service programs for recertification purposes to already existing requirements for local master plans (Florida State Department of Education, 1987). Most state policy, however, is still limited and fragmented.

Suggestions for State Law

Suggestions to guide legislative action for ISE are shown in Exhibit 10–1. These are highlights of major features of desired legislation. Suggestions for law such as these are not intended as a blueprint. They are intended, however, as an educator's conception of what might be translated into legislative form with due regard for differing circumstances in different states.

The purpose expressed in law by a legislature sets the tone for all provisions that follow and for policies and regulations that are later formulated. Exhibit 10–1 gives emphasis to four goals or purposes: (1) equality of educational opportunity, (2) continuous improvement, (3) performance changes, and (4) ISE for all personnel. Any such law should give clarity to the responsibilities of the local boards and their staffs.

LOCAL DISTRICT POLICY

Local district policy regarding in-service education tends to be nonexistent or fragmentary in most school systems. This is true in spite of the widespread delegation of authority by state law or policy to local school districts. In their study of six school systems of considerable diversity, Sealy

EXHIBIT 10–1. Abstract of Suggestions for State Law for In-Service Education

Purpose

To assure quality educational opportunity for all children and youth by promoting continuous improvement of personnel performance on the job.

Part A: The Comprehensive State Program. Provides authority for state board policy and guidelines. Defines responsibilities of local boards of education for providing in-service education. Creates a state office for coordination and planning. Creates a state advisory council. Requires a statewide needs study within each five-year period.

Part B: Supplementary Educational Services Program. Requires the creation of regional organizations to supplement local district programs. Defines these supplementary services. Provides for diverse organizational arrangements and for democratic control.

Part C: Leadership Training and Innovations Program. Authorizes the state board of education to plan for leadership training throughout the state to assure competent personnel to implement in-service education programs. Provides for the identification, funding, dissemination, and evaluation of innovative approaches to in-service education to improve practices throughout the state.

Part D: Instructional Program Development and Improvement Fund. Creates a separate state fund for in-service education and related instructional support services. Specifies the level of funding for these services at 5 percent of the personnel costs of the schools of the state. Specifies allocations to local districts, supplementary educational service organizations, and other agencies. Defines and delimits purposes for which funds may be allocated.

and Dillon (1976) found not a single one with board policy on in-service education. The absence of such policy is made more interesting by the rapid growth of teacher centers, service centers, and other quasi-legal or unofficial agencies that are in effect developing their own policies for and with local personnel.

In the past decade, school districts have been adopting policy statements relating to in-service education as a part of their plans for teacher evaluation and supervision of instruction. The ASCD National Commission on Instructional Supervision (1986) reported on such developments in a survey catalog. The need for local policy for such programs in their own right clearly persists.

The Need for Policy

If in-service education is to be related to the job, is to be responsive to institutional as well as individual staff needs, is to be coordinated with other program development efforts, is to be a commitment of the school system, and is to use local resources, then local board policy is essential. Effective assumption of local responsibility without policy guidelines cannot be anticipated.

The importance of local board policy that clearly reflects commitments is stressed by McLaughlin and Berman in their analysis of federal programs supporting or promoting educational change (1977). They point to the "hodgepodge" that is typically staff development as a serious deterrent to change. They found "successful" projects operating as "staff development projects," and warned that "institutional support from administrators" is essential. But administrators cannot be expected to initiate, command resources, and give priority to in-service education in the absence of policy. A study by Christian clearly supports the notion that "commitment by school officials" is essential to school improvement efforts (1981).

A very brief yet well formulated local district policy is shown in Exhibit 10–2. The several specific provisions make this policy relatively comprehensive and conveys, as policies should, the commitment and intent of the Board. See Appendix F for still another illustration of policy statements.

Policy Guidelines

Since little exists to guide educators or school board members in developing local policy, it might be appropriate to consider the statements of principles presented previously in this chapter. Some of those speak to policy at nearly any level, but they can nonetheless be viewed from a local perspective. Florida's Dade County Board of Education can be used to illustrate a fully developed policy. Exhibit 10–2 excerpts the main sections from the policy statements of that school system.

Five kinds of intents need to be specified in a policy that will clearly resolve issues and still offer guidelines for implementing high-quality programs. Such intents include the following:

1. *Expectations of Improvement.* The policy must clearly indicate the expectations that all personnel will seek to improve their performance.
2. *Provision of Opportunities.* The policy must clearly indicate responsibility for providing plans and programs for personnel growth for all.
3. *Personalized Growth Process.* The policy clearly recognizes the right of personnel to personalized treatment in planning and implementation of growth activities.
4. *Allocation of Resources.* The policy clearly indicates the sources and general magnitude of resources (funds, staff, time) to be allocated for programs of personnel growth.
5. *Continuity and Flexibility in Programming.* The policy provides for the use of allocated resources in ways that assure the appropriate growth activities, offered to selected individuals, at the most opportune time, under the most suitable conditions for maximum growth.

EXHIBIT 10–2. Excerpts from a Board Policy

Staff Development Programs

The Board recognizes the need to provide a comprehensive staff development program for the personnel of the Dade County Public Schools. The Board considers staff development as the educational support service designed to improve and review the competencies of personnel in the school system so that they may demonstrate the knowledge, skills, and attitudes necessary for effective performance of their assigned duties or duties to be assigned.

The Master Plan for Inservice Education is prepared according to state specifications. It is the district plan that provides personnel in this school system with the criteria for planning, implementing and evaluating staff development programs.

Section I	contains state and district requirements.
Section II	contains components leading to certificate renewal.
Section III	contains components not leading to certificate renewal.
Section IV	contains the Beginning Teacher Program Plan.
Section V	contains the Summer Inservice Institute Plan.

Sections IV and its addendum of the district's *Master Plan for Inservice Education 1984–1989* are incorporated by reference in this Board Rule and are a part hereof.

Dade County Public Schools, Miami, Florida. Board Policy as amended 6/24/87. Used with permission.

A policy statement that is carefully drawn should make commitments to guide school administrators and others in planning and implementing programs of high quality with relatively little dissonance or misunderstanding regarding the basic issues involved. (See Appendix F.)

Priority Setting

Several sources of information are utilized to provide clear guidelines for giving priority to in-service programs in a given situation. Assuming that all possible programs cannot be accommodated, selections must be made and priorities assigned. Sources of information include the following:

1. *Policy provisions:* laws, court decisions, contract provisions, local board policy, and so on.
2. *Program evaluations:* accreditation reports, program analyses, testing data, public concerns, and so on.
3. *Individual evaluations:* classroom observation reports, personnel records, needs assessment, and so on.
4. *Program proposals:* new programs, changes in organizational arrangements, community changes.

One of the major responsibilities related to program management involves organizing and implementing procedures whereby priorities for in-service education are established in an orderly fashion. Much emphasis has been given to the importance of *needs assessment*.

The term "needs assessment" has many connotations, ranging from diagnosing individual staff members' needs to assure individually relevant in-service activities to community opinion analysis, student achievement testing, to selecting in-service objectives to be emphasized. For administrative and supervisory personnel responsible for in-service programs, the key is *not* to be found in any single assessment system, review committee procedure, or survey of opinions of community or staff. A set of procedures is developed in which a responsible and representative body carefully reviews a variety of kinds of relevant information and selects priorities that represent informed professional judgments about the best use of limited resources for improving instruction. In the small-town setting, these procedures may be largely implemented by a single "Staff Development Council" with principals, teacher representatives, and special program directors comprising the group (Kilgore, 1984). In larger systems with more diversity in programming, a staff development council may be supplemented by school-level committees, special advisory committees, project teams, teacher center councils, regional service center boards, and teacher association committees (Wood, Thompson, and Russell 1981).

Identifying Major Programs

A clearly defined program provides the basis for translating long-range goals into objectives, delegating responsibilities, and operationalizing training in response to policy and priority. Special projects often operate under such arrangements, but when they emerge under the influence of outside funding, they tend to reflect special interests better than prioritized needs and are often *not* a part of a coordinated system for in-service education. Officials directing in-service operations for a system need to struggle constantly to keep special-interest programming integrated into the overall plans, policies, and priorities of the larger organization. In recent years state-mandated requirements represented the most serious threats to sound planning (Smith 1981).

A program can be defined in many ways. One way to think about and clearly designate programs is to specify the following characteristics:

1. High-priority training goal(s) associated with ideals of the organization are clearly specified.

2. An extended time frame is designated to adequately provide a life span necessary for goal attainment.
3. A target group is identified whose on-the-job responsibilities make many of them likely participants for training related to the goals designated.
4. Staff member(s) are clearly designated as responsible for the training operations.
5. A plan of action for implementing training activities and evaluating outcomes is in evidence.
6. Resources are allocated for implementing the plan.

These six characteristics of *programs* are not unlike those specified to define a *session*. Certain distinctions are important, however. A program focuses on long-range or intermediate-range goals, not on specific objectives of a short-term character. Accordingly, the time frame tends to be quite long—weeks, months, or years—in contrast with only a few hours or a day. Planning characteristics at this level of programming tend to be strategic and logistical rather than tactical as in session plans. These terms are used here to distinguish between plans that must be given much more detailed expression by the individuals actually leading the training sessions from those plans that specify selected goals, relate them to target groups, identify strategies, arrange for scheduling and resource allocating, delegate further planning, and design for evaluating.

Wide latitude is still provided for programs to be identified and structured on the basis of a very limited or a very extended operation. If a limited goal is defined, a short time frame provided, and a small target group designated, a program may well be little more than a series of sessions. Such limited, or "special," programs are in fact often structured and may be quite appropriate ways of responding to certain needs. Unfortunately, when programs are repeatedly characterized in this way, it may reflect lack of effective leadership in planning and organizing. Such ad hoc programs tend to be numerous when priorities are not carefully established, when staff in charge are reactive rather than proactive, and when crises dictate operations.

At the other extreme, programs can be defined so broadly and with such long time frames that they become a bureaucratic unit within the larger organization. These become permanent organizations with their own staffs, traditions, resources, and policies. They manufacture their own priorities out of context with the larger operation. Since they have permanent staff members, traditions, clearly developed operating procedures, and evidence of past success, they can be strong advocates for self-perpetuation. New priorities have little chance of competing with such well-organized interest groups.

Organizing Programs

Programs should be structured to avoid the evils of both *ad hocracy* and *bureaucracy*. Every program should have clearly attainable, specific goals, not vague missions or ideals alone. A time frame of proper length for accomplishing goals should be clearly specified and staff resources allocated accordingly. In addition to normal monitoring of the operation from within and without the program, a full-scale review should be provided at least once during the designated life of each program. The review should be conducted to determine *when* the program should be terminated and how; *not if* it should be terminated. Obviously, by terminating programs, resources are released for reallocation to new, higher priorities.

These suggestions for maintaining flexibility in implementing in-service programs, so as to be responsive to needs and priorities, are based upon concepts of management by objective (MBO). These concepts have their greatest validity in *temporary systems* as distinguished from *continuous systems*. When an organization and its staff is assigned responsibility for continuous response to inputs in efforts to produce a continuous flow of outcomes, a system is developed that has rather regularized procedures. In fact, such systems become so regularized and their procedures so standardized that traditions and habit patterns tend to dominate decision making. They become unresponsive to changing conditions that might warrant changes in procedures. Even so, when held responsible for continuous production, regularized procedures are essential, and continuous systems emerge.

In-service education shares with virtually all developmental operations (curriculum development, materials development, staffing, and evaluation) in schools and colleges the distinction of being a *discontinuous operation*. Gant, Smith, and Hansen (1977) refer to them as "temporary systems." Their virtue is found in being able to respond to changing priorities, to concentrate resources for short time periods on urgent or difficult problems, to avoid the constraints of traditions, to "borrow" human talents otherwise unavailable, and to attend to change rather than to maintenance. The price the organization must pay for these virtues is loss of *direct productivity* (Harris et al. 1985) from these resources allocated to change process. To be sure, these activities—in-service education and others—directed by such temporary programs will be *indirectly* productive. Students will learn more or more appropriately because teachers and others have learned to perform better. But in the short run, temporary systems are always under attack, being challenged and often deprived of resources because they are not seen as directly productive.

Because continuous systems produce and temporary systems *seem* not to do so, the latter always face a precarious existence. The natural tendency is to become more permanent, less temporary! Herein lies the danger of losing all the special advantages of being temporary for the sake of greater security, more acceptance, and a sense of belonging. These tendencies are natural enough. The challenge to staff members in charge of in-service programs involves providing for those assigned to a program the satisfactions they need without corrupting the system. Harris (1985) has conceptualized an approach to this in describing the "amplified team" approach to improving instructional programs. Others advocate decentralization at the building and grade level to make in-service programs integral parts of the school operation (Zigarmi 1979). Others suggest elaborate means for isolating or insulating in-service education from the dominant influences of school governance. Some of these suggestions are reflected in advocacy for teacher centers and professional control of in-service education. Unfortunately, these alternatives are not likely to be generally effective. While offering some limited advantages, they add problems of loss of continuity, political instability, and organizational fragmentation.

STAFFING AND ORGANIZING

Any operational unit that is expected to maintain and develop in-service education offerings for school personnel has a large, complex responsibility. The best ways to staff and organize for the "delivery" of such in-service education opportunities are largely unknown at the present time. Proposals and current practices range widely from the sublime to the ridiculous. Even larger school districts have only recently developed offices or departments for in-service education purposes, and these are a diverse and precarious array of arrangements.

An enormous array of special programs and projects involving in-service education as referred to in Chapter 1 has given rise to the proliferation of diverse organizational arrangements with staffing patterns of similar diversity (Nelson 1976, 71–77). While there may well be merit in such diversity, the impression an observer is likely to get is one of unbelievable chaos.

Other, less transient notions about organizing for the delivery of in-service education are being implemented and tested. The regional education service center movement has resulted in well-established service organizations in many states with heavy responsibility for supplementing and supporting local school district in-service programming efforts (Stephens 1977).

On the assumption that in-service education will largely remain a responsibility of the local school district, organizational arrangements and staffing patterns will be discussed in the next section with these units of operation in mind. To be sure, other units will always be involved in various ways. Colleges, professional associations, state agencies, service centers, consortia, and private firms will undoubtedly provide manpower, materials, developmental efforts, technical support, and funding for in-service education. The challenges to the local school district are to retain control, respond to needs, and assure steady growth in quality of programs. This involves staffing and organization for the orchestration of a very complex operation not unlike that described by Nelson (1976, 75–78) as the Montgomery County "systematic corporate model."

Programs must be spawned under the leadership of an organizational unit—office, department, division—that is directly associated with the larger school system at the highest administrative and policy-developing levels. Such an office must be a *permanent* one for purposes of assessing needs, deploying staff, initiating programs, allocating resources, and coordinating efforts. However, major training programs can and should be developed as temporary systems.

A Complex Systems View

In-service education needs to be seen as one of a complex of interrelated systems. Both developmental and operational systems of various kinds are involved. Exhibit 10–3 shows such a complex schematically depicting the total educational operation as a system. Central to this system is the subsystem 2.2 *Instuctional Operations System* (IO). This may be represented as the classroom if oversimplified. Actually it is a system that has many subparts in the form of classroom, laboratory, library, reading clinic, resource room—any operation that takes students, materials, space, time, and staff to use directly in promoting learning. Both instructional and noninstructional support systems are shown as 2.3 and 2.4, which are directly associated with the *Instructional Operations System*. The *Administrative Support System* (2.1) is likewise directly related to the IO system. Each subsystem is directly linked with others in functional relationships as shown by the solid lines with arrows suggesting the direction of flow of responsibility and/or service. The dashed lines, on the other hand, show information flow for feedback for monitoring purposes. Hence the solid line from 2.5 *Evaluation Support System* to 2.2 *Instructional Operations System* indicates the responsibility of the former system for evaluating the latter. However, the dashed line from evaluation (2.5) to (2.1) *Administrative Support System* indicates responsibility for providing information to the latter system to help guide its decision-making operations.

The set of *Instructional Development Systems* (2.6) has been discussed in a previous context. Here they are shown as being linked to each other (see double arrows), directed by the administrative subsystem, informed by the evaluation subsystem as well as others, but directly serving the needs of the Instructional Operations System. *In-Service Education* is subsystem 2.63—only one of several, but enormously important.

EXHIBIT 10–3. A Systems View of the Total Educational Operation Associated with ISE

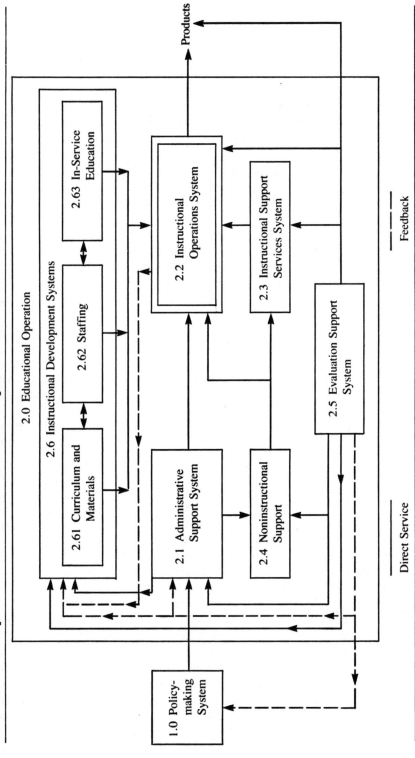

Ben M. Harris, *Supervisory Behavior in Education*, 2d ed., © 1975, p. 53. Reprinted by permission of Prentice-Hall, Inc., Englewood Cliffs, N.J.

The In-Service Delivery System

A closer look at this one developmental subsystem, *In-Service Education* (2.63), is provided in Exhibit 10–4. This important subsystem is shown here as an operating unit with various subsystems of its own. Again, solid arrows show responsibility and service relationships, and dashed lines suggest major sources of information and the direction of flow. Four operating units are identified as functionally interrelated in producing *in-service training operations*. This schematic is referred to later in this chapter with reference to staffing and organizing programs of in-service education. Obviously, one might consider the possibility of staffing each of these four subsystem operations separately. However, planning, designing, and operating (2.632–2.634) might be viewed as sequenced tasks to be performed by the same undifferentiated staff members. Still another approach is to consider the unique competencies required to assure the efficient functioning of each subsystem. In most instances, some kind of team approach is likely to be most promising, even though staff specialists may well be assigned key responsibilities.

Relating Developmental Systems

Some of the problems inherent in any complex organization with somewhat discrete subsystems are those of coordination. Coordination problems are always present. Even when all aspects of an operation are the sole responsibility of a single individual, some tasks are neglected, and time frames overlap. When numerous persons are involved, when tasks are more numerous, and when interdependencies are essential, the coordination problems may grow increasingly severe. To some extent, these problems are avoided by clearly delegating responsibilities as suggested in Exhibits 10–3 and 10–4. Close working relationships in a team structure can increase communications among those responsible and thereby reduce misunderstandings, encourage sharing of information, and so on.

 Goal specification has been widely advocated as an approach to assuring that various operating units will produce according to plan. The term "management by objectives" (MBO) has promise as more than a tool of accountability for outcomes. Subsystems need to be guided not only by their own objectives but by those shared goals and objectives that are superordinate. The sharing of responsibilities for designated portions of an operation cannot be avoided. An innovative program, to be implemented, may require curriculum and materials development as well as in-service education. The materials may have no chance of making a contribution without in-service training in their use, but they may not even be properly developed unless field trials are conducted with trained users. In-service education cannot be regarded as the solution to all problems, and simul-

EXHIBIT 10–4. In-Service Education as a Delivery System

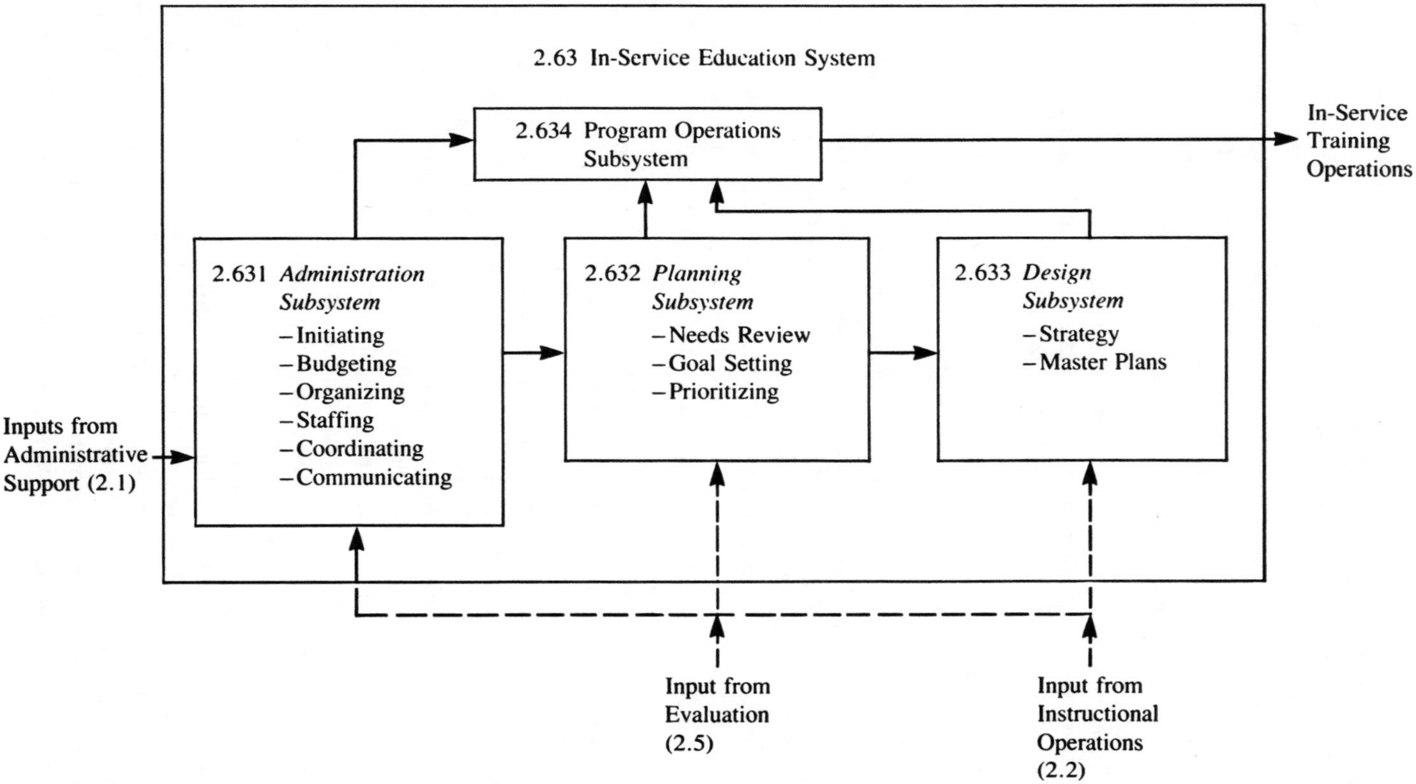

In-Service Training Operations

2.63 In-Service Education System

2.634 Program Operations Subsystem

2.633 *Design Subsystem*
  – Strategy
  – Master Plans

2.632 *Planning Subsystem*
  – Needs Review
  – Goal Setting
  – Prioritizing

2.631 *Administration Subsystem*
  – Initiating
  – Budgeting
  – Organizing
  – Staffing
  – Coordinating
  – Communicating

Input from Instructional Operations (2.2)

Input from Evaluation (2.5)

Inputs from Administrative Support (2.1)

taneous developmental efforts are nearly always required to assure the effectiveness of training (see Exhibit 10–5).

Superordinate goals should be specified early in any planning for an in-service education operation as a way of identifying the other developmental systems that need to be involved. To illustrate this approach using the high school English team vignette from Chapter 1, suppose the faculty and principal, together with feedback from Ann, the librarian-reading specialist on the team, define a training goal as follows:

> To develop competence in using individual educational plans with students to assure that diagnostic data will be translated into individually prescribed activities guided by programmed learning packets.

Such a goal could be seen as one involving a set of training objectives. Some of these might be the following:

1. To utilize at least one diagnostic instrument or procedure with an individual or small group to generate a reliable diagnostic profile.
2. To select from among an array of learning packets those that best relate to specific diagnostic needs.
3. To confer with individual students, using nondirective, positively reinforcing techniques, in planning a study sequence to assure that the student (a) accepts assigned tasks and (b) understands expectations.

Other objectives could be inferred as necessary or appropriate to the training outcome or goal. However, such training, no matter how carefully specified as a set of objectives or how well implemented as workshop, laboratory, or clinical experience, is likely to lack transfer capability for our team of English teachers at Swift High School. Where are these diagnostic instruments our trainees will be learning to use? Has preselection already been completed? Should these teachers get involved in defining the learning problems that need diagnosis? What about these learning packets? Do we have a good collection available for these English teachers to use? If not, can we get them, or will they need to be developed? In any case, will some curriculum planning need to precede training, or should we work on all fronts simultaneously?

Exhibit 10–5 suggests an approach to the problem of relating training and other developmental efforts to each other via a superordinate goal. This goal statement is shown as "to operate an individual education plan." This is an operational goal and is detailed as three different operational objectives—to diagnose, to develop IEPs, and to use LAPs. Each of these three objectives are shown as being implemented by the accomplishment of a combination of training, curriculum, and other objectives.

EXHIBIT 10–5. Logical Relationships between a Superordinate Goal and Objectives of Different Kinds

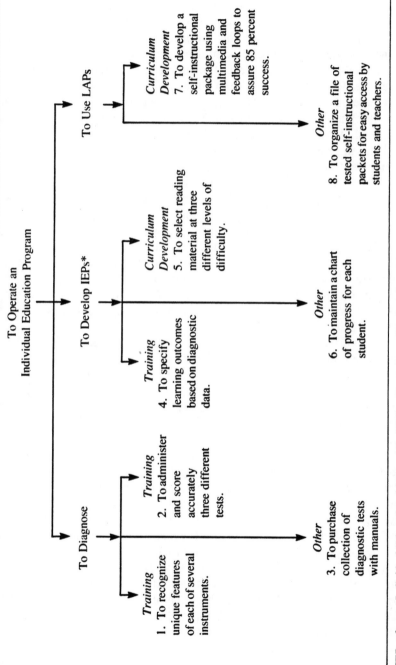

To Operate an
Individual Education Program

To Diagnose

Training
1. To recognize unique features of each of several instruments.

Training
2. To administer and score accurately three different tests.

Other
3. To purchase collection of diagnostic tests with manuals.

To Develop IEPs*

Training
4. To specify learning outcomes based on diagnostic data.

Curriculum Development
5. To select reading material at three different levels of difficulty.

Other
6. To maintain a chart of progress for each student.

To Use LAPs

Curriculum Development
7. To develop a self-instructional package using multimedia and feedback loops to assure 85 percent success.

Other
8. To organize a file of tested self-instructional packets for easy access by students and teachers.

*IEP refers to Individual Educational Plan while LAP refers to Learning Activity Packet.

Planned Variation

The search for an ideal approach or perfect model for organizing in-service education is surely fruitless. The school-based approach to in-service education may have strengths in the closeness of staff to decisions and funds, in the diversity of approaches stimulated, and in the freedom from bureaucratic controls. However, decentralized in-service education can become inflexible, too. School staffs can be unresponsive to needs defined through other eyes. Isolation of staff groups within self-contained schools can be as stultifying as isolation of individual teachers in self-contained classrooms has been. Teacher Corps director Bill Smith (1978) may have sensed this problem in reference to the school-centered in-service education projects as he insists on "the community council" for each school with elected parent representatives. Goodlad's assertion that "the single school is the largest and the proper unit for educational change" (1975, 110–11) may not be true. Certainly, such immutable rules are likely to promote rigidities in our view of alternatives, and hence could lead to undesirable uniformity.

Perez's (1979) study comparing school-based and other organizations for in-service education was not able to find the advantages so often claimed. Almanza (1980) found school-level programs heavily supported by in-service training from outside the school. A Virginia survey of in-service practices was not supportive of school-based programs (Virginia Department of Education, 1978).

Planned variation may well be a more useful principle of organization than many others. Rivlin contrasts variations in programs (1975, 170) as an alternative to experimental efforts. "Instead, these efforts are pilot studies of models forced into substantial use. Their merit lies in their exposing the difficulties of implementing . . . programs." In a field like ISE where a great deal of promising practice has been developed, the need for such pilots seems obvious.

Lawrence's (1974) study of effective in-service education programs contrasted the school-based and the college-based programs, favoring the former. However, he found quite a variety of organizational variations to be effective. Yarger suggests seven "organizational types" (1976, 19–22) including the independent program, the almost independent program, the professional organization program, the single-unit program, the free partnership program, the free consortium program, and the legislative political program. These are admittedly not pure types. They do suggest an array of variations that might be encouraged and utilized. As Yarger defines these types, he sees all local school district operated programs as falling into the single-unit in-service program. This tends to obscure two important possibilities for planned variation: internal and external.

Within a school system, with whatever resources, an individual, a group of individuals, a school or a part of it, a district or a part of it can be organized in diverse ways to generate and consume in-service education. Clinical supervision, although essentially an individualized delivery system, can be utilized as a schoolwide operation, be limited to individuals in a school, or be available in many schools. The teacher center facility that serves as a place where staff personnel can engage in training encounters may serve a school, a project, a district, or a region. What is more basic, however, is the need to organize in response to real, high-priority training needs in effective and efficient ways. In so doing, a program plan should allow for a great variety of alternatives and combinations. The teacher being assisted today in his or her own classroom via clinical supervision may well want to be in a teacher-training facility for skill development a bit later. Futhermore, a regional service center or university or professional organization may or may not be involved with this teacher in various ways.

Organizing for Collaborative Decisions

The highly personal nature of in-service education creates a demand for collaboration in all facets of program operations. Collaborative decisions involve more than just representation of interests. It requires that those to be affected and who have contributions to make shall be involved in decisions. This helps to assure that interests are balanced without loss in the quality of the program. In local school districts, such bodies as advisory councils, planning committees, in-service self-study committees, and other groups are being utilized more and more to oversee the planning, implementing, and evaluating of the in-service programs for the entire school district. These groups usually operate under the direction of the superintendent guided by local policy or district master plan. Such groups almost always include classroom teachers in substantial numbers as the most affected group in the system. Administrators, supervisors, school board members, and lay citizens or parents are also included. The size of the group may range from nine to fifteen persons without becoming unwieldy for effective action.

Collaborative decision making involving a variety of groups and individuals at different levels of the organization can create problems unless responsibilities are rather carefully delineated. Each decision-making group needs a charter clearly indicating rights, responsibilities, and restrictions. A comprehensive master plan for in-service education can serve as a guide for decision by various groups. Plans review procedures, funds allocation controls, and board-approved priorities are a few of the various ways to assure delegation and involvement without creating chaos or waste.

Staff Competencies Needed

Every program is likely to have need for certain specific competencies in planning, organizing, designing, implementing, and evaluating training operations. Fairly routine activities directed toward simple basic generic skill development may be arranged by those with sophisticated teaching competencies. More complex problems or more elaborate in-service programs will certainly call for staff personnel with an extensive array of special competencies.

A competency-guided program for leadership training (SEST Project) has identified five "critical" and a larger number of major competencies directly associated with in-service education. These were specified as minimally essential and not comprehensive at all. They included clinical, planning, conducting, coordinating, and leader-training competencies (1974, 73–75). The school-based teacher educator project mentioned earlier (Warner et al. 1977, 11) specifies twenty competencies that are largely those expected in any teacher. Five of the twenty do suggest special skills and knowledge in evaluating instruction, individual growth planning, conferencing, making referrals, demonstrating, and facilitation of research.

William R. Tracy (1984), in reference to industrial training programs, suggests a series of steps that imply competencies for those directing such programs. These include identifying training needs, analyzing job data, selecting and writing objectives, constructing instruments, selecting content, selecting training strategies, and selecting training aids. These tend to reflect the more specific operating needs of program implementation and do not prescribe a particular approach or organizational structure. Some of the competencies that might well be most important among the staff group giving regular direction to in-service education are described below (Lozano 1980):

PLANNING

1. To produce an assessment of needs for training.
2. To develop a master plan that provides clear guidelines for specific programs.
3. To write program or project proposals for responding to specific training priorities.
4. To assist teachers in the preparation of individual professional growth plans.

DESIGNING

5. To design or adopt a training session plan.
6. To produce a self-instructional training packet.
7. To lead a group in planning and designing a series of training sessions.

IMPLEMENTING

8. To select a training plan, make arrangements, and lead participants through a sequence of meaningful learning activities.
9. To lead teachers through individually planned clinical cycles.

10. To train personnel in specific procedures for conducting in-service training sessions.

EVALUATING

11. To utilize systematic procedures instrumentation for observations in classrooms.
12. To construct a questionnaire eliciting objective, reliable, discriminating responses.
13. To conduct an interview for gathering objective, reliable, and discriminating data from personnel.
14. To analyze data derived from more than one source, using several graphic techniques for drawing different interpretations.

Each kind of in-service program operation will tend to present requirements for staff competencies different from the requirements of other operations. The need for cooperative or participative decision making as well as other kinds of teacher involvement in many in-service education operations suggests the need for personnel who have competencies in group leadership. Clinical supervision strategies for in-service education would tend to emphasize competence in face-to-face interpersonal communications. In contrast, a program that emphasizes use of independent study packets creates a heavy demand for staff competencies related to instructional design, materials development, programming, graphics, and test construction. Still different competencies will be needed in staffing for in-service programs that emphasize individual growth planning as utilized in the De-TEK system (Harris and Hill 1982). Here diagnostic and supportive intervention teams must have competence in classroom observation, data analysis, demonstrating, and consulting.

Since the character of all programs should be different in response to differing needs of individuals, differing purposes, and changing conditions, it is usually unwise to develop a permanent staff on the basis of highly specialized competencies. Instead, rather basic competencies relating to planning, observing, working with groups, and working with individuals may be the ones most clearly required. The amplification of the permanent staff's competencies by creating ad hoc training teams for specific in-service education endeavors makes it feasible to utilize a great variety of competencies beyond those possessed by a small staff group.

Much emphasis has been given to teacher involvement in in-service education (Cooper 1977; Yarger 1976; and Yeatts 1976). Involvement of any person in decision making, in assessing needs, in evaluating, and in implementing in-service activities is, of course, desirable only to the extent that it contributes to the quality of the in-service education program. The emphasis on *teacher* involvement is appropriate, to be sure, because the teachers are so large a part of the reason for in-service education. However, viewed as a concern for full effective use of human resources (Nadler 1976, 1982), the emphasis shifts to involvement of staff, not just teachers. Furthermore, the emphasis can and should shift from involvement for representation purposes to involvement for purposes of assuring competencies needed.

Borrowing Competencies

The need to make fullest possible use of available competencies for planning, designing, and especially implementing in-service education programs has been mentioned in various sections in this chapter. In arguing for a fully assigned, responsible staff group at the central office level, a small group is also projected. This is possible, of course, only if the office or division responsible for in-service education has authority and resources for borrowing personnel.

Borrowing staff resources can and should take a variety of forms. Central staff personnel in all instructional development offices should be utilized. Hence, curriculum development specialists, program evaluation personnel, and special service personnel all have contributions to make toward in-service education. Arrangement for borrowing their services for specific assignments must be made. Conversely, of course, these staff members will often be directing in-service education programs within their own areas of responsibility, and their efforts will need support and coordination.

Classroom teachers are among the most promising staff members to be borrowed for in-service education. Not only is this a very large body of highly educated personnel with a great variety of competencies, but most classroom teachers need opportunities for experiences outside the confines of the classroom. As the recipients of most in-service education they also need to be heavily involved in many aspects of planning, implementing, and evaluating. Borrowing teachers for in-service education may involve released time from classroom duties, overtime paid for as such, or an extended contract for additional days, weeks, or months beyond the regular contract year.

Perhaps the most widely neglected and potentially most promising human resource is to be found among the parents and other individual citizens of every school and college community (Harris et al. 1985). In stereotyping such people as laymen, we ignore the many kinds of expertise possessed by a large percentage of the public. The problem is one of identifying these talents and finding means for utilizing them in appropriate ways. Fortunately, most citizens, especially parents, are usually eager to contribute time to school program improvements of nearly any kind. Hence, a very inexpensive human talent pool is readily available.

DELIVERY SYSTEMS

The design of specific programs for the delivery of educational experiences to a target group goes beyond the policy that provides a framework and support. It also goes beyond the general concern for effective planning process as discussed in Chapter 9. There are many strikingly different ways of designing for the delivery of in-service education. Many designs are in operation; new ones continue to emerge. The state of the art is not sufficiently advanced to clearly discern the superiority of some systems over others. In fact "planned variation," as discussed earlier, seems preferable even in the face of statewide mandates and pressures for uniformity (Rivlin and Timpane 1975).

Different design configurations are presented here to illustrate a variety of promising alternatives as well as to give attention to the application of some principles of good practice discussed in Chapter 9. Delivery systems have been characterized in many ways. School-based in-service education has been widely advocated (Perez 1979; Freiberg and Olivarez 1978; Smith 1978). Teacher center approaches once had substantial support, especially through union advocacy and federal funding (Cooper 1977; Mertens and Yarger 1981). Clinical supervision as a delivery system has had over two decades of widespread attention (Cogan 1973; Goldhammer, Anderson, and Krajewski 1980). Management by objectives (MBO) programs (Redfern 1980), quality circles (Ouchi 1981), organization development (Schmuck et al. 1975), differentiated supervision (Glatthorn 1984), coaching (Joyce and Showers 1980, 1982, 1983), and many other approaches have been advocated and tried, and have produced some worthwhile results. The problem for in-service education planners and trainers is not a lack of alternatives. On the contrary, even in the absence of adequate funds, without clearly designated staffs, and with little clear legal or policy structure, many creative variations for delivering ISE have been spawned. The challenge is to learn to utilize this rich variety more systematically and refine their application, while evaluating for differential effects.

Differentiating Designs

Delivery systems vary in some very fundamental ways. Some are temporary, others are permanent. Some are very special in purpose, concerned with highly restricted problems or needs as in school desegregation efforts (King 1980), while others serve a broad array of purposes (Ramakka and Huddleston 1986). Delivery systems can focus on specific behavior changes in the trainees (Munroe, Buchanan, and Grigg 1981) or be much more broadly conceived to enhance their education (Kilgore, Reichert, and Curtiss 1984). Delivery systems can be personalized or not (Zigarmi 1979).

EXHIBIT 10–6. Summary Estimates of Principles of Design Applied to Three Distinctive Delivery Systems

	SELECTED DELIVERY SYSTEMS		
CATEGORY OF OPERATING PRINCIPLES	SUPERMARKET	INDIVIDUALLY GUIDED IMPROVEMENT	INTENSIVE TRAINING CENTER
1. Policy Provisions	High	High	High
2. Planning Involvement	Medium	High	High
3. Content for Learning	Medium	High	Very High
4. Clients Served	Medium	Very High	Very High
5. Time for Training	Very High	Medium	High
6. Location for Training	Low	Low	Very High
7. Evaluation Process	Low	Low	Very High
8. Resource Allocations	Very High	Very High	Very High
9. Incentives Provided	Very High	Very High	Very High
10. Decision Making	High	Very High	High

Adapted from Hagen 1981. Estimates reflect comparisons of operating characteristics of the programs with the principles designated.

They can be largely self-directed or controlled by others. They can be prestructured or evolving in character (Gay 1980; Petrosky 1986).

Hagen (1981) utilized ten general principles of design as a framework for studying and contrasting in-service education delivery systems in operation. Exhibit 10–6 summarizes the findings from this study. Three clearly contrasting systems operating in different school settings were selected. It appears that some principles do differentiate among designs while others are common to otherwise very distinctive program designs. (See Chapter 2, "Guiding Principles.")

The detailed analysis of these three programs in operation suggests that no program conforms well to all principles utilized in this study. Great variations were also shown in the effectiveness of these programs. All three were judged, nonetheless, to be consistently high on policy provisions, resources allocations, incentives provided, and effectiveness of decision making.

Supermarket Design

The Supermarket delivery system analyzed by Hagen was a well-organized example of programs widely instituted by teacher centers, larger school systems, service centers, and professional associations. In brief, these delivery systems utilize a survey process to identify workshop topics of interest to teachers. A small planning and coordinating staff organizes workshops or short courses or other presentations around each topic that is chosen or identified with frequency. Workshop and other presenters are selected from among peers when available, and outside consultants are hired as needed. Workshop sessions are scheduled months in advance and publicized. Teachers attend voluntarily, making their own selections, with or without guidance from administrators or supervisors. Released time is sometimes provided, but more commonly, the workshops and other kinds of sessions are scheduled for late afternoons, evenings, Saturdays, and during school vacations. Teachers are given "credit" for attending these sessions in terms of salary schedule advancement or "equivalent time off" from nonteaching duties.

The IGI Design

The Individually Guided Improvement system studied by Hagen was an example of a well-structured individualized MBO program. Teachers and principals develop individual growth plans based on mutual agreements on teacher needs and interests. The plans are written with goals, objectives, schedules, and review processes made explicit. Teachers are allowed much freedom to exercise individual initiative in implementing their own individual plans. Principals are responsible for providing support services as needed and monitoring progress toward objectives. Central office supervisory personnel are made available as consultants, and funds are budgeted for travel, released time, and materials as needed on an individual basis.

The Training Center Design

The Intensive Training Center system studied by Hagen provides in-service training for faculty groups with a specific kind of instructional change designated as the overriding focus. A team of trainers, working full time in central location, design a program of training and offer it as a service to faculty groups. These groups become trainees, committing themselves to several weeks of intensive laboratory training followed by guided implementation over a period of many months in each school. The principal is required to participate as a full member of the faculty group and must agree to coordinate the implementation phase within his/her school. The training team follows each faculty group into their respective schools, observing, conferring, suggesting modifications, and assisting with plans and preparation of new materials for implementation. The consistent superiority of this highly structured training center design should be studied more carefully.

Design features emphasizing both high levels of experience impact (Harris 1985, 68–70) and explicit provisions for follow-up activities are clearly important for delivery systems promoting transfer of training. A study of seventy-four selected systems in operation by Cavender (1986) verified many of the principles and practices cited in this chapter and introduced in Chapter 2. The indications are, however, that special attention needs to be given to assure that the training activities provided are high-intensity, realistic, focused, practical, and structured for application. Similarly, this study reflects the critical importance of on-site follow-up and support as advocated by Joyce and Showers (1983). It appears that given these elements of design in the operation, needs assessments and related features are much less important.

Leadership for implementing high-quality in-service education and maintaining such programs in operation has been needlessly neglected. Neither the charisma of the principal nor the good intentions of willing teacher "coaches" are likely to be adequate for either implementing or maintaining a quality ISE program. Berry's (1987) study indicates in a preliminary way some of the leadership competencies associated with high-quality programs:

Leadership from both the principal and outside specialists is important.
Principal leadership needs to be expressed as *technical* competence related to in-service training, not just as general leadership skill.
Principals utilizing outside specialists with high levels of technical competence in in-service education maintain better programs of training.

These preliminary findings are consistent with those of previous scholars emphasizing the importance of both *inside* and *outside* change agents (Hall and Guzman 1984; Fullan 1982; Bailey 1985).

SUMMARY

Standardized "models" of in-service delivery have much appeal to busy practitioners and are being widely utilized. Clinical supervision, the simulation workshop, individual growth plans, quality circles, and so on are but a few delivery system models from the immediate past. Perhaps the most exciting "model" of recent vintage is one proposed by Joyce and Showers (1980, 1982, 1983). These researchers present convincing evidence to support a delivery system involving presenting of theory, demonstrating related practices, providing intensive laboratory training for skill building, and applying to real situations with observations, corrective feedback, and supportive services. This "model" is widely misunderstood and misapplied as "coaching." Nonetheless, the fully designed delivery system has promise because it incorporates so many recognized principles of good practice.

The DeTEK system is carefully detailed elsewhere (Harris and Hill 1982; Harris 1986). It deserves brief attention here simply as another illustration of the dramatic variations in delivery systems which do, nonetheless, seem to work. These two fairly recent developments in designing for the delivery of training experiences that improve teaching serve to emphasize the importance of diversity in working with human affairs. There are no patent medicines to be taken. An open-minded view of well-conceived alternatives is essential to progress in this field.

Even so, nearly all studies of effective training programs, regardless of form, have some design characteristics in common. All have structure and functional utility. All require continuity of experience. All are time-consuming and expensive.

STUDY SOURCES

Bergquist, Constance C. 1985. "The Teacher Education Center Program in Florida." In *What Works in In-Service Education Programs for Teachers?*, ed. Elva G. Galambos. Atlanta, Ga.: Southern Regional Education Board.
   This is a brief report on a systematic evaluation study of the teacher center operations in Florida. Many of the problems unique to this type of delivery system are documented and discussed.

California State Commission for Teacher Preparation and Licensing. 1981. *Comprehensive Plan for Coordination of Preservice and In-Service Professional Preparation of Educational Personnel in the State of California.* Sacramento, Calif.: California State Department of Education. ERIC ED 201 047
   A comprehensive plan that outlines problems, goals, components, and suggested mechanisms for coordinating preservice and in-service education. The plan addresses removing barriers, identifying needs, funding, communications, and evaluation. The planners emphasize client-centered, flexible, realistic training programs that allow for institutional autonomy.

Christian, Jerry D. 1981. "The Operational Effects of the Five-Year Priorities Plans of Texas School Districts as Functions of Commitments to and Strategies for Process of Change." Ph.D. diss., The University of Texas at Austin (August).
   Commitments of superintendents and boards of trustees were studied in relation to effectiveness of implementation of 5-year, districtwide school improvement plans. Variables studied related to commitment but also to principal leadership, training provided, extent of change attempted, quality of evaluation and feedback provided, extent of communications with staff and community, and overall quality of "operationalization" of the programs.
   Christian found commitments to be of overriding importance while principal leadership and training were relatively weak influences. However, with a reanalysis of the data, eliminating very inconsistent respondents, commitment, leadership, and training all emerge as strong predictors of success.

Gall, Meredith D., and R. S. Renchler. 1985. *Effective Staff Development for Teachers: A Research-Based Model.* Eugene, Ore.: Clearinghouse on Educational Management, College of Education, University of Oregon.

These authors identify 27 "dimensions" as related to effective in-service programs. While drawing on only a few studies and ignoring many others, the authors usefully present the dimensions as relating to 6 aspects of planning.

Three very brief "case studies" are presented toward the end of this monograph. While not clearly related to the "model," they are interesting in their own right.

Glatthorn, Allan A. 1984. *Differentiated Supervision*. Alexandria, Va.: Association for Supervision and Curriculum Development.

This author uses the term "supervision" to mean in-service education "facilitating the professional growth of the teacher" (p. 2). As such, four "differentiated approaches" or strategies are proposed: (1) clinical, (2) cooperative, (3) self-directed, and (4) monitoring. Each approach is discussed in some detail.

All except the last of these four approaches illustrate well-accepted alternatives for individualizing in-service education. The author suggests a differentiated rationale for using each strategy which may be too mechanistic but is worthy of consideration.

Joyce, Bruce R., and Beverly Showers. 1983. *Power of Research on Training for Staff Development*. Alexandria, Va.: Association for Supervision and Curriculum Development.

A review of several studies suggesting more emphasis on a training sequence directed toward application of skills to practice. The authors argue for more laboratory training, direct "coaching," and supporting services to assure transfer.

Kilgore, Alvah M., Ronald Reichert, and Pamela Curtiss. 1984. "The Application of Research Generalizations from Staff Development to a Rural District: A Case Study Research Report." A paper presented at the Annual Meeting of the Association of Teacher Educators (January). ERIC ED 241 466

The paper describes the effects of applying research-based generalizations about in-service education to local school practice. Seven generalizations provided focus for the study. The case report reveals interesting applications that seem to support collaborative planning with teachers and university personnel to assure flexible scheduling, practical outcomes, and full use of human resources.

Munroe, M. J., Barbara Buchanan and Nora Grigg. 1981. "Linking Teacher Behavior with Learning Style: Tucson Model for Effective Staff Development." A paper presented to the National Council of States on In-Service Education (November). ERIC ED 209 235

The development of a bilingual and multicultural program for staff development is described. The focus is on the Tucson model for utilizing a combination of intensive summer "institute" training followed by weekly workshops reinforcing summer skills.

Pankratz, Roger. 1980. *Planning for Institutionalization: The Continuation of New Programs and Practices*. Omaha, Nebr.: Center for Urban Education, University of Nebraska at Omaha. Teacher Corps Developmental Training Activities.

This author deals with "political" as well as technical problems related to making educational improvements. He emphasizes processes involving awareness, acceptance, preparation, limited installation, and institutionalization. In a closely related document (Pankratz and Martray 1981), the emphasis is placed on collaboration as well as other "critical steps."

Peper, John B. 1986. "Implementing Computer-Based Education in Jefferson County, Colorado." Chap. VII in *Microcomputers and Education*, ed. J. A. Culbertson and L. L. Cunningham. 85th Yearbook of the National Society for the Study of Education, Part I. Chicago: The University of Chicago Press.
A case report is presented on the implementation of computer education in a large suburban school system. "Staff education" is discussed explicitly (pp. 146–50), illustrating a 3-phase program structure. A key strategy for promoting computer utilization appears to have involved the identification, training, and assigning of building-level coordinators.
This case also raises interesting questions about the formal versus the informal aspects of the training process.

Rawitsch, Don G. 1981. "Lessons Learned on the In-Service Trails." *Classroom Computer News* 2 (September-October): 16–17.
The work of the Instructional Services Staff of the Minnesota Educational Computing Consortium are described briefly in this report. Three approaches are reported including scheduled workshops, individual consultations, and assisting local schools in developing their own follow-up training plans.

Schuler, Randall S., and Stuart A. Youngblood. 1986. *Effective Personnel Management*, 2d ed. St. Paul, Minn.: West Publishing Company.
Chapter 12 of this volume deals with "Training and Development," defined as "any attempt to improve . . . employee performance by increasing . . . ability to perform through learning" (p. 388). Despite a commitment to a deficit model, this chapter is useful in designating and describing programs such as OJT, apprenticeships, job rotations, and so on.

Smith, Douglas J. 1981. *A State Funding Model for In-Service Training of a School Staff*. Ann Arbor, Mich.: Unpublished document (August). ERIC ED 206 619
A review of the 1979 Michigan legislation allocating funds to staff development programs is presented. The features of the legislation stressed relate to management training, voluntariness, and cooperative planning.

Von Gilinow, Mary Ann, Michael J. Driver, Kenneth R. Brosseau, and J. Bruce Prince. 1983. "The Design of a Career Oriented Human Resource System," *Academy of Management Review* 8.
These authors propose an "integrated human-resource system" in which identification, assignment, development, and career-path planning are managed in a long-term, comprehensive way. The authors present a model for linking various organizational and personnel functions in strategic planning to personnel development and training.

Washington State Department of Education. 1981. *The Washington State System for Coordination of Staff Development Coordination Study: A Final Report*. Olympia, Wash.: Office of the State Superintendent of Public Instruction. ERIC ED 209 240

This report outlines the roles and responsibilities of the Superintendent of Public Instruction (SPI) in the State of Washington in regard to the improvement and coordination of statewide teacher in-service. After a field-based research study was conducted, a system was devised by which the SPI can improve coordination of staff development programs and resources among the major agencies involved.

Wood, Fred H., S. R. Thompson, and Frances Russell. 1981. "Designing Effective Staff Development Programs." In *Staff Development/Organization Development*, ed. Betty Dillon-Peterson. Alexandria, Va.: Association for Supervision and Curriculum Development.

A systematic proposal for a 5-stage planning, implementing, maintenance model for general use in school settings. The authors summarize with a list of principles.

Zigarmi, Patricia. 1979. "A Model for an Individualized Staff Development Program." In *Staff Development: New Demands, New Realities, New Perspectives*, ed. Ann Lieberman and Lynne Miller. New York: Teachers College Press.

In addition to a brief description of a program operation in South Dakota using the individual project approach to staff development, the authors discuss a variety of operating issues. This portion is especially useful in identifying practical problems of effective operations.

The staff development coordinators' roles are described in some detail. The tensions in program operations are analyzed.

11.

Evaluation Techniques

INTRODUCTION

The evaluation of in-service education operations should not be taken lightly. As one of the most important developmental operations, ISE deserves careful, systematic evaluation. As an operation that is *sensitive* in the sense that personnel are very much concerned about the quality of in-service education, ISE should be evaluated rather closely and regularly. As an operation that can be enormously influential, yet one that is expensive and disruptive in nature, ISE deserves evaluation that is truly rigorous.

To speak of what evaluation should be as it relates to in-service education is one thing, but the mounting of evaluation efforts that are truly productive is a difficult endeavor. Limited resources must provide extensive information regarding a host of diverse facets of the operation. The intermittent nature of ISE makes timing a critical problem. The widespread involvement of personnel of all kinds makes ISE evaluation feedback an elaborate process in which findings must be in the most readily usable form.

PURPOSES OF EVALUATION

By recognizing the specific purposes that can be served and selecting from among them, evaluation efforts are made more efficient and are simplified. Obviously, evaluation is intended to improve operations (Thompson 1975, 76). However, such improvements can be accomplished in a variety of ways (Borich and Madden 1974, 313). Improvements need to be sustained by providing reinforcing evidence. This is quite different from go–no go decisions that are to be made on the basis of some overall assessment.

Detecting defects in a program or session is still another focus for evaluation that is essential to improving the quality of training. The clear determination of operational strengths is also important to assure their maintenance even as some revisions are undertaken (Harris 1986, 171–74).

In addition to differentiating purposes to be served, plans for evaluation have to be developed differently for programs and for sessions. Session evaluation data may be quite useful in program evaluation, if planned for. However, session evaluations should be useful in themselves, regardless of larger programmatic purposes to be served. Conversely, session evaluations can rarely be used for program evaluation purposes by simple aggregation of data. Program evaluation requires a special design and entails numerous decisions regarding the evaluation questions to be answered.

Providing Reinforcement

The people directly involved in any aspect of in-service education can profit from, and often need, the reinforcement that evaluation can offer. Traditionally, evaluation data are perceived as threatening, and they may well be. However, when people are planning well, getting results, and satisfying needs of their colleagues, they need feedback that is reassuring and supportive. Such feedback, like all evaluation outcomes, should be as clearly objective as possible. "Snow jobs" are neither ethical nor effective for reinforcement purposes. However, even the mediocre ISE program or session has some strengths, and these should not be neglected.

Evaluation efforts that are clearly useful for reinforcement purposes must be diagnostic as well as objective to assure that strengths will be detected even when many weaknesses prevail. Hence, data of different kinds, about different aspects of the operation, and from different sources need to be gathered. In the analysis of these data, the reinforcement potential must be retained by avoiding aggregates and retaining a diagnostic profile. For instance, participant responses on a series of five-point scales could be reported as a mean or median for all responses of 3.1. However, reporting a range of responses from 2 to 5 is a bit more informative. Showing a frequency distribution for each of several items may be even more helpful if in fact there are substantial differences in the responses to different aspects of the session. (See Exhibit 11–1.) Finally, a scattergram showing relationships of objectives of participants to their responses may help still more to reinforce with the selectivity that guides improvements as well.

The use of carefully analyzed data in providing feedback to individuals and groups for reinforcement purposes is of course crucial. Obviously, feedback should be as rapid as possible, consistent with careful analysis of data. If those most in need of feedback can undertake the analysis process themselves, then feedback is likely to be prompt and also more meaningful.

EXHIBIT 11–1. Illustration of a Frequency Distribution of Participant Responses to Several Items (N = 46)

	FREQUENCY OF RESPONSES					
	1	**2**	**3**	**4**	**5**	
ITEMS	**SLIGHTLY**	**SOME-WHAT**	**SUBSTAN-TIALLY**	**HIGHLY**	**EX-TREMELY**	**MEAN RATING**
5. How stimulating did you find the session activities?	0	1	2	8	35	4.7
7. How relevant to your job situation did you find the session content?	0	3	2	2	39	4.7
8. How useful (practical) for you was the skill or information gained in this session?	5	10	13	12	6	3.1

When machines or computers are utilized, turnaround time needs to be planned for the shortest possible interval, and the printout or other documents utilized for feedback purposes need to be clear, simple, and readily interpretable.

Often, feedback for reinforcement purposes is as important to the participants as it is to the officials in charge. A much-neglected use of evaluation involves giving participants information that helps them more accurately assess the worth of the ISE activities they have been a part of. Too often participants see evaluation as perfunctory—an exercise in opinion giving—but not as a systematic process for responsible assessment of an important part of school operations for which all parties *share* responsibilities and benefits.

Go–No Go Decisions

The basic program of a school rarely faces decision making involving the serious possibility of discontinuing an operation entirely. When such decisions are faced, the circumstances are often of an emergency kind; hence, evaluation data are not highly influential. Decisions regarding temporary systems such as ISE programs can be of the go–no go type, however. There is no rational reason to continue any particular type or form of inservice education year after year. In fact, changing circumstances nearly always make discontinuance of an ISE program worthy of consideration at some point in time.

The tendency for staff groups to become associated with a program or project and to perpetuate it is a tendency which makes evaluation of the kind that can support a no go decision important. Bank and Bury (1978) in studying evaluation efforts in 409 school districts throughout the United States comment that such efforts rarely involve what they call "make or break" decision-making purposes.

The emphasis on evaluation for the improvement of ongoing operations should not blind evaluators to this special purpose of informing decisions where discontinuation is a potential alternative. It is not realistic to view any ISE program as a permanent operation. Needs are so numerous that even relatively successful programs judged on the basis of the accomplishment of their own objectives may be less than top priority when judged in terms of a broad array of program alternatives for meeting other needs.

The emphasis given to needs assessment in much of the literature on planning in-service education can be seen as related to the problem of deciding to discontinue, as well as to initiate, new efforts. Unfortunately, many needs assessments approach the problem as though there were only one kind of decision to make regarding what to initiate in the way of new ISE. Such a one-sided view of the problem may well be counterproductive. Decisions to mount new programs may inadvertently force decisions in favor of discontinuing already operating programs. Instead, the evaluation efforts should be such that needs assessment data are carefully utilized in concert with other data reflecting ongoing program efforts. Under such arrangements, existing programs will be discontinued only when they are ineffective, have accomplished their purposes, or have become low in priority.

Diagnosing

The most promising purpose of in-service education evaluation is the clear identification of operational *defects* that can be eliminated or *ameliorated*. While this purpose may seem negatively oriented, it need not be. On the contrary, recognition of the complexities surrounding ISE makes it quite logical to expect that sessions and programs will always be far from perfect. To make the best possible use of scarce resources is an urgent need because of the scarcity of such resources and also because of the important contributions to be made by ISE when it is of high quality.

Evaluation efforts directed toward identifying defects must be highly diagnostic in nature. Vague or generalized references to difficulties are not adequate for this purpose. Data gathering must assure as much validity as possible. Instrumentation should be such that reliable data are provided. But data analysis techniques must be sophisticated enough to assure that diagnostic interpretations rather than general impressions result. The survey approach and branching diagram analysis presented later in this chapter are both useful for diagnostic purposes.

EVALUATION AS PROCESS

The foregoing discussion about the various purposes of evaluation implies a data-gathering and analysis process. But evaluation is generally recognized to be much more than this process. In the past, many viewed evaluation as an act of judging something or someone, which is of course a very archaic use of the term. However, recent trends associated with technological developments in testing, measurement, and educational research have emphasized research design, data gathering, and statistical analysis to the point of creating confusion about the utility of evaluation. Evaluation is not research. The two have much in common, but the differences are extremely important (Stake 1969, 372–80). Some of the differences have been well expressed by experts in both fields. Thompson (1975) reflects the position of Stufflebeam (1971) and others in defining evaluation as "the marshalling of information for the purpose of improving decisions." Obviously, in the real world decisions are made with or without organized evaluation efforts. Hence, Thompson's stress on improving decisions is important.

A Sequence of Processes

Evaluating in-service education involves systematically implementing a set of sequenced processes, as follows:

1. *Selecting,* defining, and specifying *evaluative criteria.* What specific measurable events do we anticipate as evidence of success?
2. *Selecting,* designing, or adapting *instruments and procedures* for measuring events related to the evaluative criteria.
3. *Gathering (recording) data,* using appropriate instruments and procedures.
4. *Analyzing data* in ways that reduce and array them in relation to evaluative criteria.
5. *Interpreting results* (findings) by comparing and contrasting findings with each other, by classes, and against criteria.
6. *Valuing findings* by relating them to values and expectations of the individuals or institutions being served.
7. *Deciding* on one or more *actions* that should logically follow.
8. *Acting* on the decisions so as to improve and maintain the best of the operation.

While these eight processes are numbered in sequence and are generally followed in sequence, they may also overlap one another. Criteria are sometimes revised, refined, added, or deleted after instrumentation, data gathering, and analysis are well along, because new insights may be produced in process. Interpretation and analysis may overlap, with some new analyses being undertaken as the result of insights gained in preliminary efforts. Valuing is most dangerous out of sequence. Until analyses are thoroughly completed and thoughtful interpretations are drawn, valuing is premature and usually leads to faulty decisions.

An Illustration

This sequence of evaluation processes in simple application can be described for a single-session training program as follows:

EVALUATIVE CRITERIA
1. At least twenty-five teachers will voluntarily attend.
2. Teachers attending will include at least one-third secondary and one-third elementary.
3. Participants (80 percent) will report activities as stimulating and relevant to a high degree.
4. Participants (75 percent) will estimate utility (practicality) of learning outcomes as high or extremely high.
5. Participants (90 percent) estimating utility of learning outcomes as limited will report need incongruence with objectives.

INSTRUMENTATION. A simple questionnaire is designed to elicit postsession information as follows:

1. extent of voluntariness in attendance;
2. level of assignment—elementary or secondary;
3. extent of stimulation of activities;
4. extent of perceived relevance of content to job;
5. extent of perceived utility (practicality) of skills and knowledge;
6. a checklist of objectives to be prioritized according to perceived needs.

DATA GATHERING. Present questionnaire at end of session, requesting each participant to complete it and deposit it in a basket on departing, to retain anonymity.

ANALYSIS
1. Tabulate voluntary versus involuntary participant responses.
2. Count elementary and secondary participants. Determine percentage of each.
3. Tabulate frequency of responses on five-point scale for item on extent of stimulation.
4. Tabulate frequency of responses on five-point scale.

5. Tabulate frequency of responses on five-point scale for item on extent of utility of learned outcomes.

6. Compute mean ratings for items 3, 4, and 5 by assignment level, and voluntariness.

7. Score the checklist of objectives for each respondent giving plus and minus values to objectives as prioritized according to their relationship to those of the session. Compute a total congruence score for each participant.

8. Prepare a scattergram showing relationships between individual participant responses to items tabulated in item 5 and the congruence score computed in item 7.

INTERPRETATION

Compare analysis 1 above (A–1) with criterion 1 (C–1).

Compare A–2 with C–2. Compare A–3 and A–4 with C–3.

Compare A–5 with C–4. Compare A–8 with C–5.

Determine whether each criterion was in fact attained.

If not, determine for which group criteria were attained by comparing and contrasting A–1 and A–2 with A–6.

VALUING

Where criteria have not been attained or exceeded, determine how serious you and others regard the discrepancy.

Where criteria have been met, estimate the importance of these in terms of overall expectations.

DECIDING. For each serious discrepancy, *review factors* associated with it. What level was most clearly associated with it? To what extent was incongruence in objectives associated with discrepancies?

Specify at least two alternative actions that might relate to each discrepancy or set of discrepancies. For instance, if all criteria are far short of attainment, then:

Action Alternative 1. Scrap the entire effort. Redesign and repeat training.

Action Alternative 2. Modify training design and extend training to a sequence of sessions.

However, if only a limited number of discrepancies is detected, then other action alternatives might be in order. For instance, suppose criteria 1, 2, and 3 are fully attained, but for criterion 4 data analysis reveals only 68 percent of participants rating the session as "high" or "extremely high." Furthermore, it appears that lower-level responses are from respondents who are (1) secondary (26 percent) and (2) involuntary (22 percent). Now action alternatives of somewhat different kinds emerge:

Action Alternative 3. Confer with secondary principals and director of secondary education in an attempt to secure voluntary participation in future sessions.

Action Alternative 4. Plan another training session directed toward secondary personnel with special emphasis on voluntariness and unique needs designated in the evaluation (A–7).

Action Alternative 5. Combine alternatives 3 and 4.

ACTING

Implement decisions made.

The overly simplistic illustration of the eight processes of evaluation as described here can become much more elaborate as the complexity of the session or program being evaluated varies. Also, more critical decisions require more rigorous specification of criteria, instrumentation, and data analysis. Regardless of the complexity of the evaluation required, however, the eight processes seem to remain a useful guide.

Dangers in Simplification

Both researchers and evaluators tend to offer overly simplistic approaches to evaluation that needlessly restrict their usefulness in improving in-service education. Pretest and post-test comparisons are often advocated as if controlled experimental conditions prevail, but they never do. Another common error is simply to compare objectives with outcome measures. Still another variant of such overly simple approaches is one that simply focuses on perceptions of outcomes or satisfaction by participants. Whereas any one of these approaches might be useful as a way of generating or analyzing data, none can be regarded as a useful evaluation plan or design. Furthermore, the inadequacies of these approaches remain even when sophisticated computerization statistics and language are employed.

A satisfactory evaluation design must direct our attention to at least three kinds of questions and offer some hope that answers will be forthcoming to each:

1. What kind of operation as observed (or as perceived) actually exists or existed?

All too often we evaluate an operation presuming that it has or had certain characteristics when in fact something quite different actually was implemented. When this is true, we draw faulty conclusions regardless of outcomes or pre- and post-changes. This can be illustrated by an ISE program designed to develop interpersonal skills utilizing a whole array of demonstrations, role-playing, and microteaching activities. However, a controversy before the school board the night before the first session generated a great deal of spontaneous discussion among participants. This was wisely accommodated by session leaders, but as a result demonstrations were eliminated and role-playing involvement was substantially reduced in subsequent sessions. Finally, videotape equipment for use by one third of the total group did not function properly, and those participants received little feedback of this self-viewing kind.

A comparison of pretest scores with post-test scores in the case illustrated might well indicate substantial gains in knowledge but little in skill or attitude. Valid interpretations cannot be drawn regarding the relationships between discrepancies and ISE operations unless those events described are carefully documented as part of the evaluation scheme.

2. What kind of outcomes are (were) produced for what participant subgroups?

All too often we gather and analyze outcome data from an ISE session or program as though participants were a homogeneous group of sponges just waiting to absorb what is offered. Obviously, such a view is naive. Participants are a very diverse lot. Their needs, levels of experience, job assignments, learning styles, intelligence, attitudes, and so on are very different. Accordingly, if pre- or post-gain scores show limited effects or if self-reports by participants are not overwhelmingly positive, we have no clear way of interpreting these findings. Was the experience actually faulty, or was it in fact quite effective with some and not so effective with other participants? If the latter is to be determined objectively and not used simply as a basis for rationalization of results, then the evaluation plan must provide for gathering data about participants as individuals.

3. What are the relationships between *controllables*—resources and procedures—and *consequences,* both planned and inadvertent?

All too often evaluation efforts concentrate on isolated sets of data rather than on relationships among them (Borich and Madden 1974, 328–30). For instance, in the illustrative program described, the relationship between amount of skill gained and the extent of use of the videotape in microteaching should be analyzed. Such a relationship might lead to an interpretation regarding the contribution of video feedback to the growth or lack of growth shown in the data. The emphasis on relationships between those things that are controllable and the outcomes produced are crucial because of the purposes discussed earlier.

A BASIC EVALUATION MODEL

The enormous variety of evaluation problems that need to be addressed does not permit a simple "cookbook" evaluation method. In fact, even one basic model or design will not suffice for all purposes. However, since in-service education always involves people engaging in planned activities to produce new learnings, it is possible to approach a great variety of sessions and programs with a single basic model. A systems model is widely advocated and seems especially appropriate for temporary systems like in-service education where inputs, processes, and products are fairly clearly discernible and predeterminable.

The Black Box

Almost all evaluation models can be viewed in relation to the basic schematic representation of a system in operation. This basic system diagram includes three boxes, as shown in Exhibit 11–2. The *inputs* box (1) represents needs, resources, objectives, and people, which are introduced into the system according to purpose and plan. The *processes* box (2) represents a complex of events, interactions, procedures, activities, and so on, which constitute the planned operation. The *products* box (3) represents outcomes anticipated and desired.

Three overly simplified evaluation plans are shown in Exhibit 11–2 in schematic form. The weaknesses in these approaches as shown have already been discussed. Each deals with only one kind of input and not that which can be readily controlled or manipulated. Furthermore, the processes are ignored in every instance. The black box is a complete mystery as far as the evaluation plan is concerned. Hence, findings in the form of answers to the three questions may be either positive or negative, but they have no consequence in either case. When needs are satisfied, the processes associated with that result are indeterminant. When objectives are not attained, no clues are provided regarding probable causes. When test score gains are large, no basis for reinforcement is provided except in a very gross way.

A Multivariate Approach

An approach to making better use of basic systems concepts in evaluating in-service education is derived from the CIPP model pioneered by Stufflebeam (1971). CIPP stands for context, input, process, product evaluation. In adapting and simplifying this model for use in in-service education, context data are treated in only informal ways while careful attention

EXHIBIT 11–2. Schematic View of a Simple System with Three Associated Evaluation Plans

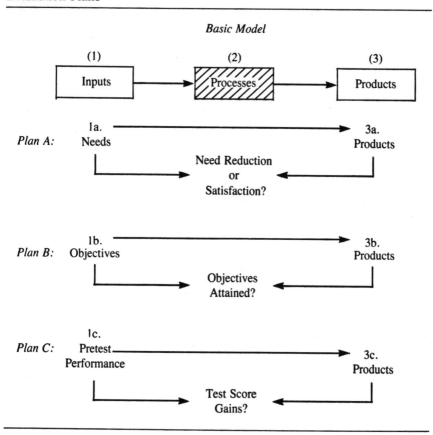

Basic Model

is given to input, process, and product data, and the analysis of each such data set to reveal relationships that are meaningful and useful. In doing this, a limited number of selected, important, measurable products or learning outcomes are specified in advance as desired and probable. Data regarding these are sought as objectively as possible. (See Exhibit 11–3.)

The evaluation plan also provides, however, for the careful selection of processes that are both important to the planned operation and are controllable in the sense that they could be increased, decreased, substituted, or changed in quality. Data regarding these processes are then sought in as objective a form as possible.

Finally, one or more inputs that are rationally and logically related to the processes of the operation are selected. These inputs must also be control-

EXHIBIT 11–3. A Schematic View of a Multivariate Model

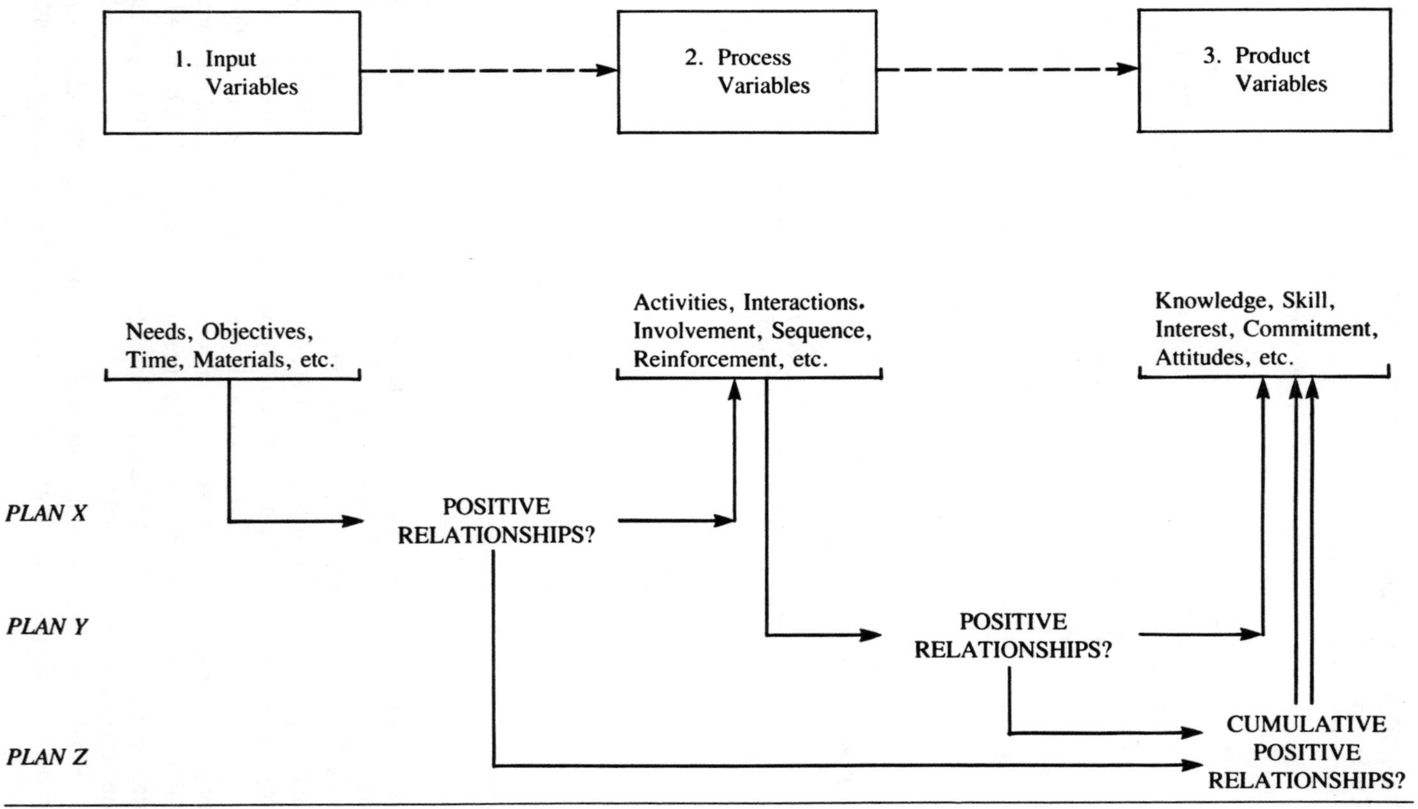

Flowchart showing three boxes connected by dashed arrows: "1. Input Variables" → "2. Process Variables" → "3. Product Variables"

1. Input Variables — Needs, Objectives, Time, Materials, etc.

2. Process Variables — Activities, Interactions, Involvement, Sequence, Reinforcement, etc.

3. Product Variables — Knowledge, Skill, Interest, Commitment, Attitudes, etc.

PLAN X

PLAN Y — POSITIVE RELATIONSHIPS?

PLAN Z — POSITIVE RELATIONSHIPS?

CUMULATIVE POSITIVE RELATIONSHIPS?

lable in the sense that they can be increased, decreased, substituted, or improved in quality. Data regarding these inputs are gathered as objectively as possible.

When these three sets of data are made available, an array of analyses can be undertaken, all data can be analyzed in traditional fashion, but multivariate analyses are made possible. Schematically, each analysis can be represented as follows:

Plan X attends to the relationships between one or more inputs and the processes that follow. Evaluation questions include: Are the needs of participants related to the activities provided, interactions stimulated, or involvement secured? Similar questions can be addressed for each kind of input for which there is data.

Plan Y attends to relationships between processes—activities, interactions, involvement, and so on, and outcomes or products that follow. Finally, *Plan Z* attends to the possible cumulative effect of positive relationships between both inputs and processes, and processes and products.

The unique values derived from such a multivariate view of the in-service operation are also multiple. (1) Any number of variables can be utilized in the evaluation plan, so long as there are at least three. (2) Positive or negative relationships signal more than good or sad feelings; they indicate possible influencing factors. (3) Cumulative effects can be considered.

INSTRUMENTATION

Instrumentation for in-service education evaluation tends to be dominated by the use of simple questionnaires. Questionnaire design can draw on well-developed survey techniques from the social and behavioral sciences. When well designed and well administered, they can provide useful data. When poorly designed, they can be useless. Furthermore, questionnaires offer only one kind of instrumentation.

Other approaches to data gathering having implications for instrumentation include interviews, observations, artifacts (McGreal 1983), and tests. Each can be utilized in a variety of ways. Each calls for careful instrumentation to assure relevant and reliable data. Technical assistance with instrumentation is available in sources by Cook (1976), Rattenburg and Pelletier (1974), and Sonoquist and Dunkelberg (1977). However, the source of the data and the kind of data gathered are both important considerations in instrument selection and design.

These four approaches or types of instrumentation are briefly described in Exhibit 11–4, along with indications of the *kinds* of data generally provided and the various sources from which such data can be secured.

EXHIBIT 11–4. Four Types of Useful Instrumentation by Kind of Data and Source

TYPE OF INSTRUMENTATION	KINDS OF DATA	SOURCES OF DATA
Questionnaire		
Provides abbreviated, precategorized data, but also provides for a variety of kinds of responses including ratings, ranking, and open responses.	Attitudes Opinions Information	Participant Student Observer Trainer
Test		
Provides abbreviated, precategorized data.	Information Skills Concepts	Participant Student
Interview Schedule		
Provides for verbal responses to many of same kinds of questions offered by the questionnaire. Permits more in-depth data gathering.	Attitudes Opinions Information Reactions	Participant Student Observer Trainer
Observation Record		
Provides for data on observable events. Does not rely on the responses of individual. Records behaviors regardless of form.	Events Interrelation-ships	Observer

Questionnaires and interviews provide much the same kind of data and utilize similar sources, unless special interview techniques are employed to produce more in-depth responses and to secure focused reactions. Obviously, the interview may have a special contribution to make where respondents cannot read and will not respond readily to a questionnaire. Interviews are costly ways of gathering data compared with questionnaires.

Tests have much in common with questionnaires but focus on securing knowledge or skill data while minimizing options and attitudes. Teachers seem every bit as uncomfortable with knowledge and skill tests as most other adults. In fact, considerable resistance to tests is often encountered in in-service training situations. For this reason, their use tends to be minimized despite the unique contributions they could make in evaluating ISE outcomes. Of course, tests given to students can conceivably be useful when evaluating ISE outcomes that are expected to have direct impact on student learning in rather specific ways. This latter use of testing has very limited utility. A more practical approach is to build the testing into the activities of the training session or program, with self-scoring, diagnosis, and self-analysis provided as incentives to encourage acceptance by participants. Another technique incorporates a few test items into a questionnaire or interview schedule so that they do not generate the anxieties associated with taking a test. There are, of course, certain standardized tests that might be useful, especially as input measures. These are illustrated by the Graduate Record Examination and the National Teachers examination tests, which measure academic aptitude and knowledge with considerable reliability.

Observation records are of many kinds and varieties (Harris 1985, 1986). They provide unique data, unlike those offered by any of the other instruments. Observation data can be highly reliable and valid. When classroom events—behaviors of students, teachers, or interactions among materials and people—are important kinds of data, then observations are uniquely well suited to obtaining such information. The cost of gathering observation data is, like interview data, rather high. Accordingly, observations are employed most often for the more elaborate or crucial ISE evaluation purposes.

Artifacts as a source of evaluative information have been most persuasively advocated in recent years by McGreal (1984). Artifacts have much to tell us about any program operation. Plans help reveal objectives, sequences, activities, and content. Transparencies and handouts emphasize content presented. Tests as artifacts, and test scores both provide insight into the objectives and the outcomes. Bulletin boards, reading lists, displays, records, and reports are still other useful artifacts.

Interestingly, carefully constructed questionnaires, designed to elicit descriptions of events *previously observed* by teachers and students, can generate usually reliable data of the kind that observation records provide. To make effective use of a questionnaire in this way, each item must be carefully constructed to discourage opinions, attitudes, and guessing while stimulating *recall* and *estimation*. To illustrate this last point, consider and contrast these three ways of eliciting a response:

1. Did you make use of the new self-instructional materials with your students? (check one)
   (   ) yes   (   ) no
2. To what extent did you use the new self-instructional materials with your students? (circle one numeral)

None	Some	Much	Constantly
0	1	2	3

3. Tell us about your use of the new self-instructional materials:
   a. Did you previously use these materials with your students? (check one option)
      (   ) no   (   ) yes, some   (   ) yes, a lot
   b. How much have you used the new self-instructional materials with your students *since* the workshop session? (circle one numeral)

None	Some	Quite a lot	A great deal
0	1	2	3

The first way of asking gives little information about *extent of use.* Furthermore, it encourages invalid responses, since few people like to admit that they have not followed through on training objectives. The second way of asking is little better than the first. While phrased to provide an estimation, it offers only four crudely specified response options. Since "none" is not likely to be utilized often, and "constantly" is an unrealistic estimate to be discounted if offered, the item provides little useful information. The third way of asking is more complex, of course. Part a provides the participant with a frame of reference for thinking and hopefully stimulates responses that are somewhat thoughtful. Part b provides clear guidance for the participant to estimate one of four levels of *extent of use.* The information provided by both parts 3a and 3b is useful, but a *comparison* of part 3a with part 3b provides uniquely useful information about the possible impact of the training in stimulating extent of use.

A Simple Questionnaire

Relatively simple questionnaires can provide rich sources of data for in-service education evaluation. It is not necessary, even though it might be interesting, to ask a lengthy array of questions in order to produce useful evaluative interpretations leading to decisions for improving an ISE session or program. Unfortunately, lengthy questionnaires often produce lots of data that are not useful for various reasons. Poorly designed instruments yield poor results. But more important, data gathered must be relevant and must lead to interpretations that can guide decisions and actions. Put another way, we need to focus on the controllable or *modifiable* elements in the situation as much as possible.

The basic model discussed and illustrated in the previous section calls for a minimum of three kinds of data, with at least one kind—input or process—subject to modification. Hence, the simplest instrument and design would call for only three bits of information, as follows:

an important bit of information about an input (age, experience, position, voluntariness, need, interest, etc.)

an important bit of information about a process (activities, group size, involvement, stimulation, work group, etc.)

an important bit of information about product or outcome (knowledge gain, intent to try, new performance, objectives achieved, enthusiasm, etc.)

A simple three-item questionnaire would generate all of this information. The participant could provide it all. A single branching diagram analysis would yield interpretations with which to consider decisions for improving the program or session.

Without trying to illustrate each variation of this simplest of all instruments, an example can serve to emphasize design considerations that are important. Suppose an instrument emerges, looking something like this:

PARTICIPANT REACTIONNAIRE
1. Your age? (circle one)
   20–30   31–40   41–50   50+
2. Your subgroup assignment? (check one)
   (   ) Group A—with teacher leader
   (   ) Group B—with principal leader
   (   ) Group C—with local supervisor leader
   (   ) Group D—with visiting consultant leader
3. How well motivated are you to try to implement the _____?
   (check one that fits best)
   (   ) I am definitely going to implement.
   (   ) I am considering implementing, may try.
   (   ) I am considering implementing, have doubts.
   (   ) I am very skeptical. I may. I may not.

This instrument consists of just three items. They include an input item (age), a process item (subgroup), and a product item (intent to implement). Little time is consumed in data gathering. A set of traditional analyses can be undertaken, and a more useful analysis based on the multivariate model in Exhibit 11–4. The three sets of questionnaire responses illustrated in Exhibit 11–1 also provide input, process, and product data for useful evaluation. Since the job is a given, it can be treated as the input. The extent of stimulation provided by the session constitutes process, while estimates of usefulness of outcomes are product data. Hence, these simple questionnaire responses lend themselves to multivariate analysis.

A More Elaborate Questionnaire

It is not the author's intent to urge ISE evaluators always to utilize the simplest of instruments. Just as questionnaires may not be either the best or the only instrumentation needed, so neither very simple nor very complex instruments are best. A few guidelines to consider call for the following:

1. Use the simplest, clearest, most objective instrumentation consistent with the data desired.
2. Ask only for data really needed and actually to be used.
3. Be sure each data bit is an important one, in the sense that it is relevant to the in-service effort being evaluated.
4. If in doubt, utilize more than one data source and instrument type.

Exhibit 11–5 provides an illustration of a questionnaire that utilizes only a single source (the participant), generates more data than the three-item one previously presented, but still remains quite simple and easy to utilize. It is intended for use at the end of a session, but it could be modified easily for use with a program of limited duration. Items 1, 2, 3, and 4 would generally be considered input items. Items 5 and 7 might be considered process items. Items 6 and 8 are product items; however, relating responses to items 3–6 generates still another variable that can be considered a process measure.

Obviously, this instrument has serious limitations. While providing four different input items, the process items are not likely to be very useful. They both ask for perceptions that are likely to be unreliable. They are not likely to yield two quite distinct kinds of data. On the contrary, one is very likely to contaminate the other. The product item 8, in asking for an estimate of usefulness, is likely to produce data of limited validity, since it asks for opinion only. Overall, the instrument suffers from depending on a single data source. Even so, such an instrument is likely to be useful for evaluation purposes and makes practical demands on participants and planners alike.

EXHIBIT 11–5. Illustration of a Single-Source Instrument

Session Feedback Instrument

Session Topic: Using Self-Instructional Learning Packets   Date: 8/10/—
Leader: W. R. Wuthridge

1. Participant code: 1   (Do not use your name. Remain anonymous!)
2. Participant Assignment: Teacher (✓)   Other (   )
   Level: Elementary (   )   Middle School (✓)   Senior High (   )
   Other (   )
3. Objectives: On the left check (✓) only the one, two, or three statements that *best* represent *your* needs or interests *prior* to coming to this session.

		Ranks
Checks (✓)	*Objectives*	*1 to 9*
( )	To recognize the major features of a learning packet that distinguish it from a workbook.	6
(✓)	To construct test items that are highly diagnostic.	4
( )	To recall the titles of available learning packets that are appropriate to my class group.	8
( )	To estimate reading level of material using both formal and informal techniques.	7

EXHIBIT 11–5. (continued)

Checks ( )	Objectives	Ranks 1 to 9
( )	To sequence a set of activities for learning to conform to accepted principles.	2
( )	To schedule group work for an entire week to provide for balance and variety for students.	3
( )	To design a self-scoring key for use with independent study activities.	1
(✓)	To prepare laminated materials for nonconsumable use in study packets.	5
( )	To recall five principles of human growth and development.	9

4. How did you happen to attend this session? (check one reason below that *best* fits you).
( ) Told to by principal (or supervisor); had no choice.
( ) Expected to; suggested by principal (or supervisor).
(✓) Decided to; it seemed to fit my interests.
( ) Agreed to; it fit with my growth plans.
( ) Convenient to attend; others going too.
( ) Had to complete requirements.
( ) Sounded exciting; promising.

5. How *stimulating* did you find this session? (check only one).
( ) Extremely stimulating.
(✓) Highly stimulating.
( ) Substantially stimulating.
( ) Somewhat stimulating.
( ) Slightly stimulating (or less).

6. Respond to the objectives listed in item 3 above again! This time, please rank from 1 to 9 the extent to which those objectives were accomplished for you! Rank 1 = most completely accomplished or gained outcome. Rank 9 = least completely accomplished.

7. How *relevant* to your job-situation did you find the contents of the session?
( ) Extremely relevant.
(✓) Highly relevant.
( ) Substantially relevant.
( ) Somewhat relevant.
( ) Slightly relevant (or less).

8. How *useful* (practical) for you was the skill or information gained in this session?
( ) Extremely useful.
( ) Highly useful.
(✓) Substantially useful.
( ) Somewhat useful.
( ) Slightly useful (or less).

Additional instrumentation of relatively simple kinds could be developed for use along with the *Session Feedback Instrument* presented in Exhibit 11–5. A follow-up survey of participants could offer a checklist of classroom practices to be completed providing data on self-observed events. This would supplement and make more concrete the actual usefulness of data that were sought in item 8 as merely an opinion. Of course, an observer recording in participant classrooms would provide still another way of substituting evidence of events for opinions.

Still another way of supplementing the data provided by the instrument shown in Exhibit 11–5 would be to secure more detailed information regarding the experiences of participants in the session. Regardless of the perceived stimulation from the session activities, data on verbal participation, extent of task attentiveness, and subgroup leader style could be useful for process analysis. These kinds of data are available, of course, by using an observer. In the absence of an observer who can be entirely free for such data gathering, it may be desirable to add a few items to the questionnaire to obtain participant estimates of these kinds.

Self-Evaluation

Self-reported data can be utilized from the trainers and planners of in-service education programs just as they are utilized from participants. Of special value is self-evaluation that focuses on preplanning rather than on actual operations. Many problems can be avoided by preevaluation of the plans and arrangements themselves. Instruments for use in evaluating plans were discussed in Chapters 4 and 9 and are illustrated in Exhibits 4–1 and 9–2. One of these instruments focuses on session planning; the other applies to program plans. Both make explicit the kinds of provisions that are likely to be essential for operations to be implemented successfully. They focus heavily on input specifications. If these checklists are utilized systematically prior to finalizing plans and actual implementation, fewer problems of routine kinds emerge to frustrate initial efforts at implementation. Preoperational evaluation of plans followed by replanning assures that evaluative feedback on inputs are likely to be largely positive and reinforcing in early stages of the program operation. Furthermore, evaluation efforts can focus more quickly and thoroughly on *process* evaluation.

The planning documents discussed in considerable detail in Chapter 4 are still another kind of instrument for evaluation and monitoring. To the extent that the *plans* themselves have been well documented, they serve as guides to monitoring the operation as a basic reference for instrumentation. If schedules call for certain events on certain dates, these schedules should be used to monitor events. The Gantt chart discussed in Chapter 9 most clearly illustrates this use of plans/operations comparisons as a way of monitoring. However, discrepancies observed in the process of monitoring should become the focus for more detailed data gathering. Why are events behind schedule? What can be done with resources saved? How does one delay affect another event?

GRAPHIC ANALYSIS AND DISPLAYS

In previous chapters and in the illustrations given in this chapter, a number of analysis and data display techniques have been shown. There is, of course, an enormous array of options available for *both* analyzing and displaying data in forms that assist with interpretations and decision making. The use of simple frequency distributions and scattergrams is widespread. They are useful and generally easily interpretable. Bar graphs and line graphs are also in widespread use in education, business, and government. The branching diagram analysis technique illustrated earlier is one that we think deserves more attention because it is multivariate and not well known. Others, of course, need to be utilized when needed.

Scattergrams

Any two sets of data that can be paired can be displayed in scattergram form. To be meaningful, the two kinds of data need to be logically related to each other. In effect, the scattergram is a graphic way of looking at correlations between two sets of events. Correlations often occur by chance or because each of the two sets of data is related to a third. Hence, it is foolish to simply correlate all sets of data with each other.

Bar and Line Graphs

Perhaps the least complicated graphic display is the bar graph. The line graph can also be used with few complications. Both permit easy interpretation and comparisons among an array of data.

Evaluation results for an entire program utilizing an array of criteria can be displayed using bar graphs. This can be illustrated with the scores produced in applying the twenty criteria of the *Descriptive Observation Record for In-service Sessions.**

The summary profile in Exhibit 11–6 of a two-day workshop for teachers

---

*See Appendix G.

EXHIBIT 11–6. Summary Profile for a Workshop

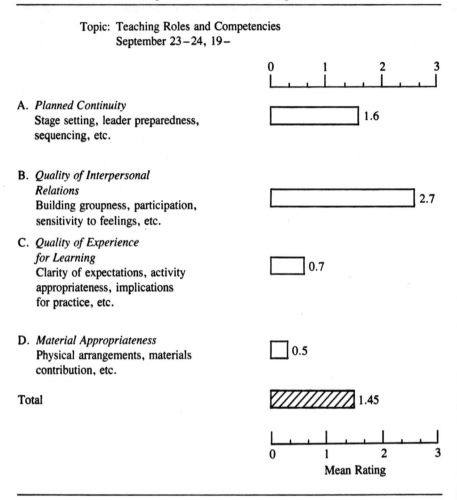

Topic: Teaching Roles and Competencies
September 23–24, 19–

A. *Planned Continuity*
Stage setting, leader preparedness,
sequencing, etc.

1.6

B. *Quality of Interpersonal
Relations*
Building groupness, participation,
sensitivity to feelings, etc.

2.7

C. *Quality of Experience
for Learning*
Clarity of expectations, activity
appropriateness, implications
for practice, etc.

0.7

D. *Material Appropriateness*
Physical arrangements, materials
contribution, etc.

0.5

Total

1.45

0   1   2   3

Mean Rating

in an elementary school combines observer ratings on twenty descriptions, clustering them to form only four bars.

The histogram is an adaptation of the bar graph that permits relating two measures to each other. In a histogram, the height of the bar represents one measure while the width of the bar reflects another measure. This is illustrated in Exhibit 11–7, using data from a program of activities in a Teacher Corps project. In this illustration, the histogram is designed as the *Impact/ Sequence Graph* by Harris for use with any in-service education session or limited program of sessions. The experience impact levels of activities are

EXHIBIT 11-7. Relating Experience Impact to Training Activity Sequence

The IMPACT/SEQUENCE GRAPH©
Session or Program: "Roles and Competencies in Teaching"
Date(s:) 9/23–24/ —
Client Group: Elementary school teachers and aides. N = 38
Place/Sponsor: Allison Elementary School/Teacher Corps
Leaders: Dr. Rubin Olivarez and Teacher Corps team

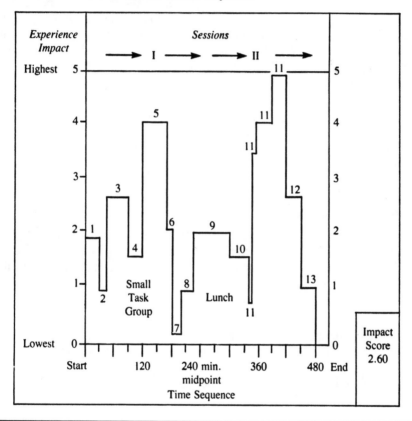

represented by the height of the bars. (See Chapter 4 for a discussion of experience impact and techniques for computing these values.)

The width of each bar reflects the number of minutes that a specific kind of activity at a *given impact level* was in progress. The activity sequence is designated by numbers at the top of each bar and is further described in the supporting planning documents. Some of the main events are labeled to assist in easy interpretation. At the top of the *Impact/Sequence Graph* is identifying information about the whole program. An impact score is computed using this histogram simply by computing the area for each bar (impact × minutes), adding all of these together, and dividing by the total minutes of activity.

Line graphs do much the same simple graphic display job that bar graphs do. A line graph can substitute for any simple bar graph. They have special value, however, when two or more sets of data need to be compared. Line graphs have their greatest value when several sets of data are being displayed and their *slopes* and *relationships* are both important. For instance, experience impact scores, attendance rates, or effectiveness measures for different projects or consultants over time can be analyzed and displayed with a series of lines. Exhibit 11–8 presents hypothetical data on participant satisfaction levels over a two-and-one-half year period. The lines show both ups and downs in three of the various components of the program for individualization presented in Appendix D. Such a graphic display provides a retrospective view of satisfaction levels. However, it suggests trends that are generally encouraging for all components shown.

Branching Diagrams

In previous sections of this chapter, the importance of multivariate analysis technique has been stressed. Branching diagram analysis was developed to facilitate such analyses in nonstatistical ways. The essential features of this technique include:

three clearly differential measures of importance to the in-service operation and independent of each other
a logical basis for interpreting each measure as an input, process, or product measure
a common source or other linkage between each bit of data of the three kinds

In a study of an ongoing program for the in-service training of teachers in the use of the *Taba Teaching Strategies* for elementary social studies, Carthel (1973) utilized questionnaire data from teachers about the "voluntary vs. involuntary" nature of their participation to secure a single "voluntariness" score for each teacher as an *input* measure. Then he utilized attendance records, observation records, and a questionnaire to produce an index of extent of "involvement" as a *process* measure. Finally, he used observation reports and student responses combined to generate an estimate of "extent of use" as a *product* measure. Each of these

EXHIBIT 11–8. Satisfaction Level of Teachers by Project Component 1974–1976

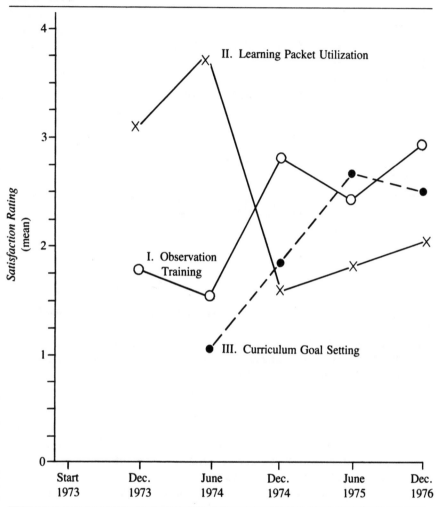

three sets of data came from different instruments and sources. However, they were related to each other because they were concerned only with voluntary participation and involvement in Taba training and the use of those strategies. Each bit of data was linked to relate bits by focusing on the individual teacher in each instance.

Plotting scores on the branching diagram simply involves inserting a frequency tally for each teacher on the three branches. When such plotting has been completed, a full diagram may look like the one below:

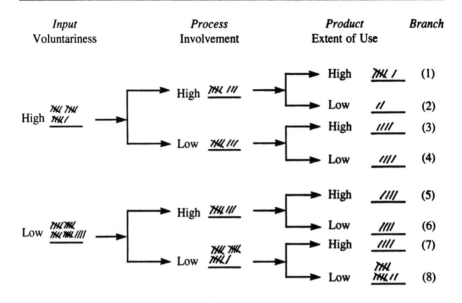

Input	*Process*	*Product*	*Branch*
Voluntariness	Involvement	Extent of Use	

As a final display, the tally marks are replaced with arabic numerals. (See Exhibit 2–6.)

Interpreting branching diagrams is a thoughtful exercise in logic. The procedure involves interpreting each branch separately and then interrelating these separate interpretations to draw one or more conclusions. The diagram just shown can be interpreted as follows:

(1) (2)* Highly voluntary teacher participants (sixteen individuals) who were *also* highly involved in the in-service training program, made more extensive use of Taba strategies in their classrooms in six out of eight instances.

(7) (8)   Less voluntary teacher participants (twenty-four individuals) who were also *not* highly involved in the in-service training program, made *less* extensive use of Taba strategies in their classrooms in twelve out of sixteen instances.

(3) (4)   Highly voluntary teachers who were *not* highly involved were equally split in extent of use.

(5) (6)   Less voluntary teachers who *were* highly involved were also equally split in extent of use.

*Numbers in parentheses refer to branches being interpreted.

Conclusions: Voluntariness is highly and consistently associated with extent of use. Involvement is also highly associated with extent of use.

(1) (3) Highly voluntary teachers make more extensive use of Taba strategies in ten out of sixteen instances.

(5) (7) Less voluntary teachers make more extensive use of Taba strategies in eight out of twenty-four instances.

However:

(1) (5) Highly involved teachers make more extensive use of Taba strategies in ten out of sixteen instances.

(3) (7) Less involved teachers make more extensive use of Taba strategies in eight out of twenty-four instances.

Therefore: Both voluntariness *and* involvement are associated with extent of use.

Decision: Both voluntariness and high levels should be promoted in in-service program plans and implementing procedures, if extent of use of strategies is to be maximized.

The illustration presented here was simplified to provide the reader with an easy-to-understand example. Appendix H includes a branching diagram analysis worksheet for readers to use in gaining experience with this analysis technique.

Other Analyses

Numerous analytical techniques of tabular and graphic kinds have much promise. Statistical methods also have merit when circumstances, time, and available resources warrant. Sanders and Cunningham (1974) discuss such techniques as Q-sort, task analysis, and Delphi. More than one analytical technique is nearly always desirable both because new insights can emerge and because different formats appeal to different users.

Various tabular displays have been shown here but not discussed in detail. Obviously, tables are nearly always utilized. When large displays of detailed data need to be presented, tables are essential. Furthermore, summarizing and comparing a few selected pieces of data can often be displayed in tabular form with great advantage.

Data analysis and display should facilitate interpretation, valuing, and decision making (Thompson 1975, 26). The techniques chosen should be dictated by the kinds of interpretations, values or orientations, and decisions that are appropriate to the situation. Above all else, however, analyses must promote communications. We cannot interpret what we do not understand. Hence, multiple approaches, graphic displays, and systems-related techniques are likely to be most valuable.

INFORMAL AND QUALITATIVE PROCEDURES

Systematic, objective, data-based evaluation efforts are emphasized in this chapter as essential to improving in-service education. Less formal, more qualitative evaluation efforts are also important because they can supplement the more formal efforts and are sometimes necessary substitutes.

Informal, qualitative procedures for evaluation include debriefing sessions, group discussions, interviews, and follow-up observations. They are informal in the sense that they may not produce quantifiable data. They are used qualitatively in the sense that fairly open-ended questions are used to guide the inquiry.

Debriefing Sessions

Leaders as well as participants of a training session or program series have vivid impressions of events and opinions regarding both processes and perceived outcomes. These are readily lost unless recorded promptly. A brief, semistructured group-sharing session can capture many impressions and opinions for review in making evaluative decisions.

Debriefing involves a small group comprised of leaders and participants. The group should include only five or six persons, so that each will have ample opportunity to verbalize. Multiple debriefings can be used if necessary to keep the group size small.

The debriefing should be scheduled immediately after a session or at the end of a series. Twenty to thirty minutes is generally adequate. A discussion leader and a recorder should be designated to encourage expressions of opinions and assure that they are recorded and made available to evaluators in useful form.

A few open-ended questions are useful in guiding the debriefing. Examples of questions commonly used include:

What do you think was most clearly accomplished? (outcome)
What seemed most useful and/or stimulating in promoting any accomplishments? (process)
What objectives were unclear, unrealistic, not well accomplished, or not properly addressed? (input-process)
How could this session (or series) be improved? (process-input)
What did you learn that was distinctively new, worthwhile, or useful? (product)

Debriefing sessions should be brief in time allocated, but also in the way impressions and opinions are expressed. There is no need to try to reach consensus or to argue about ideas being expressed. Instead, all ideas should be considered, recorded, and acknowledged.

Group Discussions

The evaluation of a series or program can be enhanced by extended discussion in a formal group setting. The focus for discussion can be both the formal evaluation report and the informal, qualitative information provided by debriefing, interviews, or observations.

Group discussions can vary from an hour to an extended series of sessions that may take many hours. Ideally, the work of a group is structured to serve the evaluation purpose, but procedures are flexible and informality is retained to allow for the free exchange of ideas, the interpretation of analyses, and the reaching of consensus regarding improving the ISE program.

Discussion groups should rarely exceed ten persons. A formal leader is usually designated. The task or tasks of the group need to be clarified in the early portion of the discussion session, and a schedule of activities adopted for accomplishing these tasks.

Perhaps, the most promising place for group discussions in the evaluation process is in synthesizing analyzed data, reviewing interpretations of findings, and offering value judgments for decision making and future planning. In these ways, evaluation becomes an integral part of the planning process (Borich and Jemelka 1981).

Interviews

Follow-up interviews with selected participants in a training program permit focused, in-depth questioning about inputs, processes, and outcomes. Since such interviews are individual, they require a great deal of time when used with a substantial number of participants (Harisun 1984).

The advantages of interviews over the more economical use of questionnaires or debriefing sessions is found in the use of open-ended questions and the opportunity to probe for deeper meanings that may lie behind simple answers. These advantages can be realized, of course, only when the interviews are rather carefully structured. In this sense, they are not really such informal procedures after all.

Observations

To the extent that ISE outcomes are changes in behavior, then observations may well be one of the most important ways of gathering outcome data (Harris 1986, 127–54). Like interviews, observations are highly individualized and require considerable time to gather sufficient information to be reliable in making decisions.

Classroom observations are often undertaken for so-called teacher evaluation purposes. As such, the focus is exclusively on the individual teacher. Both summative and developmental efforts in teacher evaluation utilize classroom observations. For purposes of evaluation of in-service education programs, the focus need not be on the individual teacher. But since such observations are widely conducted, the recorded data can sometimes be utilized as a source of information. Any objective teacher evaluation system utilizing classroom observations provides a record of teaching practices or their omission. Some review of these records after specific training efforts have been completed may be a useful way to consider outcome possibilities.

EVALUATING ONGOING OPERATIONS

Sessions come and go; they change constantly in terms of topics, participant objective, materials, and presenters. Special programs and projects have their own unique features too, with fairly explicit time frames that lend themselves to tailor-made evaluation plans. When an array of ongoing efforts at in-service education is to be evaluated, a survey research approach may be needed.

School districts, regional centers, colleges, and private consulting firms are only a few entities busily engaged in the delivery of a variety of ISE sessions, programs, workshops, courses, field experiences, and so on. Client groups may range widely. Goals and objectives are usually diverse and they change in-process. Trainers, time, resources, and materials also range widely. Under such conditions, highly goal-oriented or outcome-based evaluations are often not feasible. Routine use of questionnaires by participants for specific sessions may be interesting but only nominally useful. Instead, a periodic, comprehensive survey, using a standardized instrument, may be useful.

One approach to such a survey is comparable to a *general physical examination* of a healthy person. The evaluation is designed to be utilized with standard procedures, based on basic principles of good practice, and testing actual conditions against such standards or principles. (See prior references to McLendon 1977; Lozano 1980; Lawrence et al. 1974; Joyce, Howey, and Yarger 1976; Hagen 1981; Cavender 1986.)

To undertake such a survey, basic principles need to be operationalized with attention to specific criteria. There need to be ways of sampling from among a wide variety of practices, and selecting those that seem most relevant. There also need to be ways of scoring these selected practices using specific criteria. Finally, the criteria need to be applicable to a wide variety of programs and delivery systems.

An illustration of a survey instrument for possible use in evaluating ongoing, highly complex ISE programs is shown in Appendix L. A few illustrative portions of the instrument are reported and discussed here to clarify scoring and profiling procedures.

The *In-Service Program Evaluative Criteria* detailed in Appendix L are drawn from the principles of good practice and the studies on effective training highlighted elsewhere in this book. General principles and practices are made operationally useful for survey purposes by selecting those that have been shown to discriminate well among higher- and lower-quality programs. Six categories of practice are utilized in this instrument. Within each category, a dozen or more criteria of good practice are specified. All together, seventy-six criteria are provided. Some illustrations follow.

Category I. *Policy*
   1. To what extent do policy statements regarding ISE exist?
   8. To what extent are laws, regulations, and policies flexible in permitting participants . . . to tailor ISE to individual . . . needs?
Category III. *Designing*
   27. To what extent are ISE activities selected and designed for direct impact on . . . present practice?

The seventy-six criteria detailed in Appendix L are categorized and selected to provide knowledgeable assessors with an instrument whereby a diagnostic profile of relative strengths and weaknesses can be produced without elaborate data gathering. Exhibit 11–9 outlines the contents of the entire instrument. The six categories represent the major headings under which most of the literature considers the problems of in-service education. This author, in addition to specifying criteria in operational terms based on an array of recent studies, has also clustered these criteria to reflect twenty-four practices. This makes for a manageable scoring process without losing diagnostic power.

Exhibit 11–10 shows a portion of the *ISE Assessment Profile* completed for an ongoing program. Procedures for utilizing this survey instrument in evaluating an in-service program can vary depending upon the rigor desired and the time and resources available. An individual who is thoroughly familiar with all aspects of the program operation might complete the instrument using his or her store of firsthand information. Such an assessment might require only an hour or two of a person's time.

Obviously, reliance on the memory and information of only a single source is always risky. An *outside team* of experts might utilize the survey instrument as their frame of reference while observing, interviewing, checking records, and reviewing available data from various sources. The instrument would then also serve to report on the estimates of consensus of such an expert team.

Less elaborate, but still somewhat rigorous procedures might involve

EXHIBIT 11–9. Outline of Categories, Practices, and Specific Criteria for ISE Program Assessment

CATEGORIES AND PRACTICES	NUMBER OF CRITERIA
I. Policy (12)	
A. Clarity and structure are provided	5
B. Flexibility is provided	4
C. Funds allocations are clear and realistic	3
II. Planning (13)	
A. Personnel are assigned	3
B. Participant involvement is assured	2
C. Needs assessments are utilized	3
D. Goals and priorities are clarified	2
E. Strategies are developed	3
III. Designing (13)	
A. A variety of forms for training are used	2
B. Direct impact is emphasized	5
C. Individual needs are served	2
D. A variety of targets for change is included	2
E. Active participation is emphasized	2
IV. Organizing (11)	
A. Locations and groupings are arranged	6
B. Schedules and timetables are planned	2
C. Personnel and resources are well utilized	3
V. Implementing and Following Through (13)	
A. Plans and goals are related	2
B. Timetables and schedules are realistic	4
C. Incentives, sharing, and support are provided for	3
D. Follow-up, feedback, and applications are emphasized	4
VI. Evaluating (14)	
A. Systematic and purposeful procedures are used	3
B. Participants are served and involved	2
C. Focus includes input, process, and product	6
D. Measures are used effectively	3

a panel of knowledgeable individuals—teachers, administrators, supervisors, and others—who would make independent assessments, using the in-service survey instrument (Appendix L). These several instruments as completed would be reviewed, compared, and contrasted with each other. Then, differences in estimates would be resolved by resort to interviews, data gathering, and argumentation until consensus is reached. The *profile* would represent the best overall professional judgments based on both firsthand experience and thoughtful discourse. The recommendations for improving the in-service education program that emerged from the collaborative yet systematic efforts of such a panel of local personnel would surely be worthy of serious consideration and action.

EXHIBIT 11–10. Illustration of a Portion of the ISE Assessment Profile for an In-Service Program

D. Variety of change targets   ⌊ *7* ⌋
   31 (*3*)   36 (*4*)

E. Activity emphasis   ⌊ *4* ⌋
   32 (*2*)   37 (*2*)

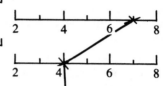

IV. ORGANIZING

A. Locations and groupings   ⌊ *13* ⌋
   39(*1*)   40(*2*)   41(*4*)

   42(*3*)   49(*1*)   43(*2*)

B. Schedules and timing   ⌊ *2* ⌋
   44(*1*)   48(*1*)

C. Personnel and resources well utilized   ⌊ *11* ⌋
   45(*3*)   46(*4*)   47(*4*)

D. Follow-up, feedback and applications   ⌊ *9* ⌋
   56(*2*)   57(*1*)   60(*4*)   62(*2*)

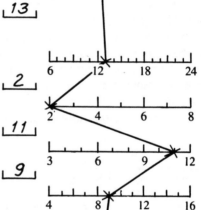

V. EVALUATING

A. Systematic and purposeful procedures   ⌊ *6* ⌋
   68(*2*)   67(*2*)   69(*2*)

B. Participants served and involved   ⌊ *4* ⌋
   64(*3*)   74(*1*)

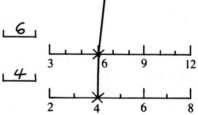

SUMMARY

Evaluation of in-service education has only been introduced here. The science and art of program evaluation is in its infancy. New tools of evaluation are at our disposal. In-service education demands evaluations of the most rigorous kinds because it is such a sensitive and important aspect of the school.

This writer sees little to be gained by continuing to adopt and adapt research methods to evaluation of in-service education in most day-to-day operations. Practitioners should borrow from the experiences and techniques of researchers, but forge their own methodologies.

This chapter has tried to provide a beginning for those who want practical approaches. New and promising alternatives are being developed. We should be exploring, refining, and avoiding standardization. Whatever our approaches, they should be objective, systematic, and open-ended. The problem is one of constantly seeking to understand what the in-service efforts are, and acting on that growing understanding. The problem is *not* one of finding the correct answers, using a particular test, developing a simple instrument, or even adopting one evaluation model. A variety of approaches, thoughtfully employed, will be most revealing.

STUDY SOURCES

Borich, Gary D., and R. P. Jemelka. 1981. *Programs and Systems: An Evaluation Perspective*. New York: Academic Press.
An in-depth analysis of instructional programs as operating systems is combined in this volume with systematic consideration of evaluation processes in such operations. These authors offer some of the most imaginative and creative ideas in the field.

Burden, Paul R. 1982. "Teachers' Perceptions of Their Personal and Professional Development." A paper presented at the Midwest Educational Research Association meeting, Des Moines, Iowa (November).
The author reports on one of the more recent efforts to systematically analyze teacher self-perceptions directly related to teaching. A useful study with implications for teacher needs assessment in a developmental context is revealed.

Burstein, Leigh. 1984. "The Use of Existing Data Bases in Program Evaluation and School Improvement." *Educational Evaluation and Program Analysis* 6 (Fall): 312–13.
A brief review of the notion that schools are developing data bases of substantial kinds. Their potential use in the evaluation process is discussed. Test scores, dropout reports, teacher evaluation reports, and many other kinds of data are more readily available now and need to be considered for improvement purposes.

Duke, Daniel L., and Lyn Corno. 1981. "Evaluating Staff Development." In *Staff Development/Organization Development,* ed. Betty Dillon-Peterson. Alexandria, Va.: Association for Supervision and Curriculum Development.
These writers discuss problems of superficial evaluation and stress need for formative efforts.

Guba, Egon G., and Yvonne S. Lincoln. 1981. *Effective Evaluation.* San Francisco, Calif.: Jossey-Bass Publishers.
Chapter 1 is especially useful in reviewing a variety of evaluation models including those by Tyler, Eisner, and others. These authors stress the use of evaluations to improve operations.

Harris, Ben M. 1985. *Supervisory Behavior in Education.* 3d ed. Englewood Cliffs, N.J.: Prentice-Hall, Inc.
Chapter 8 on "Evaluating Instructional Programs" provides additional discussion of evaluation models, illustrates various uses of branching diagram analysis, and also illustrates data envelopment analysis.

Korinek, Lori, Rex Schmid, and Martha McAdams. 1985. "In-Service Types and Best Practices." *Journal of Research and Development in Education,* 18 (Winter): 35–38.
A survey report of common practices and professional opinions about their effectiveness. The authors identify 14 "best practices." The study adds detail to the growing consensus on what makes training effective.

May, Leslie S., Carol Ann Moore, and Stephen J. Zammit, eds. 1987. *Evaluating Business and Industry Training.* Boston: Klower Academic Publishers.
A series of 15 chapters is provided by various authors on specific aspects and approaches to evaluation of training. This is perhaps the most diverse set of ideas yet published. The volume includes chapters on evaluation products, content validity, cost/benefit analysis and personnel decisions.

APPENDIXES

Appendix A

HARRIS'S ESTIMATES OF EXPERIENCE IMPACT POTENTIAL FOR TWENTY-EIGHT ACTIVITIES BY CHARACTERISTICS

ACTIVITY	1 SENSES INVOLVED	2 MULTIPLE INTERACTIONS	3 EXPERIENCE CONTROL	4 FOCUS	5 ACTIVENESS	6 ORIGINALITY	7 REALITY	TOTAL
1. Analyzing and calculating	2	2	2	3	3	1	1	14
2. Brainstorming	1	1	3	2	1	2	2	12
3. Buzz session	2	3	2	1	2	2	2	14
4. Demonstrating	1	1	3	1	1	2	3	12
5. Discussing, leaderless	2	2	1	1	1	1	2	10
6. Discussing, leader facilitated	2	2	1	2	1	1	2	11
7. Film, TV, filmstrip viewing	2	1	1	2	1	1	2	10
8. Firsthand experience	3	3	3	3	3	3	3	21
9. Group therapy	2	3	1	2	2	3	3	16
10. Guided practice	3	3	3	2	3	2	3	19
11. Interviewing, informative	1	2	2	1	1	1	1	9
12. Interviewing, problem solving	2	3	2	2	2	2	2	15
13. Interviewing, therapeutic	2	3	2	2	2	3	3	17
14. Lecturing	1	1	1	1	1	1	1	7
15. Material, equipment viewing	3	2	1	1	2	2	1	12
16. Meditating	1	1	1	2	2	3	2	12
17. Microteaching	3	2	2	3	3	2	3	18
18. Observing systematically in classroom	2	2	1	1	2	2	3	13
19. Panel presenting	2	1	1	1	1	1	1	8
20. Reading	1	2	3	3	2	1	2	14
21. Role playing, spontaneous	2	2	1	2	3	3	3	16
22. Role playing, structured	2	2	3	3	3	2	3	18
23. Social interaction	3	2	1	1	2	3	1	13
24. Tape, radio, record listening	1	1	1	1	1	1	1	7
25. Testing	2	2	3	3	1	1	1	13
26. Videotaping or photographing	3	2	1	2	3	2	3	16
27. Visualizing	2	1	1	2	1	1	1	9
28. Writing or drawing	2	1	1	2	3	2	1	12

Appendix B

ILLUSTRATION OF A PLANNING DOCUMENT FOR AN ISE SESSION

INTRODUCTION TO CLASSROOM OBSERVATION

Corpus Christi Schools   Spring 19—

Phase II—Sessions 1 and 2 Wednesday, January 15, 19—

GOAL A-1
"To promote the development of new administrative staff members as instructional leaders."
To develop skilled observer-analysts.

OBJECTIVES

A-1.1 To observe and record in live classroom situations with objectivity and reliability.

    a. To recognize objectively recorded evidence given samples from observation records showing ratings, feelings, opinions, etc., as well as descriptions of objects and events.

    b. To record evidence in a live classroom situation (or filmed), given a structured comprehensive observation guide, for a period of thirty-five to forty-five minutes, so that no opinions, judgments, or conclusions are expressed.

    c. To record evidence in a live classroom as in (b) so that 80 percent of the entries are substantively the same as those produced by an experienced observer.

    d. To record evidence in a live classroom as in (b) so that the teacher reading the edited record would object to no item as evidence of fact and would have only a few items of evidence to add.

General Information

Place: Administrative Building,
    1305 Leopard Street
Group Size: 20–25
Contact Person: W. Davis

Phone: 939–5811
Participants: New administrators
    and supervisors. Mostly assistant
    principals.

Sequence of Events—Session 1, "Introduction to Classroom Observation"

TIME	ACTIVITIES	MATERIALS	LEADERS
8:30 A.M.	**Introductions** of visiting consultants, etc. Brief orientation to project.	Scratch pads	Williams Davis
8:45 A.M.	**Getting Acquainted.** Name plaques, code numbers, positions, etc.	Session-rating sheets, colored paper (8½" × 11"), envelopes (9" × 4"), flow pens, pencils	Harris
9:00 A.M.	**Overview of the Day.** Review time schedule. Indicate sequence: 1. Learning about observation techniques. 2. Learning about one observation instrument. 3. Learning to use one observation instrument.	Chalkboard outline Time schedule	Harris
9:15 A.M.	**Introducing the Observational Problems** Relevance, objectivity, reliability. Brief reference to the need for observations that we can trust to base efforts at improvement of instruction. Brief reference to three problems. Introduce film-viewing activity. Show sixth-grade film with observation guide. Give quiz of objective evidence. Self-score quiz. Lead discussion of the teaching observed and problems in answering. Prepare transparencies.	16-mm film 16-mm projector Answer sheet Sixth-grade test Quiz key transparency	McIntyre
10:00 A.M.	**Coffee Break**		

Sequence of Events (*continued*)

TIME	ACTIVITIES	MATERIALS	LEADERS

10:20 A.M.	**Feedback on Test Results**
	Present lecturette on implications
	1. Unstructure; observations lack reliability, accuracy, or details. We seek too little, do not remember enough, and draw conclusions that might be faulty. Different individuals see quite different things.
	2. The problem is this:
	  a. There is too much to see, so we select.
	  b. We value different things to select.
	  c. We cannot remember details, so we generalize.
	  d. We get preoccupied with certain events and ignore others.
		Feedback transparencies	Harris

10:30 A.M.	**Presentation of Comprehensive Observation Guide (COG)** Brief lecturette visualized to show basic features of the COG. 1. There are four main sections to focus observer attention on sequentially. 2. "I. The Classroom." 3. "II. The Teacher." 4. "III. The Pupils." 5. "IV. The Lesson." 6. Under each section is a series of very specific questions (examples). 7. The observer simply describes what he sees in response to each question as he constantly scans the events and objects of the classroom.	Transparencies of NEWCOG format Overhead projector and screen Flow pens, pointer, three-prong adapter, blank transparencies	Harris

284

Time	Activity	Materials	Presenter
10:45 A.M.	**Distribute and Scan NEWCOG** Allow time for all participants to scan material. Brief participants on several key points by calling attention to examples. 1. Notice that events are described. No value judgments, opinions, or ratings are called for. Questions ask for *evidence!* 2. Notice that some questions are blank. 3. Notice that evidence is described as vividly as possible to convey meaning for one who was not an observer. 4. Notice that the absence of events that might be expected is objective "negative evidence."	NEWCOG Sample showing actual recording	McIntyre
11:00 A.M.	**Present Procedures for Using NEWCOG** 1. Write while in classroom. 2. Read every item sequentially from front to back and record all that is observable. 3. Use shorthand note-taking procedures. 4. Avoid getting too engrossed in a portion of the lesson—keep attention roving. 5. When all items have been used initially, use time to concentrate on "IV. The Lesson" and other new events that arise. 6. Go back to all blank items and try to add evidence.	Handout—Four Problems in Recording Evidence	Harris
11:05 A.M.	**Questions**		
11:20 A.M.	**Discuss plans** for final briefing on observation practice after lunch. Give directions on reassembling at school where observation practice sessions are planned.	Maps	Davis
11:30 A.M.	**Adjourn**		

285

Appendix C

EVALUATIVE CRITERIA FOR AN IN-SERVICE EDUCATION PROGRAM PLAN*

I. GOAL SPECIFICATION

( ) A. *A problem of importance is clearly described.*
The problem is related to the real world of the school program operation. The problem is documented by references to research, theory, or authoritative opinion. The problem is illustrated with specific examples or other clarifying information.

( ) B. *A need for training is clearly designated.*
The problem is *translated* into training-related approaches. A client or participant (group or individual) is clearly designated as appropriately related to the problem. Discrepancies are designated between *what is* and *what could be* in client performances.

( ) C. *Long-range outcomes are defined.*
Performance outcomes are clearly indicated for the client(s). Performance outcomes related to the problem in I.A. above. Performance outcomes are complex patterns of change in behavior not readily accomplished except over time.

( ) D. *Specific goals and related major objectives are specified.*
Goals are specified as performances which are portions of long-range outcomes. Goals are more explicitly defined as a set of specific performances. Goals and major objectives are sequenced and/or prioritized.

*Refer to Chapter 9 for the checklist based on this set of criteria.

II. STRATEGY

( ) E.   *The overall training strategy is clearly developed.*
The format for the entire sequence of program events is described. The logical relationship of each different kind of event to the outcomes is explained. The relationship of each event to those before and after it are explained.

( ) F.   *Influences or conditions conducive to (or inhibiting) the strategy are indicated.*
Essential preconditions for success of the program strategy are described. Conditions or circumstances that might threaten the program's effects are indicated. Special conditions that would be most facilitative are described.

( ) G.   *Cautions and limitations of the strategy are made explicit.*
Any truly serious negative side effect is clearly indicated. Errors of omission or commission are explained when serious consequences could ensue. The ways in which the strategy cannot be expected to be most promising are described.

III. DESIGN

( ) H.   *A series of clearly designated sessions is sequenced.*
More than one session is clearly designated according to time, place, and time frame required. All sessions are shown in relation to all other sessions over time. The rationale for sequencing, spacing between sessions, and specifying the length of each time frame is made clear.

( ) I.   *The various sessions are clearly related to specific goals and/or major objectives.*
Each session is logically shown as related to one, or more than one, goal and/or objective. When more than one session relates to a single goal or major objective, the progression or purpose of duplication is justified. When the same session relates to more than one goal or major objective the rationale for such dualism is justified.

( ) J.   *The various sessions are related to clients to differentiate experiences.*
A diverse set of experiences is provided in different sessions. Participants are provided with choices and alternatives for participation in session activities. Specific interests and characteristics of clients are clearly reflected in subgroup activities.

( ) **K.** *Resources required for each session are designated.*
Personnel are clearly designated as leaders and resource persons for each activity. Materials designated include all major items plus supplementary materials. Special resources are identified and budget provisions shown.

( ) **L.** *Logistics relating time, space, people, and materials to each other have been described.*
Sequences of events as described indicate people, space, and materials of crucial importance. Lists of people and other resources are cross-referenced to time schedules. Diagrams or descriptions of space indicate time, material, and people to be involved.

IV. IMPLEMENTATION

( ) **M.** *Responsibilities for each major component of the program have been assigned.*
Lists of persons with responsibilities include cross-references to activities and objectives. Memos or letters to responsible individuals clearly describe expectations. Flowcharts or other displays show responsibilities of different individuals.

( ) **N.** *Schedules of events and their coordinate relationships have been carefully detailed.*
Schedules are provided which show multiple relationships (time, space, people, events). Schedules are easily interpreted by different persons with different purposes.

( ) **O.** *Procedures for monitoring and providing corrective feedback are described.*
Critical "check points" are clearly designated in each major sequence of events. The criteria of "successful" operations are made explicit for each sequence. Plans for providing feedback to those involved during the program operation are described.

( ) **P.** *Provisions have been made for more detailed planning, training, and orientation activities for leadership personnel.*
Follow-up training needs are identified (hypothesized) and scheduled during implementation. Monitoring and feedback provisions are such that they are used for follow-up training purposes. Training time, staff, and other resources are allocated in advance, in anticipation of need.

( ) Q. *Communications have been prepared to use in informing all persons involved.*
Memos, letters, news releases, bulletin boards, reminders, etc. are prepared and prescheduled for use. Meetings are planned and scheduled to provide face-to-face sharing of problems and progress. On-site visits by important officials are planned to provide opportunities for them to see the program in operation.

V. EVALUATION

( ) R. *Instrumentation and procedures for gathering data on the program in operation are available.*
Instruments are named and sources identified or samples shown. Use of each instrument is described. Rationale for making use (or omitting) some data is presented.

( ) S. *Analytical procedures have been described for processing data.*
General analytical plans are outlined. Main tabular displays are shown. Special analytical techniques (statistical, graphic, etc.) are described.

( ) T. *Procedures for utilizing evaluation findings are designated.*
Kind of reports to be developed are indicated. Timetables for periodic releases are developed. Formats for different users are suggested.

VI. MATERIAL

( ) U. *Materials to be utilized throughout the program are fully developed and ready for use.*
Handouts are illustrated and clearly designated as to time and purpose. Transparencies are sketched if not completed and designated by purpose. Other materials (films, books, kits, videotapes) are *both* listed and described.

( ) V. *Facilities and equipment to be required are listed and/or described.*
Equipment needs are clearly specified by time and place. Special equipment to be rented or borrowed is so designated. Responsibilities for setting up and operating equipment are delegated.

( ) W. *Resource lists of materials and equipment that might be useful are provided.*

Materials to locate or purchase for use are designated. Materials to be prepared are described. Lists of known supplementary materials for follow-up are developed.

( ) X.   *Facilities arrangements that are to be required (or are desirable) are described.*

Room arrangements are shown as diagrams. Special arrangements are described as needed.

VII. OTHER

( ) Y.

( ) Z.

Appendix D

A COMPREHENSIVE PLAN FOR INDIVIDUALIZING INSTRUCTION

Rock Meadows Public Schools
Part A: The In-Service Education Plan*
1985 to 1990

CONTENTS

   I. The Long-range Goal
  II. Overview of the Program Rationale. The program plans.
 III. Comprehensive Program Goals
     A. In-service education
     B. Curriculum and materials development
     C. Facilities and equipment
     D. Community involvement

I. THE LONG-RANGE GOAL

By the end of the instructional year, in June 1990, all classroom teachers will be making full, high-quality use of five approaches to individualization of instruction in their classrooms and laboratories. Sixty percent of all instructional time will evidence some form of individualization in operation. Eighty percent of the high-priority goals and objectives of the curriculum will provide for individualization in three or more ways.

---

*Other parts of the complete plan include: Part B—Curriculum and Materials Development and Acquisition Plan; Part C—Facilities and Equipment Plan; and Part D—Community Involvement Plan.

Other evidences that a truly high-quality, full-scale program of individualization is in operation will be the following:

1. Learning resource centers will be in full operation, staffed and regularly used by students, teachers, and aides.
2. Learning activity packets will be in evidence in use and available in all content areas at all levels.
3. Observations will report a full range of individualizing practices in evidence.
4. Teacher self-reports will indicate growing use of all five approaches.
5. Student descriptions of their instructional life will report use of individualization consistent with observations.

II. OVERVIEW OF THE PROGRAM

Rationale

Students are very different one from another. They differ in interests; prior experiences; prerequisite learnings; and physical, social, and emotional development.

Learning expectations and modes of instruction should be different for every student. Differences should be those that are needed to create optimum conditions for the maximum amount of the most relevant learning for each individual.

Teachers are very different in their interests, competencies, and ways of working with students. These differences should be utilized to provide all students with the most suitable kind of instruction and also to assist all teachers to become more versatile and more fully competent.

Materials, assignments, tests, time limits, grades, and grouping arrangements should all reflect the best interests of the individual learner.

The Program Plans

Four separate but related plans for individualizing instruction are to be implemented.

A. The In-Service Education Plan
B. The Curriculum and Materials Development Plan
C. The Facilities and Equipment Remodeling Plan
D. The Community Development Plan

All plans will be implemented during the period from August 1985 through July 1990. Since all plans are related to the single, long-range superordinate goal of individualizing instruction for all students, specific objectives and all activities of each plan will be related to this single goal.

III. COMPREHENSIVE PROGRAM GOALS

A. *In-Service Education*
   1. To develop a comprehensive understanding of the meaning of individualization of instruction (II) among all staff personnel.
   2. To become skillful in utilizing five different approaches to II in the classroom for all teaching personnel.
   3. To become analytical in the use of observations and other data sources for diagnosing growth needs of all teaching personnel.
B. *Curriculum and Materials Development*
   1. To develop a selected set of high-priority goals and objectives for student learning for each content area on an ungraded basis.
   2. To produce, test, and provide for the distribution of self-instructional learning activity packets for each priority goal and objective.
   3. To select and purchase a collection of multimedia instructional aids for use in relation to each priority goal.
   4. To organize and make operational one or more learning resource centers for purposes of storing, cataloguing, distributing, and using a full array of instructional materials and equipment to facilitate individualization of instruction.
C. *Facilities and Equipment*
   1. To select, purchase, and arrange for the storing and maintenance of instructional equipment to assure ready access to multimedia by both students and teachers.
   2. To remodel at least one area in every school for special use as a learning resource center for multimedia utilization.
   3. To remodel up to 60 percent of all classrooms to facilitate their use for individualization of instruction.
D. *Community Involvement*
   1. Same as A–1 for a broadly representative group of parents and other citizens.
   2. To secure acceptance of four out of five major approaches to individualization of instruction by 70 percent of parents and 80 percent of students.
   3. To secure active involvement of a representative group of citizens as aides, tutors, visiting specialists, and advisory committee members.

IV. PLAN A OVERVIEW: IN-SERVICE EDUCATION

Components

The in-service education program will include four fairly distinct, though related, operational components, as follows:

Component I. *Observing and Analyzing Classroom Practices*
   The entire staff will develop skill in using a systematic set of classroom observation procedures with a focus on specific individualization practices. Furthermore, teachers will provide feedback to other teachers on observed events. Self-reports on practices will be developed.
Component II. *Using Learning Activity Packets (LAPs)*
   The teachers will learn to make selected use of LAPs with individuals and small groups.
Component III. *Individual Growth Planning*
   Teachers in consultation with principals and consultants will learn to develop diagnostic analyses of teaching performance patterns and develop growth plans to guide improvement efforts on an individual basis. Cooperative implementation of growth plan activities will be provided.
Component IV. *Learning Resource Center Utilization*

Phasing

Components I and II will get top priority during 1985 and 1986 with learning resource center utilization, component IV becoming more of a priority by the summer of 1987, and into the 1987–88 school year. Component III will get little attention until 1988–89.

Staffing and Coordinating Responsibilities

Each of the four components will have an individual acting as coordinator throughout the school district. Similarly, a coordinating committee for each component will have a teacher representative from each school and program level as well as a principal, consultant, or assistant principal on each committee.

   The superintendent will serve as chairman of the districtwide council for the program, which will have an administrative and teacher representative from each school. (Attachments for staff assignments for 1985–86 and for Guidelines for Committees and Councils not shown here.)

Released Time

To the fullest possible extent teachers will be released from regular classroom duties to allow for the activities of the program that are scheduled

EXHIBIT D–1. In-Service Education: Goal/Component Relationships

		IN-SERVICE COMPONENTS		
GOALS	**I** OBSERVING AND ANALYZING CLASSROOM PRACTICES	**II** USING LEARNING ACTIVITY PACKETS	**III** INDIVIDUAL GROWTH PLANNING	**IV** LEARNING RESOURCE CENTER UTILIZATION
1. To develop comprehensive understanding of the meaning of individualization of instruction.	Observers gain a variety of insights into the kinds of practices already in operation.	Users gain experience with diagnostic techniques for assigning appropriate packets.	(Not necessarily related.)	Teacher gains new respect for students' ability to direct own learning. Teacher develops appreciation of, and knowledge about, a great variety of materials for instruction. Teacher develops skill as organizer and coordinator of diverse learning activities.
2. To become skillful in utilizing five different approaches to individualizing instruction in the classroom.	Observers compare and contrast their practices with others. Feedback provided assists in refining practices.	Users learn about both values and limitations of packets, and other approaches that need to be used in relation to packets.		
3. To become analytical in the use of observations and other data sources for diagnosing growth needs.	Observers become fully aware of specific events associated with each approach and gain ability to be explicit about improvements to be sought.	(Not necessarily related.)		(Not necessarily related.)

during the instructional day. Released time will be planned by: (1) arranging for aides, student assistants, principals, counselors, librarians, and duty-free teachers to assist; (2) employing substitute teachers; and (3) releasing students from classes for all or portions of the instructional day. (See attachment for suggestions on Released Time Planning, not shown here.)

A substantial amount of the activity planned for components II, III, and IV can and will be concurrent with teaching activities. After-school hours will be utilized as needed, and selected teachers will be given opportunities for overtime contracts when serving on the program on Saturdays and during vacation periods.

Time requirements for the program are presented in great detail in Attachment C (not shown here). On the average, thirty to fifty hours per teacher per year are estimated to be required during the life of the program.

Visiting Consultants

A general consultant will be selected to serve for all aspects of the program. This person will be a distinguished scholar serving with a major university who can contract for a minimum of two days per month on-site. A team of visiting consultants will be selected and organized to work with the local staff in implementing the various components. It is anticipated that the *team* of visiting consultants will vary from three to five persons serving fifty to sixty days a year.

V. OBJECTIVES FOR COMPONENTS

Objectives for Component I:
Observing and Analyzing Classroom Practices

The staff will learn:

1.0. To develop a comprehensive understanding of II by:
   1.1. Identifying at least twenty specific practices that can be observed in classrooms that relate to individualization of instruction.
   1.2. Categorizing an array of thirty specific practices within a set of five approaches or modes of individualization.
   1.3. Identifying specific events in classrooms that are clearly evidence of individualization.
   1.4. Recording descriptively and scaling objectively the extent of individualization observed in any classroom.

2.0. To become skillful in utilizing five approaches to II by:

    2.1. Identifying similarities and differences between the array of practices observed and those in one's own classroom.

    2.2. Using feedback provided by observer reports for making specific changes in practices.

3.0. To become analytical in the use of observations and other data sources for diagnosing growth needs by:

    3.1. Analyzing a series of observation reports over time to identify recurrent events that suggest improvement needs.

    3.2. Comparing and contrasting self-reports with observation reports to detect discrepancies between perceptions.

    3.3. To translate an identified need into a vividly descriptive statement of improved performances that are desired.

Objectives for Component II:
Learning Activity Packets

(Not shown.)

Objectives for Component III:
Individual Growth Planning

(Not shown.)

Objectives for Component IV:
Learning Resource Center Utilization

(Not shown.)

VI. DESCRIPTIONS OF OPERATIONS

As has been indicated, the four components of the in-service education program plan will parallel the developmental efforts outlined in plans B, C, and D. All in-service education will be directed toward goals and objectives specified.

Component I:
Observing and Analyzing Classroom Practices

    a. The entire faculty will have an opportunity to become familiar with the purposes to be served by classroom observations, the instruments to be utilized, and the training and other procedures planned. A general faculty meeting will be planned. This will be followed by school-level discussions.

b. A coordinating committee for component I will be organized. Each building and grade level will have an elected teacher representative on the committee. Each building will have an administrative representative. The central staff will be represented by an instructional supervisor from each of the elementary and secondary divisions, and the superintendent will serve as chairman at least for the first year.

c. A local training team will be organized and trained as observation trainers in each building. Most if not all of these trainers will also be members of the Coordinating Committee. At least three trainers in each building will be selected, provided with released time, and trained in the use of systematic classroom observation techniques. They will also be given training in the use of standardized training procedures and provided with consulting services from a visiting consultant.

d. As training teams are ready, they will proceed to work with one fourth of the faculty in each building to train them in the use of classroom observation procedures.

e–h–j. As each group of the faculty gains skill in the use of observation techniques, interobserver reliability checks will be scheduled to secure agreements of high order. Training will be conducted in workshop settings but will quickly move to classrooms, where small groups will practice on each other.

i. A visiting consultant will be holding regular conferences with training team leaders (trainers) to discuss problems, reactions, and concerns they may be encountering.

k. Demonstrations will be planned and presented to provide opportunities for observers to see specific practices under high-quality conditions. If necessary, some of these demonstrations will be scheduled in schools in other districts to assure only top-quality displays of practices.

f. As trainers certify a substantial portion of the faculty as qualified observers, routine observations with individual feedback will be scheduled. Observations will provide each faculty member no less than five feedback reports by five different observers, one for each of an array of lessons.

n. Principals will have debriefing sessions with small faculty groups to determine concerns and problems and obtain suggestions for revisions in procedures during the following year.

Procedures for subsequent years will be much like those described here, with only a few exceptions: (1) new teachers will be trained as soon as possible; (2) rechecking of reliability levels will be provided; (3) growth planning will be related to observation and feedback processes beginning early in the second year as a part of component III.

Component II: Using Learning Activity Packets

(Not shown.)

Component III: Individual Growth Planning

(Not shown.)

Component IV: Learning Resource Center Utilization

(Not shown.)

VII. STAFF ASSIGNMENTS

(Not shown.)

VIII. BUDGET

(Not shown.)

Appendix E

ILLUSTRATIONS OF INDIVIDUAL
PROFESSIONAL GROWTH PLANS

DeTEK INSTRUMENT VI
PROFESSIONAL GROWTH PLAN

Teacher __C. Henry__   School __Jones Elementary__   Date __Oct. 29, 198-__

Teaching Assignment: Grade __5th__   Subject(s) __Language Arts__

FIRST — REFERENCE ACCOMPLISHMENTS: Behavior # __3c__   Indicators Accomplished __(None)__
(Designate behavior and indicator numbers accomplished.
Refer to Data Analysis Worksheet, Instrument V)

___ # ___ # ___
___ # ___ # ___

SECOND-DESIGNATE BEHAVIORS AND INDICATORS AS NEEDS (Refer to Instrument V)		THIRD-LIST ACTIVITIES TO BE UNDERTAKEN (Describe specific activities for each indicator. Refer to Resource File and Activities List for suggestions of activities, materials and sources.)	FOURTH-MAKE DECISIONS*	
Number	**DEVELOPMENTAL LEVEL**		**Collaborator Responsible**	**Date to Complete**
3c(3)	Uses an array of question types, ranging from [K]	-- Secure a copy of Bloom's taxonomy of educational objectives... "cognitive domain", Read and review w. Supv.	Helen Johnson	11/10/19-
			C. Henry	11/20/19-
	Simple recognition and recall to analysis, synth., eval. [K]	-- Secure a copy of Wm. H. Banaka's "Training in Depth Interviewing", chap. 7. Harpers (1971). Read and bring to conference.	Wm. B. Noyes	11/10/19-
			C. Henry	11/15/19-
	[E]	-- Arrange for a visit with Jerry Canon at Hillsdale Elem. or Fred Akers at Eisenhower JHS to observe classroom discussion.	Wm. Noyes C. Henry and H. Johnson	11/5/19 - 11/7-15/
	[T]	-- Plan a discussion lesson to incorporate new techniques. -- Present discussion lesson w. observer.	C. Henry and H. Johnson	11/22/19- 11/23/19 -

*INDICATE the proposed date for STEP 10-REVIEW DIALOG SESSION.   Time: __3__ : __00__ to __3__ : __40__   Date __11/23/198-__

Teacher's Signature __C. Henry__   Principal's Signature __Wm. B. Noyes__

301

Growth Agreement for ————————————————, Teacher

School ———————————— Assignment ————————

District ———————————— Date ————————————

Collaborator(s) ————————————————————————

Title(s) ————————————————————————————

THE INDIVIDUAL TEACHER
GROWTH AGREEMENT
by Ben M. Harris

Directions:

This agreement form is intended for use by classroom teachers in collaboration with a principal, supervisor, department chairman, or team leader. The purpose is to guide and maintain a record of systematic efforts at improvement of performance on the job. The ITGA has been designed and tested for use under certain specific conditions:

(1) There is a willingness on the part of the teacher to improve job performance.

(2) There is a collaborating official willing and able to assist in planning and facilitating the improvement activities.

(3) Classroom observation data and/or other objective data related to teacher performance have been collected.

CYCLE I. RECORDING, ANALYZING AND DECIDING

I–A   Record and review data from instruments used:

DATE	OBSERVER	INSTRUMENTS	SCORE(S)

I–B   Diagnostically analyze cumulative data.

STRENGTHS	IMPROVEMENT NEEDS

I–C   Decide whether a plan for meeting improvement needs is required.

Yes _____   No _____

If *yes*, teacher will draft a plan for improvement to be discussed.
If *no*, complete item IIIG(3) below and sign-off on item III-H.

CYCLE II. PLANNING

II–A   Review and plan for improvement. Revise plan as needed. Propose plan.

II–B   Approve plan for improvement (attached).

Signature: _____

Title: _____

Date: _____

CYCLE III. REVIEWING PROGRESS AND REPLANNING

III–F   Progress report on improvement plan in operation.

Which objectives have been accomplished? _____; _____; _____

Which objectives are in progress? _____; _____; _____

What changes (revisions, additions, substitutions) are needed?

_____

_____

III–G Next Steps

(1) Continue to implement plan until _____

(2) Revise improvement plan on _____ (refer to II–B above)

(3) Initiate new Cycle I with new agreement by _____ (refer to I–A above)

III–H Approved by:

Signature: _____

Title: _____

Date: _____

Appendix F

ILLUSTRATION OF A LOCAL DISTRICT ISE POLICY

STAFF DEVELOPMENT

A. In-Service Education for All Personnel

The continuous efforts to improve instruction for all students shall be promoted by a program of in-service education (ISE).

1. Definition. In-service education includes planned learning opportunities provided under the direction of the staff for improving performance in already held or assigned positions.
2. All personnel are entitled to, and responsible for, participating in in-service education throughout the period of tenure with the district.
3. The administration shall provide for an ISE program or programs that assure: (a) attention to the most urgent needs of the district for improving its operations, and (b) attention to the specific needs of individual staff members for improving performance on the job.
4. The administration shall develop a long-range plan for the ISE of personnel and shall update it annually.
5. All affected personnel will be provided opportunities to influence the character of the ISE program(s) by direct or representative participation in planning, evaluating, and implementing.
6. Training opportunities developed by colleges, teacher centers, professional associations, and other agencies may be utilized for ISE purposes so long as they are coordinated with, and guided by, the ISE program plans of the district.
7. All required ISE activities shall be on time specified under the contract of the personnel involved. Activities necessitating overtime or out-of-contract time periods (summer or holidays) shall be authorized under mutual agreements for extra pay or compensatory time exchanges.

Appendix G

DESCRIPTIVE OBSERVATION RECORD FOR IN-SERVICE SESSIONS (DORIS)

Directions:

This instrument is designed in two parts. (1) An observation form is provided with twenty criteria specified to guide the observer in recording the events as they transpire during an in-service training session. (2) A profile sheet is provided to convert evidence recorded into a set of ratings.

The observation form should be utilized throughout a specific session. The observer should record narrative descriptions of any events that relate to any one of the twenty criterion statements.

When the session ends, the observer reviews the recorded notations carefully. **Then,** the observer checks each item on the profile sheet **in the one box** that most accurately reflects what happened in the session.

Assigned values are recorded for each item on the profile sheet as designated for the one box that is checked.

Category scores are determined by adding all assigned values for the item in each category and dividing that sum by the number of items. Category scores calculated to one decimal place are recorded in the boxes at the left margin.

No total score is to be computed. Each item score and category score should be utilized diagnostically to focus on strengths and weaknesses in the session.

DESCRIPTIVE OBSERVATION OF IN-SERVICE SESSIONS

DORIS

Topic _Techniques for Evaluating Inservice sessions_

Location _Lemoyne, PA._ Date _3/10/87_

SUMMARY PROFILE for the Analysis and Interpretation of the DORIS

		Evidence		
Category	Assigned Values	Not Observed	Uncertain	Abundantly Observed

A. Planned Continuity

	Assigned Values	Not Observed	Uncertain	Abundantly Observed
2. Stage setting	3	☐ 0	☐ 1	☒ 3
4. Leader preparedness	5	☐ 0	☐ 2	☒ 5
6. Sequence	2	☐ 0	☐ 1	☒ 2
9. Timing	1	☐ 0	☒ 1	☐ 2
16. Feedback	1	☐ 0	☒ 1	☐ 3
17. Summarizing	0	☒ 0	☐ 1	☐ 2
18. Generalizing	3	☐ 0	☐ 1	☒ 3
20. Follow-through	2	☐ 0	☒ 2	☐ 4

[2.1] Scoring: A = Sum of $\frac{17}{8} = 2.1$

B. Quality of Interpersonal Relations

	Assigned Values	Not Observed	Uncertain	Abundantly Observed
3. Building groupness	1	☐ 0	☒ 1	☐ 3
10. Participation	2	☐ 0	☒ 2	☐ 4
12. Sensitivity to feelings	0	☒ 0	☐ 1	☐ 2
14. Participant autonomy	1	☐ 0	☒ 1	☐ 3

[1.0] Scoring: B = Sum of $\frac{4}{4} = 1.0$

C. Quality of Experience for Learning

	Assigned Values	Not Observed	Uncertain	Abundantly Observed
5. Clarity of expectations	1	☐ 0	☒ 1	☐ 2
7. Appropriateness of activities	2	☐ 0	☒ 2	☐ 4
11. Seriousness	1	☐ 0	☒ 1	☐ 2
13. Acceptance of participants' ideas	3	☐ 0	☐ 1	☒ 3
15. Differentation of tasks	0	☒ 0	☐ 1	☐ 3
19. Implications for practice	0	☒ 0	☐ 2	☐ 4

[1.2] Scoring: C = Sum of $\frac{7}{6} = 1.2$

D. Material Appropiateness

	Assigned Values	Not Observed	Uncertain	Abundantly Observed
1. Physical arrangements	1	☐ 0	☒ 1	☐ 2
8. Contribution of materials	4	☐ 0	☐ 2	☒ 4

[2.5] Scoring: D = Sum of $\frac{5}{2} = 2.5$

Presenter(s) _B. HARRIS_   Observer _SELDEN_

1. *Physical Arrangements.* What indicates that the leader has provided for the arrangement of the physical environment prior to the beginning of the session? How do the allocations of space and arrangements of the furnishings fit the specific needs of the group? *The chairs and tables were in straight rows, conference style. Agenda were in front of each participant on arrival. Overhead projector and screen in place -- focused.*

2. *Stage Setting.* How does the leader set the tone for the session, build expectations, and inform participants of the structure of the session and the rationale for group membership during the session? *Leader gave overview of entire day -- distinguished a.m. from p.m. goals. Warned about morning involving much review.*

3. *Building Groupness.* How does the leader develop a feeling of closeness and unity of purpose among the participants or encourage healthy competition and mature controversy when appropriate? *No evidence in a.m. p.m. session involved completing diagrams -- individuals invited to work alone or together.*

4. *Leader Preparedness.* What indicates that the leader has prepared for the session and is informed on its subject? *Materials organized in a packet. Each item utilized. Transparencies used to illustrate key ideas. Extra handouts ready.*

5. *Clarity of Expectations.* Indicate ways in which participants are informed of specific anticipated outcomes of the session. *Each session outlined on a separate sheet. Objectives for each session listed.*

Are the outcomes to be discovered or clearly designated in advance? *-objective related to branching technique to be discovered. Presenter warned "Before long, you'll get a chance to try this yourself."*

How does the leader make sure that participants know whether discovery is involved or not? *(see above.)*

6. *Sequence.* Describe the sequence of activities for each portion of the session. List the full variety of activities offered participants.
Overview in lecture form with handout used as frame of reference. Key concepts presented via overhead transparencies. Participants given tasks, allowed to get started, but feedback presented as they progressed to assure correct procedures.

7. *Appropriateness of Activities.* Indicate the appropriateness of the activities as related to the objectives of the session and the needs of participants.

Practice with diagrams led directly to answers on techniques. No small group interaction. Questions promoted only at the end of each session.

8. *Contribution of Materials.* How do the materials used in the session contribute toward the accomplishment of the objective?

Transparencies heavily utilized to present ideas, review, provide feedback and illustrated. Handouts in a packet organized for reference as presentation required.

9. *Timing.* How does the timing and pacing of the session affect the learning situation?

Morning session moved on schedule but interaction very limited. P.M. session paced smoothly except some slow to complete exercise and others had to wait.

10. *Participation.* At four different times during the session, observe the group at work and record in the spaces provided the information called for below. Divide session into four parts — list the time of observation.

9-10:15 - Mostly listening. Attentive. Handouts to read. Transparencies guide events. 10:30 - 12:00 - still mostly listening. Handouts less utilized. 1:00 - 2:00 - Lots of action. Individuals and teams interact. 2:00 - 3:15 - Mostly listening, questions.

11. *Seriousness.* Describe manifestations that indicate participants are serious about the activities at hand.

Attentiveness. Returned from lunch on time. Had to ring school bell after break. Few questions raised in morning.

12. *Sensitivity to Feelings.* What evidence suggests that the leader is sensitive to anxieties, tensions, and conflicts, among peers?

Very little here. Presenter refers several times to local conditions. Critical question (only 1) allowed time for discussion.

13. *Acceptance of Participant Ideas.* What evidence suggests that the leader accepts and utilizes contributions of participants?

Few questions or comments. One participant having trouble with practice exercise -- presenter said: "You can do it that way but it may be easier if ..." Challenging question about distorting facts handled positively.

14. *Participant Autonomy*. How does the leader provide participants with alternatives, freedom to choose, or otherwise encourage individual initiative?

Mostly all doing the same ... Listening, practicing, etc. Presenter did suggest working in groups as voluntary.

15. *Differentiation of Tasks*. What variations from assigned tasks are suggested and supported?

No variations. All doing the same.

16. *Feedback*. Describe the process used by the leader for giving and receiving evaluative feedback during and after the session.

Practice exercises interrupted to allow for "progress checks" with transparencing Key for all to use. Little interaction. Questions limited mostly at end of session.

17. *Summarizing*. Describe the approach used by the leader to summarize or synthesize the session's events.

End of session summary, each one brief, largely verbal. One transparency used in summarizing form.

18. *Generalizing*. Describe the ways in which the leader develops or evokes valid generalizations about the session's content or outcomes.

Many references to applications of techniques to sessions, programs, and other circumstances. A wide variety of illustrations provided on transparencies.

19. *Implications for Practice*. In what ways are participants led to relate generalizations to their individual work situations?

Presenter suggests most implications. Only a few questions relate to implications.

20. *Follow-through*. Describe the ways in which the stage is set for follow-up, future sessions, further study, etc.

List of sources for further reading provided with brief quotations. Extra Worksheets and additional materials provided for follow-up practices.

Appendix H

WORKSHEET FOR HARRIS'S
BRANCHING DIAGRAM ANALYSIS

Worksheet

INPUT VARIABLE   **PROCESS VARIABLE**   **PRODUCT VARIABLE**

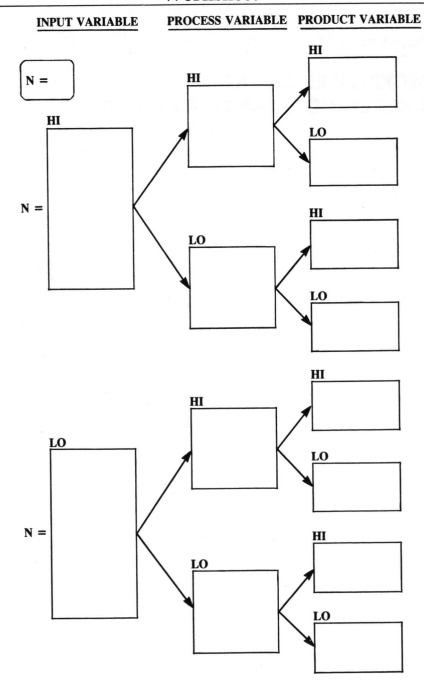

See Chapter 11, section on "Branching Diagrams," for illustrations and explanation.

Appendix I

CHECKLIST FOR THE PREPARATION OF AN IN-SERVICE SESSION PLAN

Directions:

This checklist is intended for use with *Guidelines for Preparing an In-Service Session Plan*. As the preliminary planning documents are being developed, that checklist serves to alert the planners to the contents of the plan. Check every item from A to Z. Designate each item in the space at the left, using the number code shown below.*

( ) **I. STATEMENT OF THE PROBLEM**

    ___ **A.** Clearly identified. (2)†

    ___ **B.** Described as concrete, documented, important. (1)

    ___ **C.** Defined as responsive to training. (1)

    ___ **D.** Translated into staff needs. (1)

( ) **II. CLIENT SPECIFIED**

    ___ **E.** Individuals and groups specified; background described. (2)

---

*Designate items as: "0" = Non-existent.
                    "1" = Limited or incomplete, but clearly included.
                    "2" = Clearly, adequate, completely included.

†See Chapter 4 for a list of detailed guidelines relating to each item (A–Z).

— **F.** Relationship to problem indicated; differences estimated. (1)

— **G.** Rationale for focus on these clients presented. (1)

( ) **III. GOALS AND OBJECTIVES**

— **H.** The major outcomes specified, observable, and related to the problem. (2)

— **I.** Specific objectives specified, related, and differentiated by need. (3)

— **J.** Selected as realistic, important, and significant. (1)

( ) **IV. SCHEDULE OF EVENTS**

— **K.** Master calendar for preplanning, implementing, and follow-up. (1)

— **L.** Agenda for the session includes timetable and allocations. (4)

— **M.** Sequence, time, activity relationships shown. (2)

( ) **V. DESCRIPTION OF PROCEDURES**

— **N.** Activities carefully described. (3)

— **O.** Activity selections justified. (2)

— **P.** Illustrations included to clarify. (1)

— **Q.** Alternatives or variations described. (1)

( ) **VI. EVALUATION**

— **R.** Procedures clearly described. (3)

— **S.** Instruments selected or prepared. (2)

— **T.** Analytical procedures shown. (2)

( ) VII. FOLLOW-UP PLANS

— **U.** Follow-up plans outlined and/or described show continuity. (1)

— **V.** Immediate next steps carefully detailed. (3)

( ) VIII. EXHIBITS

— **W.** Materials to be used illustrated. (5)

— **X.** Equipment and arrangements listed. (2)

— **Y.** Resource persons designated. (2)

— **Z.** Budget prepared. (1)

Title of Session ———————————————— Date ————————

Prepared by ———————————————— Planned for ————————

TOTAL QUALITY SCORE

Further Directions:

REVISE those portions of the plan that are coded "0" or "1." When the plan has been revised, reassess as follows:
  a. Code all times A to Z as before.
  b. Multiply weights designated in parentheses by each code value.
  c. Sum the weighted values for each cluster of items.
  d. Sum all weighted values for a total quality score.

Appendix J

PLANNING WORKSHEET FOR IN-SERVICE SESSION

I. GENERAL INFORMATION

Topic, Theme, or Title _____ Date(s) _____

_____ Phone _____

Place _____

Participants: Number _____ Positions _____

    Levels _____ Other Facts _____

II. ANTICIPATED OUTCOMES

Goals: A _____

      B _____

      C _____

Objectives:

    1.

    2.

    3.

    4.

    5.

III. AGENDA

Activity Number	Start Time	Activity Description	Materials, Equipment, & Arrangements	Code*

*Code each activity to a specific goal *and* objective as specified in Part II.

IV. MATERIAL, EQUIPMENT, AND ARRANGEMENTS

	Check	Seating and Other Ar-
Check Need:	Reserved ( )	rangements: (Describe
	Ready ( )	seating, furniture, and
		other arrangements)

Equipment Needed:
( ) 16-mm projector   ( )   _____
( ) Projection screen   ( )
( ) Overhead projector   ( )   _____
( ) Marking pens &
    pencils   ( )   _____
( ) Chalkboard, chalk,
    eraser   ( )   _____
( ) Microphone & PA
    system   ( )
( ) Tape recorder,
    sound   ( )
( ) Recorder, video   ( )
( ) Slide projector   ( )
( ) Other _____   ( )

		Check	
		Ordered __	
Materials Needed for Handouts:	Quantity	Received __	Code*
_____	_____	____	___
_____	_____	____	___
_____	_____	____	___
_____	_____	____	___

	Check	
Materials to Have Available:	Ready ( )	Code*
Transparencies _____	( )	
_____	( )	
_____	( )	

*Code each item with the initials of the responsible persons shown here:

_____   _____   _____

Videotape ———————————————— ( )

Sound-tape ———————————————— ( )

Film ———————————————— ( )

Slides ———————————————— ( )

Other ———————————————— ( )

Appendix K

CHECKLIST FOR PRESESSION ARRANGEMENTS

Topic/Event _____ Date(s) _____

Location _____

Contact Person _____ Phone _____

Address _____

_____ Zip _____

Directions:

Use the spaces at the left of each item to indicate initiation (_√_), then check again to indicate completion (_√ √_). Use the parentheses at the right of the items to code person assigned.

A. INITIAL PLANNING

___ Identify target group ( )

___ Assess priority needs ( )

___ Draft tentative plans ( )

___ Inform participants of tentative plans ( )

___ Secure suggestions ( )

___ Revise tentative plan ( )

___ Develop handouts ( )

___ Prepare/select visual/audio aids ( )

___ Arrange for consultants and other resource persons ( )

___ Arrange for briefing consultants ( )

___ Develop evaluation plan ( )

B. LOGISTICS

Transportation

— Self ( )

— Consultants ( )

— Others _____ ( )

Communications

— Reproduce program ( )

— Advance mailing to participants ( )

— Publicity release ( )

— Signs ( )

Physical Arrangements

— Meeting place ( )

— Furniture needed ( )

— Seating arrangement ( )

Services

— Coffee order ( )

— Meal reservations ( )

C. MATERIALS

Registration

— Name tags ( )

— Place cards ( )

— Pencils ( )

— Extra mail-outs ( )

— Registration list ( )

Handouts (List)

— _____

— _____

— _____

— _____

Transparencies (List)

— _____

— _____

— _____

— _____

Miscellaneous Material

— Blank acetates ( )

— Marking pens ( )

— Marking pencils ( )

— Other material ( )

— _____ ( )

— _____ ( )

D. EQUIPMENT

___ Overhead projector ( )

___ Spare projection
lamp(s) ( )

___ Projection screen ( )

___ Cassette recorder(s) ( )

___ Tape recorder, reel ( )

___ Chalkboard, chalk ( )

___ Extra cassette(s), tapes ( )

___ Microphone ( )

___ 16-mm projector ( )

___ 16-mm take-up reel ( )

___ Extension cords ( )

___ Three-prong adapter ( )

___ Other equipment

___ _____ ( )

E. SPECIAL ARRANGEMENTS

Appendix L

IN-SERVICE PROGRAM EVALUATIVE CRITERIA AND ASSESSMENT PROFILE (IPECAP)

Directions:

An assessor should circle either a 1, 2, 3, or 4 opposite each criterion statement. Each assessment should represent a clearly supportable estimate of actual operating reality (1 = very limited or uncertain; 4 = clearly, extensively, or completely). If in doubt, use lower ratings.

I. POLICY

ASSESSMENT
RATINGS

1. To what extent do policy statements regarding ISE exist?   1   2   3   4

2. To what extent is a comprehensive plan or organization in place to direct (facilitate) ISE planning?   1   2   3   4

3. To what extent does policy designate ISE as both a right and a responsibility of all staff?   1   2   3   4

4. To what extent does policy assure differentiated opportunities for ISE staff?   1   2   3   4

5. To what extent does policy assure some freedom of choice for staff in pursuing ISE activities?   1   2   3   4

6. To what extent does policy call for ISE planning, participation, and evaluation as a part of the regular duties of staff members?   1   2   3   4

7. To what extent does policy require resource allo- 1 2 3 4
    cations for ISE to assure time, material, person-
    nel, travel, and other requirements can be met?

8. To what extent are laws, regulations, and policies 1 2 3 4
    flexible in permitting participants and other staff
    to tailor ISE to individual and local needs?

9. To what extent are ISE needs of all participants 1 2 3 4
    provided for at no personal cost?

10. To what extent does policy offer incentives to 1 2 3 4
    staff to participate fully in ISE programs?

11. To what extent do officials (Board members, su- 1 2 3 4
    perintendents, others) publicly communicate sup-
    port for ISE?

12. To what extent does policy promote ISE pro- 1 2 3 4
    grams to serve a variety of professional and in-
    stitutional purposes?

II. PLANNING

13. To what extent are knowledgeable and respon- 1 2 3 4
    sible individuals assigned to plan ISE program
    activities?

14. To what extent are participants involved in the 1 2 3 4
    planning of their own ISE?

15. To what extent is formal systematic needs assess- 1 2 3 4
    ment undertaken for individuals?

16. To what extent are staff members in various types 1 2 3 4
    of positions (principal, supervisor, evaluator) in-
    volved in planning ISE?

17. To what extent are ISE plans clearly related to 1 2 3 4
    high-priority, long-range goals?

18. To what extent are teacher and program evalua- 1 2 3 4
    tion reports utilized in ISE planning?

19. To what extent are individual staff member needs 1 2 3 4
    given priority in ISE planning?

20. To what extent are outside consultants involved in planning ISE at local levels?   1 2 3 4

21. To what extent is ISE planning clearly differentiated and coordinated at district, building, and individual levels?   1 2 3 4

22. To what extent are the complexity and the magnitude of the training goals considered in developing a strategy and plan?   1 2 3 4

23. To what extent are alternative ways of utilizing personnel, programs, and institutions built into the ISE plans?   1 2 3 4

24. To what extent are plans reviewed and adapted to assure feasibility and relative advantage?   1 2 3 4

III. DESIGNING

25. To what extent do staff member participants serve also as planners, presenters, and evaluators in their ISE?   1 2 3 4

26. To what extent do designs for ISE programs utilize a wide variety of formats—courses, workshops, visits, demonstrations, etc.?   1 2 3 4

27. To what extent are ISE activities selected and designed for direct impact on the staff members' present practice?   1 2 3 4

28. To what extent are objectives guiding the design specific in designating performance changes anticipated?   1 2 3 4

29. To what extent are objectives guiding the design related to specific diagnosed needs of individuals and programs?   1 2 3 4

30. To what extent are differences in clients as individuals and as groups recognized in the design of specific ISE programs?   1 2 3 4

31. To what extent are ISE programs directed toward   1 2 3 4
curriculum change, methods, and materials use,
evaluating students and classroom management?

32. To what extent are ISE activities selected and   1 2 3 4
designed for active rather than passive participation?

33. To what extent are activities selected to assure   1 2 3 4
change in behavior (not just knowledge or at-
titude)?

34. To what extent are activities selected for use   1 2 3 4
specifically related to an objective?

35. To what extent are ISE programs designed to al-   1 2 3 4
low for flexible and alternative uses of time to
assure appropriate and varied experiences?

36. To what extent do ISE program designs respond   1 2 3 4
to needs for retraining, renewal, innovations, and
improvement in basic skills?

37. To what extent do designs for programs include   1 2 3 4
systematic use of a wide variety of activities?

38. To what extent do program designs call for use of   1 2 3 4
activities with highest experience impact—role
playing, simulations, directed practice, etc.?

IV. ORGANIZING

39. To what extent are locations for training deter-   1 2 3 4
mined by training requirements rather than convenience and cost of arbitrary preferences?

40. To what extent are training groups organized for   1 2 3 4
optimum learning, rather than for convenience,
economy, or traditions regarding levels, subjects,
experience, etc.?

41. To what extent are a variety of group and individ-   1 2 3 4
ualized arrangements utilized—tutorials, small
groups, large groups, mass media?

42. To what extent do locations utilized include class- 1 2 3 4
rooms, meeting rooms, other schools, colleges,
state or national conferences?

43. To what extent are expectations that staff mem- 1 2 3 4
bers will participate directly related to job assignments?

44. To what extent are ISE programs scheduled to 1 2 3 4
utilize a variety of time frames—summer, during
school hours, after school, Saturdays, etc.?

45. To what extent are arrangements for presenta- 1 2 3 4
tions and support personnel provided to include
college consultants, other education agencies,
central staff, as well as local personnel?

46. To what extent are arrangements made for using a 1 2 3 4
variety of resources for support services—going
beyond those individuals regularly involved?

47. To what extent do local building personnel serve 1 2 3 4
as presenters, organizers, and facilitators (including teachers, principals, and others)?

48. To what extent are schedules arranged so that re- 1 2 3 4
leased time, individual consultations, and access
to classrooms are readily available?

49. To what extent are consultants, visiting resource 1 2 3 4
persons, and experts utilized with small groups
and individuals (not just for large group presentations)?

V. IMPLEMENTING AND FOLLOWING THROUGH

50. To what extent are preplanning documents ac- 1 2 3 4
tually utilized to guide and direct implementation?

51. To what extent are time allocations made to ac- 1 2 3 4
commodate a full schedule of diverse in-service
activities?

52. To what extent are training activities scheduled to assure in-depth study and continuity of experiences over time?   1 2 3 4

53. To what extent are training sessions scheduled to provide two- or three-hour blocks rather than short meetings?   1 2 3 4

54. To what extent are participants expected to commit to a training series extending twenty to thirty or more hours during a school year rather than attending isolated, short sessions?   1 2 3 4

55. To what extent are a variety of incentives offered—released time, travel, expenses, compensatory time—to encourage full participation?   1 2 3 4

56. To what extent do in-service sessions include those that assure follow-up into actual application situations with hands-on, guided practice?   1 2 3 4

57. To what extent is follow-up training, emphasizing actual application of skills, a major portion of the total program?   1 2 3 4

58. To what extent are support services available to trainees as they attempt to apply new skills or techniques (released time, aides, materials, etc.)?   1 2 3 4

59. To what extent do individual needs get attention in the implementation process so that amounts and kinds of training are varied?   1 2 3 4

60. To what extent are implementers provided with observation, feedback, and reinforcement when applying new skills?   1 2 3 4

61. To what extent are participants provided with opportunities to share ideas, information, and concerns as regular parts of the program?   1 2 3 4

62. To what extent are mutual assistance or peer coaching arrangements provided to facilitate implementation?   1 2 3 4

VI. EVALUATING

63. To what extent is evaluation of in-service programs systematic, objective, and carefully planned? 1 2 3 4

64. To what extent are participants actively involved in the process of evaluating in-service experiences? 1 2 3 4

65. To what extent is evaluation process focused upon determining increases in skills as well as knowledge and information of participants? 1 2 3 4

66. To what extent is improved performance the primary basis for designating needs and evaluating in-service effects? 1 2 3 4

67. To what extent is evaluation of in-service activities related to specific needs of the participants as a group? 1 2 3 4

68. To what extent is evaluation process focused upon determining actual changes in practices of participants? 1 2 3 4

69. To what extent are evaluation activities conducted along with implementation as well as afterwards? 1 2 3 4

70. To what extent is evaluation process focused upon attitudes and opinions of participants? 1 2 3 4

71. To what extent is evaluation process focused upon the skills and techniques of leaders? 1 2 3 4

72. To what extent is evaluation process focused on the appropriateness of materials, activities, and grouping arrangements? 1 2 3 4

73. To what extent are evaluation measures utilized to provide objective, descriptive data rather than opinions, feelings, or speculations? 1 2 3 4

74. To what extent is evaluation process focused on individual participants as well as group outcomes? 1 2 3 4

75. To what extent do the evaluations attend to "side effects" as well as intended outcomes? 1 2 3 4

76. To what extent are evaluation data analyzed, reviewed, and carefully reported to leaders? 1 2 3 4

ISE ASSESSMENT PROFILE

A Profile of Assessments:
In-Service Education Program Operations

School _____ Date _____

Program(s) _____

Profile estimates based on: Assessor(s) are:

____ Individual assessor *or*   ____ Teacher(s)

____ Team of assessors   ____ Supervisor(s)

                                           ____ Administrator(s)
Time Frame of Operations:
                                           ____ Program Director(s)
____ Immediate past (less than one
     year)   ____ Others (specify) _____

____ Past year   _____

____ Past several years

Directions:

Record each of the seventy-six assessments in the parentheses with a corresponding number. When multiple assessors are invited, use a consensus or a mean assessment for each entry.

Sum all assessments on each line (IA, IB, IC, etc.) and record these totals in the space at the end of each line.

Place an "x" on the grid for each sum of assessments.

Example:

B. Flexibility
   4 ( ) 5 ( ) 8 ( ) 12 ( )   ____ ┤┼┼┼┼┼┼┼┼┼┼┼┤
                                              4   8   12   16

I. POLICY   Low   High
                                             ─────────────────────

   A. Clarity and structure
      1 ( ) 2 ( ) 3 ( ) 6 ( ) 11 ( ) ____ ┤┼┼┼┼┼┼┼┼┼┼┼┼┤
                                                5   10   15   20

Low   High

B. Flexibility provided
4 ( )   5 ( )   8 ( )   12 ( )

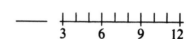

C. Funds allocations
7 ( )   9 ( )   10 ( )

II. PLANNING

A. Personnel assigned
13 ( )   16 ( )   20 ( )

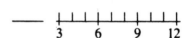

B. Participant involvement
14 ( )   29 ( )

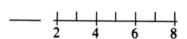

C. Needs assessment
15 ( )   18 ( )   19 ( )

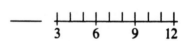

D. Goals and priorities
17 ( )   22 ( )

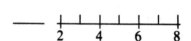

E. Strategies
21 ( )   23 ( )   24 ( )

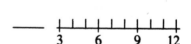

III. DESIGNING

A. Variety of forms
25 ( )   35 ( )

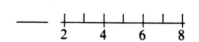

B. Direct impact emphasis
26 ( )   27 ( )   33 ( )   34 ( )
38 ( )

C. Individual needs served
28 ( )   30 ( )

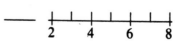

Low   High

D. Variety of change targets
31 ( )   36 ( )

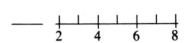

E. Activity emphasis
32 ( )   37 ( )

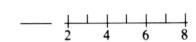

IV. ORGANIZING

A. Locations and groupings
39 ( )   40 ( )   41 ( )   42 ( )
43 ( )   49 ( )

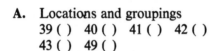

B. Schedules and timing
44 ( )   48 ( )

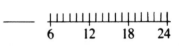

C. Personnel and resources well
utilized
45 ( )   46 ( )   47 ( )

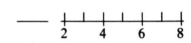

V. IMPLEMENTING AND FOLLOWING THROUGH

A. Preplanning and scheduling
50 ( )   51 ( )   52 ( )   53 ( )

B. Commitment and incentives
54 ( )   55 ( )

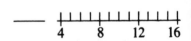

C. Follow-up, feedback, and
applications
56 ( )   57 ( )   60 ( )   62 ( )

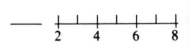

D. Support and individualization
58 ( )   59 ( )   61 ( )

	Low	High

VI. EVALUATING

A. Systematic and purposeful procedures 67 ( )   68 ( )   69 ( )

—— |++++++|++|++++|
        3   6   9   12

B. Participants served and involved 64 ( )   74 ( )

—— |+|+|+|+|+|
        2   4   6   8

C. Focus includes input, process, and product
65 ( )   66 ( )   68 ( )   70 ( )
71 ( )   72 ( )

—— ||||||||||||||||||||
        6   12   18   24

D. Measures used effectively 73 ( )   75 ( )   76 ( )

—— |++++++|++|++++|
        3   6   9   12

Appendix M

IN-SERVICE EDUCATION LEADERSHIP COMPETENCIES

A. Supervising in a Clinical Mode
   1. Conducts interviews.
   2. Leads clinical cycles.
   3. Observes in classrooms.

B. Planning for Individual Growth
   4. Develops activity schedule.
   5. Assists in selecting objectives.
   6. Interprets performance data.

C. Designing In-Service Training Sessions
   7. Plans variety of activities.
   8. Develops evaluation plan.
   9. Specifies realistic objectives.

D. Conducting Training Sessions
   10. Leads meaningful activities.
   11. Makes arrangements.
   12. Selects training strategy.

E. Training for Leadership Roles
   13. Organizes debriefings.
   14. Trains teacher leaders.
   15. Identifies teacher leaders.

F. Assessing Needs
   16. Consults with planners.

17. Analyzes assessment data.
18. Selects and adapts instruments.

G. Developing a Master Plan
   19. Designates strategies.
   20. Identifies resource needs.
   21. Relates training to priorities.

H. Writing a Project Proposal
   22. Coordinates proposal writing.
   23. Constructs visual displays.
   24. Writes clearly defined goals.

I. Designing Self-instructional Packets
   25. Programs activity sequences.
   26. Selects/develops media.
   27. Sequences content, objectives, and activities.

J. Designing a Training Program
   28. Designs to accommodate individual differences.
   29. Guides the planning process.
   30. Leads groups in the planning.

REFERENCES

Acevedo, Mary A., Carol Elliott, and Leonard A. Valverde. 1976. *A Guide for Conducting an Effective Feedback Session.* Document No. 15, Special Education Supervisor Training Project, Department of Educational Administration. The University of Texas at Austin.

Allen, Dwight W. 1980. "Merging Resources of the IHE and the LEA for the Improvement of Inter-Institutional Programs." In *Professional Development Occasional Paper 2.* Syracuse, N.Y.: National Council of States on In-Service Education, Syracuse University.

Allen, Dwight, and Kevin Ryan. 1969. *Micro-Teaching.* Reading, Mass.: Addison-Wesley.

Almanza, Helen K. 1980. "A Study of In-Service Education Programming Associated with Highly Innovative Programs in Selected Elementary Schools." Ph.D. diss., The University of Texas at Austin.

Alpert, Judith L., and Associates. 1982. *Psychological Consultation in Educational Settings.* San Francisco: Jossey-Bass Publishers.

American Association of Colleges for Teacher Education. 1976. "Report of Survey on Competency-Based In-Service Education." A report sponsored by the Performance-Based Education Committee. Washington, D.C.: Association for the Accreditation of Teacher Education. Mimeo.

————. 1979. "In-Service Education: Opportunities and Options." *Journal of Teacher Education* 30 (January-February).

Amidon, Edmund, and E. Hunter. 1966. *Improving Teaching: The Analyses of Classroom Verbal Interaction.* New York: Holt, Rinehart and Winston.

Anderson, Robert H., and Karolyn J. Snyder. 1981. *Clinical Supervision: A Coaching Technology.* Lubbock, Tex.: Pedamorphosis, Inc.

Andros, Kathleen F., and Donald J. Freeman. 1981. "The Effects of Three Kinds of Feedback on Math Teaching Performance." Paper presented at the Annual Meeting of the American Educational Research Association, Los Angeles, Calif. (April 13–17).

Argyris, Chris. 1982. "How Learning and Reasoning Processes Affect Organizational Change." In Paul S. Goodman and Associates, *Change in Organizations.* San Francisco: Jossey-Bass Publishers.

Arwady, Joseph W. 1984. "Improving Training Results through Behavior Modeling." *Performance and Instruction* 23 (March): 23–25.

Association for Supervision and Curriculum Development. 1957. *Action Research: A Case Study.* Washington, D.C.: Association for Supervision and Curriculum Development.

Bailey, Danita. 1985. "Relationships among Supervisor Competencies, Job Expectations, and Position Types." Ph.D. diss., The University of Texas at Austin.

Bailey, Gerald D. 1983. "Implementing a Self-Directed Staff Development with a District-Based Leadership Model." ERIC ED 238 848.

Bales, Robert F. 1950. *Interaction Process Analysis—A Method for the Study of Small Groups.* Cambridge, Mass.: Addison-Wesley.

Bang-Jensen, Valerie. 1986. "The View from Next Door: A Look at Peer Supervision." In *Improving Teaching,* 1986 ASCD Yearbook, ed. Karen K. Zumwalt. Alexandria, Va.: Association for Supervision and Curriculum Development.

Bank, Adrianne, and James Bury. 1978. "Directions in Testing and Evaluation: CSE, 1978." *Evaluation Comment* 5 (July): 1–9. UCLA Center for the Study of Evaluation.

Barell, John. 1981. "Developing Professional Improvement Plans: A Strategy for Staff Development." ERIC ED 211 449.

Barr, A. S., W. H. Burton, and Leo J. Brueckner. 1938. *Supervision: Democratic Leadership in Improving Learning.* 2d ed. New York: Appleton-Century-Crofts.

Bedient, D., and M. Rosenberg. 1981. "Designing Instruction for Adult Learners: A Four-Stage Model." *Educational Technology* 21 (November): 25–27.

Beegle, Charles W., and Roy A. Edelfelt. 1977. *Staff Development: Staff Liberation.* A report of a conference jointly sponsored by ASCD and the Department of Administration and Supervision, School of Education, University of Virginia. Washington, D.C.: Association for Supervision and Curriculum Development.

Bergquist, Constance C. 1985. "The Teacher Education Center Program in Florida." In *What Works in In-Service Education Programs for Teachers?,* ed. Elva G. Galambos. Atlanta, Ga.: Southern Regional Education Board.

Berman, Louise. 1977. "Curriculum Leadership: That All May Feel, Value, and Grow." Chap. 11 in *Feeling, Valuing, and the Art of Growing: Insights into the Affective,* ed. L. M. Berman and Jessie A. Roderick. Washington, D.C.: Association for Supervision and Curriculum Development.

Berman, Paul, and Milbrey McLaughlin. 1975. *Federal Programs Supporting Educational Change,* Vol. 4. *The Findings in Review.* Santa Monica, Calif.: The Rand Corporation.

Berry, Gloria. 1987. "A Study of Instructional Leadership Competencies and In-Service Education Programs Associated with Innovative Programs in Selected Elementary Schools." Ph.D. diss., The University of Texas at Austin.

Bessent, E. Wailand. 1967. "In-Service Education—A Point of View." In *Designs for In-Service Education,* ed. E. W. Bessent. Austin, Tex.: Research and Development Center for Teacher Education.

Bessent, E. W., B. M. Harris, and M. P. Thomas. 1968. *Adoption and Utilization of Instructional Television.* Austin, Tex.: The University of Texas.

Bessent, E. W., et al. 1974. *A Computer-Assisted Instruction Module.* Vol. 1, *Student Manual for Instructional Decision-Making.* Austin, Tex.: Special Education Supervisor Training Project, The University of Texas.

Blessing, Buck. 1979. "Ptolemy, Darwin and Change." *Training and Development Journal* 35 (July): 28–30.

Bloom, Benjamin S. 1976. *Human Characteristics and School Learning.* New York: McGraw-Hill.

Bloom, Benjamin S., 1956. *Taxonomy of Educational Objectives. Handbook I: The Cognitive Domain.* New York: David McKay.

Borich, Gary D., and R. P. Jemelka. 1981. *Programs and Systems: An Evaluation Perspective.* New York: Academic Press.

Borich, Gary D., and Susan K. Madden. 1974. *Evaluating Classroom Instruction: A Source Book of Instruments.* Reading, Mass.: Addison-Wesley.

Bork, A. 1987. "The Potential for Interactive Technology." *BYTE Magazine.* 12:201–04.

Borrero, Maria G., et al. 1982. "Research Based Training for Organizational Change." *Urban Anthropology* 11 (Spring): 129–53.

Boyan, Norman J., and Willis D. Copeland. 1978. *Instructional Supervision Training Program.* Columbus, Ohio: Charles E. Merrill.

Brookover, Wilbur B., et al. 1980. *Measuring and Attaining Goals of Education.* A document of the ASCD Committee on Research and Theory. Alexandria, Va.: Association for Supervision and Curriculum Development.

Bunderson, C. Victor, and Gerald W. Faust. 1976. "Programmed and Computer-Assisted Instruction." *The Psychology of Teaching Methods,* 75th Yearbook, Part I, ed. N. L. Gage. Chicago: National Society for the Study of Education.

Burden, Paul R. 1982. "Teachers' Perceptions of Their Personal and Professional Development." A paper presented at the Midwest Educational Research Association meeting, Des Moines, Iowa (November).

Burstein, Leigh. 1984. "The Use of Existing Data Bases in Program Evaluation and School Improvement." *Educational Evaluation and Program Analysis* 6 (Fall): 312–13.

Butts, David P. 1967. "The Classroom Experience Model." In *Designs for In-Service Education,* ed. E. W. Bessent. Austin, Tex.: Research and Development Center for Teacher Education Monograph, The University of Texas at Austin.

California State Commission for Teacher Preparation and Licensing. 1981. *Comprehensive Plan for Coordination of Preservice and In-Service Professional Preparation of Educational Personnel in the State of California.* Sacramento, Calif.: California State Department of Education. ERIC ED 201 047.

Carthel, James T. 1973. "An Application of a Systems Analysis Model to the Evaluation of an Instructional Improvement Program." Ph.D. diss., The University of Texas at Austin.

Cavender, Steven. 1986. "In-Service Education Design Features for Transfer of Training in Selected Schools." Ph.D. diss., The University of Texas at Austin.

Christensen, Judith C. 1985. "Adult Learning and Teacher Career Stage Development." Chap. 8 in *Career-Long Teacher Education,* ed. Peter J. Burke and R. G. Heideman. Springfield, Ill.: Charles C. Thomas, Publishers.

Christian, Jerry D. 1981. "The Operational Effects of the Five-Year Priorities Plans of Texas School Districts as Functions of Commitments to and Strategies for Process of Change." Ph.D. diss., The University of Texas at Austin (August).

Cline, Daniel. 1984. "Achieving Quality and Relevance in In-Service Teacher Education: Where Are We?" *Teacher Education and Special Education* 7 (Fall): 199–208.

Cloutier, Marc G. 1986. "The Relationship of Medical Knowledge and Psychological Type to Aggressive Leadership Performance of Senior Medical Students in a Stressful Environment." Ph.D. diss., The University of Texas at Austin.

Cogan, Morris L. 1973. *Clinical Supervision*. Boston: Houghton Mifflin Company.

Conrad, M. J., Kenneth Brooks, and George Fisher. 1973. "A Model for Comprehensive Planning." *Planning and Changing* 4 (Spring): 3–14.

Coody, Betty. 1967. "A Study of the Impact of Demonstrating Teaching on Experienced and Inexperienced Teachers under Various Supervisory Conditions." Ph.D. diss., The University of Texas at Austin.

Cook, Desmond. 1966. *Program Evaluation and Review Technique: Applications in Education*. Washington, D.C.: U.S. Department of Health, Education, and Welfare, U.S. Government Printing Office.

Cook, Stuart W. 1976. *Research Methods in Social Relations*. 3d ed. New York: Holt, Rinehart and Winston.

Cooper, Myrna. 1977. "In-Service Training Projects of the United Federation of Teachers." *NCSIE In-Service*. National Council of States on In-Service Education. Syracuse, N.Y.: Syracuse University, College of Education (November).

Corey, Stephan M. 1957. *In-Service Education for Teachers, Supervisors and Administrators*, 56th Yearbook, Part I, ed. Nelson B. Henry. Chicago: National Society for the Study of Education.

Crawford, John, and Jane Stallings. 1978. "Experimental Effects of In-Service Teacher Training Derived from Process-Product Correlations in the Primary Grades." In Gage, N. L., et al. 1978. *An Experiment on Teacher Effectiveness and Parent-Assisted Instruction in the Third Grade*. Stanford, Calif.: Center for Educational Research at Stanford University (May 1978) ERIC ED 160 648.

Creekmur, Jimmie L. 1977. "A Descriptive Analysis of In-Service Education Programs of Selected Texas School Systems Utilizing Operational Criteria." Ph.D. diss., The University of Texas at Austin.

Cropley, A. J., and R. H. Dave. 1978. *Lifelong Education and the Training of Teachers*. Advances in Lifelong Education, Vol. 5. UNESCO Institute for Education. Oxford: Pergamon Press.

Cruickshank, Dr. R. 1977. *A First Book of Games and Simulations*. Belmont, Calif.: Wadsworth Publishing Company, Inc.

Cunningham, William G. 1982. *Systematic Planning for Educational Change*. Palo Alto, Calif.: Mayfield Publishing Co.

Davis, Larry N., and Earl McCallon. 1974. *Planning, Conducting and Evaluating Workshops*. Austin, Tex.: Learning Concepts.

De Kalb County Schools. 1975. *Performance-Based Certification Supportive Supervision Model*. Doraville, Ga.: De Kalb County Schools.

DeVries, David L. 1976. "Teams—Games—Tournament: A Gaming Technique That Fosters Learning." *Simulation and Games* 7 (March): 21–33.

Dillon, Elizabeth A. 1976. "Staff Development: Bright Hope or Empty Promise?" *Educational Leadership* 34 (December): 165–70.

Duke, Daniel L., and Lyn Corno. 1981. "Evaluating Staff Development." In *Staff Development/Organization Development*, ed. Betty Dillon-Peterson. Alexandria, Va.: Association for Supervision and Curriculum Development.

Duke, Daniel L., and R. J. Stiggins. 1986. *Teacher Evaluation: Five Keys to Growth*. A joint publication of the American Association of School Administrators, National Association of Elementary School Principals, National Association of Secondary School Principals, and the National Education Association. Washington, D.C.: National Education Association.

Edelfeldt, Roy A. 1976. "Can Competency-Based Teacher Education Be Applied to In-Service Education? Should It Be?" A draft manuscript prepared for the Association for the Accreditation of Teacher Education (July). Mimeo.

Edelfeldt, Roy A., and Margo Johnson, eds. 1975. *Rethinking In-Service Education*. Washington, D.C.: National Education Association.

Edmonds, Fred, James R. Ogletree, and Pat W. Wear. 1963. *In-Service Teacher Education: A Conceptual Framework*. A theoretical base for the second phase of teacher education. *Bulletin of the Bureau of School Service*, Vol. 36, no. 2 (December). College of Education, University of Kentucky, Lexington, Ky.

Ellington, Henry, Eric Addinall, and Fred Percival. 1981. *Games and Simulations in Science Education*. London: Kogan Page.

Engel, Herbert M. 1973. *Handbook of Creative Learning Exercises*. Houston, Tex.: Gulf Publishing Company.

Enos, Donald F. 1976. "A Cost-Effectiveness Analysis of Competency-Based and Non-Competency-Based Teacher Education at San Diego State University." Ph.D. diss., The University of Texas at Austin.

Evans, Michael C., Ben M. Harris, and R. L. Palmer. 1975. *A Diagnostic Assessment System for Professional Supervisory Competencies*. Document no. 11. Austin, Tex.: Special Education Supervisor Training Project, The University of Texas at Austin.

Fever, Dale. 1986. "Training by Committee at Good Samaritan Hospital." *Training* 23 (March): 73–76.

Finkel, Coleman. 1986. "Pick a Place, But Not Any Place." *Training and Development Journal* 40 (February): 51–53.

Flanders, Ned A. 1970. *Analyzing Teaching Behavior*. Reading, Mass.: Addison-Wesley.

Florida State Department of Education. 1975. *Criteria for Designing, Developing and Approving a District Master Plan for In-Service Education*. Tallahassee, Fla.: State Department of Education.

Florida State Department of Education. 1987. A+ Program: Certification "+" Competencies. Tallahassee, Fla.: State of Florida, Department of Education (August 28).

Freeman, Robert E. 1983. "Effective Workshop Processes for Global Education." *California Journal of Teacher Education* 10 (Winter): 40–56.

Freiberg, H. Jerome, and Ruben D. Olivarez. 1978. *Dimensions of In-Service Education: The Texas Teacher Corps Experience*. San Antonio, Tex.: Trinity University, Teacher Corps Network.

Friant, Ray J., Jr. 1983. *Preparing Effective Presentations: How to Make Presentations Pay Off*. Babylon, N.Y.: Pilot Industries, Inc.

Friedlander, Madeline S. 1972. *Leading Film Discussions: A Guide to Using Films for Discussion, Training Leaders, Planning Effective Programs*. New York: League of Women Voters, City of New York.

Friedman, Myles I., Patricia S. Brinlee, and Patricia B. Dennis Hayes. 1980. *Improving Teacher Education: Resources and Recommendations*. New York: Longman.

Fullan, Michael. 1982. *The Meaning of Educational Change*. New York: Teachers College Press.

Fullan, Michael, and Allan Pomfret. 1977. "Research on Curriculum and Instruction Implementation." *Review of Educational Research* 47 (Winter): 335–97.

Gage, N. L. 1978. *The Scientific Basis of the Art of Teaching*. New York: Teachers College Press.

Gage, N. L., et al. 1978. *An Experiment on Teacher Effectiveness and Parent-Assisted Instruction in the Third Grade*. Stanford, Calif.: Center for Educational Research at Stanford University (May). ERIC ED 160 648.

Gall, Meredith D., and Joyce P. Gall. 1976. "The Discussion Method." In *The Psychology of Teaching Methods*, 75th Yearbook, Part I, ed. N. L. Gage. Chicago: National Society for the Study of Education.

Gall, Meredith D., and R. S. Renchler. 1985. *Effective Staff Development for Teachers: A Research-Based Model*. Eugene, Oreg.: Clearinghouse on Educational Management, College of Education, University of Oregon.

Gant, Jack, Oron Smith, and John H. Hansen. 1977. *Temporary Systems*. Tallahassee, Florida.

Gay, Geneva. 1980. "Conceptual Models of Curriculum-Planning Process." Chap. 7 in *Considered Action for Curriculum Improvement*, ed. A. W. Foshay. Alexandria, Va.: Association for Supervision and Curriculum Development.

Geffert, H. N. 1976. *State Legislation Affecting In-Service Staff Development in Public Education*. Model Legislation Project. Washington, D.C.: Lawyers' Committee for Civil Rights Under Law (March).

Georgia Department of Education. 1980. *Planning Education Improvement*. Atlanta, Ga.: Research and Development Utilization Project, Department of Education.

Georgia Department of Education. 1983. *Guidelines for the Implementation of Performance-Based Certification by the Georgia Department of Education, Regional Assessment Centers, and Local School Systems*. Atlanta, Ga.: Division of Staff Development (June). Mimeo.

Gibbs, G. I., ed. 1974. *Handbook of Games and Simulation Exercises*. London: E. and F. N. Spon Ltd.

Gite, Lloyd. 1983. "Giving That Winning Presentation." *Black Enterprise* 14 (September): 49–52.

Glatthorn, Allan A. 1984. *Differentiated Supervision*. Alexandria, Va.: Association for Supervision and Curriculum Development.

Glickman, Carl D. 1985. *Supervision of Instruction: A Developmental Approach*. Newton, Mass.: Allyn and Bacon, Inc.

Goldhammer, Robert. 1969. *Clinical Supervision*. New York: Holt, Rinehart and Winston.

Goldhammer, Robert, Robert Anderson, and Robert Krajewski. 1980. *Clinical Supervision: Special Methods for the Supervision of Teachers*. 2d ed. New York: Holt, Rinehart and Winston.

Goldstein, William. 1982. *Supervision Made Simple*, Fastback 180. Bloomington, Ind.: Phi Delta Kappa Educational Foundation.

Good, Thomas, and Jere Brophy. 1978. *Looking in Classrooms*. 2d ed. New York: Harper & Row.

Good, Thomas L., and R. S. Weinstein. 1986. "Teacher Expectations: A Framework for Exploring Classrooms." Chap. 6 in *Improving Teaching*, ed. Karen K.

Zumwalt. Alexandria, Va.: Association for Supervision and Curriculum Development.

Goodlad, John I. 1975. "Schools Can Make a Difference." *Educational Leadership* 33 (November): 110–11.

Goodman, Paul S., and Associates. 1982. *Change in Organizations: New Perspectives on Theory, Research and Practice.* San Francisco: Jossey-Bass Publishers.

Gordon, E. W., Lizanne DeStefano, and Stefanie Shipman. 1985. "Characteristics of Learning Persons and the Adaptation of Learning Environments." In *Adapting Instruction to Individual Differences,* ed. Margaret C. Wang and Herbert J. Walberg. Berkeley, Calif.: McCutchan Publishing Corp.

Grant, Carl A., ed. 1981. "Staff Development: State of the Scene and Possibilities." *Journal of Research and Development in Education* 14 (Winter). Athens, Ga.: University of Georgia, College of Education.

Grant, Carl A., and Kenneth M. Zeichner. 1981. "In-Service Support for First Year Teachers: The State of the Scene." *Journal of Research and Development in Education* 14 (Winter): 99–111.

Greenblat, C. S., and R. D. Duke, eds. 1975. *Gaming—Simulation: Rationale, Design, and Applications: A Text with Parallel Readings for Social Scientists, Educators, and Community Workers.* New York: Sage Publications.

Gryna, Frank M., Jr. 1981. *Quality Circles: A Team Approach to Problem Solving.* New York: AMACOM, A Division of American Management Association.

Guba, Egon G., and Yvonne S. Lincoln. 1981. *Effective Evaluation.* San Francisco, Calif.: Jossey-Bass Publishers.

Hagen, Nancy Joyce. 1981. *A Comparative Analysis of Selected In-Service Education Delivery Systems.* Ph.D. diss., The University of Texas at Austin.

Hall, Gene, and Frances Guzman. 1984. "Sources of Leadership for Change in High Schools." A paper presented at the Annual Meeting of the American Educational Research Association, New Orleans, La. (April).

Hall, Gene E., and S. Loucks. 1978. "Teacher Concerns as a Basis for Facilitating and Personalizing Staff Development." *Teachers College Record* 80 (September): 36–53.

Harisun, Marelle. 1984. *Commonwealth Schools Commission Professional Development Programme (S.A.).* A Survey of Professional Development Practices in South Australian Schools: Report to the Professional Development Committee. Adelaide, South Australia: State Professional Development Committee. Mimeo.

Harris, Ben M. 1963. *Supervisory Behavior in Education.* Englewood Cliffs, N.J.: Prentice-Hall, Inc.

Harris, Ben M. 1966. *A Research Study of the Effects of Demonstration Teaching upon Experienced and Inexperienced Teachers.* Cooperative Research Project No. S–384, U.S. Office of Education. Austin, Tex.: The University of Texas at Austin.

Harris, Ben M. 1975. *Supervisory Behavior in Education.* 2d ed. Englewood Cliffs, N.J.: Prentice-Hall, Inc.

Harris, Ben M. 1976. "Limits and Supplements to Formal Clinical Procedures." *Journal of Research and Development in Teacher Education* 9 (Winter): 85–87.

Harris, Ben M. 1980. *Improving Staff Performance through In-Service Education.* Boston, Mass.: Allyn and Bacon, Inc.

Harris, Ben M. 1985. *Supervisory Behavior in Education*. 3d ed. Englewood Cliffs, N.J.: Prentice-Hall, Inc.

Harris, Ben M. 1986. *Developmental Teacher Evaluation*. Newton, Mass.: Allyn and Bacon, Inc.

Harris, Ben M., E. Wailand Bessent, and Kenneth E. McIntyre. 1969. *In-Service Education: A Guide to Better Practice*. Englewood Cliffs, N.J.: Prentice-Hall, Inc.

Harris, Ben M., and Jane Hill. 1982. *Developmental Teacher Evaluation Kit*. Austin, Tex.: Southwest Educational Development Laboratory.

Harris, Ben M., K. E. McIntyre, Vance Littleton, and D. F. Long. 1985. *Personnel Administration in Education*. 2d ed. Boston: Allyn and Bacon, Inc.

Hart, Louis B., and J. Gordon Schleicher. 1979. *A Conference and Workshop Planner's Manual*. New York: ANACOM.

Hasazi, Susan E., et al. 1983. *Vocational Education for the Handicapped: Perspectives on In-Service Personnel Development*. Personnel Development Series, Doc. 6. Washington, D.C.: Division of Personnel Preparation, Office of Special Education and Rehabilitative Services. ERIC ED 224 939.

Heie, Harold, and David Sweet. 1984. "Faculty Development through Growth Contracts." In *Andragogy in Action,* ed. Malcolm S. Knowles. San Francisco: Jossey-Bass Publishers.

Heitzmann, William Ray. 1983. *Educational Games and Simulations*. 2d ed. What Research Says to the Teacher. Washington, D.C.: National Education Association.

Henderson, Jeff. 1987. "On the Value of Simulated Reality." In *Innovations Abstracts* 9 (September 25): 1–2. Austin, Tex.: Community College Leadership Program, The University of Texas at Austin.

Heyman, Mark. 1975. *Simulation Games for the Classroom*. Bloomington, Ind.: The Phi Delta Kappa Educational Foundation.

Heyman, Mark. 1978. "Experimental Learning: Some Thoughts about It, Leading to Categorization." *Simulation Gaming* 5 (January–February): 4–5.

Hite, Herbert. 1976. "Three Scenarios for In-Service Education." A paper prepared for the Committee on Performance-Based Teacher Education. Washington, D.C.: American Association of Colleges for Teacher Education (October). Mimeo.

Hite, Herbert, and Pat McIntyre. 1980. *Planning for In-Service Education (Revised): A Resource Guide*. Washington, D.C.: Office of Education, Teacher Corps. ERIC ED 185 031.

Horn, R. E., ed. 1977. *The Guide to Simulation/Games for Education and Training*. Cranford, N.J.: Didactic Systems, Inc.

House, Richard M. 1983. *Standards of Practice in Continuing Education: A Status Study*. A research report of the Project for the Development of Standards and Criteria for Good Practice in Continuing Education. Silver Spring, Md.: Council on Continuing Education Unit.

Howey, Kenneth R., Sam Yarger, and Bruce Joyce, eds. *School-Focused In-Service: Descriptions and Discussions*. Reston, Va.: Association of Teacher Educators.

Howsam, Robert B. 1977. "The Profession of Teaching." In *Issues in In-Service Education: State Action for In-Service,* pp. 9–13. Syracuse, N.Y.: National

Council of States on In-Service Education, Syracuse University, College of Education (November).

Hundley, Anna, and Martha Hartzog. 1981. *Characteristics of Effective In-Service Education.* Austin, Tex.: Southwest Educational Development Laboratory.

Hutson, Harry M., Jr. 1981. "In-Service Best Practices: The Learnings of General Education." *Journal of Research and Development in Education* 14 (Winter): 1–10.

Ingber, Phil. 1987. "Graphics, Sound Make the IIGS an Apple to Eye." In *Electronic Learning* 41 (February): 18.

Iwanicki, Edward F., and Lucille McEachern. 1983. "Teacher Self-Improvement: A Promising Approach to Professional Development and School Improvement." *Journal of Staff Development* 4 (May): 62–77.

Iwanicki, Edward F., and Lucille McEachern. 1984. "Using Teacher Self-Assessment to Identify Staff Development Needs." *Journal of Teacher Education* 35 (March–April): 38–41.

Jackson, Phillip W. 1974. "On Becoming a Teacher." *Today's Education* 63 (March–April): 37–38.

Janis, Irving L. 1972. *Victims of Groupthink: A Psychological Study of Foreign-Policy Decisions and Fiascoes.* Boston: Houghton Mifflin.

Jones, K. 1980. *Simulations: A Handbook for Teachers.* London: Kogan Page Ltd.

Joyce, Bruce R. 1977. "Structural Imagination and Professional Staff Development." *NCSIE In-Service,* National Council of States on In-Service Education. Syracuse, N.Y.: Syracuse University (March): 3.

Joyce, Bruce R., K. R. Howey, and Sam J. Yarger. 1976. *Issues to Face,* In-Service Teacher Education Concepts Project, Report No. 1. Syracuse, N.Y.: The National Dissemination Center, Syracuse University.

Joyce, Bruce R., and Beverly Showers. 1980. "Improving In-Service Training: The Message of Research." *Educational Leadership* 37 (February): 379–85.

Joyce, Bruce R., and Beverly Showers. 1982. "The Coaching of Teaching." *Educational Leadership* 40 (October): 4–10.

Joyce, Bruce R., and Beverly Showers. 1983. *Power of Research on Training for Staff Development.* Alexandria, Va.: Association for Supervision and Curriculum Development.

Kello, John E. 1986. "Developing Training, Step-By-Step." *Training and Development Journal* 40 (January): 50–52.

Kibler, Robert J., L. L. Barker, and D. T. Miles. 1970. *Behavioral Objectives and Instruction.* Boston, Mass.: Allyn and Bacon, Inc.

Kilgore, Alvah M., Ronald Reichert, and Pamela Curtiss. 1984. "The Application of Research Generalizations from Staff Development to a Rural District: A Case Study Research Report." A paper presented at the Annual Meeting of the Association of Teacher Educators (January). ERIC ED 241 466.

King, Nicelma J. 1980. *Staff Development Programs in Desegregated Settings—Executive Summary.* Santa Monica, Calif.: Rand Corp. ERIC ED 198 198.

Kintsfather, David. 1985. "Using Simulation to Teach." *Feedback* 27 (Summer): 17–19.

Knowles, Malcolm S. 1975. *Self-Directed Learning: A Guide for Learners and Teachers.* New York: Association Press.

Knowles, Malcolm S., and Associates. 1984. *Andragogy in Action.* San Francisco: Jossey-Bass Publishers.

Korinek, Lori, Rex Schmid, and Martha McAdams. 1985. "In-Service Types and Best Practices." In *Journal of Research and Development in Education*. 18 (Winter): 33–38.

Ladwig, Dennis J. 1983. "Quality Circles Improve School Operations." *School Business Affairs* 49 (October): 37–39.

Lawrence, Gordon, Dennis Baker, Patricia Elzie, and Barbara Hansen. 1974. *Patterns of Effective In-Service Education*. Gainesville, Fla.: University of Florida, College of Education (December).

Lawrence, Gordon, and D. Harrison. 1980. *Policy Implications of the Research on the Professional Development of Education Personnel: An Analysis of Fifty-Nine Studies*. Washington, D.C.: Feistzer Publications.

Lewis, Karron G., and J. T. Povlacs, eds. 1988. *Individual Consultant Techniques for Faculty Development Personnel*. Vol. 1. Stillwater, Okla.: New Forums Press.

Lieberman, Ann. 1982. "Practice Makes Policy: The Tensions of School Improvement." Chap. X in *Policy Making in Education*, Part I, 81st Yearbook of the National Society for the Study of Education, ed. Ann Lieberman and M. W. McLaughlin, Chicago: The University of Chicago Press.

Lieberman, Ann, and Lynne Miller, eds. 1979. *Staff Development: New Demands, New Realities, New Perspectives*. New York: Teachers College Press.

Lieberman, Ann, and Lynne Miller. 1984. *Teachers, Their World and Their Work: Implications for School Improvement*. Alexandria, Va.: Association for Supervision and Curriculum Development.

Little, Judith L. 1981. *School Success and Staff Development: The Role of Staff Development in Urban Desegregated Schools—Executive Summary*. Boulder, Colo.: Center for Action Research, Inc. ERIC ED 205 628.

Lovell, John T., and Kimball Wiles. 1983. *Supervision for Better Schools*. 5th ed. Englewood Cliffs, N.J.: Prentice-Hall, Inc.

Lozano, Judith A. 1980. "Relationships between Characteristics of Planning Documents and Selected Indicators of Quality Operations for In-Service Education Programs in Public School Systems." Ph.D. diss., The University of Texas at Austin.

Luke, Robert A. 1976. "Collective Bargaining and In-Service Education." *Phi Delta Kappan* 57 (March): 468–70.

Luke, Robert A. 1980. *Teacher-Centered In-Service Education: Planning and Products*. Washington, D.C.: National Education Association.

Lutz, John E. 1976. "In-Service Personnel Development: A Systematic Approach to Program Planning." *Educational Technology* 16 (April): 44–47.

Lynch, Pat. 1979. "Prompt Cards End Those Transparency Fumbles." *Training/HRD* 16 (June): 34, 36.

McCleary, Lloyd E., and Kenneth E. McIntyre. 1972. "Competency Development and University Methodology." *National Association of Secondary School Principals Bulletin* 56 (March): 53–68.

McGreal, Thomas L. 1983. *Successful Teacher Evaluation*. Alexandria, Va.: Association for Supervision and Curriculum Development.

McGreal, Thomas L. 1984. "Artifact Collection." *Educational Leadership* 41 (April): 20–21.

McIntyre, Kenneth E. 1967. "The Laboratory Approach." In *Designs for In-*

Service Education, ed. E. W. Bessent. Austin, Tex.: Research and Development Center for Teacher Education, The University of Texas at Austin (February).

McIntyre, Kenneth E., Wailand Bessent, Ben M. Harris, and Jack Roberts. 1970. *Shady Acres In-Basket.* Washington, D.C.: National Association of Elementary School Principals, NEA.

McKibbin, Michael, Marsha Weil, and Bruce Joyce. 1977. *Teaching and Learning: Demonstrations of Alternatives.* Washington, D.C.: Association of Teacher Educators.

McLaughlin, Milbrey, and Paul Berman. 1977. "Retooling Staff Development in a Period of Retrenchment." *Educational Leadership* 35 (December): 191–94.

McLendon, Dan P. 1977. "A Delphi Study of Agreement and Consensus among Selected Educator Groups in Texas Regarding Principles Underlying Effective In-Service Education." Ph.D. diss., The University of Texas at Austin.

Mager, Robert F. 1968. *Developing Attitude toward Learning.* Palo Alto, Calif.: Fearon Publishers.

Mager, Robert F. 1975. *Preparing Instructional Objectives.* Palo Alto, Calif.: Fearon-Pitman Publishers.

Mager, Robert F., and Peter Pipes. 1970. "Is Non-Performance Rewarding?" In *Analyzing Performance Problems or "You Really Oughta Wanna."* Palo Alto, Calif.: Fearon Publishers.

Mai, Robert P. 1981. "The Advisory Approach as a Form of Professional Growth." In *School-Focused In-Service: Descriptions and Discussions,* ed. Kenneth R. Howey, Sam Yarger, and Bruce Joyce. Reston, Va.: Association of Teacher Educators.

Maidment, Robert, and William Bullock, Jr. 1985. *Meetings: Accomplishing More with Better and Fewer.* Reston, Va.: National Association of Secondary School Principals.

Main, Dana. 1975. *Exper Sim: A System for Teaching Research Design through Computer Simulation.* New York: Exxon Education Foundation.

Manolakes, Theodore. 1975. "The Advisory System and Supervision." In *Professional Supervision for Professional Teachers,* ed. Thomas J. Sergiovanni. Washington, D.C.: Association for Supervision and Curriculum Development.

Margolis, Fredric H., and C. R. Bell. 1985. "How to Break the News That You're Breaking Them into Small Groups." *Training* 22 (March): 81–85, 88–89.

Martin, D., and P. J. Saif. 1985. "Curriculum Change from the Grass Roots." A paper presented at the Annual Meeting of the Association for Supervision and Curriculum Development (March). ERIC ED 254 913.

Marshall, Jon C., and S. D. Caldwell. 1984. "How Valid Are Formal Needs Assessments?" *NASSP Bulletin* 68 (November): 24–30.

Marx, Raymond J. 1982. "Videodisc-Based Training: Does It Make Economic Sense?" *Training/HRD* 19 (March): 56–65.

Maslow, Abraham H. 1971. *The Farther Reaches of Human Nature.* New York: Viking Press.

Massey, Sara R. 1979. "Staff Development: Teaching Adult Professionals." *NCSIE In-Service* (April): 18–20. National Council of States on In-Service Education, Syracuse University, Syracuse, N.Y.

Mathis, Robert L., and John H. Jackson. 1985. *Personnel: Human Resource Management.* 4th ed. St. Paul, Minn.: West Publishing Company.

Matthews, Doris B., Howard Hill, and Jim Frank Casteel. 1984. *Staff Development: A Matter of Survival*. A paper presented at the annual conference of the Association for Supervision and Curriculum Development. New York (March). ERIC ED 241 510.

May, Leslie S., Carol Ann Moore, and Stephen J. Zammit, eds. 1987. *Evaluating Business and Industry Training*. Boston: Kluwer Academic Publishers.

Megarry, Jacquetta. 1977. *Aspects of Simulation and Gaming: An Anthology of SAGSET Journal, Volumes 1–4*. London: Kogan Page Limited.

Meier, John. 1968. "Rationale for and Application of Microtraining to Improve Teaching." *Journal of Teacher Education* 19 (Summer): 145–57.

Melnik, Michael A., and Daniel S. Sheehan. 1976. "Clinic to Improve University Teaching." *Journal of Research and Development in Education* 9:68–74.

Mertens, Sally. 1983. "The Basics in In-Service Education: Findings from the Rand and Teacher Center Studies." *Action Teacher Education* 4 (Spring and Summer): 61–66.

Mertens, S. K., and S. J. Yarger. 1981. *Teacher Centers in Action*. New York: Syracuse Area Teacher Center.

Metz, Edmund J. 1982. "Do Your Quality Circle Leaders Need More Training?" *Training and Development Journal* (December): 198.

Miller, Gerald V. 1979. "Individualizing Learning Objectives." *Training and Development Journal* 35 (July): 40–42.

Milroy, Ellice. 1982. *Role-Play: A Practical Guide*. Aberdeen, England: Aberdeen University Press.

Mitman, Alexis L. 1978. "Teacher Self-Reports in an Experiment on Teacher Education and Effectiveness." In N. L. Gage, *An Experiment on Teacher Effectiveness and Parent-Assisted Instruction in the Third Grade*. Stanford, Calif.: Center for Educational Research at Stanford University (May).

Moran, Charles F. n.d. "The Conpar Method of Conducting a Workshop." Unpublished paper prepared for executive development purposes. Detroit, Mich.: Fisher Body Division, General Motors Corporation.

Mouton, Jane S., and R. R. Blake. 1984. *Synergogy: A New Strategy for Education, Training, and Development*. San Francisco: Jossey-Bass Publishers.

Munroe, M. J., Barbara Buchanan, and Nora Grigg. 1981. "Linking Teacher Behavior with Learning Style: Tucson Model for Effective Staff Development." A paper presented to the National Council of States on In-Service Education (November). ERIC ED 209 235.

Munson, Lawrence S. 1984. *How to Conduct Training Seminars*. New York: McGraw-Hill Book Company.

Nadler, Leonard. 1974. "Implications of the HRD Concept." *Training and Development Journal* 28 (May).

Nadler, Leonard. 1976. "Learning from Non-School Staff Development Activities." *Educational Leadership* 34 (December): 201–04.

Nadler, Leonard. 1982. *Designing Training Programs: The Critical Events Model*. Reading, Mass.: Addison-Wesley.

Napoli: Participant's Manual 1965. La Jolla, Calif.: Western Behavioral Sciences Institute.

National Advisory Council on Education Professional Development (NACEPD).

1973. *Vocational Education: Staff Development Priorities for the 70s.* A report. Washington, D.C.: National Advisory Council (January).

National Commission on Instructional Supervision. 1986. *Catalog of Policies, Practices, and Programs in Instructional Supervision.* Arlington, Va.: Association for Supervision and Curriculum Development.

National In-Service Network Task Force. 1980. *Quality Practices Task Force: Final Report.* Bloomington, Ind.: Indiana University, School of Education (July).

Naumann-Etienne, M., and J. W. Todd. 1976. "Applying Organizational Development Techniques to In-Service Education." A paper presented to the American Educational Research Association, San Francisco, Calif. (April). ERIC ED 122 357.

Nelson, Marilyn. 1976. "Creating Organizational Structures for the In-Service Training of Teachers." In *Cultural Pluralism and Social Change,* a collection of position papers by Richard M. Brandt et al. Report No. 5. In-Service Education Concepts Project. Palo Alto, Calif.: Stanford Center for Research and Development in Teaching (June).

Nevi, Charles. 1986. "Against the Grain: Half-Truths That Hinder Staff Development." *Principal* 65 (January): 44–46.

Ober, Richard. 1969. "The Nature of Interaction Analysis." *High School Journal* 51 (October): 7–16.

Onore, Cynthia, and N. B. Lester. 1985. "Immersion and Distancing: Ins and Outs of In-Service Education." *English Education* 17 (February): 13–17.

Oregon Teacher Standards and Practices Commission. 1977. "Continuing Professional Development: A Discussion Paper." Prepared by the Committee on Professional Growth. Salem, Oreg.: The Commission (September). Mimeo.

Ouchi, William G. 1981. "Theory Z: How American Business Can Meet the Japanese Challenge." Reading, Mass.: Addison-Wesley.

Pankratz, Roger. 1980. *Planning for Institutionalization: The Continuation of New Programs and Practices.* Omaha, Nebr.: Center for Urban Education, University of Nebraska at Omaha. Teacher Corps Developmental Training Activities.

Pankratz, Roger, and C. Martray. 1981. "A Collaborative Involvement Strategy for Educational Improvement." A paper presented at the Annual Convention of the Association of Teacher Educators, Dallas, Tex. (February). ERIC ED 200 576.

Pareek, Udai, and T. V. Rao. 1982. "Role Playing: The Basic Tool of Behaviour Simulation." In *Developing Motivation through Experiencing.* New Delphi: Oxford and IBH Publishing Co.

Pareek, Udai, and T. V. Rao. 1982. *Developing Motivation through Experiencing: A Trainer's Guide for Behaviour Simulation in Motivation Training.* New Delhi: Oxford and IBH Publishing Co.

Pedler, Mike, ed. 1983. *Action Learning in Practice.* Aldershot, Hants, England: Gower Publishing Company Limited.

Pedras, Melvin J. 1984. *The Conceptualization and Design of a Staff Development Model for Community College Part-Time Faculty.* A paper presented to the American Vocational Association Convention, Anaheim, Calif. (December).

Peper, John B. 1986. "Implementing Computer-Based Education in Jefferson County, Colorado." Chap. VII in *Micro-Computers and Education,* ed. J. A. Culbertson and L. L. Cunningham, 85th Yearbook of the National Society for the Study of Education, Part I. Chicago: The University of Chicago Press.

Perez, Roberto. 1979. "A Comparison of Centralized and Decentralized In-Service Education Programs: Teacher Involvement, Program Characteristics and Job Satisfaction." Ph.D. diss., The University of Texas at Austin.

Performance Learning Systems. 1986. *We Can Show You the Secrets of Creating a Championship Teaching Staff.* Emerson, N.J.: Performance Learning Systems, Inc.

Peterson, P. L., and H. L. Walberg, eds. 1979. *Research on Teaching.* Berkeley, Calif.: McCutchan Publishing Company.

Petrosky, Anthony R. 1986. "On the Road to Shanghai: A Three-Year Project with the Public Schools." In *The Teaching of Writing,* ed. A. R. Petrosky and David Bartholomae, 85th Yearbook, National Society for the Study of Education, Part II. Chicago: The University of Chicago Press.

Pollak, Gertrude K. 1975. *Leadership of Discussion Groups: Case Material and Theory.* Holliswood, N.Y.: Spectrum Publications, Inc.

Principles of Good Practice in Continuing Education. n.d. Silver Spring, Md.: Council on the Continuing Education Unit.

Race, Philip, and David Brook, eds. 1980. *Perspectives on Academic Gaming and Simulations 5.* The proceedings of the 1979 Conference of the Society for Academic Gaming and Simulation in Education and Training. London: Kogan Page Ltd.

Ramakka, Vicky, and Robert Huddleston. 1986. "Countywide In-Service Training Day." *Phi Delta Kappan* 67 (May): 682–83.

Rattenburg, Judith, and Paula Pelletier. 1974. *Data Processing in Social Sciences with OSIRIS.* Ann Arbor, Mich.: Survey Research Center, Institute for Social Research, University of Michigan.

Rawitsch, Don G. 1981. "Lessons Learned on the In-Service Trails." *Classroom Computer News* 2 (September–October): 16–17.

Reavis, Charles A. 1976. "Clinical Supervision: A Timely Approach." *Educational Leadership* 33 (February): 360–63.

Rebore, Ronald W. 1982. *Personnel Administration in Education: A Management Approach.* Englewood Cliffs, N.J.: Prentice-Hall, Inc.

Rebore, Ronald W. 1987. *Personnel Administration in Education.* 2d ed. Englewood Cliffs, N.J.: Prentice-Hall, Inc.

Redfern, George B. 1980. *Evaluating Teachers and Administrators: A Performance Objectives Approach.* Boulder, Colo.: Westview Press.

Rivlin, Alice M., and P. M. Timpane, eds. 1975. *Planned Variation in Education: Should We Give Up or Try Harder?* Washington, D.C.: The Brookings Institution.

Rodriguez, Sam, and Kathy Johnstone. 1986. "Staff Development through a Collegial Support Group Model." Chap. 7 in *Improving Teaching,* ed. Karen K. Zumwalt. Alexandria, Va.: Association for Supervision and Curriculum Development.

Rogers, Carl R. 1969. *Freedom to Learn.* Columbus, Ohio: Charles E. Merrill.

Rogus, J. F., and Mary Martin. 1979. "The Principal and Staff Development: Countering the School Culture." *The Clearing House* 53 (September): 28–30.

Rosenblum, Shiela, and JoAnn Jastrzab. 1980. *The Role of the Principal in Change: The Teacher Corps Example.* Cambridge, Mass.: Abt Associates, Inc.

Ryor, J., A. Shankee, and J. T. Sandefur. 1979. "Three Perspectives." *Journal of Teacher Education* 30 (January–February): 13–19.

Sanders, James R., and Donald J. Cunningham. 1974. "Formative Evaluation: Selecting Techniques and Procedures." In *Evaluating Educational Programs and Products*, ed. Gary D. Borich. Englewood Cliffs, N.J.: Educational Technology Publications.

Sauer, Stephen F., and R. E. Holland. 1981. *Planning In-House Training: A Personal System with an Organizational Perspective*. San Diego, Calif.: University Associates, Inc.

Schiffer, Judith. 1980. *School Renewal through Staff Development*. New York: Teachers College Press.

Schmuck, Richard A., et al. 1975. *Consultation for Innovative Schools: O. D. for Multiunit Structure*. Eugene, Oreg.: University of Oregon Press.

Schroeder, James E. 1983. "A Pedagogical Mode of Instruction for Interactive Videodisc." *Journal of Educational Technology*, Vol. 12, pp. 311–17.

Schuler, Randall S., and Stuart A. Youngblood. 1986. *Effective Personnel Management*. 2d ed. St. Paul, Minn.: West Publishing Company.

Sculli, Domenic, and Wing Cheong Ng. 1985. "Designing Business Games for the Service Industries." *Simulation/Games for Learning* 5 (March): 16–27.

Sealy, Leonard, and Elizabeth Dillon. 1976. "Staff Development: A Study of Six School Systems." A report to the Ford Foundation. New York: The Ford Foundation. Mimeo.

Seidner, Constance J. 1976. "Teaching with Simulators and Games." In *The Psychology of Teaching Methods*, ed. N. L. Gage. Part I, 75th Yearbook of the National Society for the Study of Education. Chicago: The University of Chicago Press.

Shaftel, Fannie, and George R. Shaftel. 1967. *Role-Playing for Social Values. Decision Making in Social Studies*. Englewood Cliffs, N.J.: Prentice-Hall, Inc.

Showers, Beverly Kay. 1980. "Self-Efficacy as a Predictor of Teacher Participation in School Decision Making." Ph.D. diss., Stanford University, Palo Alto, Calif.

Showers, Beverly. 1985. "Teachers Coaching Teachers." *Educational Leadership* 43 (April): 43–48.

Shubik, Martin. 1975. *The Uses and Methods of Gaming*. New York: Elsevier Scientific Publishing Company, Inc.

Silverblank, Fran. 1979. "Analyzing the Decision-Making Process in Curriculum Projects." *Education* 99 (Summer): 414–18.

Silvern, Leonard C. 1972. *Systems Engineering Applied to Training*. Houston, Tex.: Gulf Publishing Company.

Simon, Alan E. 1977. "Analyzing Educational Platforms: A Supervisory Strategy." *Educational Leadership* 34 (May): 580–84.

Singer, Robert N. 1977. "To Err or Not to Err: A Question for the Instruction of Psychomotor Skills." *Review of Educational Research* 47 (Summer): 479–98.

Skinner, Michael. 1984. *Red-Flag: Air Combat for the '80s*. Novato, Calif.: Presidio Press.

Smith, Douglas J. 1981. *A State Funding Model for In-Service Training of School Staff*. Ann Arbor, Mich.: Unpublished document (August). ERIC ED 206 619.

Smith, William L. 1978. "Changing Teacher Corps Programs." *NCSIE In-Service*.

Syracuse, N.Y.: National Council of States on In-Service Education, Syracuse University.

Smith, William L. 1979. "Collaboration: A Decision Making Framework for In-Service Education." In *NCSIE In-Service* (April). Syracuse, N.Y.: National Council of States on In-Service Education, Syracuse University.

Sonoquist, John A., and William C. Dunkelberg. 1977. *Survey and Opinion Research: Procedures for Processing and Analysis*. Englewood Cliffs, N.J.: Prentice-Hall, Inc.

Sowden, Susette, and Ronald Harden. 1984. "The Use of Two Innovation Games in a Staff Development Programme." *Simulation/Games for Learning* 14 (August): 113–21.

Sparks, Georgea M. 1983. "Synthesis of Research on Staff Development for Effective Teaching." *Educational Leadership* (November): 65–72.

Special Education Supervisor Training Project. 1974. *Professional Supervisory Competencies*. Austin, Tex.: The University of Texas.

Sprinthall, Norman A., and Lois Thies-Sprinthall. 1983. "The Teacher as an Adult Learner: A Cognitive-Developmental View." In *Staff Development*, 82d Yearbook, Part II, National Society for the Study of Education, ed. Gary A. Griffin. Chicago: The University of Chicago Press.

Stadsklev, Ron. 1974. *Handbook of Simulation Gaming in Social Education. Part I, Textbook*. Tuskaloosa, Ala.: Institute of Higher Education Research and Services, The University of Alabama.

Stake, Robert E., and Terry Denny. 1969. "Needed Concepts and Techniques for Utilizing More Fully the Potential of Evaluation." Chap. 16 in *Educational Evaluation: New Roles, New Means*, 68th Yearbook, Part II, ed. Ralph Tyler. Chicago: National Society for the Study of Education.

Stephens, E. Robert. 1977. *Regionalism: Past, Present and Future*. Executive Handbook, Series No. 10. Arlington, Va.: American Association of School Administrators.

Strother, George B., and John P. Klus. 1982. *Administration of Continuing Education*. Belmont, Calif.: Wadsworth Publishing Company.

Struening, Elmer L., and Marilyn Brewer. 1983. *The University Edition of the Handbook of Evaluation Research*. Beverly Hills, Calif.: Sage Publishers.

Stufflebeam, Daniel L., et al. 1971. *Educational Evaluation and Decision Making*. Phi Delta Kappa Study Committee on Evaluation. Itasca, Ill.: F. E. Peacock Publishers.

Sullivan, Cheryl Granade. 1980. *Clinical Supervision: A State of the Art Review*. Alexandria, Va.: Association for Supervision and Curriculum Development.

Sullivan, Debra K., and Joseph C. Basile. 1983. "Implementation of the Stallings Classroom Management Staff Development Demonstration Project in Putnam County, West Virginia." Charleston, W. Va.: Appalachia Educational Laboratory. ERIC ED 225 976.

Swenson, Thomas L. 1981. "The State-of-the-Art in In-Service Education and Staff Development in K-12 Schools." *Journal of Research and Development in Education* 15 (Fall): 2–7.

Taylor, D. W., Paul C. Berry, and Clifford H. Block. 1957. "Does Group Participation When Using Brain-Storming Facilitate or Inhibit Creative Thinking?" *Administrative Science Quarterly* 3 (June): 23–47.

Taylor, John L., and Rex Walford. 1978. *Learning and the Simulation Game.* Beverly Hills, Calif.: Sage Publications, Inc.

Thomas, Michael P., Jr. 1967. "In-Service Programs as Organizational Learning." In *Designs for In-Service Education,* ed. E. W. Bessent. Austin, Tex.: Research and Development Center for Teacher Education, The University of Texas.

Thompson, Mark S. 1975. *Evaluation for Decision in Social Programmes.* Lexington, Mass.: Lexington Books, D.C. Heath Co.

Tom, Alan R. 1984. *Teaching as a Moral Craft.* New York: Longman, Inc.

Tracy, William R. 1984. *Designing Training and Development Systems.* Rev. ed. New York: American Management Association.

Tropman, John E. 1980. *Effective Meetings: Improving Group Decision-Making.* Beverly Hills, Calif.: Sage Publications (Sage Human Services Guide #17).

Tyler, Ralph W. 1985. "Conditions for Effective Learning." Chap. XI in *Education in School and Non-School Settings,* ed. Mario D. Fantini and Robert Sinclair. Part I, 84th Yearbook, National Society for the Study of Education. Chicago: The University of Chicago Press.

Ulmer, Dale. 1986. "Interactive Video for the Electronics Age." *Workplace Education* 4 (March–April): 6–7.

Vaughan, Joseph. 1983. "Using Research in Teaching, Schools and Change to Help Staff Development Make a Difference." *Journal of Staff Development* 4 (May): 43–51.

Virginia Department of Education. 1978. *In-Service Education for School Personnel in Virginia: Guiding Principles.* A Priority in Pursuit of Quality Education. Richmond, Va.: Office of Curriculum and Instruction, Department of Education, Commonwealth of Virginia (March).

Von Glinow, Mary Ann, et al. 1983. "The Design of a Career Oriented Human Resource System." *Academy of Management Review* 8.

Wade, Ruth K. 1984. "What Makes a Difference in In-Service Teacher Education?: A Meta-Analysis of Research." *Educational Leadership* 42 (December–January): 48–53.

Warner, Allen R., 1977. "Developing Competencies for School-Based Teacher Educators." *NCSIE In-Service.* National Council of States on In-Service Education. Syracuse, N.Y.: Syracuse University, College of Education (November): 5–11.

Washington State Department of Education. 1981. *The Washington State System for Coordination of Staff Development Coordination Study: A Final Report.* Olympia, Wash.: Office of the State Superintendent of Public Instruction. ERIC ED 209 240.

Watkins, Karen. 1986. "When Co-workers Clash." *Training and Development Journal* 40 (April): 20–27.

Wircenski, Jerry, and David Just. 1984. "An In-Service Staff Development Program for Vocational Teachers Working with Disadvantaged Students." *Research in Education* (June). ERIC ED 239 068.

Wolf, Steven. 1981. "The Alaska Special Education In-Service Training Center." *Journal of Staff Development* 2 (November): 2–18.

Wood, Fred H., S. R. Thompson, and Frances Russell. 1981. "Designing Effective Staff Development Programs." In *Staff Development/Organization Develop-*

ment, ed. Betty Dillon-Peterson. Alexandria, Va.: Association for Supervision and Curriculum Development.

Yarger, Sam. 1976. "An Exploratory Model for Program Development in In-Service Education." In *Creative Authority and Collaboration,* a collection of position papers by Sam Yarger et al. Report No. 4. Palo Alto, Calif.: In-Service Teacher Education Concepts Project (June).

Yarger, S. J., K. R. Howey, and B. R. Joyce. 1980. *In-Service Teacher Education.* Palo Alto, Calif.: Booksend Laboratory.

Yarger, Sam J., and Sally K. Mertens. 1976. "About the Education of Teachers—A Letter to Virginia." In *Issues in In-Service Education: State Action for In-Service.* National Council of States on In-Service Education. Syracuse, N.Y.: Syracuse University, College of Education (November).

Yeatts, Edward H. 1976. "Staff Development: A Teacher-Centered In-Service Design." *Educational Leadership* (March): 417–24.

Zemke, Ron, and John Gunkler. 1985. "28 Techniques for Transforming Training into Performance." *Training* 22 (April): 56–63.

Zigarmi, Patricia. 1979. "A Model for an Individualized Staff Development Program." In *Staff Development: New Demands, New Realities, New Perspectives,* ed. Ann Lieberman and Lynne Miller. New York: Teachers College Press.

Zumwalt, Karen K. 1982. "Research on Teaching: Policy Implications for Teacher Education." Chap. IV in *Policy Making in Education,* ed. Ann Lieberman and M. W. McLaughlin. Part I, 81st Yearbook of the National Society for the Study of Education. Chicago: The University of Chicago Press.

Zumwalt, Karen K., ed. 1986. *Improving Teaching.* ASCD Yearbook. Alexandria, Va.: Association for Supervision and Curriculum Development.

Index